KING, LORDS AND PEASANTS

IN MEDIEVAL ENGLAND:
The Common Law of Villeinage
in the Twelfth and Thirteenth
Centuries

BY

PAUL R. HYAMS

CLARENDON PRESS · OXFORD
1980

Oxford University Press, Walton Street, Oxford OX2 6DP

OXFORD LONDON GLASGOW
NEW YORK TORONTO MELBOURNE WELLINGTON
KUALA LUMPUR SINGAPORE JAKARTA HONG KONG TOKYO
DELHI BOMBAY CALCUTTA MADRAS KARACHI
NAIROBI DAR ES SALAAM CAPE TOWN

*Published in the United States
by Oxford University Press, New York*

British Library Cataloguing in Publication Data

Hyams, Paul R
    King, lords and peasants in medieval England. –
    (Oxford historical monographs).
    1. Serfdom – England – History
    I. Title   II. Series
    301.44′93′0942   HT781   79–42923

ISBN 0–19–821880–X

Typesetting by Parkway Group, London and Abingdon
Printed by Lowe and Brydone Ltd, Thetford

To Judy as I said I would

PREFACE

Law has always attracted my interest as an attempt to apply reasoned logic to the organization of human affairs. As a solicitor's son (who narrowly escaped my father's fate), I never found the Law strange or frightening, though I recognized the artificiality of its intellectual system and the gulf that could separate it from the realities of everyday life. When I went on to read History as an undergraduate, I had high hopes of the Law. Why should one not quarry the social history of the past directly out of legal records? Could not Law be treated as a 'mirror' of Society? The *naïveté* of my ill-considered musings is now obvious to me. The relationships between Law, Society, Social Theory, and so on (all in capital letters) are complex far beyond anything I then understood. All the same my undergraduate self has periodically looked over my shoulder as I worked on this book. I chose villeinage as the subject for a doctoral thesis in the expectation that I should write it partly from royal and common-law records and partly from manorial and estate records. But legal villeinage proved so fascinating and presented so many problems that I have not so far fulfilled my original intention to compare it with economic serfdom on its manorial home ground.[1] This book thus contains more Law and less descriptive sociology than I once intended. All the same I have throughout striven to relate the legal doctrines I expound to the community of lawyers or the intellectual traditions from which they sprang, and to trace where possible the influence of and the effects on the social and economic trends of the day. Lawyers and social historians will each pick up technical errors or defects of balance and interpretation in their areas of interest. The archaeological reconstruction of the legal artefact, from the incomplete potsherds of the common law's distant past, is a trick of a very different kind from the (?cliometric) analysis of secular change in a mixed pre-industrial economy like medieval England. Like

---

[1] It is worth mentioning right from the start that I have endeavoured to use the words 'villein', 'villeinage', etc. exclusively in a legal context throughout this book. When I have wished to refer to dependent social classes or an economic context, I have talked of 'serfs' and 'serfdom'. This analytical distinction will become important when I discuss the origins of villeinage at the end of the book.

Stephen of Tournai, I have invited two different guests to the
feast, fully aware that I am likely to satisfy neither.[2]

For the legal core of this book, I was fortunate in having two
fine guides. Vinogradoff's basic study, *Villainage in England,* as
modified by Maitland's farseeing shrewdness in his *History of
English Law* (and later works), can be felt on every page. Much
of this book, indeed, consists in an amplification and reworking
of their vision of villeinage in the light of a more extended
reading and analysis of cases from the plea rolls than their wider
concerns permitted them. I have read all the extant plea rolls
before 1250 and sampled quite widely from rolls of the second
half of the century. Some readers may find the book's major
merit to be its presentation of case material. To increase its utility,
I have included the names of participants and venues wherever
possible. A's suit against B over Whiteacre may give the lawyer,
intent on the reconstruction of doctrine, all he needs. Historians
ought to go further. Anecdotes are more than just attractive;
they give concrete existence to theoretical possibilities.

After this book was essentially complete and ready for the
press, two major scholarly bombshells dropped on its author. I
refer to the appearance late in 1976 of Professor S. F. C. Milsom's
The Legal Framework of English Feudalism and a few months later
of the third and fourth volumes of Professor S. E. Thorne's
translation—a new edition in all but name—of the treatise *De
legibus* traditionally associated with the name of Bracton. Each
constitutes a major advance in the field and demanded the most
careful consideration.

On reflection, Milsom's bold and imaginative essay required
the less adjustment for two reasons. First, although I certainly
cannot claim to have anticipated this most original revision of
Maitland's forms of action, Professor Milsom's previous work
had forewarned me to some extent. Even without the warning,
my own views are often compatible with his, especially in
Chapter 13, and may be left to stand on their own merits. And
secondly, Milsom's bold and imaginative model is controversial
and likely to trouble scholars for some time to come.[3] Hasty
amendment of a book on another subject is the wrong way to

---

[2] Stephan von Doornich, *Die Summa über das Decretum Gratiani*, ed. J. F. von Schulte
(Giessen, 1891), prol.

[3] See my review in *EHR* xciii (1978), 856–61.

attempt judgement. I content myself, therefore, with brief footnote references where appropriate.

Thorne's Bracton is quite another matter. The treatise *De
legibus* is a crux of legal archaeology quite central to this book,
which might in one sense be described as a monograph on the
treatise's view of villeinage. Moreover, until now even Professor
Thorne has accepted the traditional attribution in print, though
the occasional rumour did trickle out of Cambridge, Mass.,
from time to time. One reading of the 'Translator's Introduction'
to vol. iii sufficed to convince me that the new understanding of
the treatise and its context carried the ring of truth. This
revision was on a scale far too grand to be dealt with in defensive
footnotes or an apologetic appendix. I have therefore completely rewritten Chapter 8 and some part of every other chapter.
I willingly concede that this was a blessing in disguise. Much
that seemed formerly to present unceasing difficulties now makes
much better sense. I merely note that authors do not need many
such blessings at so late a stage. My consolation is that I have,
in my turn, provided my share of new data to take Bractonian
studies on a little further still.

It has been an inordinate length of time since I launched into
the serious study of villeinage. The publication of one's first
piece of substantial research is, moreover, a moment to record
gratitude to all those who helped an academic tiro on his way.
Derek Hall read drafts of every part of this book (some in several
guises) but never saw the work completed. Mine is among the
majority of studies in English legal history written over the last
decade or so that simply would not have reached their present
form without him. Derek viewed my 'burrowings' with good
humour, and was always ready with common-sense advice to
guide them back into more or less the right direction. Right up
to his early death in September 1975, he schooled me soundly in
techniques of legal research and saved me from a host of errors.

Barbara Harvey and Professor S. F. C. Milsom examined the
D. Phil. thesis which still skulks within this book. Each offered
advice and inspiration. Barbara Harvey, in particular, has been
unstinting in her encouragement and willingness to discuss
everything from fine points of interpretation to secular trends of
the economy.

To James Campbell must go the blame for enticing me into medieval history when he was my undergraduate tutor, and for teaching me how difficult it is to do well. His profound and virtuoso criticism of various parts of this book in draft long exasperated me before I could incorporate it—to the book's great gain. I have been fortunate also to sit at the feet of Sir Richard Southern, informally as well as at lecture and colloquy. His teachings, of broad horizons and imaginative art, I found impossible to follow, but an inspiration none the less. To return from an evening with either of these two is—for me—to vow to read more deeply and to worry ever more fiercely at the texts and authorities.

From my six months in 1975 as a Robbins Senior Fellow at the Institute of Medieval Canon Law in the University of California Law School at Berkeley, I learnt a little about the learned laws, and much about the special position of Professor Stephan Kuttner in the world of the Canonists. Had my visit been earlier, this book would have found a very different shape. Among the many others who contributed to it, I must single out Mr John Barton, Drs Paul Brand, Michael Clanchy, Barbara Dodwell, Edmund Fryde, Sally Harvey, Brian Kemp, Ian Kershaw, Mrs Vivienne Killingsworth, Dr Edmund King, Professor Peter Landau, Dr Henry Mayr-Harting, Professor Kenneth Pennington, and Mr John Prestwich.

I have accumulated the much valued membership of three Oxford colleges *en route*, Worcester, Jesus (where I was Scurry Jones Junior Research Fellow, and picked up from Dr David Rees the quotation that heads Chapter 1), and my present home, Pembroke. Each has supported and nourished me in irreplaceable ways. Similarly, I have almost always been treated well by the men and women who conserve the books and documents I use. My special thanks for many kindnesses go to the librarians of the Bodleian and Codrington libraries and their assistants (Mr Webb, Miss Aubertin-Potter, and Mr Britton) in Oxford, and the staff at the British Library and Public Record Office. I owe too special warm thanks to those who have typed out drafts and portions of this book at Pembroke College and the History Faculty Office (especially Mrs Marion Stowell).

My feelings toward my wife Elaine rest on a much firmer

basis than a mere academic publication. Had her relationship
to me been restricted to her part in this book, she would still
deserve to head the list of those I thank. I hope my parents, who
could write better books, feel that this is a reasonably adequate
return for the time and effort invested.

CONTENTS

PART IV

ABBREVIATIONS

Ab. Plac.	*Placitorum . . . abbreviatio, temp. regum Ric. I . . . Edw. III* (Rec. Comm., 1811)
Beaumanoir	P. de Rémi, Sire de Beaumanoir, *Les Coutumes de Beauvaisis*, ed. A. Salmon (Paris, 1899–1900; resissued 1970)
BHRS	*Bedfordshire Historical Records Society*
BL	British Library
Bloch, *Mélanges*	M. Bloch, *Mélanges historiques*, Paris, 1963
BNB	*Bracton's NoteBook*, ed. F. W. Maitland, London, 1887
Br.	Bracton, *De Legibus et Consuetudinibus Angliae*, ed. H. N., London, 1569
BRB	*Buckinghamshire Archaeological Society*, Records branch
Brev. Plac.	*Brevia Placitata*, ed. G. J. Turner and T. F. T. Plucknett, *SS*, lxvi, 1947
Britton	*Britton*, ed. F. M. Nichols, Oxford,1865
Buckland, *Slavery*	W. W. Buckland, *The Roman Law of Slavery*, Cambridge, 1908
Cal. Pat. R.	*Calendar of Patent Rolls*
Cas. Plac.	*Casus Placitorum, and reports of cases in the King's Courts (1272–8)*, ed. W. H. Dunham, jr., *SS*, lxix, 1950
Cl. R.	*Close Rolls, Henry III*
Cod.	*Corpus Iuris Civilis, Codex Iustiniani*
CRR	*Curia Regis Rolls*
DB	*Domesday Book*
Decretum	*Corpus Iuris Canonici, Decretum Gratiani*
Dialogus	R. FitzNeal, *Dialogus de Scaccario*, ed. C. G. Crump *et al.*, Oxford, 1902; trans. and ed. Johnson, *NMT*, 1950
Dig.	*Corpus Iuris Civilis, Digestum*
Early Yorks. Charters	*Early Yorkshire Charters*, ed. W. Farrer and C. T. Clay (12 vols.), 1914–65
Ec. H. R.	*Economic History Review*
EHR	*English Historical Review*
Fitzherbert	Sir A. Fitzherbert, *La Graunde Abridgement*, ?London, 1516
Fleta	Fleta, *Commentarius juris Anglicani*, ed. J. Selden, 1685
FNB	*The New Natura Brevium . . . of Mr Anthony Fitzherbert*, London, 1666
Gesetze	*Gesetze der Angelsächsen*, ed. F. Liebermann,

	Halle, 1903–16
Glanvill	*Tractatus de Legibus et Consuetudinibus regni Angliae Qui Glanvilla vocatur*, ed. G. D. G. Hall, *NMT*, 1965
Howell, *State Trials*	*A Complete Collection of State Trials . . . from the Reign of Richard II to the 16th year of the Reign of George III*, London, 1809–28. Vol. xx, ed. T. B. and T. J. Howell
Hoyt, *Royal Demesne*	R. S. Hoyt, *The Royal Demesne in English Constitutional History, 1066–1272*, Ithaca, N. Y., 1950
Hunter, *Fines*	*Fines, sive pedes finium . . . AD 1195–1214*, ed. J. Hunter, vol. i, Rec. Comm., 1835
Inst.	*Corpus Iuris Civilis, Institutiones Justiniani*
JI 1	Public Record Office class, plea rolls, Justices Itinerant, mainly eyre rolls
KB 26, 27	Public Record Office class, plea rolls of the central courts
LHP	*Leges Henrici Primi*, ed. L. Downer, Oxford, 1972
LQR	*Law Quarterly Review*
LRS	*Lincolnshire Record Society*
Maitland, *Coll. Papers*	*The Collected Papers of F. W. Maitland*, ed. H. A. L. Fisher, Cambridge, 1911
MGH	*Monumenta Germaniae Historica*
NAS	*Three Early Assize Rolls for the County of Northumberland, saec. xiii*, ed. W. Page, Surtees soc., lxxxviii, 1890
NMT	*Nelson's Medieval Texts*, London and Edinburgh etc., now Oxford Medieval Texts
Novae Narrationes	*Novae Narrationes*, ed. E. Shanks and S. F. C. Milsom, *SS*, lxxx, 1960
NRS	*Northamptonshire Record Society*
P&M	Sir F. Pollock and F. W. Maitland, *The History of English Law before the Time of Edward I*, 2nd ed. Cambridge, 1898
Plucknett, *Concise Hist.*	T. F. T. Plucknett, *A Concise History of the Common Law*, 5th ed., London, 1956
Powicke and Cheney, *Councils*	*Councils and Synods, with other Documents relating to the English Church*, vol. ii, ed. Sir F. M. Powicke and C. R. Cheney, Oxford, 1964
PRS	*Pipe Roll Society*
RCR	*Rotuli Curiae Regis*, ed. Sir F. Palgrave, Rec. Comm., 1835
Rec. Comm.	Record Commission, London
Reg. Omn. Brev.	*Registrum Omnium Brevium tam originalium quam judicialium*, London,1531
RHDFE	*Revue historique de droit français et étranger*
Richardson, *Bracton*	H. G. Richardson, *Bracton: the Problem of his*

Text, SS supplementary vol. ii, 1964

Richardson and Sayles,   H. G. Richardson and G. O. Sayles, *Law and*
  Law and Leg.   *Legislation from Athelbert to Magna Carta*, Edin-
                               burgh, 1966

Richardson and Sayles,   *Select Cases of Procedure without Writ under Henry*
  Procedure without Writ   *III*, ed. H. G. Richardson and G. O. Sayles,
                               SS, lx, 1941

Rot. de Ob. et Fin.   *Rotuli de Oblatis et Finibus in Turri Londiniensi*
                               Asservati, Temp. Regis Johannis, Rec. Comm.,
                               1835–6

Rot. Lit. Claus.   *Rotuli Litterarum Clausarum in Turri Londiniensi*
                               Asservati, ed. T. D. Hardy, Rec. Comm.,
                               1833–4

Rot. parl.   *Rotuli Parliamentorum . . .*, 6 vols., London,
                               1767–77

RRS   *Regesta Regum Scottorum*, ed.G. W. S. Barrow,
                               The Acts of Malcolm III, King of Scots, 1153–
                               1165, Edinburgh, 1960 (*RRS* i); ed. *idem*
                               and W. W. Scott, *The Acts of William I, King of*
                               Scots, 1165–1214, Edinburgh, 1971 (*RRS* ii)

R.S.   Rolls Series, London (Chronicles and
                               Memorials of Great Britain and Ireland
                               during the Middle Ages)

Sayles, *Select Cases in*   *Select Cases in the Court of King's Bench under*
  K.B.   *Edward I*, ed. G. O. Sayles, *SS*,lv, lvii-lviii,
                               1936, 1938–9

Selden Registers   *Early Registers of Writs*, ed. E. de Haas,
                               T. F. T. Plucknett, and G. D. G. Hall, *SS*,
                               lxxxvii, 1970

Selden YBB   *Selden Society, Yearbook series*, 1903-in progress
SRS   *Somerset Record Society*
SS   *Selden Society*
Stubbs, *Charters*   *Select Charters and other Illustrations of English*
                               Constitutional History, ed. W. Stubbs, 9th ed.
                               revised by H. W. C. Davis, Oxford, 1913

TRHS   *Transactions of the Royal Historical Society*
Van Caenegem   *Royal Writs in England from the Conquest to*
                               Glanvill, ed. R. C. Van Caenegem, *SS*, lxxvii,
                               1958–9

Vieux Natura Brevium   *Natura Brevium in Frenche*, ed. R. Tottel,
                               London, 1557

Villainage   Sir P. Vinogradoff, *Villainage in England*,
                               Oxford, 1892

WRS   *Wiltshire Record Society*
WSS   *William Salt Society, Historical Collections,*
                               Staffordshire
X   *Corpus Iuris Canonici, Decretales Gregorii IX*
YAS   *Yorkshire Archaeological Society*, record series
YB, YBB   *Yearbook, Yearbooks*

'Nor is there any reading more jejune and unprofitable to a
philosophical mind than that of our ancient law-books.'
Hallam, *Middle Ages*, ch. 8, Part 2 (vol. ii, p. 362, of the
1878 edn.)

1

INTRODUCTION

The common law of villeinage consisted in the rules and procedures by which the royal justices decided which of the king's
subjects were entitled to the tenurial protection and other legal
benefits of his courts. It was also the system of law on which the
royal courts based their rulings on the legal freedom or villeinage of those who legal status came before them. Those
directly involved in villeinage cases must have been a minute
proportion of the total number of people whose status was
unfree or doubtful. The significance of the decisions about the
few on the lives of the many, the importance of the common
law's doctrine of villeinage to medieval English lordship, these
are constant themes of this book. But my primary aims have
remained: to survey the evolution of villeinage doctrine in the
courts, to seek explanations of its form and development over a
century and a half, and to assess the relative values of technical
legal factors, widely held views about society, economic
pressures, and so on.

In Part I, I examine in turn the distinctive characteristics of
villeinage status. Royal justices had to possess a mental image
of the permissible restrictions on a villein's autonomy and the
way these differed from those appropriate to free peasants.
They used it to determine status questions from evidence about
the customs owed to the peasant's lord. The historian can use it
to illuminate the handicap of villein status in the struggle for
daily existence. English villeins were never submitted to extremes of seignorial constraint of the kind we label 'slavery'. Yet
contemporary lawyers were sometimes tempted to equate the
English villein with the Roman *servus*, to facilitate the borrowing
of civilian concepts, and just possibly also to strengthen the
hands of the lords against their peasant tenants. The preliminary survey of Part I is therefore organized round the idea of
chattel slavery. I ask how closely the known characteristics of
English villeinage correspond with the institutional model of a

slavery system based on the chattel ownership of one human being by another. This view of villeinage in terms of chattel ownership has clear limitations. Examination establishes that the model was there alright, but needed constant modification in crucial ways to accord with rural realities.

Being owned by another is not the only mark of slavery. Many would say that the slave is rightless. Part II examines the few legal rights of the villein. It starts with Bracton's[1] theory of villeinage, the most sophisticated contemporary attempt to fit villeinage into a conception of the legal system as a whole, the treatise *De legibus* (before 1236). The villein reminded this work's author, with his education in the schools, of the Roman law *ascripticius* (or *colonus*), who, though not fully free, possessed something close enough to legal rights to perplex the learned commentators. *Ascripticii* were at least different from *servi*. The *De legibus* leant far more heavily on these discussions than has been realized. More broadly, its account of villeinage combines English and Roman material in a way that deserves study as social theory. How consciously he used Roman ideas to change English law, and to what end, are difficult but essential questions, even if one only wants to know what the law was. It is much easier to demonstrate that a villein, once shown to be a villein, had but few rights enforceable in the royal courts. This is not to say that he was totally rightless even there, still less to deny his resources elsewhere. Manorial and ecclesiastical courts obstinately attributed to villeins what they thought were legal rights, while neighbours, who did not think in such terms, never treated them as rightless. Outside his own courts, not even the king pursued a consistent policy of discrimination against villeins. When convenient, he was quite happy to treat villeins on a par with other taxpayers or soldiers.

But, of course, the king's law courts, which had originated the distinctions, continued to observe them. Part III examines the main ways in which they decided cases when villeinage was

---

[1] S. E. Thorne's 'Translator's Introduction' to *Br.*, iii, in 1977 left the treatise *De Legibus et Consuetudinibus Angliae* without a known author; current learning is rehearsed below Chap. 8(i). Convention would permit the use of 'Bracton' to denote the unknown author and his book, as with *Glanvill*. To avoid undue pedantry I have occasionally followed this and rather more often use 'Bractonian' for views etc. found in the book. I therefore always refer to Henry III's judge, now a mere reviser and user, as 'Henry de Bracton'. But my normal usage is to specify the *De legibus* and its (unknown) author.

at issue. The 'action of naifty'[2] was specially designed to try questions of status. For various reasons claimant lords increasingly found it an unsatisfactory method and preferred to sue in tenure rather than status. A sketch of the workings of the action of naifty and the main method of status proof, the production in court of suit of kin, thus leads into a chapter on villeinage tenure and the courts' revealing quest for effective tests. To meet the litigants' needs, ideas from the wider world outside the courts had to be imported. With the aid of the popular association between servility and the uncertainty of life under arbitrary lordship, the courts were able to conserve for lords their villein customs without removing from freemen their all-important tenurial security. And if long after the common law preserved in its own honour the myth that it had always leaned towards liberty, this was the result of another imported idea. Part III concludes with an enquiry into the ideological bias of the common law in its treatment of villeinage cases. The introduction and diffusion of the Roman law *favor libertatis* is fairly easy to explain. This done, the prima-facie case for the bias to liberty disappears. The search for an in-built procedural advantage, in the allocation of the onus of proof for example, leads at least to the technical conclusion that the common law, without thinking too much on the matter, left the parties, lord and villein, to compete on terms of formal equality. *Ceteris paribus*, of course, this must have placed the odds on the lord getting his way.

No doubt this was only to be expected in a society as stratified as medieval England. It might seem equally plausible that villeinage originated in a conscious effort to repress a dependent peasantry for the economic benefit of the seignorial classes. The last full chapter of the book, Part IV, examines the way common-law villeinage came into existence, in the light of all the regularities and anomalies detected in the workings of the developed system of the thirteenth century. Common-law doctrines cannot have existed before there was a common law. Perhaps, then, common-law villeinage is best understood as a by-product of the legal reforms and developments that created the new, expanded royal law, born out of the courts' need to define the groups to whom the benefits of the novel royal remedies ought

---

[2] This, the basic action on hereditary unfree status (*nativitas*), is the main subject of Chapter 10. 'Naifty' (sometimes 'neifty') is the central legal topic of this book.

to be offered. If so, the law of villeinage probably attests to a general increase in the freedom of the non-noble classes, from which some, the villeins, were excluded. Even if the terms of their tenure, their rent, and other customs remained the same as before, villeins' conditions would seem to have worsened by comparison with that of their more fortunate neighbours. To test that hypothesis would require another study, which would provide a more detailed knowledge of the evolution of villeinage law in the generations around 1300. If this book thus falls short of comprehensive coverage of villeinage law, and if its conclusions omit important aspects of the relationship of King, Lords, and Peasants in Medieval England, that in itself makes a telling point about Law in medieval society.

PART I

CHATTEL OWNERSHIP AND ITS CONSEQUENCES

By the early thirteenth century, Englishmen of quite low rank were becoming accustomed to availing themselves of common-law protection. The distinction between those to whom the king allowed access to his courts and those excluded, the villeins, must already have been very significant for lawyers and of great importance to a minority in the villages. Royal justices quite frequently had to decide whether to give peasant litigants a hearing, especially at sessions before itinerant justices. They gradually worked out *en route* the criteria for legal freedom in England. With each new set of judgements, it became clearer what a 'villein' was, how to define 'villeinage'. The common law, in this area even more than elsewhere, was applying press-ure on the complex variety of local custom and attempting to reduce it to uniformity. Already common lawyers well enough grounded in the learned laws[1] sometimes turned to Roman law for help in making sense of English custom. They learnt there that, if villeins would be equated with *servi*, everyone, as the *De legibus* was to say, had to be 'aut liber . . . aut servus'.[2] The Roman *servus* was a *res* or chattel, 'the one human being who could be owned'.[3] Contemporary lords had no objection to seeing their men, occasionally, as things which they owned. Now the lawyers would press the idea towards its logical conse-quences.

This conception of peasants as chattels was, it is true, quite artificial and most inappropriate to the actual circumstances of the English countryside. Nor would English rural custom sub-mit easily to coercion by men armed with logical theories. A good deal of this book will concern the difficulties caused to the lawyers and their clients. But it is a convenient device to adopt

---

[1] See E. Rathbone, 'Roman Law in the Anglo-Norman realm', *Collectanea Stephan Kuttner* i (= *Studia Gratiana* xi 1967), 253–71, and cf. S. Kuttner and E. Rathbone, 'Anglo-Norman Canonists of the Twelfth Century', *Traditio*, vii (1949–51), 284–90.

[2] *Br.*, f. 4b. The author was aware that *coloni* or *ascripticii* might offer more accept-able analogies; see below and esp. Appendix.

[3] Buckland, *Slavery*, pp. 2–5; cf. ibid., p. 10.

the jurists' assumption that the villein can be understood as his lord's chattel, as Britton said 'purement le chatel son seignur',[4] to trace the idea through its corollaries and to elicit in particular points of doctrine which cannot be explained in its terms. These last provide clues which may enable a better understanding of the lawyers' attitude towards English serfdom and its effect on the peasantry.

In the ideal world of a thirteenth-century jurist's mind, the law of villeinage might be summarized:

The lord owns his villein as a chattel and may sell him like one. Consequently, the villein himself owns nothing; all his land and goods belong to the lord. He cannot leave his land or alienate it without the lord's permission, and he is unprotected by the royal courts against the lord raising his rent or ejecting him. Having no property of his own, he has nothing to transmit to an heir, and thus has no legal heir except—for certain purposes—the lord.

How far was such a picture from the true legal situation in the courts?

---

[4] *Britton*, I. xxxii. 5 (i. 197–8) and cf. I. xxxii. 5 (i. 204–5). His direct statement stands almost alone, though the idea is taken for granted by other writers. Cf. Vinogradoff, *Villainage*, p. 44, and see *Dialogus*, II. x (101), and *The Mirror of Justices*, ed. W. J. Whittaker (*SS* vii 1893), p. 77.

THE LORD'S RIGHT OF SALE:
THE VILLEIN AS CHATTEL

The lord's right to alienate his villein at will, regardless of the villein's own wishes, is an essential part of the idea that the villein is his lord's chattel and can be seen in the general statements which occasionally occur in the counts made in court by naifty claimants. One Alexander de Steringe, for instance, pleaded that Peter son of Simon de Langham, the man he was claiming as his villein, had once been given to his grandfather as his villein 'as him whom he could give and sell'.[1] As a judicial opinion of the 1240s put it: 'Earls, barons and free tenants may lawfully . . . sell their serfs (*rusticos*) like oxen or cows . . .'.[2] There is hardly another form of wording which could demonstrate more clearly the villein's legal dependence.

Entries on the plea rolls relating to villeinage cases contain many references to sales of villeins: the sale of a man virtually amounted to proof of his villein status. As the *De legibus* noted when discussing exceptions of villeinage against the assize utrum,[3] one way of proving that the assize plaintiff was a villein was to produce the charter of sale. And many litigants did in fact plead the alleged sales of those whom they claimed to be villeins or their close relatives.[4] Sales were not just evidence of status; they also helped to establish a claimant's title to a particular villein or alleged villein. Furthermore, an alleged sale might itself have to be proved in court before its evidentiary value was felt. For example, in an action *de fine facto*, Hugh son of Avaunt sought to make Richard Angot keep to the terms of a

[1] JI 1/560, m. 58d = 561, m. 55 (Norfolk eyre 1250).
[2] *The London Eyre of 1244*, ed. H. M. Chew and M. Weinbaum (London rec. soc., 1970), no. 346, cf. *Cas. Plac.*, p. 78/20 (Casus et judicia ?1268/72).
[3] *Br.*, f. 290.
[4] *CRR* i. 264, 383 (Wilts., *coram rege* 1201), is the earliest noted; there are many others. In *CRR* xi. 1579, 1639 (Bucks. 1225), the plea referred not to a sale but to a fine of 1205, *BRB* iv. 28 = *Fines, sive pedes finium . . . A.D. 1195–1214*, ed. J. Hunter, vol. i (Rec. Comm. 1835), p. 283. In *CRR* i. 263 (Lincs., *coram rege* 1201), an action of naifty was concorded on terms which gave one of the two rival claimants all rights in a villein; this would be good evidence to cite in any future dispute.

fine made some thirty years before.[5] Richard's defence was that Hugh was his villein sold to him by his brother Geoffrey, together with the land which was the subject of the fine under dispute. Although Richard had Geoffrey brought into court to confirm this, the court upheld Hugh's right to hold the land in peace according to the terms in the fine, since Richard could not deny the fine and had not complained about it before.[6]

The lord's right of sale was, then, considered an inherent part of villeinage. These cases do not reveal just how normally the sale of villeins occurred in country life, but a somewhat neglected source, the charters of sale, does. Hundreds of originals still exist from the twelfth and thirteenth centuries, and few cartularies do not contain one or two.[7] The many modern editions of collections of medieval charters enable the historian to get some idea of the volume of sales. Maitland and Vinogradoff, concentrating their attention on villeins sold apart from their holdings, concluded that 'in practice such transactions were uncommon'[8] and have encouraged historians to play down the numbers and frequency. This is probably wrong. Whether or not the charters mention land may not be important, for even those which purport to transfer a villein on his own may have actually envisaged that his holding would pass with him.[9] Actually the holdings were being sold with their cultivators, which largely explains the absence of any organized market in men of the kind

[5] *CRR* xiv. 336 (Norfolk 1230); the fine is *Norfolk Fines*, ed. B. Dodwell (*PRS* n.s. xxvii), no. 187. *NRS* v. 481, 545a (Northants eyre 1202), is an earlier example.

[6] JI 1/560, m. 5d = 561, m. 3d (Norfolk eyre 1250), has a similar disagreement, this time about a charter said by the plaintiff to record the defendant's sale to her but by the defendant to have been his manumission.

[7] *The Cartulary of Missenden Abbey*, ed. J. G. Jenkins (*BRB* ii, x, xii, for 1938, 1946, and 1962) contained fourteen, when completed in 1331; one of these is known only from the list of contents.

[8] Vinogradoff, *Villainage*, pp. 151–3, and *P&M*, i. 414n. The only other treatment of such charters I know is J. Parker, 'Serfdom in England and the transfer of serfs in Buckinghamshire', *Records of Bucks*. vii. 2 (1893), 137–52, of curiosity value only. See also F. M. Stenton's introductions to his *Transcripts of Charters relating to . . . Gilbertine Houses* (*LRS*, xviii, 1922) and *Documents illustrative of the social and economic history of the Danelaw* (Brit. Acad. Records of Soc. and Econ. Hist. v. 1920).

[9] In manumissions where two separate charters were made, one can sometimes confirm at this was so, e.g. *H.M.C.*, *Rutland MSS* iv (1905), p. 18, from *c*. 1240, and the transactions discussed by Stenton in *EHR* xxvi (1911), 93 ff., to be dated a little after 1200. Richardson and Sayles, *Law and Leg.*, p. 143, go a little too far, as will appear below.

known in slave societies.[10] In the twelfth century men were occasionally sold as if they were genuine chattels, apart from their holdings, and their families were split up,[11] but this soon became rare. Nevertheless, since lawyers defined villeins as men who could be sold, one is bound to ask how freemen stood in this regard.

The answer seems simple and clear. A freeman, who cannot be owned by another, equally cannot be sold; this is one of the things which distinguishes him from a villein. According to the *De legibus* a freeman cannot even be possessed by one who knows him to be free.[12] Of course, the services which a freeman owed for his land could be regarded as something capable of being bought and sold, but if the law of villeinage followed the logical lines of our jurist's ideal world, sales of villeins ought to have been distinguishable from dealings in a freeman's service. The lawyers did talk as if this were so; they referred to the 'attornment'[13] of a freeman's service, never of the sale of a freeman.

In practice, so simple a distinction could not be maintained. No doubt a society with full chattel slavery could have managed to do so. Sale in open market was humiliating and distinctive. But because this was unknown in medieval England, someone dealing with a purchase of land for a new lord, say, would hardly trouble to distinguish the transfer of a poor but free peasant's services from the sale of a villein. In consequence, the peasant's descendants might end up as villeins. We must therefore examine how the lawyers approached this problem.

One reasonable criterion would be whether the tenant had the right to give or withhold his consent to the transfer of his services. But consent never served as a general and definitive

---

[10] It is not impossible that there were slave markets in pre-Conquest England. The tenth-century laws show state protection of a comparable, though much more important, market—that of cattle. Villeinage was not influenced by Anglo-Saxon slavery, though other unfree conditions may have been important; see Chap. 13.

[11] The evidence is indirect. See *Glanvill*, v. 6, last sentence, for the division of a family between two lords, termed 'ius antiquum' by 'Glanvill Revised', Gonville and Caius College, MS 205/111, p. 75.

[12] *Br.*, f. 44b, from *Dig.*, 41.2.1.6., according to Thorne's note, ii. 137.

[13] 'Attornment' is an ambiguous term. Normally at this time, it was said to be the old lord who attorned the tenant or his homage and service to the new lord. This will be the sense used here. But men also talked of tenants attorning themselves. Cf. *P&M*, i. 348, n. 1.

6 CHATTEL OWNERSHIP AND ITS CONSEQUENCES

test. In examining transactions which later law deemed invalid unless there had been attornment of the tenants,[14] Maitland noticed that there was no evidence for a normal power of the tenant to refuse his consent,[15] and that the treatise *De legibus* thought the presence of homage made an important difference. The tenant's consent was required only when his homage was transferred; even then, the law rarely permitted him to withhold it. The tenant could be compelled to acknowledge the attornment of his service, because attornment was essentially a method of livery of seisin. In contemporary law, in order to make a valid conveyance a donor had not only to make his gift (feoffment), but also to hand over seisin of the property conveyed. Failing this, the donee would not acquire full 'ownership'. Where the donor was not in physical possession of the land (the usual situation) he could not transfer its seisin, as he had none to give. What passed to the purchaser was, rather, seisin of the tenants' service. Attornment of the tenants delivered seisin of their services to the purchaser. At the same time, it clarified the tenants' position, foreclosing obligations to the old lord and defining what was due to the new one.

From the early thirteenth century, there was a special action introduced by the writ *Per que servicia* by which a purchaser of land could summon his new tenants into court to acknowledge the services by which they held.[16] Because purchasers found this valuable, long delays sometimes ensued while attempts were made to coax important tenants into court.[17] Tenants might be deemed to have been attorned without their appearance in court[18] or they might come under pressure from interested

[14] The next paragraphs are from *P&M*, i. 346–9, and 'The Mystery of Seisin', Maitland, *Coll. Papers*, i. 374–8. See also *Br.*, ff. 81b–82b.
[15] Charters reciting a tenant's consent to the transfer of his land or services are rare. One example is F. M. Stenton, *The Free Peasantry of the Northern Danelaw* (reprd. Oxford, 1969), no. 49, pp. 44–5 (*c.* 1160). Cf. also *Early Yorks. Charters* i ed. W. Farrer (*YAS* rec. ser., extra s. 1914), no. 165 (1180/1200).
[16] *BNB* 593 and *CRR* xiv. 1778 = *BNB* 598 (Suffolk 1231) will serve as an illustration.
[17] Proceedings might have to be adjourned 'pro defectu' the necessary tenants as in *SS* liii. 338 (Lincoln eyre 1219) or *CRR* xii. 481, 1223, 1836 (Norfolk 1225). In *CRR* xi. 225, 586, 640 (Somerset and Essex 1223), there was one man 'without whom the concord cannot stand'.
[18] e.g. where a lord vouched to warranty in an action of right allowed the case to go by default (cf. *CRR* xiv. 2281, Suffolk 1232, and also below p. 11) or when rents were assigned to a lord's creditors by judgement of a local court (cf. *SS* liv. 284, Gloucester eyre 1221).

parties.[19] In the early fourteenth century the courts still seem uncertain that forced attornment was illegal.[20]

The very name of the writ *Per que servicia* shows that the purchaser of land gained more than just livery of seisin from the attornment of his tenants. Obviously, to establish the precise service owed and to obtain formal agreement with the tenants helped the purchaser to avoid possible dispute in the future. In the case of villeins, however, he had no reason to wish that they should declare their services in court. The common-law rule was that the service owed by villeins was at their lord's will.[21] To set it down on a plea roll might have been construed as an acknowledgement that the new lord was limited to taking only so much as his predecessor had. Villeins therefore merely acknowledged that they held so much land 'in villeinage'.[22] There are other indications that villeins were not on the same footing as freemen when their lordship changed hands. A free tenant could always leave his holding if he did not trust his new lord or the terms on which he was to hold.[23] If he had done homage—as most thirteenth-century freemen would expect to do—he had, according to the treatise *De legibus*, a limited right to object for good cause against the transfer of his service. None of this can have been useful to a poor freeman. Even homages were occasionally sold against the tenant's will in the twelfth century. On one famous occasion in 1105, for example, Duke Robert of Normandy granted to his brother, King Henry I of England, the Count of Evreux and everything subject to him, a high-handed act which drew forth an indignant protest from Count William who did not like being treated 'like a horse or ox'.[24] In the thirteenth century, people rarely even bothered to

---

[19] *SS* lix. 1450 (Warwick eyre 1222) may be an example of this.

[20] The better view seems that it was legitimate. Compare *YB 32 and 33 Edward I* (R.S.), pp. 42–3 (1304), with *YB 33 and 35 Edward I* (R.S.), pp. 314–17 (1306).

[21] Below Chap. 6.

[22] A good example is the fine of 1205 cited above, n. 4, which ended a case traceable from *CRR* i. 95; iii. 119, 120, 123, 150 (Bucks. 1199, 1205).

[23] See below Chap. 4.

[24] Orderic Vitalis, *Historia Ecclesiastica* xi. 10 (ed. M. Chibnall, vi, 1978, p. 58). It is unclear whether the count's protest achieved anything. Cf. the payment of 7 marks in 1130 that a lord should not grant his man's service 'nisi concessu suo', *P. Roll 31 Henry I*, p. 62, cited *P&M*, i. 349 n. 1, and *Early Yorks. Charters* i, nos. 628–9 (mid-twelfth century). For the reaction of a fictional vassal to a similar attempt to transfer allegiances without consent, see *The Nibelungenlied*, tr. A. T. Hatto (Harmondsworth, 1965), p. 96.

placate a tenant whose homage had been sold over his head.[25]

Around the year 1200, then, a lawyer would have been hard put to explain with precision how differently free and villein tenants ought to be treated when a lordship passed into new hands. Consequently, the sale of a lordship was a dangerous moment for weak or unprotected tenants. Contemporaries realized this and apparently felt (whatever the lawyers might say) that a freeman's service *ought* not to be transferred without his consent.

The tenant must have feared falling into the clutches of a hostile and grasping lord who would take advantage of the legal uncertainties to increase his burden of service and take away his freedom. In 1199, John de Wolaveston had his lord, Simon Bagot, summoned before the itinerant justices at Lichfield to explain why he was about to attorn John's services to an enemy, Eudo de Mere, despite the fact that John was a *homo francus*.[26] John succeeded, for the court agreed that he should continue his accustomed service to Simon.

Others were not so lucky. The aggressive and influential Lincolnshire magnate Alexander de Pointon, an occasional itinerant justice,[27] must have been a particularly unpleasant landlord. At least two disputes in which he was concerned reached the royal courts and illustrate the sort of problems which such a man presented to his tenants.

The first case involved a long and complex series of hearings and concords.[28] In 1198, a writ of right between Alexander and one Eudo de Garton over 11¾ bovates of land in two Lincolnshire villages, Butterwick and Freston, ended in a compromise. By the final concord, the land became Alexander's for one hundred marks. Two of Eudo's tenants, however, objected to the transaction and refused to do homage to Alexander. They were

---

[25] *SS* liii. 841 (Lincoln eyre 1219) recalls an occasion when a widower about to remarry gave a cap to a tenant of his whom he was about to grant to his future wife 'in order that he would willingly (*sponte*) do homage and service to Agnes'.

[26] *WSS* iii. 60 (Lichfield eyre 1199); *francus* is a most unusual term on the plea rolls.

[27] Cf. D. M. Stenton in *LRS* xxii, p. xxvi, and *SS* lxxxiii, pp. cxciii–cxcvi, cclx–cclxi, and J. C. Holt, *The Northerners* (Oxford, 1961), Chap. IV and *passim*.

[28] It is hard to disentangle from other connected disputes, but the main references (in chronological order) are as follows: *PRS* 1st s. xxiii, no. 162 (fine of 1198); *RCR* i. 249, 331, 376; *RCR* ii. 70, 73, 240, 252; *CRR* i. 364; *CRR* ii. 36; *LRS* xxii. 139, 1174–5, 1137, 1190; *PRS* n.s. xxix, no. 162 (fine of 1202); *LRS* xxii. 1207, 1210, 1198; *CRR* ii.190, 250, 295; *PRS* n.s. xxix, no. 204 (fine of 1205).

Alard Ruff and William de Farsell' (or Farseus), whom
Alexander thereupon sued in the royal court. Alard defended
himself by attacking the validity of the sale and the subsequent
fine, on the ground that they had been made without consulting
him.

William de Farsell's warrantor, William son of Robert de
Fenne, made a similar point. He had held the land freely, he
said, until he gave it to William de Farsell' as his daughter's
marriage portion. In consequence, his lord was not permitted to
sell his land or give his homage 'eo inconsulto vel nesciente vel
non summonito'.[29] Eudo was then summoned to appear in
court and explain his sale.[30] Alexander's father had once been
farmer of the estate, and Eudo implied to the court that Alexander
had used this fact to force him to sell his land. The transaction
in the court of their mutual overlord, William de Longchamps,
was confirmed in the fine of 1198, which is thus revealed as a
collusive arrangement to clinch a deal which the parties knew
was more than a little doubtful. Alard and the two Williams
certainly thought so,[31] and William de Fenne alleged that the
agreement had been intended to disinherit him. After several
adjournments and hearings (for many of which no evidence has
survived), the dispute apparently ended in a compromise. The
two men were able to continue holding their land, William de
Fenne from Alexander, Alard from Eudo, in return for giving a
small portion of it back to the lord.[32] The dispute required
seven years' struggle and considerable concessions for men of
some substance to secure themselves on their holdings—and
even then precariously—despite the sophisticated arguments
pleaded in court.

Alexander de Pointon initiated another case himself, complaining that two of his men, Richard son of Bine and Abraham
de Ponte, had stood surety for an unnamed enemy who was

[29] *RCR* ii. 70, 240, 252.
[30] *CRR* i. 364.
[31] *SS* lxxxiii. 278 (an essoin from Michaelmas 1201) seems to show that Alard was
also proceeding against William de Longchamps and his court by a plea of false
judgement.
[32] See the fines of 1202 and 1205. In neither case did the litigant himself hold under
the new terms. Williams's son-in-law William de Farsell' acted as his attorney for the
fine of 1202 and the fine of 1205 was made by Alard's son Roger. Its immediate origins
lay in an action of novel disseisin against Eudo in which Alard was involved as
warrantor.

appealing Alexander of robbery. One wonders what the court would have decided had it accepted Alexander's story, but his adversaries told a rather different tale. They had been attorned to Alexander by their lord, Simon le Bret, but had done him only fealty for their holdings, expressly saving their homage to Simon. They had then later acted as sureties for the appellor at Simon's command.[33] The two men each paid their half mark for licence to concord, thereby participating in the more important peace agreement between the warring magnates. The episode shows how lesser men could get drawn into the quarrels of their betters, potentially to their ruin. If you came too close to men like Alexander, it was as well to be aware of legal niceties about status, or you might end up a villein. The fact that lawyers could find no neat line to separate sales of villeins from transactions involving the lords of freemen endangered many quite substantial tenants. In order to protect tenants as well as more generally to minimize violence, the lawyers continually endeavoured to establish distinctions that would work better.

There were, moreover, four other ways in which early thirteenth-century lawyers treated villeins as the chattels of their lords. Three—the notions that (1) men might dispute with each other about who owned a particular villein, that (2) villeins could be 'stolen', and that (3) lords felt free to sell villeins even if this meant splitting up families—can most conveniently be treated here. The fourth—that villeins were property in the sense that someone who held them for a limited time could on its expiry be accused of waste if he had mistreated them—is reserved for consideration later.[34]

One of the main roots of the common law of villeinage was the need to adjudicate between rival claims to villeins and their labour. Until the first decade of the thirteenth century, most cases initiated by the writ of naifty concerned such disputes fought out between rival lords.[35] As in cases about other kinds of property, litigants had to set out clearly in court the evidence for their claim. That is, they pleaded their seisin of the villeins.

---

[33] CRR ii. 124, 154, 196 (= LRS xxii. 1230, 1241, 1276-8) (Lincoln eyre and Bench 1202-3). The appeal was by Alan of Alverstone, LRS xxii. 961, and cf. ibid., 945-5, 957. Also ibid., pp. xxvi ff., for an account of the struggle between Simon and Alexander over the village of Wrangle.

[34] Below Chap. 4.

[35] Below pp. 163, 227-8 ff.

In the second type of action of naifty, where a claimant faced someone whom he alleged to be his villein (the usual sort of case after the early thirteenth century), the claimant also had to prove his seisin if he were to succeed.[36] There were two kinds of public act which claimants could cite to show that they had acquired seisin of villeins. Both are illustrated by a Buckinghamshire case.[37] In this action of novel disseisin, the twenty-four attaint jurors told how Richard de Turville had given seven villeins with their service to the Abbey of Great Missenden. Apparently, Richard had then sent his seneschal with his charter of sale to inform the men of their transfer and to supervise the handing over of seisin. The abbot took fealty from the villeins and, as no rent was due at the time, each of the villeins was lent a few pence so that he could pay his new owner something for rent *de ingressu*. The villeins then also did some token ploughings. In this way, by the taking of fealty and esplees, livery of seisin was formally effected in public and in a manner which would satisfy any future court.

The taking of esplees presented contemporary lawyers with no problems, but fealty did entail certain difficulties. In Richard de Turville's case, for example, the jurors also had to decide whether seisin of the services of a free tenant, Hugh Champion, had been validly transferred. In their view it had not, although the seneschal had publicly proclaimed the transfer of seisin to the abbey, because Hugh had never done homage or fealty to the abbey. The jurors' finding corroborates the need for a free tenant to confirm an attornment of his service by doing homage to his new lord. If villeins are found doing fealty in analogous circumstances, might not someone wonder whether they could validly be sold without such fealty being done? And how indeed could a chattel do fealty?

Obviously, to do fealty at all, set the villein apart from other

---

[36] Seisin of chattels was of course quite feasible at this time; cf. Maitland, *Coll. Papers*, i. 329–57.

[37] *CRR* xiv. 1281 = *BNB* 524 (Bucks. 1230–1). Earlier stages are *CRR* xiv. 400, 967, 973. Missenden Abbey's charters relating to Chalfont are among those transcribed on to folios now lost from the abbey cartulary. The one referred to in this case was on the missing folios, as can be seen from the manuscript's list of contents, in vol. ii of *The Cartulary of Missenden Abbey* (*BRB* x 1946), App. A, p. 175, no. xvii: 'Littera attornati Ricardi de Turvill de tenemento et tenentibus in Chalfhunt.' Hugh le Champiun's services seem to have been transferred separately in no. xix: 'Carta . . . de redditu ii. s. de tenemento quod Hugh Champion tenuit.'

chattels; no horse or ox has been known to do fealty! That the villein should pledge his faith to his lord (even perhaps do homage to him), however empty the ceremonies may have become by the thirteenth century, clearly diminishes the extent to which villeinage can be understood by the simple chattel analogy. As so often, the evidence points to the way in which thirteenth-century villeinage came into existence. Fealty by villeins is mentioned on the plea rolls only when a claimant is trying to establish his seisin to villeins or alleged villeins.[38] Early fourteenth-century manuscripts of the treatises *Casus Placitorum* and *Modus tenendi curias* contain forms of the fealty oath to be tendered to villeins. The wording varies according to whether or not the villeins held land.[39] The form for a villein who did hold land carefully avoids any suggestion of limitations on the lord's right to customs and services, whereas this circumscription is an essential part of the form for free tenants. The villein swears that he will be faithful and loyal for the tenement he holds 'in villeinage', a phrase which leaves the details open. Whether or not he has land, the villein must promise to be justiciable to the lord in body and chattels; these words could not be used of freemen.

Homage implied a mutual and personal bond. Thirteenth-century lawyers always distinguished homage from fealty. The treatise *De legibus* warns that a lord who by his own negligence or stupidity took homage from a villein might be acting to his prejudice.[40] Certainly Bracton thought homage very important; that he hinted so hard at the dire consequences of homage done by villeins is evidence that this sometimes happened in his own day. A number of contemporary charters confirm that this was so. Charters granting the homage and the *sequela* of a named peasant are fairly common in the late twelfth and early

---

[38] In addition to the case just discussed, I have noticed JI 1/1174, m. 1 (1240), JI 1/175, m. 12 (Devon eyre 1243–4), and JI 1/560, m. 25 = 561, m. 26d (Norfolk eyre 1250).

[39] *Cas. Plac.*, p. 38/109–10; *The Court Baron*, ed. F. W. Maitland and W. P. Baildon (*SS* iv 1890), p. 104 (*c*. 1327).

[40] The well-known passage on homage, *Br.*, ff. 78, 79, does not contain a form for the swearing of fealty, and mentions villeinage only as a warning; cf. *Glanvill*, ix. 1–3.

thirteenth centuries.[41] Since *sequela* is a term normally taken to apply only to the off-spring of the unfree,[42] some at least of these grants probably purported to transfer villeins who owed homage, as well as more conventional villein service. Of course, such distinctions obviously have an unreal air about them. Yet the historian might well recall Pierre Petot's belief that the French homage ceremony had servile orgins,[43] before explaining away the charters. Petot cited a fair number of contemporary French charters to demonstrate that many serfs owed something described as homage. These French charters are quite similar to the English ones, though it should perhaps be remembered that another eminent continental legal historian, F. L. Ganshof, dismissed them as a mere imitation of free homage.[44]

If Ganshof's view is followed, the English charters fit into a familiar context. Manorial courts adopted many customs which, if interpreted according to the rules of the King's Court, should have been used only for freemen. For example, actions 'according to the custom of the manor' and analogous to the petty assizes were quite common.[45] The word *homagium* was often used as a collective noun referring to all the tenants of a manor irrespective of their status in the royal courts. In England at least, until well into the thirteenth century, clear contrast cannot be made between freemen who owe homage and villeins who must not. Petot's picture of servile homage as a survival has, therefore, something to be said for it, although the matter may

---

[41] Examples in print are *The Cartulary of Newnham Priory*, ed. J. Godber (*BHRS* xliii–xliv 1963–4), no. 65, pp. 290–1; F. M. Stenton, *The Danes in England* (Raleigh Lecture, 1927, p. 22 n. 1, of the off-print.). See also BL, MSS. Add. 46353, fo. 121, Harley 2110, fo. 103v (which grants villeins with the homage of their son), and Arundel 221, fo. 57 (homage and *sequela* of a *servus*); Add. MS 46353, fo. 199, grants the *liganciam* of a villein with all his *sequela*. I owe the references to these and other charters to the kindness of Miss Barbara Dodwell. Bodleian Library, MS charters, Norfolk a.6 (614), is a will of *c*. 1200, cited by M. M. Sheehan, *The Will in England . . . to the End of the Thirteenth Century* (Toronto, 1963), p. 287, as the only example he knew of a villein being devised by will, but the devise was in fact of 'totum servicium E. cum homagio suo et tota sequela sua', which leaves the matter in some doubt.

[42] *P&M*, i. 380–1.

[43] P. Petot, 'L'Hommage servile: essai sur la nature de l'hommage', *RHDFE* 4e s. vi (1927), 68–107, cited with approval by M. Bloch, *Mélanges*, i. 509–10. Also P. Ourliac, 'L'Hommage servile dans la région toulousaine', *Mélanges . . . L. Halphen* (Paris, 1951), pp. 551–6, and M. and A. Gouron, 'Hommage et servage d'ourine: le cas des serfs d'Agde', *Mélanges P. Tisset* (Montpellier, 1970), pp. 267–75.

[44] Ganshof, *Feudalism*, tr. P. Grierson (3rd ed., London, 1964), p. 81.

[45] Cf. below pp. 49, 69.

be more complex than he thought.[46] The absence of any English case where the doing of homage has been pleaded by an alleged villein as evidence that he is really free corroborates Petot's view. In four early cases, actions *de homagio capiendo* were successfully defeated by the plea that the plaintiff was a villein[47] or that he only held in villeinage,[48] but this is not quite the same thing as pleading that you are free *because* you have done homage. It would, therefore, be unwise to reject the notion of servile homage entirely.[49]

The taking of fealty, then, and perhaps of homage, must be seen with the taking of esplees as a method of establishing seisin to villeins. A small group of cases go further and treat the villein as a piece of property which can be wrongly diverted to the advantage of someone who is not his rightful lord. That is, they imply a view of the villein as something which can be stolen like a chattel.

Two appeals from the Cornwall eyre of 1201 allege the taking of villeins, though neither came to much.[50] Two other cases were actions *de fine facto*. In the first, Ralph son of Avelina alleged that his neighbour, Reginald son of Eadmund, had

---

[46] My present feeling is that a convincing explanation would have to take into account a number of different ceremonies used in different areas at various periods before the twelfth century to symbolize the bonds between lords and their various ranks of followers. Few of these may have been specifically free or servile. Contemporaries present at them would have been thinking more generally of dependence, protection by the lord, and the obligations due from that class of men in that particular region. Twelfth-century clerks used *homagium* or related terms to describe many of these rituals, and problems only arose towards 1200 when, under the influence of the learned laws leading them to a clearer distinction between free and serf, men began to try and define homage as something characteristic of freemen who—unlike serfs—could choose their lords and the terms on which they were prepared to serve. Petot himself drew attention to the evidence for another type of ritual in his 'La Commendise personnelle', *Mélanges Paul Fournier* (Paris, 1929), pp. 609–14, noting that most of it came from eastern France. Eleventh- and twelfth-century English references to commendation might be re-examined with this hypothesis in mind.

[47] *CRR* ii. 131 (Norfolk 1202); *CRR* iv. 259 (Beds. 1206).

[48] *CRR* iii. 141 (Wilts. 1204); *CRR* viii. 65 = *BNB* 53 (Devon 1219) whose later stages are ibid. 145, 232, 339 (1219–20), and the concord *Devon Feet of Fines*, ed. O.J. Reichel (Devon and Cornwall rec. soc., iii, 1912), no. 129, pp. 67–8. JI 1/567, m. 18 (Norfolk eyre 1257), is a later example.

[49] Voluntary enserfment is relevant here. Rare examples are the interesting story told by manorial jurors in 1297 about events from 1202/40 (probably 1218–19 or 1226) and a straight case from 1286, *Court Rolls of the Manor of Wakefield*, i. ed. W. Pailey Baildon (*YAS* xxix 1901), pp. 78, 224. And see pp. 36, 183, below for penal enserfment.

[50] *SS* lxviii. 284, 393 (Cornwall eyre 1201).

lured Ida, a villein woman, and her son William, on to his land against the terms of a fine his father had made with Avelina at a previous eyre.[51] This kind of complaint may have been much more common at an earlier time when tenants were fewer. It failed here because Ralph could not prove his right to Ida and William. In the second case, Richard son of John claimed that Reginald the Young had chased one of his men, King' off his land, though he had previously agreed by fine that the land should be Richard's.[52] Reginald disclaimed interest in the land but said that King' was his villein and had not been affected by the fine.

A lord could, then, expect compensation for the unjust loss of his villein. He also had free disposal of the villein's family. One of the harshest customs in contemporary serfdom was that by which the children of a marriage between villeins of different lords were shared by the respective lords, thereby splitting up the family. On the Continent the custom of *formariage*—where a serf made a special payment for permission to marry out of the lordship—demonstrates the importance of the question. Various methods were used to avoid the situation where children claimed by one lord lived out of his control on another lordship. Sometimes serfs were exchanged when two married across the lines of their lordships. When this was impossible, children were sometimes separated from each other and their parents, to be shared between the lords as agreement or local custom decreed.[53]

The harshness of this custom dates from an earlier age when men were scarce and land plentiful. In the later twelfth century the practice was probably becoming archaic. Glanvill says that if the situation arose the children were to be divided *pro-portionaliter* between the lords.[54] Within approximately thirty years, this statement was annotated as 'ius antiquum' by

[51] *BNB* 1834 (Norfolk eyre 1227).
[52] *CRR* viii. 110; ix. 227; x. 55 (Surrey 1219–21).
[53] See P. Dollinger, *L'Évolution des classes rurales en Bavière* ... (Paris, 1949), pp. 257–8; M. Bloch, *Mélanges,* i. 293–5 etc. J. Balon has now brilliantly shown that the word *collibertus* was used for serfs in whom two lords had an interest, 'Le Statut juridique des colliberts du Val de Loire', *Revue bénédictine* lxxvii (1967), 298–324. The theologians seem to have worried more about lords breaking up marriages than taking children away from their parents.
[54] *Glanvill,* v. 6. Hall translated this 'equally' in his edition, p. 58. Glanvill may also have in mind certain local customs, by which, for example, the husband's lord received more than his wife's.

'Glanvill Revised'.[55] When the author of the *De legibus* worked through the four topics covered by Glanvill in this chapter, he changed this one completely,[56] and assimilated it to his treatment of the children of marriage between parents of different status. For him the question became: in whose lordship was the child born? This could still entail partition in rare cases and his justification of the rule is rather artificial. Local customs can alone demonstrate actual practice.[57] Partition customs, of whatever form, left no mark on the plea rolls.

[55] Gonville and Caius College, MS 205/111, p. 75. 'Glanvill Revised' is Maitland's name for an attempt to up-date Glanvill, made apparently *c*. 1229. Hall, *Glanvill*, pp. 195–8, gives details.

[56] *Br.*, f. 5. See my article, 'The Proof of Villein Status in the Common Law', *EHR* lxxxix (1974), 733 ff., for the rest of his adaptation of Glanvill on marriages between villeins and free. I have followed the rearrangement of the text proposed by Professor Thorne in his translation, ii. 30. For Bracton's discussion of the *servus communis* in ff. 25b, 43b, see below, p. 91, n. 30.

[57] Cf. *Br.*, f. 271 *addicio*, for a Cornish custom that implies that a rule similar to Glanvill's had formerly prevailed. Woodbine doubts whether this can be Bracton himself; see his edition i. 404.

3

THE LORD'S OWNERSHIP OF
THE VILLEIN'S PROPERTY

What, then, are the corollaries of the view in thirteenth-century legal practice that treats the villein as his lord's chattel? First of all, it follows that the lord ought to be the true owner or *verus dominus* of anything which may appear to be owned by the villein. In strict logic, whether the property in question is land or chattels should not matter, but our sources deal with these in different ways, and so must we.

The account in the treatise *De legibus* mainly concerns land. It is studded with quotations of the Roman-law tag: 'Quidquid per servum adquiritur, id domino adquiritur.'[1] Thus according to the author, a lord can acquire property through his villein, even though he may not have been aware of what the villein was doing when the acquisition was actually made, providing it was done in his name. If it was not, the villein enjoyed all the rights of an owner and was capable of making a valid gift or sale of the property which would bar any future claim by his lord,[2] or of retaining a seisin which might be passed on to his heirs.[3] By his perhaps excessive logic here, the author lands himself in some difficulty. Even in his view, though, the lord becomes the owner of his villein's acquisition as soon as he takes possession of it. This he may do with impunity and the villein then has no remedy for his ejection.[4] Once in seisin, the lord, and not his

---

[1] The best place to see Bracton organizing his thought around this tag is ff. 25 ff. Cf. also ff. 43b–44, 100b, and Thorne's translation, ii. 37, 288, for the Roman-law sources; also Richardson, *Bracton: the Problem of his Text* (SS suppl. vol. ii, 1964), pp. 110–11. Buckland, *Slavery*, Chap. VI, outlines the Roman law and there are earlier discussions of this material by Vinogradoff, *Villainage*, pp. 67–8, and *P&M*, i. 416.

[2] *Br.*, f. 25b. Cf. *Fleta*, iv. 3 (194), and *Britton*, II. vii. 5 (i. 249). Once in possession, the villein's purchaser would be protected from the villein's lord by the assize; cf. *BNB* 1203 (Lincs. 1236–7), cited *Br.*, f. 31b, also *Britton* II. vi. 3 (i. 246). The position is similar to that occuring when a lessee wrongly alienates his holding without his lessor's assent; see for an example SS liii. 38 (Lincoln eyre 1218).

[3] See below Chap. 4.

[4] *Br.*, ff. 25, 193b, 196b. Cf. *Fleta*, i. 60 (128), iii. 15 (203), iv. 11 (235).

villein, is the *verus dominus* of the holding. If the lord permits his villein to retain possession and continue cultivating the land, the villein has in future no more than seisin 'in villeinage' or 'in the lord's name'.[5]

Cases on the plea rolls illustrate the point. Lords are regarded as owning land held by their villein tenants. Thus, litigants succeeded in assizes because their villeins had been ejected from their pasture [6] or had had corn stolen from their holding.[7] Another who complained *coram rege* without writ about intrusion into the land of a deceased tenant who had held of him in villeinage was advised by the court to bring an assize.[8] And Godfrey son of Nicholas's assize of mort d'ancestor failed when Ranulf the hayward confessed that he held the land in villeinage of the Countess of Oxford 'who holds that land'.[9]

The Bractonian view, though supported by these cases, cannot have emerged naturally from them. The author's actual line of thought was quite complex. First, there was Roman law. He often reiterated another tag, inspired by the *Digest*, that 'qui ab aliis possidetur, nihil possidere poterit'.[10] If anyone possessed by another cannot himself possess anything, then no villein in his lord's possession can have possessions of his own. Certainly, he can give nothing away, for no one can give what he does not have. But this conclusion is too extreme,[11] and he calls the doctrine of seisin to his rescue. Anyone who has seisin may validly give away such seisin as he has.[12] Elsewhere there is a different and preferable argument that avoids both Roman law

[5] See for example *Br.*, f. 197. BL, Add. Charter 43371 is a grant made by the Hospitallers in 1194 to one Edith and her heirs; the heirs swore that they would never lay any claim in future to 'aliquid de terris quod Lodovicus pater predicte Edithe nomine Hospitalis Ierosolomit' possedit'. The obligations included heriot, a third of the chattels.

[6] *BRB* vi. 217 (Bucks. eyre 1227). The plaintiff's attorney later acknowledged that his tenants held freely!

[7] *NRS* v. 892 (Northampton 1203).

[8] *CRR* xii. 277 (Lincs. 1225) discussed by Richardson and Sayles in *Procedure without Writ*, p. xlix, where it is no. 5.

[9] JI 1/229, m. 10 (Essex 1227).

[10] *Br.*, ff. 11b, 12, 17, 25b, 191. Cf. *Fleta*, iv. 11 (235). The source was *Dig.*, 41.2.23.1.

[11] It clashes with his own view, above p. 000.

[12] *Br.*, f. 25b. The author knows that what he is saying is controversial ('videtur . . . Respondeo') and I have seen no cases in which villeins seem to have been able to alienate their seisin without the lord's license. See further below Chap. 5.

and complications.[13] Since, he argues, the villein's property really belongs to his lord, all villein land-purchases must be made with the lord's money and therefore in his name. A case from *Bracton's NoteBook*[14] is very much to the point. On that occasion, an assize of novel disseisin failed, because the plaintiff had sold the land to one of the defendant's villeins, who had passed it on to his lord 'as land bought with his lord's chattels'. These differing accounts, scattered through the *De legibus,* always occur in a land-law context. However, the statements undoubtedly applied equally to chattels, as the last case illustrates.

Villeins occasionally heard in court that they had nothing of their own. When William son of Robert brought an assize of novel disseisin and was accused of being unfree, he claimed to have bought his manumission.[15] But, answered his opponent John de Chettewynde, 'he had nothing of his own, since he was a villein'. Then again, there was the unpleasant rejoinder of the Abbot of Burton in 1280, when charged with robbery in the course of a long dispute over the services owed by his peasant tenants. He had, he said, taken only what belonged to him, since villeins could own nothing except their bellies.[16]

These extreme statements were quiet justified in legal theory, for there is no evidence of anything like the Roman law's *peculium* in England.[17] In practice, of course, villeins were often treated or allowed to behave in ways which seem to imply that they had property rights. Lawyers were well aware that manorial custom almost always treated the villein as if he were the owner of his chattels and holding. More important, the royal administration did not forbear to tax villeins because of any logical difficulties with legal theory.[18] Yet the common law neither incorporated this knowledge into its system nor tried to

---

[13] *Br.,* ff. 196 *addicio,* 196b, 198. Cf. *Fleta,* iv. 11 (237).

[14] *BNB* 1256 (Norfolk 1238–9).

[15] JI 1/1172, m. 4d = Vinogradoff, *Villainage,* App. IV, pp. 421–2 = *Ab. Plac.,* p. 104 (?Salop 1225–6).

[16] *The Burton Chartulary,* ed. G. Wrottesley (*WSS* v. 1 1884), pp. 81–6.

[17] A Roman-law *peculium* was the property or money a master allowed his *servus* to treat as if it were his own, though ultimate ownership of course remained with the master. Bracton's one reference, *Br.,* f. 44, is lifted bodily from *Dig.,* 41.2.24, and cannot be taken seriously. Also *Fleta,* iv. 15 (203).

[18] See below Chap. 9 (ii).

rationalize it, as did other systems of slavery and serfdom law.[19] This interesting point cannot be explained merely by the logic of the lord's ownership, and is perhaps another hint that the confrontation of manorial custom with the law of villeinage was too recent in the early thirteenth century for the learned lawyers to have made impact on it.

The situation was by no means invariably to the villein's disadvantage, for in later law he could always use his unfree status to bar actions for debt and so on.[20] In general, however, the common law worked very heavily against the villein. The lord could take anything his villein held, and the villein had no redress in the royal courts. Thus in an action of replevin[21] alleging the unjust taking of animals as distress, the defendant answered that she had taken them 'as her own', and the issue became simply whether the plaintiff was her villein. Cases of this kind are discussed below; there was no case to answer once the plaintiff had been proved a villein.[22]

Since the villein had nothing of his own, if he acted to his own financial disadvantage, his lord was also the loser. Thus a lord might sometimes claim compensation in his court because his villein had cost him money. For instance, a villein who had been fined for some misdemeanour in an ecclesiastical court might be amerced in his local manorial court for 'loss of the lord's chattels'.[23] When the clergy complained to the king about lay

[19] Buckland, *Slavery*, Chap. VIII, discusses the *peculium*, which has been cited in recent argument about slavery in the Americas as one of those Roman-law features which may have made slave conditions better in Latin America than in the United States. See S. M. Elkins, *Slavery: a problem in American institutional and intellectual life* (Chicago, 1959), A. A. Sio, 'Interpretations of slavery: the slave status in the Americas', *Comparative Studies in Society and Hist.*, vii. 3 (1965), pp. 288–305; recent views have tended to be sceptical of Elkins' suggestion.

[20] Cf. *Britton*, I. xxix. 25 (i. 168): 'quant qe il ad si est a soen seignur, si qe il ne ad rien propre', and below p. 000.

[21] JI 1/560, m. 5d = 561, m. 3d (Norfolk eyre 1250).

[22] To plead that the goods taken belonged to one's own villein was an equally good defence in such cases. *LRS* xxii. 561 (Lincoln eyre 1202) is an example. In JI 1/699, m.7d (Oxford eyre 1247) the defence to a robbery plaint was that the defendant's villein had taken the goods on to his lord's land of his own free will; the parties came to a compromise.

[23] Examples are *Select Pleas in Manorial Courts*, ed. F. W. Maitland (*SS* ii 1888), pp. 97, 98, 113, 162–3; *The Court Rolls of the Abbey of Ramsey*, ed. W. O. Ault (New Haven, 1928), pp. 196, 239, 246, 250, 251, 252, 258–9 and see J. A. Raftis, 'Social structures in five East Midland villages', *Ec. H. R.* 2nd s. xviii (1965), 89. I have noticed similar steps taken when villeins got into trouble in secular courts. Since most of the cases noticed concern sexual morality, see below Chap. 11, pp. 187–8, for a possible explanation.

encroachments on what they claimed to be their jurisdiction, the laity's reply was always careful to reserve explicitly the lords' right to prevent money penalties being imposed on their villeins 'since they and their rights in their goods are their lords' '.[24] In a distress case from about 1270,[25] counsel, extending the argument, was prepared to assert that a villein could do nothing at all in court unless his lord were present.

Such a view could be justified, given the state of the law then. An action of naifty would be expensive for the lord, even if he succeeded. The villein would be amerced for false claim, and on several occasions, the lord, having just proved his claim to his villein, had then to stand surety for the half-mark amercement owed to the king.[26]

Another topic is worth considering here as a last consequence of the lord's ownership of his villein's goods. If these belong to the lord, they ought to be available to any of the lord's creditors in the same way as his other chattels to satisfy them for his debts. In Maitland's words, 'we may say that the serf, having no proprietary rights against the lord, is treated as having none against those who by virtue of legal process are enabled to claim what the lord himself could seize'. Maitland went on to compare references from the *Dialogue of the Exchequer* and the treatise *De legibus*, and concluded that 'we seem to see here a change unfavourable to the villein' during the intervening period. This tentative suggestion was probably wrong. More likely, one legal rule remained in force from the time it was established by Henry II into the thirteenth century.[27]

The *Dialogue's* reference occurs in a passage where the master is explaining to his pupil how the king may obtain money owing to him as taxation or feudal dues.[28] We cannot know, therefore, if what is said there applies to dealings between tenants-in-chief

---

[24] Powicke and Cheney, *Councils*, II. 1. 690–1, 2.1217 (1261, 1300–1). I suspect that *jura* or something similar has been omitted in the passage quoted: 'et sua (jura) in bonis suis'.

[25] *Cas. Plac.*, p. 80/22 (? 1268/72).

[26] Examples are JI 1/37, m. 23d (Berks. eyre 1241), JI 1/404, m. 4 (Lancs. eyre 1246), and JI 1/1045, m. 27 (York eyre 1241). This is the background to c. 20 of Magna Carta, protecting villeins from unrestricted amercement; see below pp. 143–4.

[27] *P&M*, i. 419–20. Maitland's suggestion was confined to a footnote, but has been taken up for example by Charles Johnson in his edition of the *Dialogus*, p. 112 n. 1.

[28] *Dialogus*, II. xiv (112).

and their own tenants[29] or, more improbably still, to transactions between parties unconnected by any feudal bond. Nevertheless, Richard FitzNeal says that the sheriff may enter the
land of a royal debtor's villeins, seize and sell their goods
(subject to the same rules as the lord's other goods) 'for these
are well known to belong to the lord', but only when all the
tenant-in-chief's saleable goods have been disposed of. Here,
apparently, is a recent innovation. A royal *constitutio* had established the rule that distress for royal debts, except scutage,[30]
should start with the lord's demesne before going on to the
debtor's other property. Richard could still remember, though,
the days when goods were quite legally sold off indiscrimi-
nately, and the bailiffs did not bother to find out whether they
belonged to the lord of the fee or to his knights or villeins. But
from the time of the *constitutio* the rule was 'prius propria, dehinc
aliena', which might even so involve villeins in unlimited though
sporadic demands.[31]

Between the *Dialogue* and the *De legibus*, there are no written
discussions of the villein's liability to be distrained for his lord's
debts and precious little other evidence. Exchequer regulations
attributed to the beginning of John's reign detail the correct
procedure for the enforcement of the king's debts but do not
mention villeins.[32] Only a few scraps of evidence facilitate a
reconstruction of the legal position of the mid-thirteenth century. In 1232 Henry III ordered the sheriff of Wiltshire not to
distrain Geoffrey de Mandeville's villeins of Highworth for his
Exchequer debts until further orders were received, but to
distrain instead on Geoffrey's own goods.[33] On 7 October 1250

[29] Magna Carta, c. 60, would suggest that it should, and the principle may have
been applied at least intermittently; cf. Henry I's Coronation Charter, c. 2, for
example.

[30] No doubt this is because scutage is associated with wartime and was virtually a
tax on knightly undertenants. See T. Madox, *History . . . of the Exchequer*, xvi. 8–9
(London, 1711), pp. 469–70, S. K. Mitchell, *Studies in Taxation under John and Henry III*
(New Haven, 1914), pp. 317–18, 335–8. It is perhaps worth remarking that the 1235
writ for the collection of scutage does not bother to recite consent by villeins, Stubbs,
Charters, pp. 357–8.

[31] In *Dialogus*, I. xi (59), Richard recalls an occasion, apparently in 1167, when
Bishop Nigel of Ely's payment for a forest assart was taken partly from his villeins. This
may well give a *terminus a quo* for the *constitutio*.

[32] *Chronica Rogeri de Hoveden*, ed. W. Stubbs (R. S. 4 vols. 1868–71), iv. 152.

[33] *Cl. R., 1231–4*, p. 51. It looks from the rubric 'Pro villanis de Hegworth' as if the
villeins themselves purchased this writ.

Henry III addressed all the sheriffs of England in the presence of his Council at the Exchequer. Among his orders to them was that 'no villein (*rusticus*) should be distrained for a debt of his lord's while the lord has anything else by which he can be distrained'.[34] The royal view still seems to be that villein property, though ultimately at the disposal of the lord's creditors, should not be used until his other assets had been tried. Of course, in practice men may often have neglected this order of availability,[35] but sheriffs were not encouraged to help them. A remark made during a case in the 1270s tends to support this view.[36] In the course of the pleadings, reference was made to the grant of a perpetual rent-charge in frankalmoign, on terms which entitled the recipient priory to distrain for any arrears on a specified villeinage tenement, whether held by the present tenant or anyone else. This statement strongly suggests that the law did not normally allow immediate distraint on villeinage.

Thus the view of the *De legibus* is quite surprising. In the section on novel disseisin, the author considers disseisins committed under colour of distraint.[37] One way in which a tres-passory disseisin can be committed, he observes *en passant*, is by not observing the correct order of availability of property for distraint, as where a man is distrained 'per res suas dominicas' when he has villeinage. This is too summary and casual to be a suggestion for reform, and may be a slip.[38] Even if it was a considered view, distress was, after all, a method of applying pressure on a debtor which did not entitle the creditor to sell the goods on which he was distraining. In medieval times, only the king could do that by his prerogative. Other creditors had to seek execution by the appropriate writ, for it did not come as of right.[39] The passage is not, then, strictly parallel to that from the *Dialogue*.

If the passage be dismissed as error, the rule would seem to

---

[34] I am grateful to Dr Michael Clanchy for bringing this to my notice. He has printed the speech from the Memoranda Roll in *History* liii (1968), pp. 215–16.

[35] Free tenants were also sometimes troubled by distress for the debts or defaults of their lord, e.g. Sayles, *Select Cases in K.B.* iii, pp. 145–7 (Lincs. 1305).

[36] *Cas. Plac.*, p. 115 (1273/8).

[37] *Br.*, f. 217, blindly followed by *Fleta* iv. 17 (250).

[38] For other slips which may be comparable, see Thorne, *Br.*, i, pp. xxxix–xi as well as the 'Translator's Introduction' to vol. iii, and below, Chap. 8.

[39] See T. F. T. Plucknett, *The Legislation of Edward I* (Oxford, 1949), pp. 55–6, 148–9, and *idem, Concise Hist.*, pp. 389–91.

have remained basically the same from the days of Henry III, and is thus yet another exception to the strict application of the logic of the lord's ownership of his villein. Once again the villein is considered a special kind of chattel. He and his goods were not to be bothered by the lord's creditors until more ordinary goods had been tried.

4

ATTACHED TO THE SOIL

The previous chapter concluded with evidence which showed the villein as his lord's chattel, indeed, but a rather special kind of chattel covered by special rules. Other material already surveyed, such as the charters recording the sale of villeins, implied that villeins were in the eyes of their lords very closely associated with the land they held in villeinage. This chapter will present further evidence for this seignorial viewpoint and examine some of its consequences.

The first writer to say directly that the villein could be regarded as part of the tenement on which he dwelt was Britton, writing at the very end of the thirteenth century. First, he described the villein as his lord's chattel pure and simple. He then modified his statement by saying that, unlike other chattels, the villein might not be devised by will because he was 'annex al fraunc tenement' and as such outside the jurisdiction of the Courts Christian where the validity of wills was determined.[1] It seems true that villeins were not devisable,[2] and this restriction on the logic of the chattel analogy is interesting because several legal systems (Roman law among them) did permit the transfer or manumission of genuine chattel slaves by will.[3] One might have expected the Church to encourage testamentary manumissions as a means of achieving salvation and to adopt this rule as canon law, though this does not seem to have happened. Britton's statement that the villein is 'annex al fraunc tenement' is therefore not to be rejected out of hand and could be correct, except that there are no similar statements from earlier writers. The attempt to explain this leads into a complex problem in the history of ideas.

Britton's statement is at least partly the product of Roman-

---

[1] *Britton*, I. xxxii. 5 (i. 197). Since many borough customs permitted land to be devised, I suppose that villeins might have been devised by the wills of burgesses. I know of no evidence on the matter.

[2] See above p. 13 n. 41 for a possible exception.

[3] e.g. Buckland, *Slavery*, pp. 442 ff., 460 ff.

law influence which he was not the first to feel. Marc Bloch long ago demonstrated that the phrase *servus glebae* began to be used by French lawyers around 1300 as a semi-official term for serfs.[4] This particular phrase was never used in the same way in England, but the *ascripticius*, carrying much the same connotation, was. Both suggest that those to whom they refer were tied to the soil. *Ascripticius* was the standard term for the unfree in the *Dialogue of the Exchequer*. One passage contrasted the *ascripticius* with the freeman, because unlike him he could not leave the condition of his status against the will of his lord. Another passage calls land possessed by *ascripticii* demesne, since the lord could remove them at will from one tenement to another, or even sell them apart from their land,[5] and an ecclesiastical canon of 1258, repeated in 1261, also used the term, when prohibiting interference with villein wills.[6]

Apart from the treatise *De legibus*, these are the only contemporary English sources that use the term *ascripticius*. They show that some lawyers conceived the villein to be attached to the soil—in the sense that he could not freely leave the land he occupied—long before Britton. But the *De legibus* emphasized a different aspect of the idea that the villein was attached to the soil. Precedents for his particular argument can be found among the glossators of Roman and Canon law.[7] He applied the phrase *glebae ascripticius* not to the ordinary villein but to the villein sokeman of the Ancient Demesne,[8] and thus his full argument is not relevant here. The author had in mind an analogy between the villein sokeman and the freeman in villeinage.[9] Each might do servile works, but did not owe them by reason of personal status, since each remained personally free. The services were owed by reason of the tenement held. Neither was to be compelled to continue holding the land if he did not wish to do so, and each could therefore withdraw at will. This distinguished

---

[4] See Appendix for the next paragraphs.

[5] *Dialogus*, I. x, xi (pp. 53, 56).

[6] Powicke and Cheney, *Councils*, II. 1. 585, 681, quoted in Appendix. See also *Regiam Majestatem*, II. 12.3, which uses the word when discussing sale and manumission of villeins. P. Stein, 'The Source of the Romano-Canonical part of Regiam Majestatem', *Scottish Hist. Review* xlviii (1969), 107–23, has given good reasons for dating the work after 1318.

[7] See below, p. 271.

[8] *Br.*, ff. 7, 203. Bloch, *Mélanges*, i. 370 n. 2, does not seem to have noticed this.

[9] This is f. 209.

both from the pure villein whose status prevented him from leaving the land.

The *De legibus'* treatment of the famous Bestenover Case illustrates the author's argument. This complex dispute is introduced into the treatise to support the distinction Bracton wished to make between tenure and status.[10] As a contemporary commentator remarked,[11] a freeman may do villein services for his holding, but he does not thereby become unfree. Why not? He gives the Bractonian answer: because he can leave the holding like a freeman. The plea-roll entry on the case does not mention this point, which must be due to later analysts, probably from the circle of William de Raleigh. The *De legibus* applies the phrase *glebae ascripticius* to the villein sokeman in much the same way.

On this topic, then, Roman law had a certain influence on English lawyers' ideas. To assess its importance, the historian needs to know how the influence reached them. How familiar was the idea of the villein's attachment to the soil in English court practice in the early thirteenth century?

One important area in which the common law did treat villeins as essentially part of their lords' land is the action of waste. The law on this subject clearly reflects the feelings and economic convenience of the landed classes. The topic recurs frequently in thirteenth-century legislation, and the gradual process by which reversioners gained a general remedy against those tenants with a more temporary interest in the land can readily be traced.[12] The aim was to preserve the land intact for the reversioner, together with any attached capital assets. Among these capital assets, the villeins needed to cultivate the land were by no means the least important. Magna Carta already prescribed that wardships were to be held 'sine destructione hominum vel rerum'.[13] In 1258 the barons, still seeking to remove the barriers against the free succession of their heirs, requested that the lord of a fee should make no waste, exile, sale,

[10] See below Chap. 8 (iii). The full references to the Bestenover Case are on p. 56 n. 28.

[11] *BNB* 70.

[12] The action of Waste is discussed by T. F. T. Plucknett in *YB 12 Edward II* (Selden YBB xxiii), p. lx, and S. F. C. Milsom, *Novae Narrationes*, pp. cxc–cxcviii.

[13] Magna Carta, 1215, c. 4 (= Articles of the Barons, c. 3 and c. 5, of the 1225 version). See also Unknown Charter, c. 3, J. C. Holt, *Magna Carta* (Cambridge, 1965), p. 303.

or alienation of, *inter alia*, men holding villeinage tenements.[14] This was granted, in a more generalized form, the next year when the Provisions of Westminster forbade *firmarii* to make waste, sale, or exile of various types of property including men, unless specifically authorized to do so in writing.[15] Somewhat earlier the *De legibus* had described restrictions on the freedom of action of holders of wardships and tenants in dower in similar terms. The writ forms and model counts he supplies include versions alleging waste of men.[16]

The plea rolls elucidate the various forms which waste of men might take. Several cases concern sales, and the *De legibus* gives a prohibition writ and specimen count for this.[17] Manumission, another possibility, was specifically mentioned by the author of the Unknown Charter.[18] Less obvious are other acts probably summarized as exile in the legislation. Sometimes the record does tell us of villeins going into exile;[19] more often the courts interested themselves in the reasons for their departure. Excessive tallage was frequently mentioned. In one case, for example, villeins had allegedly been tallaged 'ultra modum' so that some were driven into exile. But the defendant claimed to have taken tallage reasonably and once a year only, and the issue was put to a jury on the question of fact.[20] Other offences against villeins which were alleged to constitute waste of the land were the taking of their goods,[21] the exaction of excessive services,[22] and

[14] Petition of the Barons, 1258, c. 1, Stubbs, *Charters*, p. 373.

[15] Provisions of Westminster 1259, c. 20, Stubbs, *Charters*, p. 394, incorporated in Statute of Marlborough 1267, c. 23.

[16] *Br.*, ff. 87, 315–17. Cf. *Britton*, V. xiv. 5 (ii. 299–300), and *Fleta*, v. 34 (360).

[17] *Br.*, f. 315. *CRR* xiv. 1105, 1630 (Warwick 1231), JI 1/174, m. 21 (Devon eyre 1238), JI 1/560, m. 11d = 561, m. 11 (Norfolk eyre 1250).

[18] Unknown Charter, c. 3. Cf. the writ ordering a view, *Br.*, f. 31b, *CRR* xiv. 1105, 1630. Also *CRR* i. 109 (Surrey 1199), where a lord complained that his ex-bailiff had, *inter alia*, redeemed men. And *Novae Narrationes*, B263.

[19] *BNB* 632 (Norfolk 1231), *CRR* xiv. 1526, 1555 = *BNB* 574 (Surrey 1231), *BNB* 691 (Essex 1232), JI 1/561, m. 60 (Norfolk eyre 1250). Statute of Gloucester 1269, c. 5, did not mention exile but was interpreted as if it did in the early fourteenth century, *Novae Narrationes*, p. cxciii.

[20] JI 1/561, m. 60 (Norfolk eyre 1250). Other examples *CRR* xiv. 1059 = *BNB* 485 (Herts. 1231), *CRR* xiv. 1788 (Hunts., Northants 1231), *BNB* 691 (Essex 1232), JI 1/176, m. 9d. (Devon eyre 1248–9).

[21] *CRR* xiv. 1105, 1630 (Warwicks. 1232), JI 1/319, m. 14 (Norfolk case from Herts. eyre 1248), where the villeins' chattels were taken, their houses and the trees growing on the land rased, according to the plaintiff's allegations.

[22] *Br.*, ff. 87, 316d, refers to the taking of reasonable customs and services only. Cf. the similar wording of the concord in *CRR* xii. 1443 (Sussex 1225). Also *CRR* xii. 181 (Essex 1227).

the extortion of excessive amercements and sureties against the terms of a previous agreement.[23]

These cases reveal that the law at this time took a clear line on waste of men. All acts tending to impoverish villeins below the subsistence level were condemned. When men must flee in order to survive, the capital value of the land and its reversion fall. The common law in the thirteenth century was thus prepared to regard villeins as part of the value of a piece of land.[24] The most obvious consequence of this view, which was of course far from new, was to encourage the king to help lords to restrain their peasants from flight or to bring them back if they did flee. Royal writs dating back to the late eleventh century show Norman kings granting this kind of aid to favoured beneficiaries, and the writs they used were adapted by the Angevin common law into the regular writs of naifty by which status disputes were brought into the courts in the thirteenth century. How this happened is described later in this book.

The developed writ of naifty ordered the sheriff: 'Facias habere R.M. nativum suum et fugitivum . . . qui fugit de terra sua post primam coronationem', or something similar.[25] That is, the sheriff is to cause the claimant to have back his fugitive villein. In practice, however, it was only rarely that thirteenth-century àctions of naifty were about villeins who had run away from their holdings and were to be returned there. A sheriff who took the writ's wording literally would be asking for trouble.[26] Most entries about naifty actions apparently deal with peasants who denied that they are unfree while still on their land. Probably only a very few cases refer to genuine flights. The case in which Richard son of John claimed two sisters Margery and Rosa de Northcote illustrates the difficulties.[27] Richard pleaded in his count that they were his villeins and produced their two brothers, John and Geoffrey, who admitted that they were villeins. Margery said that she was not a villein nor did she flee from the land either within or before the limitation period. But she had married a freeman, Geoffrey of Northcote, forty years ago. Richard never tried to argue that she had fled from the fee but concentrated rather on disputing the date of Margery's

[23] KB 26/164, m. 12d (Norfolk 1260). I owe this reference to Dr Paul Brand.
[24] Cf. *Van Caenegem*, p. 336.
[25] This is the form in *Glanvill*, xii. 11.
[26] Cf. *Reg. Omn. Brev.*, f. 87, 6th *regula*.
[27] JI 1/174, m. 24 (Devon eyre 1238).

marriage. Very occasionally, claimants do talk of flights in ways which suggest that they really happened. Alexander de Stering' and his wife, for example, claiming Peter son of Simon de Langham as their villein, said in their count that 'they were always in seisin of the same Peter as their villein dwelling on their villeinage until the same Peter three years ago fled from their land on to the land of the Prior of Walsingham'.[28] Then again, alleged villeins who pleaded the defence of a year and a day on royal demesne had probably at least reached the towns or places whose privilege they claimed. A few genuine runaways can thus be identified, although the defence seems to have been rare before 1250 anyway.[29]

Seldom, then, do naifty cases indicate whether an alleged villein actually fled from the claimant's land. But it is sometimes quite clear that he did remain on it.[30] Some actions of trespass, however, tell more about flights. The De legibus allowed the lord only three or four days to recapture his fugitive villein. Once this time expired, the runaway could bring a plaint of imprisonment against his lord for any attempt to seize him, just as any freeman could sue for wrongful imprisonment.[31] In fact, plea-roll cases do not confirm this view, which is adapted to the Bractonian theory of villeinage.[32] But they do show a few lords obviously reacting to their villeins' attempted flight, and are probably representative of many similar incidents unnoticed by the royal justices. The plea that someone complaining of unjust imprisonment was the defendant's villein defeated the action. Among the defences noticed are pleas that

[28] JI 1/560, m. 58d = 561, m. 55 (Norfolk eyre 1250). Cf. JI 1/909, m. 8 (Sussex eyre 1248): 'et . . . predictus Radulfus qui est de sequela predictorum villanorum et natus in predicto manerio fugit de terra illa'. Also JI 1/1045, m. 27 (York eyre 1247), where the amercement of a villein who admitted his status in the course of a naifty action was said to be 'quia fugit ab eo'.

[29] It is discussed below Chap. 10.

[30] In JI 1/175, m. 29d (Devon eyre 1243–4), the alleged villeins denied that they could be the claimant's fugitives 'quia nunquam fuerunt manentes in terra sua'. In the vast majority of cases whether or not the alleged villein really had fled can never be known.

[31] Br., ff. 6b–7. He can also except to a writ of naifty etc. that he is a statuliber. No case authority exists for the four day rule. D. W. Sutherland, The Assize of Novel Disseisin (Oxford, 1973), pp. 97 ff., demonstrated that Bracton's parallel rule in novel disseisin was similarly a myth.

[32] See Chap. 8 (ii).

the defendant had merely captured a villein in the course of running away in order to extract pledges from him against any repetition[33] and that he had arrested a runaway's brother in order to take security from him that he would not follow suit.[34] An appeal of robbery illustrates the violence which must often have ensued on such occasions. One Nicholas Selage appealed a servant of the Abbot of Bury's called Adam son of Henry, who said that he had been sent by the abbot to take Nicholas's house into the abbot's hand because, he alleged, Nicholas had uprooted trees on the land and was obviously preparing to leave it. Nicholas abandoned his appeal at this stage, no doubt because he realized that there was no point in continuing. Nevertheless the justices instructed the jurors to inquire into the alleged violence, and when they reported that Nicholas's teeth had been broken, Adam was amerced.[35]

These cases demonstrate that the lords' concern to keep their peasants within their lordships occupied a central place in the thirteenth-century law of villeinage. Thus, one of the most important practical functions of the legal distinction between villein and freeman was to mark off those who could lawfully be brought back to the fee if they tried to leave it. The matter may also be usefully illustrated from the other direction by noting that free status entitled men to leave their land at will.

In the first place, manumission charters confirm that the right to recede freely was an automatic concomitant of freedom. Its grant was frequently the subject of a specific clause in the charter. The formula 'ire et redire ubicumque et quandocumque sibi placuerit', or something very similar, is found in many charters from the first decade of the thirteenth century on-

---

[33] *CRR* i. 364 (Wilts. 1200). *CRR* iii. 324; iv. 37 (Essex 1205) was similar though rather more involved and the lord was obviously mainly concerned with his customs and services.

[34] *CRR* vi. 349 (Lincs. 1212). The condition of the roll makes it impossible to know whether this plea succeeded.

[35] JI 1/818, m. 42d (Suffolk eyre 1240). The justices sometimes went to the bother of checking stories told in pleading this kind of defence. In KB 26/139, m. 2d (Salop 1250), a litigant who tried this on against an accusation of unjust distraint had to concord in order to keep himself from gaol, when the court learned that he had no land in the relevant village and had never sued in the county court to claim his opponent as a villein.

wards.[36] At the very beginning of the century, one Hugh Travers from Staunton in Nottinghamshire was freed by his lord William de Staunton in order that he could go to the Holy Land on his behalf.[37] Of course, many other manumissions do not mention the right to recede; their draftsmen either took it for granted or regarded the possibility that a tenant would wish to leave as too theoretical to bother about. Legal discussion is generally confined to the special case of the freeman who held land by villeinage tenure. Unlike those tenants who were villeins, they could in theory leave their holdings if they wished.

Once again the *De legibus'* discussion of the Bestenover Case is helpful, if set into its system.[38] There the careful distinction between tenure and status implies that the holding of land by villein tenure does not affect the status of a free tenant. A freeman holding land in villeinage should therefore have all normal rights of other freemen, including the right to leave his land if he wishes. The one apparent exception does not affect the main argument. If the freeman entered the villein tenement to marry a villein woman, this ensnarement, as the treatise terms it, would prevent his leaving; the reason is that the husband's free status is obscured for the duration of the marriage, so that the wife's lord is able to reclaim him if he flees from the fee in the same way as he can reclaim the wife herself.[39] Another royal justice, Master Roger de Seaton, writing a generation later, followed the Bractonian line with some additions. According to him, a free tenant might leave his villeinage tenement, but he might take with him only those goods that were not raised there and he had first to perform the service due to the head lord.[40]

Both men were in a good position to know the current law; their statement represents contemporary practice in the courts.

---

[36] The charter quoted is *Registrum Antiquissimum*, ed. C. W. Foster and K. Major (*LRS* 11 vols. 1913–73), vi, no. 1938, dated 1215/25. Other examples are T. Madox, *Formulare Anglicanum* (London, 1702), p. 417, no. 754 (1200/10), BL, Add. Charters, 16614 (*c.* 1246), *Registrum Antiquissimum* vi, no. 1858 (1240/57), BL, Harleian charters 45 E 48 (1286), Selby Abbey Chartulary, Leeds Central Library, fo. 20, no. 99 (1290), *Select Pleas in Manorial Courts* (*SS* ii), p. 175 (1298).

[37] F. M. Stenton printed this charter in *EHR* xxvi (1911), 95. It cannot be as early as the Third Crusade.

[38] See below pp. 56 ff. and Chap. 8 (iii).

[39] *Br.*, ff. 26, 194.

[40] *Cas. Plac.*, p. 56/5 (? 1273/8).

When assize jurors report that a tenant in villeinage left his holding of his own free will because he was reluctant to continue doing the villein customs due from it, we may be certain that his status was free.[41] If the tenant had been unfree, they would not have bothered to tell the story; the roll would merely have recorded that the assize failed because of the plaintiff's status.

Nevertheless, no source says outright that a villein may never leave his lord's land. A set of services, almost certainly unfree, recorded by the jurors in an assize, lays down that the tenant's son might not leave the land unless he spoke with the lord.[42] No doubt most villeins lived their lives out in their home village, but the prohibition on travel was never absolute. Villeins were not tied to the soil in a strict sense, and some occasionally travelled around the countryside in circumstances where formal manumission probably had not occurred. For example, two different cases show Buckinghamshire villeins spending considerable lengths of time in Wycombe;[43] and the lure of towns must have frequently tempted impoverished villagers, whatever their legal status. Not all villeins had full-time secure jobs on their own or others' land. Travel in search of jobs might often take them around the countryside. Thus a Norfolk villein was said to be an itinerant carpenter working for the Prior of Norwich, and coming and going as he pleased.[44] A second carpenter from Buckinghamshire but working in Wales was also alleged to be unfree though the assize jury eventually decided that this was not true.[45] Another villein left his native village of Barton Stacy in Hampshire and crossed the Channel to the Abbey of St. Denis which owned much of the land in the village. He too was probably in search of work, and finally acquired a holding.[46] A litigant alleged to be unfree failed to appear in court on the day fixed; he had embarked on a pilgrimage to St. James of Compostella in Spain.[47]

[41] JI 1/300, m. 2 (Hereford eyre 1221); cf. *SRS* xi. 327 (Somerset eyre 1225) for a tenant driven off his villein-holding by the incursions of deer.

[42] *CRR* iii. 143 (Oxon. 1204). *CRR* i. 46 also illustrates tenure in this village, Aston Rowant.

[43] JI 1/62, m. 24d (Bucks. eyre 1232), *BNB* 1167 (Bucks. 1235–6). The first villein had wrongly thought that his stay made him free; the second may have been free.

[44] *BNB* 632 (Norfolk 1231).

[45] JI 1/62, m. 16 (Bucks. eyre 1232).

[46] JI 1/775, m. 8d (Hants eyre 1235–6). See further p. 113 below.

[47] *SS* lxviii. 432 (Cornwall eyre 1201).

Wandering villeins were uncommon in the thirteenth century, though the ones just mentioned can hardly be more than a small proportion of those who did stray from home.[48] Most peasants, free or unfree, only rarely left their own immediate neighbourhood. Still, the wanderers may have become more numerous in the course of the century, and lords had to be aware of the risk of losing their valuable rights over them. Consequently, lords wanted to establish rules by which they could safely licence villeins to leave their homes. No doubt most such arrangements were merely local and never reached the royal courts. Licences, usually unwritten, were seldom recorded on the plea rolls. Their occasional enrollment, however, always stipulated that the lord retained his legal seisin of the villein despite the villein's physical absence from the lordship. This can be illustrated by an action of naifty which ended in a concord whereby the alleged villein admitted that he was unfree 'ita tantum quod libere possit ire et redire et sibi perquirere ubicumque voluerit'.[49] Much can be learnt about seignorial licences from manorial sources.[50] The plethora of material suggests the magnitude of the problem. A late thirteenth-century memorandum from the Gloucester Cartulary, for example, forbade the issue of fresh licences;[51] in future, villeins would not be allowed to leave the land unless their services were up to date and the Superior's permission had been obtained. We do not know if the rule was enforced.

Perhaps the lords' most important method of keeping track of their absent villeins was the periodic recognition payment exacted from absentees. This is often called chevage, and merits some attention here because of the confusion which has sur-

---

[48] Bracton in the passage to be discussed below mentions *mercatores* and *mercenarii* as the kind of villeins likely to be travelling around. A wandering villein presented the courts with a problem when he came to rest in a new village as an *adventicius;* cf. below pp. 209ff.

[49] JI 1/909, m. 10 (Sussex eyre 1248). Cf. JI 1/575, m. 92 (Norfolk eyre 1286), cited by W. Hudson, *Leet Jurisdiction in Norwich* (SS v 1891), p. 68.

[50] Some of the evidence is collected by H. S. Bennett, *Life on the English Manor* (Cambridge, 1937, repr. 1962), pp. 285 ff.

[51] *Historia et Cartularium Monasterii Sancti Petri Gloucestriae*, ed. W. H. Hart (R.S. 1863–7), iii. 218. Cf. Bennett, pp. 307 ff., and Vinogradoff, *Villainage*, pp. 157–8.

rounded it in the past.[52] This arose because groups of peasants made different kinds of periodic payment, some of which were called chevage and some not. On the other hand, the several kinds of payment which were called chevage differed from each other too. Our concern here is only with the payment of small amounts[53] by absentee villeins in recognition of their status— often but by no means always called chevage.

The increasing tendency in the later thirteenth century for the prevalence of chevage was probably due to the *De legibus'* influence.[54] The treatise refers to chevage in explaining that *servi* were within the *potestas* of their lords (or masters), until they somehow escaped from it. In spite of the Roman-law terminology used, the treatment is down to earth and rationalized in terms of the 'thoroughly English' doctrine of seisin. The author asks a series of practical questions. How long does a lord remain in legal seisin of a villein outside his direct physical control? How is this seisin maintained and broken? That is, at what point does a fugitive gain seisin of freedom? Characteristically, his solution adapts a piece of Roman doctrine not from the law of slavery, but from the rules governing the care of domestic animals. A villein begins to be a fugitive, he says, when he ceases to have the *consuetudo revertendi*.[55] Villeins absent from the fee can proclaim that they retain this habit of returning by

[52] The view expressed by M. Bloch, *Mélanges*, i. 290 ff., 316, that chevage was a distinguishing mark of serfdom owed by all serfs has been convincingly refuted by L. Verriest; see below p. 187 n. 9 for references.

[53] Even in the thirteenth century these could be in kind. Examples are *NRS* v. 793 (Bury St. Edmund 1203) and *Court Rolls of the Manor of Hales*, ed. J. Amphlett (Worcs. Hist. Soc. 1910–33) ii. 361, 485 (1297, 1304).

[54] This is the opinion of R. E. Latham, 'Minor Enigmas from Medieval Records', *EHR* lxxvi (1961), 639–45, considering *Br.*, f. 6b, and other references. He distinguishes six senses of chevage from that discussed here, but one of these, chevage as a payment made by suitors at a view of frankpledge, must often have been closely associated. Cf. *Select Pleas in Manorial Courts* (*SS* ii 1888), p. 94, a case from the Abbot of Ramsey's courts at Elton, Hunts., 1278, cited in Vinogradoff, *Villainage,* p. 66; also JI 1/575, m. 92d, cited above n. 49. For more about the Abbot of Ramsey's use of tithings to enforce seignorial rights, see J. A. Raftis, *Tenure and Mobility* (Toronto, 1964), pp. 101–4, 131.

[55] See W. W. Buckland, *A Textbook of Roman Law* (2nd ed., Cambridge, 1931), p. 205, and compare Buckland, *Slavery*, pp. 267–8, for the quite different rule on the moment when a *servus* became a *fugitivus:* he had to have started to run away and formed the intention not to return.

paying chevage at regular intervals, in recognition of their subjection and of the 'diminution of their heads'.[56]

Britton characteristically extended the Bractonian treatment somewhat and added a flavour of his own. He advised the lord to differentiate between villeins who held land and those who had none. If they possessed a holding, it was enough for the lord to remain in possession of the service due from it. But from the landless, he should take a penny a year 'chefage' plus a day's work at the harvest or some other service within the villein's capacity.[57] This is quite compatible with the *De legibus,* and emphasizes that chevage was but one method of retaining seisin, which conveniently enabled the seisin to be proved in court if necessary. Because of this, chevage payments were sometimes taken from villeins who had no intention of leaving the fee. The device must have been especially useful for dealing with landless villeins, particularly, perhaps, when combined with an oath of fealty. That this usage went back to the beginning of the century at least is shown by the form of King John's threats in 1205 to ensure a good military turn-out against any French invasion. Defaulters without land were to become 'servi . . . in perpetuum, reddendo singulis annis iiii denarios de capitibus suis'; those with land were to forfeit it.[58]

Chevage then cannot be neatly defined or explained. It enabled lords to retain their seisin while permitting villeins to leave their homes. Simply to compare the prominence in the legal theory of the idea that the villein is attached to the soil by his status with the number of villeins who can be found absent from their land from the latter part of the thirteenth century onwards is quite striking. There is thus a natural temptation to argue for the existence of a strong pressure towards peasant mobility during the thirteenth century, forcing the surrender of an earlier seignorial position. This may be so, for other sugges-

---

[56] This interpretation depends on Thorne's reading 'diminutionis' as against Woodbine's 'dominii', *Br.,* ed. Thorne, ii. 36. *Capitis demunitio* was a familiar idea in Roman law; cf. Buckland, *A Textbook of Roman Law,* pp. 134–41. Bracton's intention may have been to suggest to his readers the change in a villein's status, when he escaped from or was brought back into the seisin of the lord. This would accord with his treatment of legal status in general in terms of seisin; see below Chap. 8. His readers would recognize the phrase, also found in *Br.,* ff. 123b, 412b; and for example in Gregory IX's Decretals, *X* 5.1.24.

[57] *Britton,* I. xxxii. 9 (i. 201). *Fleta,* i. 7(3), merely abbreviates the *De legibus.*

[58] Stubbs, *Charters,* pp. 276–7.

tive evidence will appear in the course of this book. It suffices here, however, to note that the shadow of the legal 'attache au sol' survived, if not the substance, as the chattel analogy would have demanded.

In conclusion, then: peasant labour was required to give land its full value, and writs of naifty were used from the first to help lords keep their peasants within their lands. When lawyers came to rationalize this, they found a convenient Roman-law analogy for the villein in the *ascripticius* (or *colonus*), who was bound to the soil. For certain purposes, the villein was even treated as part of the landed property. At any rate, villeins did not have the right to recede freely until they attained free status by manumission. In practice, however, it was impossible to enforce a complete ban on peasant mobility and recognition payments were used to preserve the lord's theoretical legal rights over the absentees.

5

RESTRAINT ON ALIENATION BY VILLEINS

The common law did not permit villeins to sell or otherwise alienate their land. In theory the prohibition was absolute and followed from the now familiar legal doctrine that regarded the lord, not his villein tenant, as the owner of the land. Of course, for many purposes the villein tenants were treated in their own villages as if they did own their holdings, and the historian's main interest in the legal restraint on alienation lies in the attempt to assess the rigour with which lords insisted upon it, the opposition they met, and the measure of their success.

At any rate the legal theory is clear and can be derived through a simple chain of logic from the idea of the lord's chattel ownership of his villein. According to the *De legibus*,[1] no tenant holding in villeinage or villein socage can make a *de iure* donation of his land. If he tries to do so, the lord can reclaim his land without the need to acquire a writ and sue in court, provided that he does this within a reasonable time. Alienations, if necessary, should be made through the lord's manorial court, because they do not affect the freehold, which belongs to the lord. Later textbooks add little to this,[2] but a few cases illuminate the court's treatment of the restraint on alienation by villeins.

A set of customs claimed in court in 1206 by the Hospitallers included the provision that the tenant 'cannot marry his daughter outside their fee nor sell or give his lands without their licence'.[3] Conversely, an assize of novel disseisin succeeded in spite of the allegation that the holding concerned was villeinage, for the jurors returned that the plaintiff's predecessors had

---

[1] *Br.*, ff. 25b, 26–26b, 30b–31b, 209. He is actually discussing privileged villeinage, but what he says is of general application.

[2] *Britton*, II. vi. 3 (i. 246); *Fleta*, iii. 12 (192), takes a moral tone, declaring that villein alienations ought not to be left undisturbed.

[3] *CRR* iv. 266, 284 (Essex 1206). The mention of merchet makes it almost certain that the lords, the Knights Hospitaller, were claiming the tenure to be villeinage. And see below n. 21 for *CRR* v. 94 (Norfolk 1207).

held it freely and that they 'could sell and give the land both *in maritagium* and any other way'.[4]

Restraint on alienation was more a matter of tenure than villein status. The question before the justices was likely to concern whether or not a particular tenant held his land in terms which permitted him to alienate it. The only case noticed in which the restraint on alienation is related to status concerns a gage. Nicholas of Rigton, a villein of Kirkstall Abbey, borrowed from a Jew called Manasser on the security of his holding, of which Manasser seems to have taken seisin. The abbey obtained a royal writ ordering the sheriff to return seisin to the abbey, after an inquisition had established that Nicholas was a villein 'so that he cannot gage (*invadiare*) to jews'.[5]

The ability to control the land transactions of one's villeins was obviously a valuable asset. By possessing this legal right of veto, a lord could demand that transfers were made only under his supervision. This simplified the collection of entry fines and other payments. Above all, it helped to ensure that tenants did not act in ways which might involve him in the loss of land or rights. Thus villeins were supposed to conduct their land dealings in the manorial court, where holdings were first surrendered to the lord, or his agent, who would then give seisin to the new tenant, often by a ceremony involving a rod[6] and usually referred to as Surrender and Admittance. This ritual reminded the villeins present that it was not they, but rather the lord, whom the common law regarded as the owner of the land. When such transactions were mentioned in the royal courts, they were said, significantly, to have been effected 'per gretum et permissionem domini' or something similar.[7]

---

[4] JI 1/870, m. 8 (Surrey eyre ?1248). The jury verdict makes it clear that the suggestion had been that the tenure was ordinary villeinage, though the village, Bramley, was Ancient Demesne; cf. *V. C. H. Surrey* iii. 80 ff., *P. Rolls 33 Henry II*, p. 214, *8 Richard I*, pp. 200–1.

[5] *Coucher Book of Kirkstall Abbey*, ed. W. T. Lancaster and W. P. Baildon (Thoresby soc. viii 1904), nos. 4, 64. Many charters included a clause expressly excluding alienation to Jews or the religious, because both categories of tenant threatened the rights of the head lord or donor. Henry III forbade tenants of the royal demesne in East Anglia to gage holdings in socage or villeinage to Jews in 1234, *Cl. R., 1231–1234*, p. 592; in 1242 two Jews were alleged to have broken this ban, *Cl. R., 1237–1242*, p. 465. *Cl. R., 1272–1279*, p. 297, is another example.

[6] Cf. *Britton*, III. 12 (ii. 13–14).

[7] *CRR* vii. 62 (Northants 1214).

This control was nowhere near absolute; practical procedures and problems are examined below. Yet thirteenth-century landlords, worried by their tenants' alienations, would have been happy to have had some claim to treat the land of their free tenants as if it were demesne in this way. Perhaps twelfth-century lords had indeed behaved like this even towards tenants of some standing. By the thirteenth century, however, the right of free tenants to deal with their land as owners was established in law, if not yet accepted with good grace.[8] Thus, although Surrender and Admittance was not yet restricted to villeins, it certainly smacked of servility. As early as 1203, the defendant to an assize of novel disseisin thought it worth-while to say that the plaintiff was his villein and had come before a full session of his court to give up the land in question to a nephew who was also a villein.[9]

Clearly, there were often occasions when peasants wished to transfer land in circumstances in which seignorial approval would not have been forthcoming. Their interests were frequently in direct opposition to the lord's.[10] Peasants might wish to avoid the inconvenience or expense of legitimate transfers, or have an urgent need for cash which could not await the next session of the manorial court. The purchase of land outside the village might also presage the peasant's removal or his claim to free status. We can only guess at the scale on which evasion was practised. The closeness of the village community and the legal requirement for public livery of seisin ensured that the lord would eventually hear about outright sales. Informal leases for a short term could escape his notice more easily. If he did find out, a good deal was at stake and violence often resulted,[11] as

[8] See on this E. Miller, 'The State and the Landed Interest in Thirteenth-century England and France', *TRHS* 5th s. ii (1952), 109–29; S. E. Thorne, 'English Feudalism and Estates in Land', *Cambridge Law Journal* xvii (1959), 193–209; J. M. W. Bean, *The Decline of English Feudalism* (Manchester, 1968), Chap. 2. Sutherland, *Assize of Novel Disseisin*, Chap. III, argues that there was some reaction after 1250.

[9] *NRS* v. 663 (Northampton eyre 1203). The truth of the plea is doubtful, for the defendant later handed the land over.

[10] The forces working for and against a peasant land-market are discussed by Professor Postan in his introduction to *Carte Nativorum*, ed. C. N. L. Brooke and M. M. Postan (*NRS* xx 1960), esp. pp. xxxiii ff., xli ff. Cf. my 'The Origins of a Peasant Land Market in England', *Ec. H. R.* 2nd s. xxiii (1970), 18–31. The subject is by no means exhausted.

[11] *CRR* xii. 465 = *BNB* 713 (Herts. 1225) tells of a forced sale during the civil war when the lord was presumably unable to act.

two Buckinghamshire appeals show. In the first, the appellant, Richard son of Udard, said that seven men had broken into his house, taken and whipped his wife, and shut him out of his own home. Robert of Broughton, the chief of the accused, explained that he claimed Richard as his villein holding of him in villeinage. When he heard that Richard was making himself out to be free and trying to sell the land, he went down there to hold his court on the spot, so he claimed, and that was how the trouble started.[12] In the other case, an attempt was made by the apellee, Walter of Woughton, to justify violence (including this time the imprisonment of the tenant, Adam le Kenteis) on similar grounds. Walter said that Adam was his villein holding of him in villeinage as his father had before him and that he had alienated his tenement. Walter thereupon imprisoned him because there was nothing on which he could distrain.[13]

Since thirteenth-century law still assumed that the lord had a right to self-help in this situation, such violence was almost inevitable. The textbooks say only that he ought to act at once ('incontinenti') without specifying a time limit.[14] If he waited too long, the villein's alienee would be able to recover his seisin by the assize; this actually happened in a case *coram rege* cited in the *De legibus*[15] when the court told the lord that he ought to have proceeded 'per legem terre', and found against him.

The *De legibus* says that once the period for legitimate self-help has passed, the lord should obtain a writ. This was the writ of entry sometimes called entry *per villanum*, and the action introduced by it has hardly been noticed by legal historians.[16] Bracton includes it among a group of writs of entry, which deals with a series of different situations where somebody who occupies land, but has no freehold, takes it upon himself to alienate his seisin to a stranger.[17] Our writ is described as that concerned with entry 'per eum qui tenuerit in villenagio' and its form is the

[12] *CRR* xii. 1579, 1639 (Bucks. 1225). Richard admitted villeinage and dropped his appeal. It is hard to say whether his account of the violence ought to be believed; it is so different from Robert's story.

[13] JI 1/54, m. 12 = *BRB* vi. 444 (Bucks. eyre 1227). Adam succeeded on the imprisonment when Walter gave up his villeinage allegation, but the robbery accusation failed. See below pp. 158 ff. for more about the dispute.

[14] *Br.*, ff. 26, 31b. Cf. *Britton*, II. vi. 3 (i. 246), *Fleta*, iii. 2 (192); and see above p. 30.

[15] *BNB* 1203 (Lincs. 1236–7) cited *Br.*, f. 31b.

[16] I summarized its history briefly in 'The Origins of a Peasant Land Market', 25.

[17] *Br.*, f. 323b.

Precipe normal for writs of entry envisaging process by summons. Other writ forms have been found in only three registers of writs, the earliest of which was written after 1259.[18] It is also mentioned by *Brevia Placitata* in a long list of different types of writ of entry.[19] And that is the sum total of what the professional literature has to say about the writ of entry *per villanum*. Undoubtedly, as one among several writs of entry which appeared in the first half of the thirteenth century, it was neglected, then soon declined or atrophied.

The earliest example of the action noted dates from 1224.[20] Exactly when entry *per villanum* was invented is unknown, but it probably did not exist in 1207 when William de Pinkeney proceeded by plaint without writ against his tenant, and did not sue Coxford Priory by writ of entry as he would presumably have done a few years later.[21] It never seems to have gained wide popularity. Only six references to actions have been found on the plea rolls before 1240,[22] although the rolls of the Norfolk eyre of 1250 contain over fifty, many in groups brought by the same plaintiff.[23] Very soon a simpler alternative became available. Lords would bring an assize of novel disseisin; they argued that alienation by the tenant amounted to disseising them. Just when the justices began to allow this is unclear. It received statutory sanction in 1285 when the Second Statute of

---

[18] This is Maitland's CB (Cambridge University Library, Kk v. 33), no. 36; cf. Maitland, *Coll. Papers*, ii. 143. G. D. G. Hall thought that this part of the register (Writs 1–90) dates from before 1236, though the forms given may be those of the 1250s, *Selden Registers*, p. xxxiv, n. 4. The form from about 1272 in the Berne MS, fo. 39 (no. 33), differs only in minor details from that given by the *De legibus*. According to Hall, *Selden Registers*, p. cvi, Inner Temple MS 511.9, from a little after 1285, has another example.

[19] *Brev. Plac.*, p. 198. This is the atypical Harvard text of the early fourteenth century.

[20] *CRR* xi. 2145; xii. 330 (Cambs. 1224).

[21] *CRR* v. 94 mentioned by Richardson and Sayles, *Procedure without Writ*, p. cii. *CRR* v. 95 is another plaint brought by William about pasture rights in the village and the plea-roll entry reveals that Ralph was among the free tenants who had common on William's land. It suggests no alternative reason why William brought a plaint rather than a writ.

[22] *CRR* xii. 465 = *BNB* 713 (Herts. 1225), *CRR* xiv. 468, 529 (Middlesex 1230), JI 1/80, m. 2d (Essex from Cambridge eyre 1234–5), JI 1/536, m. 4d (Middlesex eyre 1234–5), KB 26/116A, m. 8 (Essex 1236), KB 26/119, m. 6d (Norfolk 1238). The last reference is to a large number of writs brought by John Luvel against his tenants in Docking.

[23] JI 1/560, ms. 7d, 57d are the two largest groups brought by the Abbess of Caen and Baudri de Taverham respectively. East Anglian rolls might, however, be expected to show more evidence of peasant land-dealings than would be found elsewhere.

Westminster allowed lords to choose an assize or a writ of entry *sur disseisin* to sue either the alienating tenant or his alienee,[24] but it may have been law earlier. Entry *per villanum* may already have been rare in 1285, although a last example is known from the beginning of the fourteenth century.[25] All that reached the printed *Register of Writs* was a couple of notes, one in French, the other in Latin, explaining the effect of the enactment of 1285.[26]

Like most writs of entry, the writ of entry *per villanum* usually introduced a case which was decided on the basis of a jury verdict.[27] Defences were of two kinds. The defendant might defend on the facts, denying that his title depended on the entry alleged against him or his predecessor-in-title.[28] More frequently, the defendant or his warrantor denied that the alleged alienor had held in villeinage.[29] Juries summoned to pronounce upon tenure in these cases gave a simple verdict, without going into detail about the services, presumably because the defence was regarded as merely a peremptory exception whose result did not bind the parties in the future.

The law's attitude, then, was quite straightforward: villeins were not permitted to alienate their land without the lord's consent. Small wonder, then, if popular thought denied to villeins the use of the honourable instruments by which freemen transferred their land, charters and seals. Grants evidenced in this way were felt to be more binding and permanent than those affected by Surrender and Admittance alone. A lord who allowed his villeins to use sealed writings risked losing his land irrevocably. Conversely, their use by villeins might be taken in court as evidence of freedom. This cannot be shown to be strict

---

[24] Stat. Westminster II, c. 25. Cf. *Br.*, f. 161b *addicio* ('most certainly came from Bracton', Woodbine, i. 391) and *P&M*, ii. 54n.

[25] Fitzherbert, *La Graunde Abridgement*, Counterple de vouch 121 (1302–3), wrongly dated 31 Edward III in *FNB* 191C.

[26] *Reg. Omm. Brev.*, f. 231v *regula*.

[27] The defendant might of course admit the entry alleged (as in JI 1/560, ms. 41d, 55) or deny that he held the land at all (as in ibid., ms. 36d, 50d).

[28] In JI 1/536, m. 4d (Middlesex eyre 1234–5), the defendant successfully pleaded that his entry was not as the plaintiff alleged. In JI 1/560, m. 53 (Norfolk eyre 1250: Prior of Binham v. Richard de Sancta Fide), the jury decided that there had been no entry as alleged by the prior.

[29] *CRR* xii. 465 = *BNB* 713 (Herts. 1225) was decided by the alienors coming into court and admitting that they were the plaintiff's villeins and had held from him in villeinage.

law, but their is no doubt that lords were right to fear the consequences of their neglect.

The dangers were more obvious in eastern England where the land market reached peasants rather earlier than elsewhere.[30] An assize of novel disseisin illustrates the kind of situation common in Norfolk for example. It arose from the enfoeffment of a villein holding made by one Godman, father of Lesqueva the assize plaintiff, 'per assensum et voluntatem' of John of Watlington whose villein he was. The occasion was Lesqueva's marriage, the enfeoffment being made at the church door before the religious ceremony. It reserved to Godman a small annual money rent, part of which was described as forinsec service, and had to be passed on to John as the head lord. To the onlookers the whole transaction must have resembled an ordinary grant of free dower. The arrangement worked perfectly satisfactorily for twenty years until Lesqueva's husband had been dead for some time, when John's son, also called John, ejected her from the holding. The question before the justices now was: ought she to recover it from him by the assize? Unfortunately for Lesqueva, the jurors remembered that Godman and his holding had been unfree. Even so the court hesitated before finding in John's favour.[31]

Lesqueva was not amerced because 'pauper est'.[32] Presumably she had no means of support other than the holding which was now lost. Her neighbours, some of whom had been present at her wedding and acted as jurors of the assize, perhaps shared her resentment at hard justice. Like many other ordinary people, they probably believed that the mere possession of a charter implied freedom. Perhaps this was why the court did not reach judgement at once. Its eventual decision, however, was correct in law. Of course, a litigant alleged to be his opponent's villein could safeguard himself by producing in court a charter of enfeoffment made to himself or a direct ancestor by his opponent or some ancestor of his.[33] When a lord had once treated

---

[30] See my 'The Origins of a Peasant Land Market', 24–5.

[31] JI 1/560, m. 37d = 561, m. 43d (Norfolk eyre 1250).

[32] Cases where amercements are pardoned for poverty are discussed below, p. 76.

[33] Cf. CRR v. 94 above and JI 1/175, m. 30 (Devon eyre 1243–4), where the essential portion of the charter is enrolled. Its formula ('pro homagio et servicio suo . . . sibi et heredibus suis . . . libere quiete et in feodo et hereditate . . .') would have satisfied the Bractonian criteria for an implied manumission; for which see below.

his villein as free, arguably he forfeited his right to claim him as a villein ever again. But for this defence to be valid, the charter needed to have been made between the parties or their direct ancestors. Charters made by third parties are logically irrelevant, yet they were in fact occasionally produced in court.[34] To find a tenant in villeinage trying to argue for his freedom by producing in court the charter of his lord recording that the tenant's villein services were remitted for four years while the lord went to Jerusalem is indeed pathetic.[35]

There was never any legal basis for this belief that possession of a charter implied freedom. Yet lawyers could not be unaware of its existence. Nor could they entirely ignore it. Undoubtedly this popular belief helped to encourage the author of the *De legibus* to construe a lord's enfeoffment of his villein 'sibi et heredibus suis' as an implied manumission, an innovation which eventually won a permanent place in the common law.[36] Nevertheless, this treatment of the subject should not lead us to think in terms of courts vigorously scrutinizing any charter that an alleged villein might bring into court. The sophisticated criteria envisaged by the Bractonian argument were not employed by the courts in the first half of the century. A replevin case from the Norfolk eyre of 1250 is perhaps a little exceptional but serves to make the point.[37] The issue that soon emerged was whether Nicholas le Potter, the plaintiff, was a villein of the defendant, Rose de Lascy, as she claimed. She said that he had been sold to her with his *sequela* and chattels by John de Thyning and the sale recorded in John's charter. Nicholas remembered the transaction but claimed that John had manumitted him. Neither party nor the justices ever suggested that the charter should have been produced in court, though this would surely

---

[34] JI 1/62, m. 14d (Bucks. eyre 1232) is intriguing. The alleged villein, William son of Herbert, was held to have failed in his suit though he produced a charter of a certain Simon de Bosevill granting land to his grandfather. But the naifty claimant was also unable to produce his suit and quitclaimed all William's servitude as is recorded on a fine between William and Ralf de Aynevill, one of William's sureties in the naifty action. His other surety had been named Simon de Bosevill! SS liii.78 (Lincoln eyre 1218) was a case where the charter did not help the villein; it has 'Bractonian' sidelining on the roll. Also BHRS iii. 106, 586 (Bedford eyre 1227).

[35] RCR i. 106, 107, 230, 233, 319, 376; ii. 56; CRR i. 210, 246, 370, 461; ii. 11, 13; vii. 340 (Lincs. 1198–1210). This seems to have been the subject of a dispute which can only be known from the scanty indications of entries mainly recording adjournments.

[36] Br., ff. 23b, 24b, 192b. Cf. Vinogradoff, Villainage, pp. 70 ff. P&M, i. 418.

[37] JI 1/560, m. 5d = 561, m. 3d (Norfolk eyre 1250).

have settled the matter. The jury was left to remember the sale and Nicholas's confession of his unfree status before Rose's court in full session. Perhaps the right conclusion to draw about the importance of charters is to recall the religious aura they once had, and which survived in the countryside. Far from the doctors of the learned law, illiterate peasants felt that possession of a written document must carry with it some power or advantage.[38]

So lords were well advised to try and keep written documents away from their villeinage. Yet, they sometimes permitted charters to be drawn up about villein land; already in the early thirteenth century the situation may have been beyond seignorial control in some areas.[39] Of course, the courts supported the lords wherever possible. Hence, if faced by an awkward charter, it was always worth alleging that the man who made it was a villein. This seems to have been what Richard la Weite, his wife, and her sister, did in 1220 when suing Walter son of Viuna for the return of land they alleged to have been leased from their father Goldwin for a term of years which had now expired. When Walter said that Goldwin had enfeoffed him by charter, Richard and the others tried to refute him by declaring that Goldwin had been a villein defending his land *per furcam et flagellum* and 'never made that charter nor could have done'.[40] Proof of such allegations was not easy, and Richard and Walter concorded. Lords were better advised to trust in the strength of their own courts. The special session of the Abbot of Ramsey's court held in his presence at Brancaster, Norfolk in 1239, is one of all too few thirteenth-century courts to have left a record of its proceedings.[41] A number of the abbey's tenants had apparently been dealing in free land by charter. They were now forced to surrender both land and charters and make satisfaction for the wrong done to the abbey. Most, if not all, of them were villeins

---

[38] Cf. P. Chaplais, 'The Origin and Authenticity of the Royal Anglo-Saxon Diploma', *Journal Soc. Archivists* iii (1965), 54–5.

[39] Cf. *Carte Nativorum*, but note that the charters are analysed by E. King, *Peterborough Abbey, 1086–1310* (Cambridge, 1973), Chap. 6. He concludes that most of the land transferred in them was free, much of it assarts made in the period around 1200, and that this was kept carefully apart from the villein land.

[40] *CRR* ix. 109 = *BNB* 1419 (Kent 1220). For tenure by fork and flail, see *P & M*, i. 372.

[41] *Cartularium Monasterii de Rameseia*, i, ed. W. H. Hart and P. A. Lyons (R.S. 1884), pp. 423–9.

within the definitions of the royal court. Prominence is given to the acknowledgement by one of the villeins, at a special full session, of his status and his obligation to do all villein services according to the custom of the manor, a reiteration of a confession of villeinage he had previously made before the itinerant justices at Norwich.[42] Clearly, this was the result of a special effort by the abbey to reduce evasion of the restrictions.[43]

As with charters, so with seals. The clash of interests between lord and peasant did not proceed quite along the lines of legal distinctions. Seals were important because they were perhaps the most convincing method of authenticating documents against possible challenge in the future. Other means were available, but were more or less superseded at the higher levels of society in thirteenth-century England. Possession and use of seal had some social cachet and spread gradually down society, not without some opposition. Conservative opinion disliked this lower-class encroachment on what had been the privilege of the great.[44] Yet there is no hint of a legal prohibition against villeins or any other legal category of people using seals.[45] Hence a number of peasant seals or their impressions survive from the thirteenth century, which shows that seals were sometimes used and even possessed by villeins. The earliest are to be found on documents from St. Peter's, Gloucester, dating from between 1263 and 1284.[46] In 1285 the Statute of Exeter assumed that at least some villeins would have seals, when permitting unfree as well as free peasants to serve on the grand inquests into the conduct of coroners for which it provided.[47] No legal enactment

[42] An eyre for which no roll is extant.

[43] I have mentioned evidence for some other general enquiries of this kind in 'The Origins of a Peasant Land Market', 27–8.

[44] This process is briefly described by P. Chaplais, 'The Anglo-Saxon Chancery: from the Diploma to the Writ', *Journal Soc. Archivists* iii (1966), 160–2.

[45] *P&M*, ii. 223–4, and cf. 'The Origins of a Peasant Land Market', 28 n. 6.

[46] R. H. Hilton, 'Gloucester Abbey Leases of the Thirteenth Century', *University of Birmingham Hist. Journal* iv (1953–4), 13 ff (repr. in Hilton, *The English Peasantry in the Later Middle Ages*, Oxford, 1975). It is hard to be sure that these peasants would have been held villeins in a royal court, but the reeve, who held unfree land by cirograph in 1290–1, almost certainly was. C. R. Cheney, *Notaries Public in England in the Thirteenth and Fourteenth Centuries* (Oxford, 1972), p. 8, adds another reference.

[47] *Statutes of the Realm*, i. 211; *Fleta*, i. 18 (20). The statute's date was established by V. H. Galbraith, 'A New Manuscript of the Statutes', *Huntington Library Quarterly* xxiii (1958–9), 148–51.

forbade villeins to own seals; whether or not they did must have depended on their means and need.

Our examination of the legal restraints on villein alienation, then, has revealed yet another part of the battleground between legal theory and social change.

6

THE INSECURITY OF VILLEIN TENURE

The fact that the villein had no rights in land enforceable against his lord in the royal courts is the last corollary of the lord's ownership of his villein's land to concern us. This point applied to the common law only. The factual extent of tenurial security reached far beyond the legal remedies available to a tenant in any system of courts. In practice, most tenants in villeinage enjoyed a large measure of security even in the thirteenth century. Until much later however, this was neither assisted nor recognized formally by the king or his justices. Perhaps herein lies the greatest contrast of all between the common law of villeinage and manorial custom.

The earliest manorial court-rolls already show customary holdings protected in ways modelled on the procedure of the royal courts.[1] In practice, manorial custom must have protected many whose holdings would have been considered unfree (and therefore, as we shall see, at will) by the royal justices, almost as well as the royal courts did their greater neighbours—and much more cheaply. Not until much later did a tenant in villeinage ejected by his lord have any legal remedy other than to petition his lord for reinstatement, but then, as has often been remarked, the tenant-in-chief was in a somewhat similar position *vis-à-vis* his lord, the king. What really mattered in practice were the comparative bargaining powers of lord and tenants in the manorial court,[2] and the terms on which land was actually

[1] See examples in *SS* ii. 107, 125–6, and *SS* iv. 119, 120, with Maitland's comment on p. 112. E. Kerridge, *Agrarian Problems in the Sixteenth Century and After* (London, 1969), Chaps. 1–3, has much of interest to say on this subject, mainly with reference to a later period.

[2] W. O. Ault, 'Village By-laws by Common Consent', *Speculum* xxix (1954), 389, is one of the few writers to have sought out evidence on this question. R. H. Hilton has touched on the problem a number of times; see especially his 'Peasant Movements in England before 1381', reprinted in *Essays in Economic History*, ii, ed. E. M. Carus-Wilson (London, 1962), pp. 73–90. Generalization is obviously dangerous but it ought to be possible to delimit the range of variations more fully. To one unfamiliar with the period and sources with which he deals, Kerridge, *Agrarian Problems* pp. 77–81, seems interesting on this. A manor with a good set of court rolls might permit a more detailed study.

held, the rent and service due, entry fines payable, and the like.[3] These facts cannot be ignored. Here, however, the extent of the gulf dividing manorial courts' custom from that administered by the royal lawyers is the relevant point.[4]

The common law considered the legal insecurity of villeinage a principle which hardly required explicit statement. For many purposes, villeinage was treated as part of the lord's demesne. The *De legibus* explains that demesne can be called villeinage because it is handed out to villeins and can be resumed by the lord 'tempestive et intempestive' at his will.[5] Britton's remarks are even stronger: the villein holds his land at the lord's will by villein services 'baillé', as it were, to cultivate it to his lord's use.[6]

The effect of this doctrine is that any land claim may be barred in the courts by an exception of villein tenure. In this the defendant excepts[7] that the plaintiff ought not to be heard, since he can claim no more than a villein tenement, with which the court has no concern. He has no claim to the free tenement, the freehold. Proof of this exception will defeat any suit for land, whether it sues in the *ius* (as in a writ of right) or in seisin (as in the petty assizes). To distinguish this kind of exception from one about villein status (objecting that the plaintiff should not be heard because he is a villein)[8] is important; for although the two pleas often produced similar results,[9] they drew legal effect from different sources.

[3] Compare, for example, the views of B. F. Harvey, 'The Population Trend in England, 1300 to 1348', *TRHS* 5th s. xvi (1966), 25–7, and J. Z. Titow, *English Rural Society, 1200–1350* (London, 1969), pp. 73–8. Cf. also Kerridge, *Agrarian Problems*, pp. 38–40. Similar factors governed relations between the king and tenants-in-chief especially in the later twelfth century.

[4] J. A. Raftis, *Tenure and Mobility* (Toronto, 1964), pp. 60–1, argues that the peasant's 'law' was manorial custom, implying that the common law is irrelevant to peasant life. The simplest way to see that this kind of view is exaggerated is to note the violence behind the cases cited in this and subsequent chapters.

[5] *Br.*, f. 263. Cf. *Dialogus*, I. xi (56), and the other references cited by *P&M*, i. 363. There is no need to deny that lawyers did distinguish between villeinage and demesne when convenient. See *Br.*, f. 98, where villeinage is described as 'quasi dominicum', and, for instance, *CRR* viii. 65 = *BNB* 53 (Devon 1219).

[6] *Britton*, III. ii. 12 (ii. 13–4). Cf. *Fleta*, i. 8 (4), iv. 1 (174); *Mirror of Justices*, p. 79.

[7] 'To except' (noun: 'exception') is a term of art, originally Civilian, that denotes the defendant's raising of an allegation to defeat the plaintiff's case, usually without denying outright his course of action. One can usually grasp the general sense by substituting 'objection' or 'defence'.

[8] Chap. 8 (ii).

[9] Not always; see below pp. 62–3.

Most of the *De legibus'* discussion occurs in the section on novel disseisin, and was not intended as a general statement. Even so, the treatment runs along the now-familiar lines. The villein only possesses his holding *nomine alieno* and is therefore not entitled to succeed by assize. If a villein held in villeinage, his possession was considered to be in the lord's name. The same was true even where he held freely of a stranger, once his lord had put in a claim. Consequently, the lord could bring an assize against anyone who had disseised *him* of *his* land by ousting his villein from it.[10] The original writ was very often drafted so as to exclude from its benefits tenants in villeinage. A plaintiff in novel disseisin, for example, complains that he has been disseised from his 'free tenement',[11] and one can hardly argue that a villein holding is a 'free tenement'.

The textbooks' statements can be amply confirmed from the plea rolls. A typical successful exception to an assize was the plea by a Devon defendant that the plaintiff was his villein and had formerly held from him in villeinage the land for which he was now suing. He had now taken the holding in hand and given it with his daughter as a marriage portion. He attempted no further justification of his acts and the court accepted his plea.[12] The story behind another assize of novel disseisin illustrates the kind of heartless estate management which the state of the law made possible on villeinage land. Three unmarried sisters, Edith, Agnes, and Avice, sued three brothers, Reginald, Henry, and William, complaining that they had been unjustly disseised of three acres of land in Coventry. The brothers objected against the assize that Edith and the others had no free tenement, because the land in question was the Earl of Chester's villeinage. The earl's bailiff, present in court to safeguard his master's interests, agreed that this was so. But the three spinsters persisted in their story and were allowed to put it to a jury. Originally one of the earl's bailiffs had, according to the jurors, handed the land over to Ralf de Radeford, the women's father,

---

[10] *Br.*, ff. 167b, 197, 199. The situation is unchanged by the free status of a tenant in villeinage, f. 199b citing Bestenover's Case, considered below, p. 58 ff. A similar line of argument works in the assize of mort d'ancestor; an ancestor seised *nomine alieno* cannot be said to have died siesed 'as of demesne', f. 263b. See further pp. 95–6 below.

[11] Cf. *Glanvill*, xiii. 33, *Selden Registers*, Hib 5, CA 14, etc.

[12] JI 1/175, m. 9d, towards the bottom of the membrane (Devon eyre 1243–4). *BRB* vi. 187 (Buckingham eyre 1227) is another example.

to hold in villeinage. A later bailiff had, however, taken the land back 'as the Earl's villeinage', perhaps when Ralf died, and the three unprotected women seemed tenants of doubtful value. He then passed it on to Reginald and his brothers, also to hold in villeinage. Confronted by these facts the court had no option; it held that the three brothers were absolved of all liability. All the same the three unfortunate sisters did not pay the king the normal amercement. They were said to be *pauperes*. Their father's holding may have been the sum total of the family possessions. One may guess that they died spinsters, for without land why should anyone marry them?[13]

There are many such cases. Where the plea rolls enable details of the stories behind to be recovered, they more than adequately confirm the harsh language of the textbook writers. Tenants knew as well as their lords that by the common law they could be removed at will[14] and that the lord could deal with their holdings 'sicut de suo'.[15] Their tenure was arbitrary in the sense that it really was dependent on the lord's will.[16]

A novel disseisin from 1248 helps one to understand how this relates to life in the countryside. William and Agatha de Blithe sued William de Gorham and two other men (presumably William's servants) who had disseised them of their holding. William de Gorham's defence was simple: they had no free tenement, he said. This plea he submitted to the verdict of the assize jury. The jurors fully confirmed his view of the matter. William and Agatha held of William de Gorham in villeinage by villein customs, until he ejected them 'as from his own villeinage', because they defaulted in their service. The assize therefore failed, since William de Gorham had a perfect right to throw his villeinage tenants off *his* land; he was answerable to no-one for his action. Yet, the tenants' default on their obligations perhaps made them liable to forfeiture by local custom.

---

[13] JI 1/951A, m. 14 (Warwick eyre 1232). I deduce that Edith and her sisters were spinsters because no husbands are said to have sued with them. Note that the court did not make them pay for their jury although the evidence of the earl's bailiff would seem to have made its grant a matter of the court's favour. For a comparable case with a rather happier ending, see JI 1/404, m. 7, concorded in *Final Concords of the County of Lancaster . . . 1196–1307*, ed. W. Farrer (Lancs. and Ches. rec. soc. xxxix 1899), no. 103. And for amercements pardoned for poverty, see below p. 76.

[14] Cf. *LRS* xxii. 312 (Lincoln eyre 1202).

[15] *CRR* ix. 92 = *BNB* 1411; cf. *CRR* viii. 98, 361; ix. 265 (Dorset 1219–20).

[16] As the tenant conveniently admitted in *CRR* xiv. 1492 (Gloucs. 1231); cf. ibid., 1020 for an earlier stage.

Their eviction may even have been formally approved by the manorial court, though if so, one might expect this to have been mentioned on the plea roll. Moreover, according to the jurors, William de Gorham did not merely oust his tenants; he later gave them twenty shillings 'for their poverty' and they expressed themselves as satisfied with this sum.[17] Clearly, William de Gorham, despite his undoubted seignorial rights at common law, felt that he had to take some account of public opinion or the promptings of christian charity.[18] In later times, the failure to act in accordance with local custom would have given the tenants (copyholders) a right of action against their lord in the Chancery and later still in the common-law courts themselves.[19] But such developments still lay far in the future. What men were thinking or saying in the Hertfordshire countryside about William de Gorham in 1248 was of no concern to the royal justices—unless it had led to acts of violence, when it would have been repressed.

Nor was the situation in any way changed if the villeinage tenant were personally free. Osbert de Norbroc' showed that he was well aware of this as early as 1213 when sued by one Robert for the return of land allegedly gaged to him by Robert's father Gilbert. He was quite prepared to deny the existence of any gage if necessary, but in any case, he said, he held the land in villeinage of the Bishop of London so that the bishop could take the land into hand when he pleased. He added cautiously that his body was free. And when Robert challenged his story, obviously suspecting that it was invented in order to prevent the recovery of his land, Osbert declined the court's offer to let him call the bishop into court to confirm his story. He was afraid, so he told the court, that the bishop would indeed seize the holding into his own hand once he heard that Osbert was being sued for it. Osbert's case has a very shady air; he obviously knew his way about the law, and the case is therefore all the more convincing as authority.[20]

[17] JI 1/318, m. 14d (Hertford eyre 1248). Once again the plaintiffs being *pauperes* were not amerced.

[18] The moralists had a good deal to say about the possible sin involved in a lord's exercise of his legal rights over free tenants. Cf. for example below Chap. 11, p. 192.

[19] Cf. C. M. Gray, *Copyhold, Equity and the Common Law* (Cambridge, Mass., 1963), Kerridge, *Agrarian Problems*, esp. pp. 66–73, and D. E. C. Yale's review of Kerridge in *LQR* lxxxvi (1970), 404–6.

[20] *CRR* vii. 46, 108 (Middlesex 1213); cf. ibid. 133. The case illustrates the subtleties of legal manoeuvre in unusual detail.

The assize of novel disseisin by which Roger Aselak sought in 1250 to recover half an acre of land and a messuage (house plot) in Haketon, Norfolk, is a more ordinary type of case. The alleged disseisors, John de Sancta Fide and two others, had objected against Roger that both he and the tenure by which he had held were unfree, but this was denied by the jurors who reported that Roger was a freeman. They went on to distinguish between the messuage and the land. The messuage had, they said, been acquired freely from the Earl of Norfolk's fee and the assize consequently succeeded as far as that was concerned. The half-acre of land, however, was John's villeinage and he was therefore quite entitled to eject Roger from it.[21]

Just why were freemen unable to secure common-law protection for their tenure of villein holdings? How did the law of villein status reach the form seen on the thirteenth-century plea rolls? The present examination suggests that a major factor in its development was the feeling of the king or his justices that many peasants were too unimportant to be worth the expenditure of time and effort. The inferior classes were therefore excluded from the new extended royal legal protection.[22] The legal insecurity of villeinage tenure also probably originated in a similar way as a half-intended consequence of general legal reform. One of the reformers' aims had been to attract new business from other jurisdictions into the royal courts. Henry II and his advisers could not afford to strike directly at seignorial power, and were careful not to affront public opinion by interfering in matters accepted as the sole concern of a lord and his vassals. The lord's right to deal with his demesne as he wished was, obviously, one such matter. Any freeman who sought to acquire some of this (villeinage) land to cultivate at rent knew that he was taking a certain risk; either he had no alternative because of his need for land, or he relied on the protection of local custom. That any 'freeman' who acted thus in the later twelfth century possessed the wealth or social standing to persuade the king or his justices to listen to his complaint about ejection was in any event unlikely. It is almost inconceivable that in this early period a really wealthy burgess or a member of

[21] JI 1/560, m. 20d = 561, m. 25 (Norfolk eyre 1250). Apparently, Roger had defaulted on the service due from the land. Perhaps he was afraid that his performance of villein customs might later be cited against him as evidence of unfree status.
[22] See below Chap. 13.

a great family should have stooped to acquiring strips of demesne land, although this became common enough later.

This view makes good sense of the plea-roll evidence. The free status of a thirteenth-century tenant in villeinage did not, then, affect his legal position because the law had already been settled. By that time, freeman probably were taking villein tenements quite frequently, but they were too late to change the law. Since the writs by which the real actions were commenced had been drafted so as to apply to the *liberum tenementum* only, villeinage tenure was automatically excluded, no matter who held it.

Thus far the argument is clear and logical. From the viewpoint of the common law there was much to recommend the position that villeinage tenure was outside the purview of the common law for all purposes, irrespective of the tenant's status. Lawyers generally say that they require the law to be clear, once the relevant facts are known to the court. Something close to this had now been achieved for villeinage tenure and long remained in force. Change eventually came through the evasion, not amendment, of this principle. The most serious challenge, however, probably came on the very morrow of the principle's establishment. During the early thirteenth century, members of the lower social classes were slowly becoming a more common sight in the royal courts. Increasingly, litigants included men who were holding packets of land in villeinage. At the same time, some lawyers too saw a legal anomaly in the freeman holding in villeinage. The famous thirty-ninth chapter of Magna Carta guaranteed tenure to all freemen, without making any reservations as to the kind of tenure by which they held. If this guarantee covered the freeman holding in villeinage, it would make the anomaly permanent. But the 1217 reissue restricted the protection to disseisins 'de aliquo libero tenemento suo vel liberis consuetudinibus suis'.[23] In effect this was a sharp check to the aspirations of the freeman on villeinage. To meddle in servile property entailed treatment as a serf. But, although this view must have originated somewhere close to the judicial establishment,[24] learned clerks and lawyers round the innovating judges of Henry III's minority had other opinions. The

[23] Magna Carta 1215, c. 39; Magna Carta 1217, c. 35 = 1225, c. 29.
[24] Cf. J. C. Holt, 'Magna Carta and the Origin of Statute Law', *Studia Gratiana* xv (1972), 487–508.

author of the *De legibus* took some pains to develop an analogy with the villein sokeman of the Ancient Demesne[25] in order to argue for a distinction between tenure and status and safeguard at least the status of the freeman holding in villeinage.[26] Since his main authorities were taken from just these years after 1217, it is small wonder that Maitland was led to ask whether 'for a moment perhaps there was some little doubt'.[27]

If there was, it soon passed. In fact none of the three cases Maitland cited affords unequivocal support for his suggestion. They and the few other cases that can be added merely show that the king would occasionally listen to complaints about unfree holdings, but would take action exceptionally only if his own interests were touched.

The first case to examine is the famous Bestenover versus Montacute.[28] John of Montacute had brought an action of naifty claiming Martin of Bestenover as his villein, and the case came before the royal justices in 1219 when Martin acquired a writ of *monstravit*.[29] John asserted that he had already proved Martin to be his villein when he had successfully defended an assize of mort d'ancestor brought by Martin during John's reign. He claimed that the court had adjudged Martin to be his villein on that occasion, but Martin denied this. John therefore vouched the court to warranty. To facilitate checking John's voucher, the case was then transferred from the eyre to Westminster, where we find it first. A search of the earlier plea rolls revealed to the court that in the previous case, the jurors had found the tenement sought by Martin to be villeinage, but that nothing had been decided 'de villenagio corporis'. The plea rolls can still confirm this today, since most of the relevant ones survive. They suggest that the court of that time believed

[25] See above pp. 26–7. Kerridge, *Agrarian Problems*, documents nos. 4, 9, 11, with his curious commentary suggest that this line had some influence on the much later evolution of common-law protection for copyhold.

[26] Cf. Chap. 8 (iii) below.

[27] *P&M*, i. 359; cf. Vinogradoff, *Villainage*, pp. 79–81.

[28] Main references, in chronological order: *CRR* i. 120, *RCR* ii. 192, *CRR* i. 192, 216, *Ab. Plac.*, pp. 25, 29 (1200); *CRR* viii. 15, 88, 114 (= *BNB* 70), 211, 216 (= *BNB* 88), 384. The concord was *Sussex Rec. Soc.* ii (1902), no. 170, p. 43. Discussed at length by Bracton in ff. 199–200 and Vinogradoff, *Villainage*, pp. 78–80. It is quite possible that we possess fuller records than the author of the *De legibus*. On the other hand it is not impossible that he was actually present in court!

[29] Procedure in actions of naifty is discussed in Chap. 10; the *monstravit* is the writ obtainable by the alleged villein.

Martin to be personally free, since John's exception on status was not put to the assize; the justices had merely ordered a *jurata* to report on the services due.[30] In the Hilary term of 1220, the court therefore held that 'si idem Martinus voluerit terram predictam tenere, tunc faciat predictas consuetudines quas pater suus fecit; sin autem, faciat idem Johannes de terra illa sicut de villenagio suo quod voluerit, quia terra illa est villenagium ipsius Johannis'. John was amerced because his voucher of the court had failed to prove his case, and a day was given to both parties for them to make their proof of status if they wished. In the event, the parties came to an agreement with the court's permission in the next term, and no more was heard about John's claim that Martin ought to have been his villein.

How, then, are these facts to be interpreted? Is the case an authority for the view that the courts would protect the tenure of a freeman holding in villeinage, as has been claimed? This seems unlikely. Martin probably was a freeman, though this was never finally proved. He was certainly what Bracton would have called a *statuliber*, anyway, because of his writ of *monstravit*.[31] The land was quite clearly declared to be John's villeinage. Martin was, then, treated as a freeman holding in villeinage. The court told him that he would have to do the same services as his father had (which included tallage and merchet)[32] if he wanted to hold the land; otherwise John could do with the land as he wished, since it was his villeinage. This is not a denial of John's right to eject Martin even if he did the services which his father had owed; the common law would not intervene. When John and Martin concorded, Martin acknowledged that the land was John's right and received it back at a money rent less than his father had paid. The agreement was for Martin's life only, and after his death none of his progeny was to have any further claim in the land. Possibly John's readiness to compromise is evidence that the court's decision had left Martin with tenurial rights which could not be ignored. More probably the

---

[30] See in particular *CRR* i. 120, 216. Note also the use of *homines* to describe the group with whom Martin's father Alured was tallaged, and that this is said to have been done not annually but 'uno quoque anno'.

[31] For the *statuliber*, see below, Chap. 8. Acquisition of a *monstravit* made one a *statuliber*, because of the grant of peace pending trial.

[32] This must be a reference to his unsuccessful assize mort d'ancestor of twenty years before.

concord was just an enfranchisement of the land on terms convenient to both parties.[33]

The case was collected in *Bracton's NoteBook* and exhaustively discussed in the *De legibus*. Its treatment there suggests that the author saw its decision as implying the granting of some tenurial protection to Martin. Significantly, neither the annotator of the *NoteBook* nor the author of the treatise was interested in the case for its bearing on the question of tenurial security. Instead, both emphasized that possession of a villein tenement does not affect the freeman's status (a point for which the case obviously is good authority), because, according to the annotator, the freeman can leave the land if he wishes. This interesting point is unmentioned in the judgement on the rolls;[34] furthermore, the ability to leave the land freely may sometimes have been understood to carry security of tenure as a corollary.[35] It should be assessed together with a passage from the treatise[36] where the author discusses the rules by which exceptions of villeinage can defeat assizes. Against a freeman holding in villeinage, he says, an exception will not affect his status, but it will prevent him recovering the land. His reason here resembles that in the *NoteBook:* he can leave the villeinage and go away as a freeman. And the Bestenover Case is cited in support. The general view of the *De legibus,* then, is that the lord can eject even a freeman from his villeinage at will, since he has the exception of villein tenure against any assize the tenant might bring. The possibility of criminal or trespassory action is not discussed, but it is hard to believe that these affect the position: the tenant, though free, cannot recover his villein land.

The *De legibus* now proceeds to discuss the Bestenover Case and leaves behind the question of tenurial security to concentrate on the distinction between tenure and status. In so doing, he appears to strengthen the court's judgement in the Bestenover

---

[33] Lower rent may be explained by the absence of reference to the sheep that figured in the proceedings of John's reign. The effect of the concord was to ensure that the whole expensive dispute was finally ended by Martin's death.

[34] *BNB* 70, Vinogradoff, *Villainage*, p. 80.

[35] The idea that the tenant was free from expulsion so long as he performed the services due, a compensation for his being unable to leave the land freely, probably comes from Civilian discussions about the *coloni*. It figures in a Vacarian *distinctio* about the free *agricola* and in *Leges Willelmi*, c. 29, among other places. Further discussion in Appendix.

[36] *Br.,* f. 199b; cf. f. 197b.

Case by rearranging its wording slightly and putting it into indirect speech. 'Videtur per hoc', the author concludes, 'quod licet liber homo teneat villenagium per villanas consuetudines, contra voluntatem suam eici non debet dum tamen facere voluerit consuetudines quae pertinent ad villenagium, quia praestantur ratione villenagii et non ratione personae.' An exception will defeat the assize of a freeman holding in villeinage only if he does the villein customs on account of his status. Probably this is a slip, for he had said just before that villein tenure will harm the freeman 'ad tenementum recuperandum'. He was trying to emphasize that an exception of status would not succeed in a case where the plaintiff was in Martin's position. Such a tenant remained free notwithstanding doing villein customs. By all normal Bractonian arguments the assize would fail to an exception of villein tenure, for the plaintiff could claim no free tenement. The Bestenover Case is no authority against this proposition, for it was not an assize at all. It establishes only the first point, that a tenant's status is unaffected by the land he holds. The *De legibus'* interpretation relies on its distinction between tenure and status, which cannot be taken as representative of the view accepted by the courts.[37] In any case, the court was only indirectly concerned with the tenement in the case. Facts about the villein tenure by which Martin and his father had held the plot of land from John were relevant only if they helped to prove Martin a villein. Since the court decided that they did not, the remarks about Martin's right to hold the land should perhaps not be taken too seriously. What the justices said was probably not intended to suggest that they would allow Martin to recover by the assize if John ejected him, but that he should perform the service due if he hoped to continue holding the land at all. If the *De legibus'* interpretation is correct, the king's justices were flouting the terms of the reissued Magna Carta within a very short time of its promulgation. In the absence of protests this conclusion seems most unlikely.

The circumstances behind the case may have been similar to those which arose when a lord alleged in a writ of customs and services that his tenant held in villeinage.[38] The case was almost

---

[37] Below, Chap. 8 (iii)., esp. p. 110 where the case is further discussed.
[38] There is some discussion of this writ and the action it introduced in Chap. 13.

always decided on the evidence of a jury verdict about the services. If the judgement favoured the lord, it might seem to include a declaration of the villein services by which the tenant was to hold. Yet, obviously, this in no way destroyed the lord's legal right to eject him, even if he were in fact performing adequately the services as described by the jury. In effect the judgement of the court said no more than that the tenants held in villeinage.[39] But the distinction is a fine one and, understandably perhaps, eluded contemporaries and later commentators.[40]

According to Vinogradoff, the second case, William son of Henry versus Bartholomew son of Eustace,[41] shows the justices protecting a villein in his villeinage tenement. The facts were roughly as follows. In 1224 William brought an assize of novel disseisin against Bartholomew at the Northampton eyre. Bartholomew objected against it that William held the land in villeinage only and was his villein. William answered that he had previously pleaded elsewhere in the royal courts as a free-man about this holding and he vouched to warranty the rolls and a writ of 'Martin' de Pateshull.[42] The case was then adjourned to Westminster for judgement. What happened next is very unclear. The text of *Bracton's NoteBook* says that the record of the early case had William convicted of owing villein customs

---

[39] Cf. above p.7

[40] This must have been another of the points which were to assist the growth of legal protection for copyhold. The reason why Coke and his predecessors did not cite them is no doubt that the run of such cases ended too early for them to have been reported in the Yearbooks, and this kind of writ of customs and services never reached the printed *Register*.

[41] The evidence for the case is *NRS* v. 468, *CRR* xi. 1892 (= *BNB* 1030), 2626 (= *BNB* 916); xii. 147; *BNB* 1103 (Northants 1224–5). Cf. Vinogradoff, *Villainage*, pp. 80–1.

[42] Martin of Pateshull was not yet a royal justice when William's brothers had brought an assize of mort d'ancestor *against* him (William) in 1202 at *Simon* de Pateshull's Northampton eyre, *NRS* v. 468. It failed because the assize does not lie between brothers. If this is the case William had in mind, the whole plea may have been fraudulent and the early assize collusive. On the other hand, the report of the 1224 case does not mention the production in court of any roll relating to the earlier case. The 1202 roll ought to have been available since the rolls for that eyre still exist. Perhaps the reference is to a different case on a roll already lost. This might explain why Bartholomew sought a jury 'super recordum' in the next term. Cf. below pp. 199 ff. for a case of 1228 at which assize justices who had never had a roll came into court to give their record and the court allowed a jury to enquire further into what had happened at the original hearing; also generally S. E. Thorne, 'Notes on Courts of Record in England', *West Virginia Law Quarterly* xl (1934), 347–59.

including merchet, but the only extant original roll has William quit ('quietus') of the customs. Both versions agree that the assize failed, and according to the *NoteBook* this was because the tenement was unfree. The *NoteBook* version appears preferable despite its secondary character.[43] Apparently, the assize failed because the holding was by villein tenure. William was in mercy but the court directed that he might plead in the manor court 'per breve de recto' if he wished, a point to which we must return.

The very next term, William was again in court, at the Bench, still seeking legal redress for his ejection. This time the form of action was one which summoned Bartholomew to answer why he deforced William of land concerning which there had been an assize at the last Northampton eyre.[44] This was one of the numerous trespassory actions in *Quare* form prevalent at this time, many of which never reached permanent form in the printed Register of Writs. The essence of actions in the form *quare deforciat* seems very often to have been an attempt to review a previous court decision, or someone's rights in the light of a previous decision.[45] Here William hoped by its use to reverse the previous decisions against him. Bartholomew's defence did not refer to the assize in which he had just been successful. It denied force and injury and asserted that William was his villein and the holding his villeinage, owing villein customs which he set out. Finally he offered a mark to the king for an inquest (if there had to be a jury) to decide whether the customs had been adjudged to him by the court of John's reign, as he claimed.[46] William denied that he owed any services except a money rent, and also put himself on a jury. The jury's verdict was that William was a villein and held the tenement in villeinage of Bartholomew, so William was handed over. Yet the record continues 'si facere voluerit predictas consuetudines teneat illam bovatam terre per easdem consuetudines, sin autem

---

[43] The surviving roll (KB 26/86) is badly mutilated and the Northamptonshire cases on it, being earlier in date than the other cases, may have been copied from some other roll. Cf. *CRR* xi, p. 379 n. 1. If so neither version is a primary authority, so to speak.

[44] *CRR* xi. 2626 = *BNB* 916.

[45] Cf. *Selden Registers,* pp. lxxiii, lxxxv, and, for instance, the cases indexed under 'quare deforciat' in *BNB*.

[46] See above n. 42 for a possible explanation of this proffer.

faciat Bartholomeus de terra et de ipso Willelmo voluntatem suam ut de villano suo et ei liberatur'.

The wording is reminiscent of the Bestenover Case, but this time the court clearly intended a causal connection between the performance of services and the tenure. The reason is that the land in question was privileged villeinage. The village where the land lay was Ancient Demesne,[47] as is shown by the justices' direction to William at the end of the first case, which was a reminder that he could bring a little writ of right in the manorial court.[48] William, however, had preferred to try the king's court again, probably by plaint; this way he had the chance of obtaining a judgement which would make him and his tenement free. Once this point is understood, the case is less unusual than has sometimes been thought.[49]

The third case generally cited is from William de Raleigh's Leicester eyre of 1232. The eyre roll is lost and the case is known only from its citation in the De legibus.[50] The facts can be reconstructed as follows. A freeman brought an assize of mort d'ancestor for a tenement which—as appeared from an exception—his ancestor had held by villein customs. The court apparently held that he should not on this account be convicted as a villein, and that the exception should not prevent the assize from proceeding. If the defendant wished to bring an action about the plaintiff's status, he would need to show other proof. However, this case is largely irrelevant to the matter under consideration.[51] It was most likely inserted into the De legibus by a reviser to demonstrate that proof that an ancestor had done villein customs did not suffice to make his descendant a villein, and perhaps also, to emphasize the need to have proof at hand

[47] This is pretty certain but cannot be proved in the normal way. Pilton is not mentioned in Domesday Book but is probably included in the entry referring to Barrowden, which was Terra Regis (DB, f. 219). Cf. V. C. H. Rutland ii. 211. The justices who had just declared the holding servile could not have gone on to recommend the writ of right patent!

[48] This may be the earliest reference to the little writ of right, for it precedes by two terms the Berkshire case (CRR xi. 2878) printed by Hoyt in Royal Demesne, p. 208. See Hoyt, pp. 197–200, for procedure on the writ.

[49] Some other comparable cases are cited below.

[50] Br., ff. 199b–200. This citation is probably the work of Professor Thorne's second reviser who may or may not have been Henry de Bracton; cf. Thorne, Br., iii. xxxi.

[51] Pace Vinogradoff, Villainage, p. 80.

when alleging villein status.[52] There is little doubt that the defendant in this case erred by raising the wrong exception; he should have excepted against the villein tenure of the holding. The *De legibus* warns of this trap elsewhere,[53] and advises the wary litigant to except against both tenure and status if he can.

Close examination has shown that the cases adduced lend little support to the hypothesis that royal protection of villein tenure was under active consideration in the early thirteenth century. Similarly, other cases that seem to hint at royal protection of villeinage are merely, perhaps, further evidence of the gap between the law of the royal courts and that of the manorial courts, where customary tenure was protected.

In these cases, lords apparently grant or confirm villein holdings in such a way that the services seem to have the court's approval behind them.[54] When a lord defending his disseisin on the grounds of villein tenure bothered to add some words of explanation, such as that the ejected tenant had been about to withdraw or was incapable of performing the services,[55] this only showed that to act strictly in accordance with the law was not always enough to satisfy a lord's conscience.

Some of the cases in which the king had a special interest seem more promising. Royal interventions were on the same principle that protected villein sokemen of the Ancient Demesne,[56] that is, the justices, if they acted at all, acted to encourage the manorial courts to protect them. William son of Henry might have received tenurial protection in this way, had he not tried for the higher prize of freedom.

Examples of this kind of procedure are not frequent on the rolls, but three cases make the point. In 1210,[57] one Ralph de Chiltun complained before the king that after he 'deposuit se' from free service and put himself in villeinage, John son of Hugh came in the autumn and took away some of the corn. The bare

---

[52] He stresses this elsewhere e.g. ff. 199, 200b, 270b; cf. *SS* lix. 524 (Coventry eyre 1221).

[53] *Br.*, f. 197 *addicio*. This is said by Woodbine (his edition, i. 397) to be almost certainly Bracton's.

[54] JI 1/951A, m. 18 (Warwick eyre 1232), KB 26/117B, m. 9 (Middlesex 1237).

[55] JI 1/318, m. 14d (Hertford eyre 1248), JI 1/777, m. 14 = 997, m. 4d (a Norfolk case from Winchester eyre 1249).

[56] Hoyt, *Royal Demesne*, pp. 194–8. See also M. K. McIntosh, 'The Privileged Villeins of the English Ancient Demesne', *Viator* vii (1976).

[57] *CRR* vi. 117 (Berks., *coram rege* 1210).

entry has no sequel, but Ralph may have received some remedy, for John was a well-known royal minister whose misdeeds
at the time of the Interdict required the attention of the courts
on a number of occasions.[58] The second case concerns another
member of John's evil brood of ministers, Faulkes de Breaute,
and the events which led to his fall in 1224. It was at the special
session of inquests held by Martin of Pateshull into Faulkes's
numerous disseisins[59] that Edith, the widow of one Louis de
Hida, complained to the justices that, although she was capable
of doing the services, he had disseised her from the tenement
which her husband Louis had held before his death in villeinage.[60] She begged the king to permit her to hold it 'according to
the custom of the manor of Luton' (to which it was attached).
These words suggest that her land may have been villein
socage. If so, she could hope to recover her land only by plaint
or petition to the king himself, since the manor was in the king's
hand and the little writ of right in consequence not available.[61]
The third case also concerns land of the Ancient Demesne, at
Alvergate in Norfolk. A number of tenants from the manor
complained by *monstraverunt* that Earl Roger Bigod was distraining them to do tallage, merchet, and other villein services
different from the service which they owed and which their
predecessors had done in the days of Henry II when the manor
had been in royal hands. Earl Roger answered that the complaining tenants were his villeins who had only recently decided
to declare themselves free sokemen and had then deserted their
houses, allowing them to fall into decay. Since they were unwilling to do the service due, he had taken the lands over. The
villagers denied that they were unfree but had to admit that
they had in the past done villein services by force and compulsion. In view of the last plea and because the court felt that 'they
might by chance be free', it held that 'si velint tenementa illa
tenere de predicto comite . . . faciant ei huiusmodi servicia

[58] e.g. *CRR* vi. 14, 23, 55, 117, and cf. ibid. 381 where a litigant, despite a court
judgement in his favour, had to offer the king a hundred shillings to get his land back.
[59] For which see Richardson and Sayles, *Procedure without Writ*, pp. xxxii ff., and G.
H. Fowler and M. W. Hughes in *BHRS* ix. 57–60. *CRR* xi. 1928 is a case similar to the
one to be discussed but it was introduced along orthodox lines, by an assize met by an
exception of villein tenure raised by one of Faulkes's co-defendants.
[60] *CRR* xi. 1914 (Berks. 1224).
[61] Cf. Richardson and Sayles, *Procedure without Writ*, pp. c, ciii, and *DB*, f. 209a
Edith may well have been personally free.

villana quousque per legem terre disracionaverint versus eum quod debeant esse quieti', words with a familiar ring.[62]

These cases show the full extent of royal protection. Servile tenure almost never received any protection in the royal courts. Such exceptions as have been found were almost entirely limited to the Ancient Demesne. Even there, they affected only villein socage and never pure villeinage. The words of judgements, like the one quoted in the preceding paragraph, do not grant legal protection; they merely tell the tenants that they must do the services if they wish to have any hope of continuing in their holdings.

---

[62] KB 26/121, m. 32 (Norfolk 1240). Hoyt, *Royal Demesne*, pp. 199–200, briefly treats of the *Monstraverunt;* cf. p. 248 below.

7

HERITABILITY AND VILLEIN WILLS

One further corollary of chattel ownership remains to be discussed: the villein's inability to transmit his property to an 'heir'. If the lord owns the villein, his land, and chattels, it follows that, as Vinogradoff said, 'the villein has no property of his own, and consequently he cannot transmit property'.[1] But powerful social forces at work during the thirteenth century made the practice rather different from the legal theory, and their effects can be traced even in the common law itself.

A villein could neither be nor have an heir at common law. Litigants often alleged that their opponents were unfree, in order to defeat claims based on rights of inheritance. Nicholas Baker, for instance, was the son of one Walter Wim from a small Buckinghamshire village. When his father died he had been living for some time in the town of Wycombe and believed that this had made him free. So he brought an assize of mort d'ancestor for his father's half virgate. No, replied his opponents, he and his father were both villeins though there had indeed been a certain charter made out 'ipsi Waltero et heredibus suis de eadem terra et ipse [Nicholaus] heres esse non potest quia villanus est'. When the villein status of Walter and Nicholas was confirmed by the jury, the court held that 'heres esse non potest'.[2] In another mort d'ancestor[3] the jurors reported that the deceased had been a villein though his holding was free, and they just did not know whether the plaintiff, his son, could be his heir or not 'since his father was a villein'. The court held that he could not. This principle was always accepted and can be illustrated by many other cases.[4]

---

[1] *Villainage*, p. 159.

[2] JI 1/62, m. 24d (Buckingham eyre 1232). For the supposed borough of Wycombe, see below p. 169. Nicholas does not seem to have tried to argue that the charter had enfranchised his father; cf. above p. 45.

[3] JI 1/229, m. 3d (Essex eyre 1227), cited by *Br.*, f. 199.

[4] *BNB* 343 (Middlesex eyre 1229), 702 (Dorset 1232), 1839 (Norfolk eyre 1227) are three examples, each with it own complication. But in *BRB* vi. 378 (Buckingham eyre 1227), father's confession of villeinage did not stop his daughter recovering his holding by assize of mort d'ancestor; cf. below p. 172.

The *De legibus,* though purporting to expound the courts' view, soon gets into difficulties from trying to pursue its own logic.[5] The author's first proposition is that the villein cannot be an heir; he then fills the vacuum by saying that it is the lord who is his villein's heir.[6] By his reasoning, a villein could not have a legal claim to his ancestor's seisin even if he had been living in a city or privileged place or was outside his lord's power and even though he might seek his own seisin 'in causa spoliationis'. This was because 'he will have no heir except his lord'. At any time before or after the villein's death, the lord had the same right to take into his own hands any of his villein's acquisitions of land, free or unfree. But the *De legibus* was also committed in two ways to views not easily reconciled with this tenet. The distinction between tenure and status allowed villeins to hold free land, and the theory of the relativity of villeinage[7] gave to villeins the same rights of action as freemen against anyone except their lord. According to this argument, a villein ejected from a free acquisition could bring an assize of novel disseisin against his ejector and succeed. If so, why should the villein's 'heirs' not be able to bring an assize of mort d'ancestor and succeed similarly? Bracton seems to have felt that mort d'ancestor should be available to an heir in any circumstances where the deceased, had he survived, could have succeeded by novel disseisin. Thus the lord, as nearest heir, would have had the right to bring a mort d'ancestor on the death of his villein. The *De legibus* will not allow this, however, if the deceased villein had held land freely from someone other than his lord.[8] The dead villein's lord cannot claim the land as an escheat because it was not held of him, and escheat is an incident of tenure. On the other hand the donor, from whom the land was held, cannot claim it as his escheat either, since, in the Bractonian view, the deceased villein was free as against him and ought to have left an heir to free land, at least, 'quantum ad suum feoffatorem propter suum factum et feoffamentum'. Thus in principle a villein with free

[5] *Br.,* f. 201; cf. ff. 270, 271, 271b. Also *Fleta,* iv. 13 (193), iv. 14 (197); *Britton,* I. xxxii. 6, 26 (i. 198–9, 210). The *Dialogus,* II. xviii (115), notes that a villein's death (unlike that of a freeman) extinguishes his debts since he leaves no inheritance.

[6] Does this come from a feeling that even a villein ought to have some kind of heir? Cf. *Glanvill,* vii. 17 (ed. Hall, p. 90), for the idea that the lord is *ultimus heres* to his man.

[7] These are discussed in Chap. 8.

[8] *Br.,* ff. 25–25b. Cf. f. 192b.

land can have heirs who can successfully bring an assize of mort d'ancestor for their ancestor's land. Further, if the 'heir' is under age, there is the possibility that the donor, from whom the deceased had held, might have rights of wardship or marriage; this is a prospect which no lord of a villein could view with equanimity. The whole discussion, one feels, although taken up by later writers,[9] is far removed from the real world. Its interest lies in the Bractonian pursuit of legal logic creating insoluble complications.

Even the point about escheat is somewhat doubtful. The author of the *De legibus* probably regarded the situation at the death of a villein tenant as analogous to that when a free tenant died without traceable heirs and his land reverted to the lord by way of escheat. This would, as it were, always be the case with villeins, since they never left an heir at common law. In fact, however, the only two cases known from before 1250 in which escheat was claimed in a villeinage context are both inconclusive. The Master of the Temple sought by writ of escheat twenty acres and an acre of meadow which had been held of him in villeinage by a tenant now deceased,[10] and the Prior of Thetford complained of violent intrusion into land which ought, he said, to have been his escheat because it had been held by one of his villeins before his death.[11] Without more facts about the actual situations, we cannot know if these lords were claiming their escheats as lord of the villein's body or his holding. However, *escaeta* probably just describes the lord's well-attested right to take over land held by his villein when the villein died. It might therefore belong to the lord of the villein's body, not of his holding as the *De legibus* held. There is no way to be certain.[12]

Of course, the real difficulty was that most peasants, whatever their status, enjoyed in practice a large measure of heritability. The manorial evidence tells a very different story from

---

[9] *Britton*, II. vii. 3 (i. 248), *Fleta*, iv. 13 (194), and cf. also the Harvard MS of *Brevia Placitata*, pp. 214–15.

[10] JI 1/454, m. 12 (Lincs., from Leicester eyre 1247).

[11] KB 26/133, m. 7 (Norfolk 1244).

[12] In JI 1/695, m. 18d (Oxon. eyre 1241), the Abbot of Abingdon was confirmed by an assize of novel disseisin in his seisin of meadow land just outside Oxford which he had entered on the death of the tenant, one of his villeins. See *Br.*, f. 30, for a general account of escheat.

the plea rolls, and it is a story which many historians prefer.[13] In the villages, men whom the lawyers classified as villein inherited land as heirs and expected to pass it on to others whom they in their turn regarded as their heirs. Nor was this merely *de facto*, for the rights were enforced in the manorial courts, increasingly in forms of action which closely resembled those used by freemen in the royal courts. Royal lawyers could not have been unaware of this. Reference to peasant inheritance customs was sometimes made in court, for example as tests of villeinage.[14] Even though the lord had the right to seize land into his hand, after the death of his villein as before, the son or other nearest 'heir' might and normally would offer an extra fine to succeed in the tenancy. As a Berkshire jury reported about one villeinage tenancy in Winkfield, the son of a deceased tenant could buy back his father's land 'per rationabile precium'.[15] Fleta on one occasion refers to 'the nearest heirs' to whom the bailiffs handed over villein tenements.[16] The widow of a villein might even be awarded by local custom more than the third part of her deceased husband's land which she could recover as common-law dower.[17]

What was true of land held too for movable goods. The custom of many areas permitted villeins to make wills as a normal matter. Manorial or ecclesiastical courts dealt with any disputes over their validity or probate. Although most such wills were unwritten, a good deal can still be learnt about them,[18] and though legal theory did not recognize their exist-

[13] G. C. Homans, *English Villagers in the Thirteenth Century* (Cambridge, Mass., 1942), (repr. 1960), Part II, is the most comprehensive treatment of peasant inheritance. Also R. J. Faith, 'Peasant Families and Inheritance Customs in Medieval England', *Agric. Hist. Rev.* xiv (1966), 77–95, B. Dodwell, 'Holdings and Inheritance in Medieval East Anglia' *Ec. H. R.* 2nd ser. xx (1967), 59–64.

[14] *CRR* xi. 1600 = *BNB* 1005 (Oxon. 1224) and *CRR* xi. 850, 865; *CRR* xii. 361 = *BNB* 1062 (Sussex 1225); *BNB* 794 (Berks. 1233); JI 1/777, m. 14 = JI 1/997, m. 4d (Winchester eyre 1249); JI 1/870, m. 4 (Surrey assize 1248).

[15] JI 1/36, m. 3, *CRR* xii. 1031 (Berks. eyre and Bench 1224–5). Cf. JI 1/1177A, m. 2d (Suffolk, heard at Norwich 1249).

[16] *Fleta*, i. 73 (162), from *Seneschaucie*.

[17] In *CRR* vi. 147, 192 (Berks. 1212), a widow was awarded dower on the half cot-land which her husband had held freely, but not on the two virgates whose services the jury set out in detail, ending: 'they never heard that a woman ever had dower from such a tenure, but after her husband's death she held the whole land by doing whatever customs her husband did'.

[18] M. M. Sheehan, *The Will in England . . . to the End of the Thirteenth Century*, pp. 180, 253–4, refers to sources and secondary literature. Add *Court Roll of Chalgrove Manor, 1278–1313*, ed. M. K. Dale (*BHRS* xxviii 1940), pp. 10–11 (1279–80).

ence, they are sometimes mentioned on the plea rolls.[19]

The gap between the legal theory and the life of the countryside is wider here than at any other point in the system. This is why the *De legibus* erred. It aimed to bridge the gap. The treatment of inheritance customs necessarily presented problems to the lawyers. Death is, after all, an event which exacerbates the conflicts between the survivors' claims to the deceased's property. At this moment the lord must assert or reassert his rights, if he is not to lose them. On the other hand, men naturally hope to determine the dispositions to be made after their deaths. At the least they wish to ensure that their goods will remain in the family. By the end of the twelfth century, the royal courts protected most men in the enjoyment of their rights of inheritance;[20] exclusion from this benefit for reasons of status was a handicap which rankled more and more. Furthermore, from the religious point of view, death was the moment when the soul was in its greatest danger. The Church—not without a certain financial interest of its own—urged that all classes should be able to make material provision for the salvation of their souls after their decease. Its view was that a man was entitled to die secure in the knowledge that he had made some pious bequest for his salvation,[21] and if he chanced to die intestate some part of his goods should nevertheless be distributed on his behalf.[22]

Apparently, the Church did not make a direct bid for the unfree peasant's soul before the late twelfth century. Until then, canon law had followed the Roman-law rule which attributed no testamentary capacity to the *servus*.[23] Gratian quoted with approval the statement that 'servus testamentum facere non

[19] See JI 1/80, ms. 20d, 21 (Salop, heard at Huntingdon 1235), at the end of this chapter.

[20] S. E. Thorne, 'English Feudalism and Estates in Land', *Cambridge Law Journal* xvii (1959), 192–209, is modified now by J. C. Holt, 'Politics and Property in Early Medieval England', *Past and Present* lvii (1972), 3–52, the ensuing debate in *Past and Present* lxv (1974) and S. F. C. Milsom, *The Legal Framework of English Feudalism* (Cambridge, 1976).

[21] Cf. the words of the Exeter synodal statutes of 1287: 'cum igitur extremis decedentium voluntatibus favorem maximum impendere teneamur . . .', Powicke and Cheney, *Councils*, II. 2.1045–6.

[22] Cf. Henry I's Coronation Charter, c. 7, the Unknown Charter, c. 5 and c. 27 of Magna Carta 1215, Holt, *Magna Carta*, pp. 302, 303, 324–5.

[23] Buckland, *Slavery*, p. 83.

potest',[24] but afterwards Canonist opinion gradually changed until serfs were distinguished from *servi*.[25]

Meanwhile secular law remained obdurate. At the end of the twelfth century, Glanvill's treatment of the subject was clearly confined to freemen, but recognized that in practice the matter was usually governed by local customs.[26] A generation later 'Glanvill Revised' inserted a rider asserting that Glanvill's example of a local custom applied to villeins and holders of socage land.[27] A collection of notes and cases from the 1270s contains a case report[28] which shows that some common lawyers were thinking about the legal difficulties. It includes an opinion attributed to a Bench Justice, Master Roger de Seaton. He believed that if a freeman holding by villein services wished to leave his villein tenement, he could take with him any animals or other chattels other than those raised on it, saving any services due to the lord. To justify this Master Roger cited a supposed provision of the Statute of Merton[29] 'ke si un vilain se lest murir il purra deviser ses bens ou li plerra sauve les servises as chef seignurage'. This is a misreading of c. 2 of that statute which refers to *vidue*, not *villani*. The slip was easily made if the belief that the statute might have granted testamentary rights to villeins were plausible, and obviously it was.

Yet secular lords continued to apply the strict common-law rule, and their maltreatment of villein testators helped to stimulate a series of ecclesiastical canons against interference with the making of wills (including those of villeins). The earliest surviving example is from a Provincial Council of Archbishop Boniface of Canterbury in 1257.[30] A general enactment about

---

[24] *Decretum*, C. 23, q. ii, c. 5.

[25] See A. Dumas, *Dictionnaire de droit canonique* s.v. Testament. Late in the thirteenth century, Ricardus de Mediavilla rejected suggested analogies with married women and cited Aristotle's *Politics* to deny that a *servus* could make a will, arguing from chattel ownership, *Super Quatuor Libros Sententiarum Petri Lombardi Quaestiones Subtilissimae* (Brixen, 1591), iv. 602 (45.4.3.). He was either English or Norman and had a considerable reputation as a theologian in the schools; A. B. Emden, *A Biographical Register of the University of Oxford to A.D. 1500* ii (Oxford, 1958), 1253–5.

[26] *Glanvill*, vii. 5.

[27] Gonville and Caius College, MS 205/111, p. 96, differs slightly from Maitland, *Coll. Papers*, ii. 280. The discussion still purports to be about the *liber homo*.

[28] *Cas. Plac.*, p. 56/5 (? 1272/8).

[29] The text says the statute of Marlborough but this was a mistake. See H. G. Richardson and G. O. Sayles, 'The Early Statutes', *LQR* 1 (1934), 202, for a similar mistake made in 1277.

[30] Powicke and Cheney, *Councils*, II. 1. 534, art. ix.

the devolution of the goods of intestates was expressly said to apply to *servi*, saving the lord's customs and services. The provision, which was apparently related to a chapter of Magna Carta omitted from the reissues,[31] was intended to rule out seignorial interference, unless the deceased had been under some specific obligation still outstanding. This provision was strengthened in 1258 and 1261[32] by extension to prohibit interference with the wills of *ascripticii* and others of servile condition, in contravention of the alleged custom of the English Church. In 1280, a complaint about continuing seignorial interference with the wills of laymen, free and servile, figured among a number of clerical *gravamina* presented to parliament. Two versions of Edward I's reply have survived. In the edited Canterbury text, the king is said to have wished that wills, once made, should stand. The compiler, noting that this grants implicit permission for lords to prevent the making of at least some wills, professes his disbelief that this could represent Edward's real intention. The York text says that the king forbade any hindrance to the wills of free laymen or clerks, but allowed lords to stop their villeins from making wills, since a lord could, if he wished, take away all his villein's goods 'sine injuria'. However, once the will was made, it was valid and to be observed.[33] The York text comes close to the later position at common law, but the subject remained controversial into the fourteenth century, and the flow of similar canons continued until 1344[34] when Edward III apparently accepted the secular argument that lords had a legal right to prevent villeins and married women from making wills.[35] His decision, however, may have had little practical effect.

No doubt the friction between secular and ecclesiastical jurisdiction produced many cases in the second half of the thirteenth

---

[31] Magna Carta 1215, c. 27.

[32] Powicke and Cheney, *Councils*, II. 1. 585, 681.

[33] Ibid. II. 2.878; the clergy accept the lord's right to certain customs, heriot no doubt.

[34] Ibid. 1045–6, 1143 (1287, 1295), and see for later references H. S. Bennet, *Life on the English Manor* (paperback reprint, Cambridge, 1962), p. 250; Sheehan, *The Will in England*, pp. 253–4. W. Lyndwood, *Provinciale* (Oxford, 1679), Lib. III, tit. 13, p. 172, col. 2, distinguishes in his glosses between *ascripticii* (villeins) who are free and can make wills and *servi* who cannot 'quia nec seipsos nec bona habent'.

[35] The Commons petition complained that it was 'contre reson' for niefs and married women to make wills. The answer was that 'le Roi voet qe ley e reson eut soient faites', *Rot. Parl.*, ii. 150a, which looks like agreement.

century. Two illustrations must suffice here. The first concerns the affairs of Reginald de Culleslye, a prosperous Sussex villager, who was one of Earl John Warenne's villeins.[36] On his death in 1265 or 1266, the earl's servants made vigorous enquiries into his possessions, and summoned various people (including the executors of his will) to the honorial court at Lewes. Earl John had no intention to take over all of Reginald's property, as strict law perhaps entitled him to do, but wished to exact whatever price he could for giving his approval to the distribution. So the executors had to pay half a mark for the freedom to administer the dead man's goods. A neighbouring lord, William David, from whom Reginald had held land, brought a quitclaim of Earl John's rights in it for 46s. 8d., permitted 'because, the Lord Earl does not wish to have the *status* (estate) of the said Reginald nor to hold of the said William'. Reginald's son-in-law paid four shillings for confirmation of a legacy made to him when he married one of Reginald's daughters. Another daughter had to pay half a mark for an inquisition to confirm that her house and small plot of land were her own and not her father's. The most significant point about the case was the amount of investigation necessitated by the death of one substantial villein farmer. Many estates must have had tenants like Reginald de Culleslye.

The clash of interests between the lord and the executors, which was only incidental to the investigation into Reginald's estate, is central to an interesting case from 1287.[37] One Richard de Lovesthorpe, a Lincolnshire villein who had once been reeve for his lord Alexander de Seurbek, died leaving a will. When the executors began to administer the estate, Alexander seized Richard's flock of sheep and prevented them from completing their job, 'asserting that the same Richard had been his villein, by which he understood that all his villein's goods and chattels were his own chattels'. The executors thereupon instituted proceedings against Alexander before the bishop's official; in response, he obtained a writ of prohibition. At the eyre Alexander explained that Richard had been in arrears on his accounts as

[36] *Records of the Barony and Honour of the Rape of Lewes*, ed. A. J. Taylor (Sussex rec. soc. xliv 1939) pp. 22, 23, 27, 29, 31, 32, 33 (1266).

[37] JI 1/503, m. 8 (Lincoln eyre 1287), cited by Sheehan, *The Will in England*, p. 254. A search of the rolls of the central courts has failed to find any entries relating to later stages of the case.

reeve, and had consequently been forbidden to make a will until they had been cleared,[38] which had not been done. When questioned, the jurors denied that Richard had either been in arrears or forbidden to make the will. They then added that 'in that neighbourhood villeins were accustomed to make wills and still do make them'. At this stage, the case was adjourned for judgement to Westminster, where unfortunately it cannot be traced any further.

Even without the final verdict, the case has several lessons for the historian. A layman appeals to the full rigour of the common-law rules about chattel ownership, not to deny that villeins can ever make valid wills, but rather to safeguard himself from financial loss in one specific situation. Yet by resorting to a writ of prohibition, he was prepared to argue that he, as lord, could annul any will made by his villein, since the plea that the case in the Court Christian concerned a legitimate will was a good defence to a writ of prohibition. On the other hand, the six executors (two of them clerks) were equally willing to use the Courts Christian to coerce the lord into forgoing his financial rights. Thus the arguments propounded in court for both sides probably exaggerated the just positions of each. The case affords a solitary glimpse of the disputes underlying ecclesiastical legislation about testamentary rights.

The eventual compromise between the two laws on wills had a Bractonian flavour, related to the treatise's rules permitting villeins to acquire free land. Villeins were thereby allowed a *de facto* power of testamentary disposition, subject to the lord's right to enter the land at any time before probate of the will and seize the goods on it.[39] This compromise solution, which does not give the villein all he might have wished, was not achieved until well after the period which is our concern here.

The law of succession to personal property did, then, eventually become reasonably clear and comprehensible. What about succession to land? From the mid-thirteenth century onwards, lawyers were confronted with even more complicated questions about villeinage and land succession. As the growing land

[38] Cf. *Dialogus* II. xviii (115) that a villein's death extinguishes all his debts.
[39] See H. Swinburne, *A Treatise of Testaments and Last Wills* (5th ed., London, 1728), pp. 76–8. Swinburne bases his view on fourteenth-century Yearbook cases, mainly from secondary sources, and is cautious about committing himself on an obsolete subject.

market drew in peasants irrespective of status with increasing frequency, the common law gave way only a little. The law's very complexity hindered decisions and made inheritance suits an even greater financial risk for the peasant litigant.

Two cases will illustrate such situations. Roger de la Strete was the son of a free mother Ela de Nuthe and a father John le Ball', who had acknowledged before the justices of the Bench that he was a villein of Merton Priory and held land in villeinage from the House. On John's death, Ela had moved on to a free holding of ten acres in Reigate, Surrey, where she lived until her death. Roger now brought an assize of mort d'ancestor against one of his mother's family to recover the land. But ought he to succeed? The jurors told the tale as just recounted, said that Ela had died seised 'ut de feodo', and that Roger was her eldest son and heir. The decision was then left to the justices who adjourned the case. Their judgement, if one was ever made, has not been found.[40] The second case concerned Simon Croft, a Lincolnshire villein who acquired a holding *sibi et heredibus suis,* and was later—no doubt partly on account of his acquisition— said to have died *in libero statu.* His brother William, who was still unfree, then entered the land and held it for nearly a year before enfeoffing one Nicholas de Struby 'with his own seisin'. Simon's sister Juetta had married John of Thorp who may well have been free, and their son sued Nicholas by mort d'ancestor at the eyre of 1271–2. Once again the justices adjourned the case, and as before, no decision is known.[41] Very possibly, logically defensible decisions for these cases could have been found in the jurist's study. In open court, however, it must have been very hard indeed, for much necessary information was probably unobtainable from those present or represented there.[42]

[40] JI 1/864, m. 7 (Surrey eyre 1235).

[41] JI 1/483, m. 30d (Lincoln eyre 1271–2). The entry has a very Bractonian flavour, especially in the way the jury verdict was written up. JI 1/483, m. 52d, another mort d'ancestor from the same eyre, also shows Bractonian ideas. The justices would not accept an exception of villeinage because the plaintiff's father had been enfeoffed by an ancestor of the defendant. This would have been an 'implied manumission', above Chap. 5.

[42] In Roger de la Strete's case, for example, one would need to have known at least (1) whether Roger was free, (2) whether the land sought had been John's or, as seems likely, came from Ela or her side of the family, and (3) whether the priory had ever taken seisin of it.

The historian, so remote from the tactical requirements and politics of the day, may sense ample room here for compromise. Yet, and despite villeins' increasing control over their property as the century progressed, unfree status could still have disastrous consequences for peasants unfortunate enough to find themselves facing royal justices. For many the most important effect of villein status was to defeat their claims to property which they felt they ought to inherit. Failure in these claims invariably left them impoverished, sometimes destitute. Significantly, many of the cases in which villein litigants were not amerced in the normal way for their failure 'quia pauper est',[43] were either assizes of mort d'ancestor[44] or suits for dower.[45] Often these people would have been quite well off by their neighbours' standards, had they been able to succeed to the family land. Walter Bacum, a villein of Luffield Priory, is perhaps an extreme case. During the 1270s he engrossed numerous small parcels of land in and around Silverstone in Northamptonshire worth around £4 in all, but nearly all of this was taken over by the House when he died.[46] Many smaller estates were treated in a similar fashion.

A summary of conclusions thus far may be helpful. The general principle that common-law inheritance did not extend as far as villeins or villeinage holdings is quite clear in cases from the first decades of the thirteenth century. In practice, however, most peasants passed on to those they considered their 'heirs' much of their land and other property. The author of the *De legibus* found himself unable to ignore these social facts, and his efforts to reconcile them with the law found on the plea rolls led him to adopt conflicting lines of legal logic. Consequently, his account of villeinage and heritability is tangled, but fascinating for the historian. Strict enforcement of a simple rule, that villeins could not inherit and villeinage holdings were not

[43] See D. M. Stenton's comments in *SS* liii. lxiii ff. M. T. Clanchy has pointed out that a *pauper* was not necessarily destitute, *Civil Pleas of the Wilts. Eyre 1249* (*WRS* xxvi 1971), p. xviii.
[44] e.g. *SS* liii. 228 (Lincoln eyre 1219), *BRB* vi. 243 (Buckingham eyre 1227), and the case of Nicholas Baker, above p. 66.
[45] e.g. *CRR* ix. 172, 295, 314; x. 80 (Beds. 1220–1). There are many similar cases especially in the years around 1230.
[46] *Luffield Priory Charters*, ed. G. R. Elvey, Part I (*BRB* and *NRS* 1968), nos. 231, 246–51, 258A, 259, 288. And see below pp. 259–60 for Peter de Canley who was successful in hiding his villein origins.

heritable, would have been impossible anyway. Even the king and his justices never seriously thought of it. Enforcement often hit individuals very hard. The legal doctrines about property sucession and villeinage (especially the land law) became increasingly complex, and this development favoured those wealthy enough to afford able lawyers. In the end, however, such 'prosperous villeins' made significant gains.

This chapter will conclude with a brief survey of heriot. Historians generally think of heriot as a custom by which, on a villein's decease, his best beast (if he had one) is given up to his lord.[47] Actually, heriot cannot be confined to the legally unfree, and its line of development from Old English *heregeat* is somewhat obscure in detail. In the twelfth century, both the old noble *heregeat* and the peasant customs which would later be called heriot[48] could still be referred to as 'relief'. But by the thirteenth century heriot was restricted to peasants.[49]

Legal writers say that heriot[50] is the peasant equivalent of relief. But unlike relief, the payment is said to be made by the deceased himself, rather than by his heir.[51] The crude distinction is obviously between noble and peasant custom, not between free and unfree, and in the thirteenth century both heriot and relief are perhaps best understood as tenurial obligations. Heriot does not apply to villeins alone.[52] Thirteenth-century

[47] See for example Homans, *English Villagers of the Thirteenth Century*, pp. 109, 133.

[48] e.g. *Leges Willelmi*, 20.3 (*Gesetze*, i. 306–7); these laws have been most recently discussed by Richardson and Sayles, *Law and Leg.*, pp. 121 ff., 170 ff.; *LHP* 14. See also N. Neilson, *Customary Rents* (Oxford Studies in Social and Legal History, ii, Oxford, 1910), pp. 87–8.

[49] This is one among several pieces of evidence for the way that Old English law slid down society with those who used it after the Norman Conquest, to end as peasant custom. Other evidence for the social decline of English families during the course of the twelfth century, and the part this process played in the creation of common-law villeinage, is considered below pp. 251 ff. I know of no convincing suggestion about the way in which the Old English military *heregeat* could have been developed into the peasant custom found in the thirteenth century. Any such argument will have to take into account the survival in 'some small purely agricultural boroughs' of the Old English military heriot. The contrast with Germany where it survived much more widely and in large cities is very suggestive. M. de W. Hemmeon, *Burgage Tenure in Medieval England* (Cambridge, Mass., 1914), pp. 22–4.

[50] *P&M*, i. 312–17.

[51] Does this point to the fact that in the eleventh century, the normal situation would have been for a deceased to leave several heirs?

[52] See Dugdale, *Monasticon Anglicanum* (London, 1817; repr. Farnborough, 1970), ii. 31, for a decision of 1271 from Evesham.

lawyers searched hard for customs to use as tests of villein status, but they never cited heriot in court for this purpose because they knew that too many freemen owed it.

The legal writers always discussed heriot together with relief, but as something to be distinguished from it. The *De legibus* and its abbreviators stressed that the payment was made as of grace not as of right. Fleta added that heriot had nothing to do with the heir, but was owed by the deceased himself.[53] No writer associated heriot with the legal rule that a villein could have no heir. Little direct connection between heriot and villeinage existed.

Historians have noticed that heriot closely resembled various continental customs, often called 'mainmorte' or somthing similar. French historians have ceased to believe that mainmorte was an exclusively and characteristically servile obligation;[54] likewise heriot, too, is best considered as a system of indirect controlled inheritance for peasants.[55] On the Continent, mainmorte took two basic forms. In the first, the deceased paid a valuable chattel for the right to dispose freely of his other chattels. Often described as a payment to the lord for his permission to make a will, this type of mainmorte is reminiscent of one of the explanations suggested as the origin of the English heriot.[56] In the second form, all the deceased peasant's possessions went to his lord; this is the common-law prohibition of villein inheritance, put in a different fashion.

Thus, heriot and the legal theory that the villein has no heir except his lord may be just two aspects of the same system of indirect inheritance, inheritance outside the common law. Even where the lord takes all, to profit therefrom he normally handed the tenancy out to those who might otherwise have been con-

---

[53] *Br.*, ff. 60, 84, 86; *Fleta*, iii. 18 (212); *Britton*, III. v. 5 (ii. 51). Cf. *Glanvill*, vii. 5; he does not name it and deems it a local custom, meaning, I suppose, that it was not part of the *lex regni*.

[54] Marc Bloch's account of the three marks of serfdom (most clearly expressed in 'Liberté et servitude personnelle', *Mélanges*, i. 286 ff.) has been effectively challenged by L. Verriest and others. See below p. 187 n. 9 for references.

[55] P. Petot, 'L'Origine de la mainmorte servile', *RHDFE* 4e sér. xix (1941), 275–309; cf. Hemmeon, *Burgage Tenure in Medieval England*, p. 194.

[56] Another sees the English heriot as the symbolic return to the lord of the equipment, agricultural for the peasant, military for the Old English thegn, which he was deemed have given to his man. Of course, in the thirteenth century heriot was often paid in money; cf. M. M. Postan and J. Z. Titow, 'Heriots and Prices on Winchester Manors', *Ec. H. R.*, 2nd s. xii (1958), 393, 409.

sidered the deceased's heirs. Where this type of mainmorte held sway, the deceased's relatives often had a customary right of pre-emption of the tenancy ('retrait lignager'); thus, descent to collaterals was possible.[57] The extent to which such arrangements can be paralleled from English material is not important here.[58] One eyre case, worth citing in conclusion, was initiated by a writ of customs and services in which the Prior of Much Wenlock claimed villein customs and services from some of his tenants in the village.[59] To prove that his opponents' tenure was unfree, the prior cited an elaborate set of rules which he said governed what happened when a tenant died. These rules asserted that there was no recognized heir who succeeded as of right, but that the deceased tenant's son could, at the prior's choice, pay to succeed his father. The tenants denied that they held in villeinage and claimed, *inter alia,* that each of them could bequeath his movable goods at his own will, giving to the lord only the best beast, obviously as a heriot. If a widow or children survived the tenant, they should, according to the tenants, receive all the chattels, the youngest son being the heir. Even without a verdict, this case well illustrates the conflicting views which lords and their peasant tenants must often have taken about inheritance.

---

[57] Petot, 'La mainmorte servile', 294–6.
[58] One example from Devon is in *HMC, Various Collections,* iv (1907) p. 74.
[59] JI 1/80, ms. 20d, 21 (Salop but heard at Huntingdon 1235).

PART II

THE VILLEIN AND HIS LEGAL RIGHTS

Part I of this book has considered the various consequences of the particular view of villeinage which contended that the villein was above all his lord's chattel. The strengths and weaknesses of the view for the purposes of modern study have been examined in terms of its use by contemporary lawyers. Inevitably, the conclusion that emerges is that although the idea of chattel ownership was often present somewhere at the back of thirteenth-century legal minds, villeinage law never formed a system easily analysable in such terms. Indeed, the courts never succeeded in forcing villeinage into any well-ordered, logical system.

To do so would have required the solution of a problem that, in one form or another, faces all systems of law which permit the chattel ownership of one man by another. How can the two roles of the villein (or slave, or serf) as man and as thing be reconciled? Part II of this book is devoted to consideration of some of the ways in which thirteenth-century Englishmen sought to deal with this problem and built up the common law of villeinage. It must start with the treatise *De legibus et Consuetudinibus Angliae* so long known by the name of Bracton.

8

BRACTON'S THEORY OF VILLEINAGE

This treatise *De legibus* was by far the most accomplished attempt to expound the law administered in the king's courts; 'the crown and flower of English medieval jurisprudence', Maitland called it.[1] The book has long presented scholars with severe problems. Its doctrine cannot always be reconciled with that to be deduced from the cases themselves. Was its author in error? Or did he conceive of his work as a way of proposing reforms in the law of his day? Who indeed was he, and when and how did he work?

Professor S. E. Thorne has now provided good answers to most of these questions, and by far the most convincing suggestions for the genesis of the treatise. The *De legibus*, he argues, originated during the 1220s and 1230s in the circle of clerks and lawyers round Martin de Pateshull and William de Raleigh, successively chief justices of the Bench. The author's name, once on the first folio, was replaced by that of Henry de Bracton, a prominent justice of a later vintage who had emerged from the Raleigh circle, only in the late 1250s when an editor prepared an abbreviated form of the work for publication. Henry de Bracton's role in its production was that of a reviser. He is tenatively identified with the second (or third) of these secondary authors, who possessed the long lost manuscript of the prototype *De legibus* from at least 1234. This long association with the work left many marks on the second *De legibus*, which alone was published and is known today from the forty or so extant manuscripts. Medieval readers and modern scholars alike wrongly regarded Henry de Bracton, J., as the author. This, Thorne shows, cannot be. Many features of the work, including its basic shape and aims, make best sense only in the

---

[1] *P&M*, i. 206.

'time of bustling legal activity' between Magna Carta and the Statute of Merton.[2]

These revelations greatly complicate the task of historians seeking to comprehend the theories of Bracton[3] on subjects like villeinage. Life was much easier when, despite occasional nagging doubts, one attributed the work to one date and one author, Henry de Bracton, about whose life and career a good deal was known.[4] Understanding of thirteenth-century law and society will derive immense benefits from precise dating of the various portions of the *De legibus*, which will permit a more profound appreciation of shifts in doctrinal development under Henry III. This is not the place to rewrite the legal narrative of the reign—and certainly not the time. Yet this task is very closely connected to Professor Thorne's view of the *De legibus*. Thorne's attribution of the work to different periods and hands derives from close comparison of Bracton's pronouncements with actual cases from plea rolls in print. His unexpressed assumption must therefore be that the original author, successive revisers, and even the editor aimed primarily to describe existing law. A rule amended in 1236 by the Statute of Merton would not be repeated by any sensible author writing after that date. Nor would views embodied in the judgements of Martin de Pateshull on the 1226–8 eyre visitation, but superseded after his death, be worth recording by a writer of the late 1230s or beyond. Thorne's dazzling results by this approach almost blind one to other possibilities. One is that some of those involved in producing the *De legibus* felt free to select a preferred doctrinal line from cases decided at different dates. Doctrinal advance is never smooth and need not be unilinear. Mere description of current law, as in some dull textbook of today,

---

[2] This is the bare bones of Thorne's 'Translator's Introduction' to *Br.*, iii. i–lii, which must be read in its entirety. The 1977 conclusions differ greatly from those of 1968 in the 'Translator's Introduction' to vol. ii. Though the earlier argument is clearly overtaken by the later, it retains much of value and is still required reading.

[3] To repeat an earlier footnote, I have personified 'Bracton' to denote the unknown original author, the collective authorship and its product, the treatise *De legibus*.

[4] A good starting point for the older literature is the clear and balanced treatment of T. F. T. Plucknett, *Early English Legal Literature* (Cambridge, 1958), Chaps. 3–4. H. G. Richardson, *Bracton*, is a more partial guide and J. L. Barton, 'Bracton as a Civilian', *Tulane Law Review* xlii (1968), 566–83, also makes a serious contribution that ought not to be too overshadowed by Professor Thorne.

was not necessarily the easiest or most obvious goal for a writer
of the early thirteenth century setting out to cover the laws and
customs of England. Moreover, the author of the *De legibus* was,
in Professor Thorne's words, 'a trained jurist with the principles
and distinctions of Roman jurispurdence firmly in mind, using
them throughout his work, wherever they could be used'.[5] Such
a man might not be content merely to summarize the judgements of the bench of his day, as if all were correct and the whole
consistent. At the very least he reorganized English cases in
terms of 'Romanesque' concepts.[6]

My early work on this book led me to believe he did a good
deal more than that. Henry de Bracton, a royal justice writing
somewhere in mid-century, had apparently combined in his *De
legibus* native sources of an earlier day, Glanvill and the *vetera
judicia* of the 1220s and 1230s, with Civilian concepts and texts.
It seemed reasonable to conclude that his aims extended to
reforming as well as reordering English law. Such an hypothesis
appeared to make reasonable sense of the observable corre-
lations between the views expressed in the *De legibus* on villeinage and the relevant cases of different decades. It also fitted
more or less easily the author's famous prefatory statement of
intentions. Of course, villeinage is not necessarily a typical
topic. The author never consolidated his scattered thoughts on
the subject into a single title, as he may at one stage have
intended.[7] His organizing theory must therefore be reconstructed from passages and *dicta* all over the treatise. My early
impression of a reforming Bracton, discovered from such
material in a minor area of the law, demanded cautious presentation. Nevertheless the line of enquiry seemed worth pursuing.

Professor Thorne's 'bouleversement' of previous assumptions about the *De legibus* bypasses rather than refutes the possibility that it was written in some measure to reform as well as to

---

[5] Thorne, *Br.*, i. xxxiii.

[6] Plucknett, *Early English Legal Literature*, p. 59, notes one instance of critical
self-restraint. Although *ordines* on procedure were among the Civilian works best known
at the time, the *De legibus* never attempts to Romanize here. If it had, the book would
have been useless to English lawyers.

[7] There are cross-references at ff. 5, 7 *addicio* ('doubtful origin', Woodbine, i.
372–3), 197b. Thorne indicates in his notes that ff. 24 ff., 190 ff., may be meant. All
three references could go back to the original, the first two being cut by the editor. On
the other hand, Thorne suggested casually in a recent letter that some attempt may
have been made to concentrate material in the tract on novel disseisin, ff. 190 ff.

describe. By chance, the legal topics he uses to argue his case do not include villeinage.[8] The examination of 'Bracton's theory of villeinage' that now follows in this chapter can therefore serve as some preliminary test of Professor Thorne's case, as well as a first application of his insights.

The case for the attribution to the author of the *De legibus* of an intention to reform, or at least a willingness to countenance the modification of existing law where desirable, begins with the famous statement of purpose at the beginning of the treatise. It is worth quoting at length in a text and translation adjusted to the new view of the work.

Since . . . laws and customs are often misapplied by the unwise and unlearned (who ascend the judgement seat before they have learned the laws[9] and stand amid doubts and the confusion of opinions) and frequently subverted by the greater judges who decide cases according to their own will rather than by the authority of the laws, I [N, the unknown author],[10] to instruct the lesser judges, if no one else,[11] have turned my mind to the . . .[12] judgements of just men, examining diligently . . . their decisions, *consilia* and *responsa*, and have collected whatever I found therein worthy of note into a *summa* . . .[13]

There is none of the customary false modesty here. The unknown author does not hesitate to apply to himself words penned by Azo in praise of Justinian's authorship of the *Institutes*. He diagnosed a sickness in English legal administration

---

[8] The exception is pp. xxvii–xxviii where he discusses the effect of marriage with a villein on a free woman's rights of action over land. Both there and generally in his discussion, Professor Thorne understandably works from printed cases only. See below, Chap. 10, p. 176 ff., for my own discussion of mixed marriages.

[9] 'Leges' is ambiguous here. It could refer to education in Roman law (the *leges* par excellence) or to education in law generally. Qualified readers would pick up both nuances and probably see no clash.

[10] Thorne, *Br.*, iii. li, shows that the name of Henry de Bracton found in most manuscripts was inserted at a late stage in a gap left where the real author's name had been deleted.

[11] Thorne, *Br.*, ii. 19 n. 13, justifies the manuscript reading 'minorum' where Richardson, *Bracton*, pp. 7, 53, had amended to 'iuniorum'. He now sees the intended audience as 'members of the judicial establishment', meaning primarily clerks of Raleigh's circle but also, perhaps, sitting justices, ibid. iii. xlv; cf. ibid. i. xliv. The Romano-Canonist terminology usually distinguishes different grades of judge, however, and *iusticiarii minores* meant, in 1264, judges other than the chief justiciar, *Documents of the Baronial Movement of Reform and Rebellion, 1258–67*, ed. R. E. Treharne and I. J. Sanders (Oxford, 1973), pp. 252, 260, 288. Also Peter of Blois, Ep. 95 (Migne, Pat. Lat. 207, col. 301).

[12] I do not translate *vetera*, the general manuscript reading here, because Thorne, *Br.*, iii. lii, regards it as an editorial interpolation of the later 1250s.

[13] *Br.*, f. 1. I have used Thorne's 1968 translation, *Br.*, ii. 19, amended where necessary.

and wrote to cure it by way of instruction to the judiciary's recruits. Confusion about doctrine and principles had led, in his opinion, to arbitrary decisions on the one hand and indecisiveness on the other. He thought he knew what was needed. He would turn to the volumes of the two law learned laws, where the rational principles of *all* law could be found. This confidence—arrogance almost—in the value of his own legal education is very much a feature of the early years of Henry III.[14]

As is often the case, a sense of duty may have underlay the apparent arrogance. The christian context of the learned laws is too easily dismissed by modern commentators, and there is some evidence for the view that the author saw his task as partly religious.[15] Yet his preaching was to the small élite who administered English law at the time. The author wrote for insiders like himself and assumed his readers' technical competence in the law.[16] Probably he never expected to reach a wider audience.

Then, in the politically disturbed years of the late 1250s, along came an editor to cut the work down to a manageable size, to delete what interested only the insiders, and in general to prepare it for publication.[17] Through, or in spite of, his efforts, the edited *De legibus* enjoyed, from the last quarter of the century, the uniquely influential position in English law which it continued to hold for centuries afterwards. The generations of lawyers and others with business in the courts who bought and read the book[18] must have found it heavy going. Puzzled Edwardian readers often misunderstood the more involved ideas,[19] and modern scholars have sometimes followed in their wake. No editor could have eliminated all the difficulties, since this work written for the few was not really adaptable for a wider audience. In fact no fundamental changes were attempted.

[14] Thorne, *Br.*, i. xxxii ff., remains much the best account of the author's legal learning and its application.

[15] Richardson, *Bracton*, p. 10; G. Post, 'Bracton as Jurist and Theologian on Kingship', *Procs. Third International Congress of Medieval Canon Law . . . 1968* (Vatican, 1971), 113–30. The pious tone of passages like those on ideal justices in ff. 1b, 108, is notable.

[16] Thorne, *Br.*, iii. xlv.

[17] Thorne dates this 'after 1256' or 'Sometime after 1258', ibid. iii. xlviii, lii. The possibility of some connection with the politics of the years after 1258 demands further consideration in the light of Professor Thorne's discoveries.

[18] Ibid. i. xv.

[19] A good example is the tenemental theory of status inheritance in families of mixed blood. See below Chap. 10.

Meanwhile, English legal learning had grown more insular, so that few common lawyers now possessed a knowledge of the two laws to match that of the *De legibus'* author.[20] Yet readers do need a fair command of Roman as well as common law to get full value from the book. Even when the tone of a passage seems decisively 'English', some Civilian commonplace is often to be found lurking behind the troublesome or unlikely assertion. The more one pursues Bracton on villeinage, for example, through the glosses and texts of the two learned laws, the more clearly does its 'Romanesque' character emerge. Late thirteenth-century owners and readers of the treatise no doubt admired its learning, but they *used* more practical books, such as the two abbreviations Fleta and Britton.

The more broadly educated circle of justices and clerks around William de Raleigh earlier in the century possessed in addition a deep knowledge of the English laws they enforced. Clerks who had written or supervised the making of plea rolls had easy access to these records of previous decisions. They annotated rolls and copied out cases they deemed significant.[21] Among their number perhaps was the author of the *De legibus*. He certainly cited more than 400 cases in his treatise directly from the rolls, from his or others' transcripts, and on occasion from his own personal knowledge. Although his personal interpretation of the judgements can rarely be faulted, it remains at present an open question how he saw these case citations, as support for his views or as authoritative precedents. One can be quite clear, however, that he did not work *from* these cases, even to the same extent that *Glanvill* was written from the writs of an earlier day. His task would have been almost impossible if he had.

He marshalled these materials ably in order to convince. That he always succeeded, even within the first legal establishment group of readers, is unlikely. Some references to conflicting opinions must go back to the original core of the treatise. Disputes over doctrine within the court circles are known from as far back as the 1180s.[22] There was fierce discussion of legal

---

[20] Plucknett, *Early English Legal Literature,* pp. 79–98; Thorne, *Br.,* iii. xlv.

[21] Thorne, *Br.,* iii. xxiv ff.

[22] Hall, *Glanvill,* pp. xliii–xlvii, notes the evidence of early MSS. *Br.,* f. 164b, records the tradition of his day that hard argument had preceded the launching of the assize of novel disseisin.

reforms at the time the *De legibus* was prepared for publication around 1258. Almost certainly legal debate and argument also characterized the milieu from which the work sprang in the 1220s and 1230s.[23]

The *De legibus* is no safe short-cut to the law current in the courts during the second quarter of the thirteenth century, or at any other time. Its statements always need to be placed into the context provided by other contemporary evidence and, first of all, the cases recorded on the plea rolls. The following examination of the arguments which Maitland called 'the relativity of serfage'[24] proves the promise of this method. The rest of this chapter first expounds Bracton's doctrine of the relativity of villeinage, as I call it, and then shows how this organizing theory lies behind the treatise's associated distinction between villein tenure and status. The author of the *De legibus* emerges from examination a writer profoundly affected by his schools education in the two learned laws. To a far greater degree than previously suspected, Romano-Canonist concepts acted as his guide and furnished his framework of ideas. In particular, he benefited from the contemporary interest in the possibly anomalous status of the *ascripticius*, in which scholars had already recognized parallels with the serfs of the day. He now used these parallels to reorder the common-law status of English serfs. His originality here is worth assessing, because the methods behind the theory of villeinage in the *De legibus* are a reasonable indication of the author's methods in general. Was the aim to transform English law into a smooth, comprehensive system that could stand comparison with the *ius scriptum*? Possibly so, for there can be no doubt that to a man of his schooling, Roman law was *the* standard of comparison, but some of his apparently conscious choices are hard to explain in these terms. Perhaps, then, he desired to incorporate into the common law a better sense of the changing social reality outside the courts. Prima facie, it is possible that this was a significant minor aim as far as villeinage was concerned. The extending land market was beginning by this time to reach down to peasant holdings in some parts of the country, thus presenting the courts with knotty problems over puny plots of land. Some

[23] *Br.*, f. 282, is one reference to a 'contentio . . . inter maiores' over a tricky point.
[24] *P&M*, i. 415.

simplification was certainly in order. The possibility that this was carried out in the interests of the classes that owned land and villeins is considered in a later chapter. But to make this a major aim is to expect far too much from a royal clerk of the 1220s or 1230s. Was the author, then, impelled by some urge to technical, legal rectitude? Did he hope to assist royal justices to make respectable, rational decisions about the convoluted cases that sometimes came before them to test their still relatively simple systems of rules? This too is a real possibility, which seems to be envisaged by the statement of purpose quoted above. Members of the judicial establishment would certainly have found it a worthy aim in the second quarter of the century, when gaps on the plea-roll records of difficult cases attest to frequent hesitation on the bench.[25] This phenomenon is not so obvious in the earlier period when the original *De legibus* was written. It is thus less likely that the author was motivated by an urge to assist indecisive judges, than that his revisers were aware that such problems existed.

(II) THE RELATIVITY OF VILLEINAGE

Villeinage was unlikely to strike a thirteenth-century writer as a discrete topic worthy of special treatment without some prompting. After a brief set of definitions taken from Azo early in the treatise, *dicta* and cases on villeinage are scattered all over the *De legibus*. A commentator on English law had to give some thought to the subject, since it constantly raised questions for the courts to answer. In a sense these were basic questions about who might use the common law, though few saw things in that light at the time. The impulse to build from these diverse observations something deserving to be regarded as a theory— and the 'relativity of villeinage' is so deserving—can only have come from Roman law. The close analysis of the *De legibus* in the rest of this chapter establishes that it figured in the original core and was only slightly modified by revisers and editor. The author probably saw his task as twofold. He was to state the law

---

[25] See below, Chap. 11, and the cases cited below nn. 74, 119, 122 and p. 191. The difficulties that stalled decision here do seem to derive from legal doubts, rather than from the political pressures behind adjournments in John's reign, as in the entries highlighted by D. M. Stenton, *English Justice*, pp. 90–3. I have not noticed similar cases from the thinner rolls of the early part of the century. Enrolling conventions or changing practices are equally plausible explanations.

of villeinage as the recent cases he knew had left it, and to exclude any archaisms. And he was to reformulate the rules into learned language and forms calculated to look respectable to students of the two laws. To this end he naturally drew on Civilian ideas, notably those surrounding the *ascripticius*. How far these advances were his own and how far they emanated from well-educated colleagues is impossible to say. Even with some co-operation the job was harder than it sounds. Recent discussions did not all move in one direction. No comprehensive justification for villeinage existed, for the legal distinctions rarely coincided exactly with contemporary social categories. To rationalize even this tiny sector of English law called for a clear, sharp mind.

Those who analyse servitude generally connect the conception of a serf as a chattel with the idea of bondage as a continuing state or condition. Usually a chattel slave is unfree as regards everybody and in all circumstances, but there is no reason why this should always be the case. The situation where one man is another's chattel can just as easily be regarded as a relationship between the two people most concerned, master/owner and serf/chattel. The fact that he is a chattel does not necessarily imply anything about the serf or slave's relationship with the world apart from his master or lord. This view, which considers villeinage a relationship between *two people only*, is the prime key to the Bractonian system.

Yet Bracton starts from the Roman-law maxim that 'omnes homines aut liberi sunt aut servi', taken from Justinian's *Institutes* through the mediation of Azo.[26] Any system of law which intends that the distinction between free and unfree should have practical consequences can hardly avoid some such formulation, which amounts to little more than an affirmation that the lawyers are determined to draw the line somewhere.[27] The subsequent statement, again borrowed from Roman law, that *servi* have one *condicio substantialis* only and that each *servus* is as much a *servus* as any other, is a similar declaration of faith.[28]

---

[26] *Br.*, ff. 4b–5. See Maitland, *Bracton and Azo*, pp. 44–6, 49, 51.

[27] Cf. Charlemagne's injunction issued between 802 and 813 that 'non est amplius nisi liber et servus', *Capitularia regum Francorum* (M.G.H., LL., I, Hanover, 1883), ed.A. Boretius and V. Krause, p. 145.

[28] *Br.*, f. 5, from Azo, *Summa Institutionum*, I. 3 no. 8, according to Thorne, ed. cit., ii. 31 n. 5. Cf. *Britton*, I. xxxii. 5 (i. 197–8), *Fleta*, i. 1 (1), and *P&M*, i. 412, 413.

Both twin cores of the system derive from the idea of ownership. To say that 'I own X as a villein' may be restated as: 'I
own X's unfreedom (or bondage).' Similarly one can say that a
free man is free because he owns his freedom. In both statements, 'freedom' and 'unfreedom' (or 'bondage'), are treated as
things which can be owned; a man's status varies according to
the ownership of each. Although this is merely another way of
formulating the idea rehearsed above, it can lead to very
different implications.

First of all, analogies can easily be drawn with the ownership
of other types of property. The obvious one in medieval
England was the ownership of land. The owner (or owners) of a
piece of land had a relationship with it which was unique to
him. There could, of course, be several tenants holding different
interests—head lord, free tenant in physical control of the
tenement, even the villein who was perhaps the actual culti-
vator. Each of these held or owned something different, had a
relationship with the land that was unique to him. The head
lord was seised of the services due from it, for example, and the
free tenant seised of the land 'as of free tenement'.[29] In each
case, the word 'seisin' is used to describe the unique relationship between the owner and what he owns, the lord and his
services, the tenant and *his* land. In a similar way, one may talk
of a lord in seisin of a villein as owning the villein's 'bondage', to
describe a relationship between the two men in which outsiders
had no part.[30] But that relationship was the reason why the
villein was unfree; in a sense, it *was* his unfreedom. Hence it
could be argued that the villein was villein only to his lord,
because the lord alone owned his villein's bondage. It would
follow that the villein was free against the whole world except
his lord.

This is indeed what the *De legibus* does say in four passages,

[29] A tenant in villeinage is also sometimes said to be seised of the land in villeinage.
To discuss this would complicate the argument in the text.

[30] This is an ideal only, of course. In practice villeins might hold land of different fees
and thus have, in a sense, more than one lord. This is probably what Bracton had in
mind when he borrowed the Roman-law category of *servus communis*, ff. 25b, 43b, but
another possibility appears from JI 1/1311, m. 67 (Assize at Cambridge ?1298). The
plaintiff of this assize was a villein from a manor divided into moieties but never
partitioned. One of his lords had freed him and given him half of the disputed holding to
hold freely. The other lord was one of the assize defendants and excepted against it on
the ground of the plaintiff's villein status!

the central core around which its treatment of villeinage is organized. Nobody is *servus* to the whole world ('cuilibet de populo'). The villein's lord alone can profit from an exception of villein status, for a *servus* is only unfree *vis-à-vis* his lord; as regards anyone else he is free. 'And it is commonly said that anyone can be the *servus* of one and the *liber homo* of another.'[31] The author had probably started from some of the problems posed by villeins holding free land. In a second passage,[32] he notes that one man's villein may hold land of a stranger by permission of the lord whose villein he is. If so, he can be considered the villein of his original lord and the free man of the donor who has enfeoffed him with a free tenement. Yet there is certainly no intention to restrict the argument to land law; it is implicit at almost every point in the system.

In view of its importance, we must examine more closely the way the author formulates his argument. The four passages each come in the discussion of a practical problem of everyday English law. To these everyday issues the author applies his learned theory with a determination that the details should work. Two of the four passages contain *addiciones* which show this well. Professor Thorne has taught us to regard these insertions into our manuscript texts as originating in editorial omissions of genuine matter made to abridge an unwieldy treatise. Our two passages fully confirm his view. They elaborate the relativity of villeinage, as it were against possible objections, in an unmistakably Bractonian style. Clearly the original author valued consistency more highly than his later editor.[33] The first *addicio* supports the suggestion that the doctrine derived from an analogy with land law. In it he repeats that a man can be the *servus* of one and the *liber homo* of another, just after he has pointed out that 'est enim servus proprius et alienus ut meus, tuus, suus'. Read in conjunction with the other passage, where he says that the reason why no one is a *servus* to the whole world is 'quia sunt iura separata in servo', this does seem to recall the

---

[31] *Br.*, ff. 25, 196b, 197b, 198b. *Fleta*, iv. 2 (217), can envisage more than one lord: 'quoad dominum suum, unum vel plures, pro villano et nativo habeatur, contra tamen alios pro libero debet reputari in conquerendo'.

[32] *Br.*, f. 197b.

[33] *Br.*, ff. 196b, 197b *addiciones*. Woodbine thought the first of these early and 'probably though not certainly' Bracton's; the second more certainly his, *Br.*, i. 397. Thorne, *Br.*, iii. 46, suggests that f. 197b *addicio* was removed as repetitious; for his mature thoughts on *addiciones* generally, see ibid., pp. xliv ff.

many different interests possible with regard to one piece of land. The second *addicio* appears to be addressed to what seems an inconsistency. How can villeinage be relative, a critic might have asked, when you have stated right from the start that a man is either free or unfree, and that all *servi* are as unfree as each other, no more and no less? The apparent difficulty, previously ignored, is easily dismissed: 'sed nemo pro parte servus et pro parte liber, sed omnino servus vel omnino liber, quod esse poterit diversis respectibus'.[34] In other words, Bracton modifies the rigid distinction of the *Institutes*. A man is either free against the whole world without exception, or free against the whole world other than his lord, that is, in practice, unfree and a villein. He has redefined *servus* in the dictum quoted above, in order to satisfy himself that there were no grades of bondage in English law any more than in Roman law.[35]

This no doubt struck many readers as tiresome preoccupation with donnish trivialities. That the author himself bothered with the problem was no doubt due to Azo who, like other Civilians, was keen to assimilate the anomalous *ascripticius* to the harsh schema of 'aut liber . . . aut servus'. But Bracton's solution was technically more accomplished, partly because he was able to draw on a wider selection of recent thought about servitude. Before Aquinas, there was wide agreement among Western scholars that servitude was unnatural, contrary to the law of nature, a human reaction often attributed to the Fall. Thus christian thinkers perceived that, in a way which was important to them, all men were equal save for bonds of earthly dependence between them, such as those that joined a *servus* to his lord.[36] The step from this to the Bractonian position that a

---

[34] *Br.*, f. 197b *addicio*; compare f. 25.

[35] Bracton knew that litigants were occasionally said to be 'not so free that they could' dower their wives, sell their lands, leave them to their sons, and so on. See *SS* lix. 295 (Gloucester eyre 1221), *CRR* xii. 361 = *BNB* 1062 (Sussex 1225), KB 26/119, m. 6d (Norfolk 1238), KB 26/124, m. 1 (Staffs. 1242). Such statements mean no more than that freemen alone could do these things; they imply no degrees of common-law freedom.

[36] See on this R. W. and A. J. Carlyle, *A History of Medieval Political Theory in the West*, (Edinburgh and London, 1903–36), ii. 34–6, 111–2, 119; D. B. Davis, *The Problem of Slavery in Western Culture* (Ithaca, N.Y., 1966), pp. 8, 83, 92–7; C. J. Martin, 'Some Medieval Commentaries on Aristotle's Politics', *History* n.s. xxxvi (1951), 41 ff. Aquinas went some way towards a reconciliation of slavery with natural law, Davis, op. cit., pp. 94–7.

servus is free against everyone except his lord is obviously a short one. The Accursian gloss on *Digest* 1.5.3., which summarized Civilian thought about the status of the *ascripticius*, concluded that he was free, despite his close resemblance to the *servus*, since *ascripticii* could not be bought and sold apart from their land. Thus 'quo ad dominos servi sunt, quo ad extraneos liberi sunt'.[37] This was written at much the same time as the *De legibus*, whose author may have used some of the same Civilian glosses as Accursius. Clearly, the *De legibus*' translation of villein as *servus* has concealed from historians its use at several points of an analogy between the Romano-canonist *ascripticius* and the villein.[38]

Another possible source is the English theologian Thomas of Chobham, whose *Summa Confessorum*, written around 1215, enjoyed a wide circulation. Thomas shared the widespread view that servitude originated in Noah's drunkenness, which had led him to curse his son Chanaan and make him the *servus* of his brothers.[39] '*Naturaliter* we are all free,' he avers. Yet since 'servitude never was a sin', it remains an irregularity of birth disqualifying the *servus* from ordination in spite of his baptism. This irregularity entirely disappears, however, as soon as the *servus* is freed 'per solam voluntatem vel per vocem domini sui'.[40] Despite the wide difference between their premises, Thomas's conclusion is not very far from Bracton's.

Even if the relativity of villeinage be judged merely a rearrangement of existing ideas, the achievement was by no

---

[37] *Dig.*, 1.5.3, gl. *summa* (where a discussion of Roman *statuliberi* precedes it). Accursius proffers the view in the text as one among several ('vel melius'). Thus although this Glossa Ordinaria cannot be dated before 1234 with any certainty, it may prove possible to identify Accursius' source and clarify the relationship with the *De legibus*. Cf. also J. Gilchrist, 'The Medieval Canon Law on Unfree Persons', *Studia Gratiana* xix (1976), 286, for the curious related view that a *servus* is free as against other *servi*.

[38] It is also behind the distinction to be discussed in the next section. 'The *Ascripticius* in the Two Laws' is examined in the Appendix.

[39] *Gen.* 9:25–7. This is an alternative to the Stoic–Roman law (shared on the whole by Bracton) and Augustinian views noted above. One line of descent is through *Decretum*, Dist. xxxv, c. 8. An interesting and atypical witness of the tradition is the *Sachsenspiegel;* cf. G. Kisch, *Sachsenspiegel and the Bible* (Notre Dame, Ind., 1941), pp. 137–44. Also *Mirror of Justices*, p. 79.

[40] Thomas of Chobham, *Summa Confessorum*, ed. F. Broomfield (Analecta Medievalia Namurcensis xxv 1968), pp. 66–7, 69–70, 410. J. W. Baldwin, *Masters, Princes and Merchants* (Princeton, N.J., 1970), i. 34 ff., presents the known facts of his career.

means negligible. The accurate reorganization of legal detail from actual cases into a new scheme was no easy matter; it required a very able trained mind. Glanvill and the rest had attempted nothing comparable.[41] The best way to assess the author's approach to the practice of the courts is through his account of what happened when exceptions of villein status were raised against petty assizes. This was, after all, the context in which he made the general statements with which we have been hitherto concerned.

He considers the situation where a villein, who has acquired land from a stranger to hold freely, is ejected from the free holding. The lawyer's problem is to decide in what circumstances, if any, the court can allow a villein to recover seisin by assize. Bracton's answer was as follows: since a villein is unfree only as regards his lord, only the lord may take advantage of his villein status to defeat an action brought by him.[42] No stranger is entitled to benefit from the exception; to succeed a defendant must show not merely that the plaintiff is a villein, but that he is the defendant's own villein.[43] The stranger who does not own the villein plaintiff could not recover him by writ of naifty; consequently, he cannot succeed in the exception, for one may not gain anything by an exception (or replication) which one could not claim as principal.[44] This seems to be clear enough. The stranger's exception of villeinage fails; therefore villeins can bring assizes—and presumably other civil actions too— against anyone but their lord. But this standard interpretation of Bracton[45] ignores a difficulty raised at one point in the treatise, perhaps by a reviser.[46] A villein plaintiff faced with an exception of villein status will reply that the defendant does not have the right to raise that exception. And here he is caught in his own trap, 'because just as no-one has the right to make an exception if he has no direct interest in the subject matter of the action ("cum sua omnino non intersit") and is a stranger, so it

---

[41] Glanvill's view of manumission flatly contradicts the relativity of villeinage; see below, pp. 119 ff.

[42] e.g. *Br.*, f. 191b. The next paragraphs cite only representative passages from the discussion of the assize of novel disseisin, ff. 190 ff.

[43] *Br.*, f. 196.

[44] *Br.*, ff. 196–196b, 198b. Cf. *Fleta*, iv. 11 (237). Cf. pp. 102 ff. below.

[45] e.g. *Britton*, I. xxxii. 7 (i. 199), *Fleta*, iv. 11 (235).

[46] *Br.*, f. 191b. Compare Thorne's translation, *Br.*, ii. 87; the passage beginning 'quia sciunt' on l. 18 could belong to a revision.

will not belong to the plaintiff to make a replication, because the replication belongs to another and not to him'. Neither villein nor stranger have seisin of the villein's bondage. Consequently, the exception stands unless the villein's lord, who does own his bondage, intervenes to safeguard his own rights. Unless this happens, the stranger remains in seisin of the land until the villein's lord sues him.[47] This brings us much closer to the law of the courts.

This passage, however, stands alone and never received any attention. The view everywhere else is that only the villein's lord may successfully except against his assize on the ground of his unfree status. Whether he was entitled to plead the exception in a particular case depended on seisin. The author made the lord's seisin of his villein central to his system, perhaps because he thought it more easily ascertainable than *ius*. One example of his characteristic combination of English and Roman ideas has already been noted in his treatment of chevage.[48] He equated seisin with the Roman law *potestas*, which a master had over his slave, a *paterfamilias* over his family. At the beginning of the treatise he had denied that *servi* were *sui iuris*; they were, he said, under the *potestas* of their lords and in consequence *alieni iuris*.[49] In later parts of the treatise, further away from Roman-law guides, *potestas* is treated as something rather more than the mere physical control it had meant in Roman law.[50] Whether or not someone was within another's seisin became the crucial criterion which determined who should suffer the burdens of unfree status. An exception of villein status was to defeat actions only when brought by plaintiffs within the *potestas* of the defendant they sued, only when the defendant was seised of the plaintiff as his villein. The plaintiff's rightful status (the *ius* of his bondage) was not relevant to the case. A villein, who managed to escape from his lord and thereby to gain seisin of liberty, thenceforward received legal protection as a freeman until his lord could once more establish that he was a villein by a successful action of naifty.[51]

[47] Cf. *Br.*, f. 224.
[48] Above Chap. 4.
[49] *Br.*, f. 6, from Azo, *Summa Institutionum*, with additions according to Thorne, ed. cit., ii. 34; cf. Gilchrist, 'The Medieval Canon Law on Unfree Persons', 294.
[50] Buckland, *Slavery*, pp. 101–2.
[51] The *exceptio spoliationis*, invented by Bracton to enshrine this point, is discussed below.

The *De legibus* describes such a man as a *statuliber* (a term borrowed from Roman law where it served quite a different purpose) because he was 'in statu libero'.[52] And for the opposite case where someone was 'in status servili', he coined the term *statuservus*. A *statuliber* was outside the lord's seisin and remained 'in statu libero' until recalled by writ. A *statuservus* was 'in possessione servitutis constitutus' and, even if rightly free, could not regain his liberty without a plea in court. He was bona fide, though perhaps unjustly, possessed as a villein.[53] Britton and Fleta adopted Bracton's definitions in essentials,[54] and his view thus passed into the common law. When writing of the petty assizes, Bracton treats all men as *statuliberi* or *statuservi*, irrespective of their real status. Probably he felt that seisin was the right criterion here, whatever was done in actions of naifty.[55]

The *statuliber* will successfully recover his free tenement by assize of novel disseisin from anyone who ejects him, his lord included.[56] If he dies, his heir will also recover by mort d'ancestor, and if the heir is ejected after entering upon his seisin, he too will recover by novel disseisin.[57] The *statuliber* should however take care not to put his status on the assize.[58] On the other hand, the *statuservus* will never succeed in an assize against his lord. An exception of villeinage will always defeat his assize, because the lord is entitled to enter on his villein's

---

[52] In JI 1/174, m. 24 (Devon eyre 1238), a claimant denied that a supposed manumission was valid; the alleged villein asserted that 'in statu liberi hominis et liber homo est'.

[53] *Br.*, ff. 7, 7b, 190, 194, 197b. In ff. 7, 26, the author applies to the *statuservus* a phrase from *Dig.*, 40.13 (rubric 'quibus ad libertatem proclamare non licet'), Thorne, ed. cit., ii, 38 n. 9, 89 n. 6. He could also have read that 'fuga est quedam species libertatis' in *Decretum*, C. 12, q. 2, c. 54, gl. *fugitivi*, cited Gilchrist, 'The Medieval Canon Law on Unfree Persons', 288. *Decretum*, C. 3, q. 7, d.p.c.1, considers the problem of the 'servus dum putaretur liber' and is glossed with cross-references to texts on the effect of presumed status. The ideas are clearly commonplace.

[54] *Britton*, I. xxxii. 7 (i. 199), thinks of a *statuservus* as one of whom the lord is 'en fresche possessioun' or has at least been seised of within a year and a day. *Fleta*, iv. 2 (217), for once adds some flavour of his own: *statuliberi* are 'qui in nayvitate sunt procreati, verumtamen qui a magno tempore extra astrum suum villanum ad loca remotiora se transtulerunt et liberum tenementum perquisierint', the last point being perhaps significant.

[55] This varied. See Chap. 10.

[56] *Br.*, ff. 25b–6, 196, 197b. Cf. *Britton*, II. vii. 3 (i. 248 and note).

[57] *Br.*, ff. 165b, 271b, 273b *addicio* ('a passage of doubtful origin', Woodbine, ed. cit., i. 405).

[58] *Br.*, f. 199 *addicio* ('From Bracton', Woodbine, i. 397).

acquisitions and take them into hand as property bought with
his money; a villein could hold free land only by his lord's
permission, once the lord heard of his acquisition.[59] But the
statuservus would, in Bracton's normal view, succeed against
strangers,[60] since one who is not the plaintiff's lord will fail with
an exception of villeinage 'unless he proves both points, viz. that
he is a villein and holds in villeinage'. Although Bracton says
that such an exception defeats the assize 'quantum ad
personam suam', the decisive argument must be that the tenure
is unfree so that the plaintiff has no free tenement to recover.[61]

The Bractonian teaching on the availability of novel disseisin
to villeins is thus clear and consistent, with the one exception
noted. A villein who acquired a free tenement and was ejected
therefrom could recover by the assize unless the ejector was his
own lord still in seisin of his body. This must be the conclusion
of the *De legibus'* original author, whose theory of villeinage can
be dated before 1227.[62] The relevant passages are all of a part;
they cannot be detached from their contexts.[63]

Significantly, the villeinage passages contain very few case
citations. Professor Thorne has taught us that a great deal of
Roman law lurks in the most 'English' passages of the *De
legibus*.[64] The tract on novel disseisin and especially its passages
about exceptions of villeinage are an excellent illustration. The
author, who clearly knew the courts well, could obviously have
cited recent novel-disseisin decisions as authority had it suited
him. But the relativity of villeinage was one of his 'Romanesque'
themes, which he did not attempt to 'prove' from the cases. As
he well knew, many of the cases told against his line anyway. He
therefore confined himself to simple exposition of his view, with
little or no attempt to argue its merits against the alternatives.
In fact he never even openly acknowledged the existence of
alternative views on the subject. One of the treatise's first

---

[59] *Br.*, ff. 25 *addicio* ('probably though not certainly from Bracton', Woodbine, i.
376), 26, 190b, 191, 196b, 197b, 198b, and cf. above pp. 17 ff. Also *Fleta*, iii. 13, iv. 2
(194, 217).

[60] *Br.*, ff. 25, 193, 196, 199, 201; also *Fleta* as in the last note.

[61] *Br.*, f. 190.

[62] Below p. 121.

[63] This is probably true of the four general statements, above pp. 92 ff. It is clear
beyond doubt in the discussions of exceptions of villeinage, above, and the supposed
exceptio spoliationis.

[64] *Br.*, i. xxxii–xxxiii, xxxix.

readers, however, apparently lacked the author's confidence. The one passage that does admit that the Bractonian view had its critics comes early in the treatise, long before the tract on novel disseisin. 'If his lord ejects him (the *statuliber*) without judgement,' it reads, *'some say* restitution by the assize is not available to the villein, because if he brings the assize an exception of villeinage will bar him. But *in truth*, if that is excepted against him, he may have a replication . . .',[65] and the text goes on to put the Bractonian line. This must be the work of a reviser, perhaps Henry de Bracton, writing in the late 1230s or so. By that time cases were being regularly decided against the advice of the *De legibus*, but the line of contrary cases begins much earlier. One assize from Pateshull's Essex eyre of 1227, for example, was adjudged to fail because its plaintiff was the Abbot of Coggeshall's villein, even though the abbot was a stranger to the case and the jurors had previously reported that the ejected villein had held by free service.[66] This case is of special interest, since the *De legibus* cited it to a different end. Presumably its insertion was also due to a reviser, this time Professor Thorne's first reviser who added the results of the 1226–8 eyre visitation. Whether the original author also knew the case we cannot know, but there is no evidence that he let himself be perturbed by it or other contrary authorities. His line or argument may even have been formulated as his answer to colleagues from whom he differed.

This whiff of controversy shows how misleading it is to treat the relativity of villeinage as mere exposition of doctrine, even one current at the time of writing. The next step is to place the Bractonian exception of villeinage within the judicial trends of the whole period. This is not as easy as one might wish. Entries on the plea rolls seldom specify whether a defendant alleged that the plaintiff was his *own* villein or not.[67] They merely say something like: 'Et Prior . . . venit et dicit quod assisa non debet

---

[65] *Br.*, f. 20b = *Br.*, ii. 88, whence the translation slightly amended, italics mine. I suggest that ll. 30–3 ('dicunt quidam . . . servitutis. Item') are an interpolation by the second or third reviser.

[66] JI 1/229, m. 3d (Essex eyre 1227), cited *Br.*, f. 199 = iii. 106, of which ll. 19–26 ('Item esto . . . Goggenhale') are proposed as an interpolation.

[67] The argument that assizes were originally framed against lords, S. F. C. Milsom, *The Legal Framework of English Feudalism* (Cambridge, 1976), pp. 166–7, goes some way to explain this.

fieri eo quod Hugo [one of the plaintiffs] est villanus',[68] or
'Simon et omnes alii possunt nihil dicere quare assisa remaneat
nisi quod idem Walterus est villanus.'[69] This is no use for our
purpose, although one may suppose that the defendant would
probably mention that the plaintiff was *his* villein if he could.

The examination that follows, though necessarily imperfect,
still suggests certain conclusions. The author of the *De legibus*
could not have deduced his theory by modern scientific analysis
of the cases. Equally he can hardly have invented it unaided.
The best explanation seems to be that it represents the views
espoused by certain royal justices of Henry III's minority and
denied by others. The author of the *De legibus* was, in this
instance at least, giving learned coherence to the views of one
party among the judges.

What light, then, do the cases shed on the relativity of villeinage? We must seek out and use the clearer examples. In five of
these, the defendant's exception of villeinage, specifies that the
plaintiff was the villein of some stranger not involved directly in
the case;[70] and internal evidence from three other cases shows
that they arose from similar situations.[71] Thus each of these
eight cases is authority against the Bractonian view that only
the lord could except against an assize plaintiff on the grounds
of his villein status. The plea-roll entries for five of these[72]
contain, in addition, statements which deny that a villein can
ever have a free tenement, in further contradiction of the Bractonian line. One of these, dating from 1234–5,[73] brings out the
points at issue particularly clearly. Peter de la Derme raised two
defences against William Herward's assize of novel disseisin.
He asserted that William could have no free tenement because
he was a villein and went on to deny that he had disseised him
anyway; if there had been a disseisin, the disseisor must have
been William son of Richard who gave the land to Peter. The

[68] JI 1/36, m. 3d (Berks. eyre 1224–5).
[69] Ibid., m. 2.
[70] *RCR* i. 153 (Hertford eyre 1199), a notably early example; JI 1/863, m. 2 (Surrey
eyre 1225); JI 1/56, m. 14d, and cf. m. 19 (Buckingham eyre 1247); ibid., m. 17, where
the plea was perhaps intended to enable a lord to put in his claim without the bother of
obtaining a writ of naifty; *BHRS* xxi. 211 (Bedford eyre 1247).
[71] JI 1/536, m. 2 (Middlesex eyre 1234–5), JI 1/55, m. 5d (Buckingham eyre 1241),
JI 1/175, m. 4d (Devon eyre 1243–4).
[72] The cases cited in the last note, JI 1/863, m. 2, and *BHRS* xxi. 211.
[73] JI 1/536, m. 2.

jurors reported that William Herward had held freely but added that he was William de Say's villein, and William admitted this when the justices questioned him. Not surprisingly, the justices required an adjournment before they decided the case, but they at length found for Peter 'because it was convicted by the jury that William is a villein'. Their hesitation was not unusual; often in such cases we do not know whether a decision was ever reached. In 1250, an assize taken in default of the plaintiff's appearance reported that the plaintiff had been freely enfeoffed and was in seisin for a long time, but he was a villein. No verdict is to be found on either roll.[74]

Cases of this kind tell of perplexity on the judicial benches at how best to deal with the growing complications of peasant tenure. Yet in both of these last two, a careful student of the *De legibus* could have given the court clear counsel leading to a defensible decision. One such reader, Henry de Bracton, J., may well have been tempted to come forward in this way, and six of the eight cases just analysed come from the period of his judicial career in the late 1230s and after.[75] Although this personal connection may be impossible to prove, other cases confirm the general chronology. None has been found where an exception failed because the plaintiff, although admittedly a villein, did not belong to the defendant. Only sixteen out of a very large number of assizes where villein status was an issue contain pleas which say expressly that the plaintiff is the defendant's own villein. Once again, the chronological spread of these cases is quite striking. Thirteen came from before 1225,[76] and one of the other three has the word 'suus', to show that the defendant was claiming that the plaintiff was his own villein, interlined on the roll, perhaps a clerical afterthought.[77] These

---

[74] JI 1/560, m. 26d = 561, m. 29d (Norfolk eyre 1250). The clerk left a space for the judgement and wrote beneath: 'Dampna si que fuerunt vi s.'.

[75] The exceptions are *RCR* i. 353 and JI 1/863, m. 2, which was sidelined and marked in the 'Bractonian' fashion.

[76] *RCR* i. 84 (Lincs. 1194), *PRS* xiv. 133 (Bedford 1195), *PRS* xiv. 73 (Wilts. eyre 1195), *RCR* i. 336 (Norfolk 1199), *CRR* i. 187, 262, 278 (Lincs. 1200), *SS* lxxxiii. 905, 959 = *YAS* xliv. 3, 15 (York eyre 1204), *CRR* iii. 97; iv. 39 (Norfolk 1204), *SS* liii. 78 (Lincoln eyre 1218) with 'Bractonian' markings on the roll, ibid. 137 which also is sidelined, ibid. 215; *SS* lix. 540 (Coventry eyre 1221), ibid. 1044 (Shrewsbury eyre 1221), *CRR* xi. 1892 = *BNB* 1030 (Rutland 1224); for the last case see above, pp. 60 ff.

[77] JI 1/318, m. 2 (Hertford eyre 1248). The other two are JI 1/560, m. 23d=561, m. 27d, and JI 1/561, m. 46, both from the Norfolk eyre of 1250.

decisions about exceptions of villein status, then, show that the relativity of villeinage was clearly not established law in the 1230s, but leave open the possibility that it may have become so again at a later date.[78]

Similar conclusions emerge when one tests the other aspect of the relativity of villeinage. This is the suggestion that questions of status should be decided on the basis of the lord's seisin of the alleged villein. At various points, the *De legibus* refers to another exception, called the *exceptio spoliationis*, and declares it to be available to alleged villeins sought by writ of naifty. The alleged villein can plead the exception, Bracton says, if he is outside the claimant's power; he can then refuse to answer to the writ until the property the claimant has taken from him without judgement has been restored. As he puts it elsewhere, a lord's claim to a villein's adjuncts, his children, land, and chattels, is not to be admitted until he has proved his right to the principal, the villein's own body, 'per legem terre'. ('And it is a popular saying that you should first catch your hart, and then skin him later when he is caught!') This is a corollary of his insistence that a *statuliber* must be treated as a freeman until proved otherwise. A despoiled *statuliber* can sue for the return of his property in the ordinary way, according to Bracton, even though the despoiler might claim him as a villein. In this view, a lord who ejects from land someone of whom he is not seised as a villein, for example, cannot force the disseisee to put his status on the assize. Unless the *statuliber* is foolish enough to do so of his own choice, then, his assize will succeed. Conversely, a *statuservus* will always fail in an assize against one who is seised of him as a villein, even though it may be that he is rightly a freeman.[79]

Obviously, these tenets are very much part of the system here termed the relativity of villeinage. In rounding this off with the *exceptio spoliationis*, the author of the *De legibus* was again combining two very different kinds of material. He decked out his 'Romanesque' ideas on unjust spoliation with odd pieces of

---

[78] See *Annales de Dunstaplia*, ed., H. R. Luard (R.S. 1866), pp. 320–1, for an account of an assize at the 1285 Dunstable eyre which may imply that a villein could at this time succeed in novel disseisin against one who was not his lord.

[79] The popular saying ('vulgariter dicitur'), pre-empting Mrs Beeton, is *Br.*, f. 191; see also ff. 7, 25b, 197b, 199. Bracton takes his examples all from land tenure, despite the fact that the writ of naifty refers to *catalla* only. For other assizes, see *Br.*, ff. 224b, 290. Cf. *Britton*, IV. x. 6 (ii. 225); *Fleta*, iii. 13, iv. 11 (194, 236–7).

common-law writs and decisions. Closer examination shows once more how much creative legal thinking lies behind the relativity of villeinage.

That an unjust despoiler should not benefit from his unjust action was a long established principle of the learned laws. Thus, first of all, one who had been despoiled of his property ought to be restored to possession, and until he was, he should not be forced to plead in court about its rightful ownership. From these ideas, the Canon law had developed an *actio spolii*, first known from 1189, and an *exceptio spolii*, available to the unjustly despoiled while still out of possession, which appears first in the early thirteenth century.[80] The principles involved were quite familiar in England[81] and probably played their part in the formation of the action of novel disseisin, which may be regarded as an earlier equivalent of the *actio spolii*, although, interestingly for the present purpose, nothing like the *exceptio spolii* was known to the common law.[82]

The *De legibus* applies these ideas to villeinage law, once again treating freedom as something which might be owned by either a man or his lord. Thus, to restate once more; not until a lord had proved his claim to his villein (i.e. to the man's bondage), could he take possession of the villein's land or other adjuncts. If he went ahead none the less, the villein could oppose against his writ of naifty the *exceptio spoliationis*, and also, as a *statuliber*, recover by an assize of novel disseisin any land taken by the lord. How far, then, was Bracton extending principles already present in English practice? The *exceptio spoliationis* was Bracton's invention, a conscious development of ideas which can be found in some previous villeinage cases.

From the first, the twelfth-century precursors of the writ of

---

[80] See F. Jouon des Longrais, 'La Portée politique des réformes d'Henri II', *RHDFE* 4e s. v (1936), 547–51; Richardson and Sayles, *Procedure without Writ*, pp. cxxviii–cxxix; *Van Caenegem*, pp. 386–90; Sutherland, *Assize of Novel Disseisin*, pp. 20–1.

[81] *P&M* i. 117–8 gives a number of references.

[82] The circumstances of the common law's birth virtually ruled out the possibility that Henry II might have imposed on the courts which heard actions of right a rule by which the *exceptio spolii*, or something like it, defeated them. Both he and his predecessors had achieved the same end by writs of reseisin. Later kings had less need to act, since actions in the royal court over seisin soon became more important than actions in the right. *RCR* i. 421 (Northants 1199), cited in this connection by Sutherland, *Assize of Novel Disseisin*, p. 21, is an extraordinary case; see the later stages in *CRR*, i. 122, 172 (1200).

naifty had assumed that the reseisin of men they were designed
to effect should automatically include the runaways' chattels
and money. The lord took these with their bodies.[83] The
developed thirteenth-century writ of naifty continued to order
the handing over of the fugitive 'cum omnibus catallis suis et
tota sequela sua'.[84] Glanvill had earlier contented himself with
the observation that success in an action of naifty brought to the
claimant all the villein's chattels as well as his body.[85] No doubt
this was a simple deduction from the writ formula, which was of
the kind strictly construed in the thirteenth century. If a
claimant came into court having already recovered the alleged
villein's chattels, the formula in his writ of naifty would be, as
Fleta pointed out,[86] vain. The point looks valid by the
standards of contemporary pleading, but no litigant is known to
have argued it in court.[87]

There are in fact very few cases with any obvious relevance to
the argument. Those that have been found, however, establish
no more than a tenuous connection between the Bractonian
exception and current legal ideas. There is no reason to believe,
for example, that an alleged villein's claim to have been despoiled of his property normally stayed any action of naifty
brought against him. No such plea appears on the rolls. But this
is not the whole story. Cases where the alleged villein met a writ
of naifty by obtaining the protection of a writ of *monstravit*
pending trial at the eyre[88] also are to the point. One value of the
monstravit was that it prohibited the claimant's seizure of any
property until he had proved his right to the alleged villein.

---

[83] *Van Caenegem*, p. 343, and nos. 104, 112, 113.

[84] See the writs in *Selden Registers;* for other registers with relevant writs cf.
Bibliography I.A.3.

[85] *Glanvill*, v. 4. He had noticed that novel disseisin was the only action where
success carried with it the adjuncts to the holding; cf. ibid., xii. 18, xiii. 38–9. The
formula for his writ of novel disseisin makes this clear, ibid., xiii. 33, unlike earlier ones
apart from *Van Caenegem*, no. 95 (1154/64). Cf. *Br.*, ff. 179b, 187 ff.; *Fleta*, iv. 9 (231–2);
Britton, II. xxii. 9 (i. 358).

[86] *Fleta*, iv. 11 (236–7). This argument would, of course, have applied to many other
writ formulas.

[87] In *BNB* 1139 (Bucks., *coram rege* 1235–6), a lord who had proved his claim in the
county court was said to recover his villein's goods 'by judgement of the court'. In 1256,
the justices ordered the sheriff to hand over to a lord the chattels of his villein, who had
just acknowledged his status, without further ado, A. Harding (ed.), 'The Shropshire
Eyre Roll of 1256', (Oxford Univ. B.Litt. thesis, 1957), no. 37.

[88] For which see below, Chap. 10.

Disregard of this prohibition would be taken seriously by the courts as contempt of a royal order.[89] The claimant had to return to his opponent pending trial the property he had taken, and would have damages assessed against him, which were, of course, payable only if the alleged villein successfully proved his liberty. The authority for this is a case which may have been quite famous at the time. David del Brok was claimed as a villein by Gilbert Basset. He obtained a writ of *monstravit*, but Gilbert continued to distrain him for villein customs and services which, in his view, he did not owe. He therefore complained direct to the King's Council. Gilbert was ordered to return to David the chattels taken and not to touch them further 'until it is known whether he is free or serf'. A day was fixed for the proofs of status and 'meanwhile [David] is to have his chattels by plevin, so that if he proves his liberty he is to have the chattels *quiete*, but if he fails Gilbert is to have him *cum catallis suis*', a clear reference to the writ of naifty. The value of the goods was assessed at 10 marks, David found two sureties to guarantee his undertaking and was to receive in addition 5 marks damages if he proved himself free.[90]

Both these cases come from the period of William de Raleigh's dominance at the court *coram rege*; no later examples have been traced. Even so, they are authority for something less than the full exception of the *De legibus*. This was no standard procedure. David del Brok had complained directly to the Council; few peasants could follow that lead. Moreover, the Bractonian exception comprehended all spoliations, including those perpetrated before the acquisition of a *monstravit*, but in Raleigh's dispensation the alleged villein had to commence new proceedings for the recovery of his property *after* he had secured his personal freedom. The most that can be claimed for the two cases, then, is that they establish the Bractonian view as within a range of pleas worth trying in the courts.

Two trespass cases lend a little support to this conclusion. The action of trespass had, of course, no need for an *exceptio*

[89] See my 'The Action of Naifty in the Early Common Law', *LQR* xc (1974), 332; the only other case is *CRR* xiii. 526, 732; *BNB* 1894 (Suffolk, Bench and eyre 1228).

[90] *CRR* xv. 1344, 1434 (Berks., *coram rege* 1235). The trial of status was *BNB* 1167 (?Bucks., *coram rege* 1236), but the final jury verdict is on a lost roll. The 1235 hearing is on Raleigh's roll, much used for *Bracton's NoteBook*.

spoliationis. Lords did not sue villeins in trespass; they acted, and challenged their villeins to sue them if they dared. But on at least two occasions the courts took the view that a claimant lord was liable for any trespass to an alleged villein's goods until he proved his right. In the earlier case, the defendant was ordered to return to the complainant chattels taken from him and was reminded that he could sue later 'de vilenagio'.[91] In the other, the defendant's exception, that his opponent was his villein, failed when he admitted that he had never sought him in the county court; he had to restore the goods taken and was gaoled.[92]

If the exception had represented practice, it would further have followed that villeins outside their lord's power, the *statuli-beri* of the *De legibus*, could recover their free holdings by assize. It must have been very rare indeed for a lord to eject his villein from the villein's free holding without at the same time regaining control of the villein, and no cases reveal themselves as having arisen from such circumstances. The one relevant case discovered is authority for the less surprising side of the idea, that which supported the interests of the lord against his villein, and was known at least to one of the *De legibus'* revisers, who cited it elsewhere in another connection.[93] In it, a Bractonian *statuservus*, who may rightly have been free, failed to recover by assize. Richard de Fraxino sued Ralph Malet and his wife Lucia by novel disseisin at an eyre of William Raleigh's. Ralph being dead by the time of the eyre, his widow and son tried unsuccessfully to prove that Richard was a villein. The jurors then reported that Richard's father William, though really free, had been forced to do villein services by Ralph Malet, who had died seised of him as his villein. The court consequently held that the assize failed but reminded Richard that he might later have such recovery as he ought. Probably the justices meant that when he had recovered his free status in court, he could go on to sue for his holding too.

[91] *SS* lxxxiii. 972 = *YAS* xliv. 17 (York eyre 1203–4).
[92] KB 26/139, m. 2d (Salop 1250).
[93] JI 1/62, m. 16d (Buckingham eyre 1232), cited *Br.*, f. 200b. Coming from a Raleigh eyre, this is presumably the work of the second reviser who may be Henry de Bracton; cf. Thorne, *Br.*, iii. xxxii. It is of some special interest as an 'assize continued' which modifies Thorne's argument, ibid., p. xxiv.

This is the sum total of the relevant case material,[94] and this part of the system may now be summarized. The *exceptio spoliationis* was an invention of the *De legibus*. The ideas behind it were known to English lawyers of the later twelfth century. The very wording of the writ of naifty ensured that a successful claimant would recover chattels and other property with the body, but there is no evidence that the courts would penalize a claimant who took the adjuncts before he had proved his right to the principal. Nor do courts seem to have been particularly interested in whether one who raised an exception of villeinage was seised of his alleged villein.

These, then, are the twin ideas generally accepted as constituting the doctrine of the relativity of villeinage. The last part of the chapter expands a further aspect of Bractonian villeinage and establishes that it too belongs within the same system. But it is already obvious that we face a personal creation. Within the general exposition of English law lies this theory of villeinage, fashioned by a jurist well educated in the learned laws and seriously concerned that his arguments be logically consistent with each other. The assertion that villeins are unfree only as regards their lords echoes case decisions of a limited period, during the Minority. That later courts saw villeinage differently would doubtless not have shifted the author of the *De legibus*, though it might well have saddened or irritated him. To promote his other proposition, that villeinage cases ought to turn on seisin of the villein, he willingly invented a fictitious exception. The courts, who might have taken the hint, never adopted his suggestion. The Bractonian theory of villeinage, as revealed thus far, is learned, highly self-consistent, and prescriptive in nature. The *iuniores* who would staff the courts were being instructed how they *ought* to deal with villeinage suits.

(III) THE DISTINCTION BETWEEN TENURE AND STATUS

It is possible to restate the principle behind the *exceptio spoliationis* in rather different terms. The assize of novel disseisin, a real action, seeks a tenurial remedy, the reseisin of an ejected tenant. It aims to restore the tenurial *status quo ante*, so

---

[94] In JI 1/1178, m. 10d (Assize at Shepton Mallet 1253), a court headed by Henry de Bracton accepted that intervention by the claimants invalidated an alleged villein's assize, but would permit no claim to the property 'antequam corpus suum disracionaverint'. Bractonian views no doubt advanced in the second half of the century as the *De legibus* became better known.

that questions of the ejected tenant's personal status must be put aside as secondary, not to arise until the main tenurial question is settled. The distinction between tenure and status implied by this formulation is the other major premise of the Bractonian theory of villeinage. Discussion must begin with some consideration of its practical feasibility. Many contemporaries would, I supose, have felt that in a perfect world there would be no need for law on the subject. All villeins would hold in villeinage as their fathers did before them and as their offspring would later. That ought to be all there was to say.[95] Alas for the dreamers, the way that common-law villeinage was born[96] ensured that villeinage was never part of a world where everyone kept his place. By the time Bracton wrote, peasants in certain areas quite frequently bought and sold parcels of land.[97] Members of free peasant families were sometimes prepared to accept the servile obligations of customary land despite the obvious dangers, because they needed a holding for their support. Others acquired villeinage as part of their rise in economic position through engrossing, or even as an investment. In the other direction, the legally unfree were not always prevented from obtaining fee holdings.[98] If disputes about the ensuing situations reached the royal courts, the common lawyers could be presented with knotty problems about despicably small pieces of land. Even if the courts decided not to protect villeins' tenure of free holdings, they still had to decide between conflicting claims to the holding from the original head lord of the tenement and the lord of the villein tenant's body.[99] The professional lawyers no doubt employed by some of the disputants complicated the justices' problem further by their clever pleas, as some of the cases show. Hence the Bractonian distinction very likely aspired to simplify doctrine so that judges could decide their cases.

The initial inspiration may have come from the situation of the freeman who held in villeinage.[100] Although this was never

---

[95] For the place of heritability in the scheme, see above Chap. 7.
[96] Below Chap. 13.
[97] Cf. above Chap. 5.
[98] See recently on movements of land within villages E. King, *Peterborough Abbey, 1086–1310* (Cambridge, 1973), Chaps. 3, 6.
[99] Bracton recognizes this problem elsewhere, above, p. 67f.
[100] The converse problem of the villein acquiring free land may have been the more influential in the relativity of villeinage proper.

a major problem,[101] thirteenth-century royal justices shared the widespread feelings of disgust at the thought of freemen being wrongly condemned to servitude,[102] and were unwilling that tenure of odd villein holdings should be allowed to take away free status. Men of some substance held odd parcels of villeinage. These decisions probably signify no more than an occasional expression of comforting moral sentiment by the courts. Upon them, however, the author of the *De legibus*, inspired by his studies in the two laws, could establish the novel principle that tenure and status should be strictly distinct, each quite independent of the other.

The treatise states this specifically and clearly. 'For there is a general rule . . .,' it says, 'that a freeman confers nothing of liberty on a villeinage tenement on account of his own free person, nor on the other hand does a free tenement in any way change the condition of a villein.'[103] The author adheres to his principle with admirable consistency. The fact that a man has done villein customs for a villein tenement must not be used as proof of his villein status, he asserts, unless he owes the customs 'ratione personae'. On the other hand, a villein does not become free by holding land for free services. Nor does the tenant's status affect the land. Thus a freeman may hold a villein tenement and perform villein services for it while remaining personally free; similarly, a villein may hold a free tenement by free services.[104]

There can be little doubt that Civilian thought on the status of the *ascripticius* provided the inspiration. Medieval commentators agonized over this, impressed but not always convinced by the obvious resemblance to the *servus*. Was he unfree like the *servus*, or essentially free? Those who plumped for this second alternative argued that the *ascripticius'* resemblance to the *servus*

---

[101] Jouon des Longrais, 'La Vilainage anglaise et le servage réel et personnel', *Recueils soc. Jean Bodin* ii (1937), 216, takes a different view but cited no evidence. The question certainly arose during Henry III's minority; see above Chap. 6.

[102] See below Chap. 12.

[103] *Br.*, f. 170: 'Est enim ratio et regula generalis . . . quod liber homo nihil libertatis propter personam suam liberam confert vilenagio, nec liberum tenementum in aliquo mutat condicionem villani.' He refers to the cases where a freeman holds for villein services and where a villein holds for free service. Neither tenant will succeed in recovering his holding by assize.

[104] *Br.*, ff. 7, 24b, 26, 166, 192b, 199b–200. Cf. *Britton*, I. xxxii. 3 (i. 196, 206); *Fleta*, iii. 13, iv. 11 (193, 238).

was superficial and due only to his land tenure—he was a *servus glebae* but no more. As Azo put the matter in a passage which the author of the *De legibus* had certainly read, 'vere liber est licet quodam servitio sit astrictus'.[105] On the other hand, decisions in English cases frequently contradict the Bractonian line. Examples recur throughout the period surveyed in this book; no chronological pattern emerges comparable to those traced earlier in the chapter. Nor is it possible that the author was unaware of views opposed to his. In discussing the conditions under which donations of land may be made to villeins, he admitted the force of the view that a villein cannot have a free tenement.[106] On other occasions, he quoted the tag, frequently met on the plea rolls in exceptions and jury verdicts, that 'the plaintiff cannot have a free tenement because he is a villein'.[107] He found ways out of the difficulties, but must have known that he was being controversial. Yet this reform attempt, in the short run so unsuccessful, had found a promising beginning in the leading case, Bestenover versus Montacute.[108] The earlier comprehensive discussion of this case need not be repeated here. After John of Montacute had established his right to villein services from Martin of Bestenover, the court made it clear that the question of Martin's status still had to be determined. John would have had to pursue the question by writ of naifty if he had so wished. An annotator in *Bracton's NoteBook* summarized the court's view in the words: 'Note that a free man can do villein customs by reason of a villein tenement but on account of this he will not be a villein, because he can leave the tenement.' The case does indeed support the *De legibus'* denial that proof of tenure suffices to establish villein status, although, as we have seen, the treatise's explanation of the decision is not beyond criticism.

Three other cases from the first half of the century are also consistent with Bracton's distinction. The first of these from the year before Bestenover's Case had been marked on the plea roll for attention. Anger son of Hugh was suing his

---

[105] Maitland, *Bracton and Azo*, p. 44. See further the Appendix.
[106] *Br.*, f. 24b. See below p. 112 for the further distinction needed.
[107] *Br.*, ff. 193, 195.
[108] *Br.*, ff., 199b–200, cited two hearings, *BNB* 70 = *CRR* viii. 114, and *BNB* 88 = *CRR* viii. 216; they do support the conclusions he drew from them. See above p. 56 for full references to the case and Bracton's use of it. He also cited two other cases from rolls now lost.

second assize of novel disseisin in one day. The first had failed when the court found that the holding he sought was villeinage. Not unnaturally, the defendant in the second assize (for land in a different village) excepted against him on the ground of villein status. He failed, the assize proceeded and Anger recovered his land.[109] The other two come from Bracton's spell as an eyre justice in the 1240s. In one, Christiana the wife of Simon the clerk recovered her land by assize of mort d'ancestor although her father-in-law had once held a villein tenement.[110] And Robert the son of Ago de Gatton recovered his free tenement in Reigate despite an exception that he was villein to the chief defendant. The justices had told the court a long story about his family's being of free blood but having held for three generations a villeinage tenement in Gatton on which some of them had been born.[111]

In these four cases, the courts showed themselves unwilling to find villein status from the mere fact of having held villein land. Other such cases are no doubt concealed by the short entries which record most assizes on the plea rolls. Similarly, that freemen commonly held land in villeinage without losing their freedom is certain enough, though the number of ascertainable cases is small.[112] Legally, this made good sense. In practice a family who remained on villeinage land for more than one generation risked the obliteration of their free antecedents in an imperceptible slide into villeinage. Nevertheless, the law accepted that freemen could hold in villeinage and remain free. To a logical mind, the obvious corollary was that villeins could hold free tenements. In fact the common law was more reluctant to allow this. The association between tenure and status was too strong to be broken, especially given the powerful feeling that the servile peasantry was not the king's concern but their lords'.

Free tenure undoubtedly had very close associations with

---

[109] *SS* liii. 176 (Lincoln eyre 1218) with 'Bractonian' sidelinings; cf. also pl. 174 for the other case.

[110] *BHRS* xxi. 234 (Bedford eyre 1247).

[111] JI 1/870, m. 4d (Surrey eyre ?1248).

[112] A. L. Poole, *Obligations of Society*, pp. 18–20, discusses this subject but is too ready to conclude that a tenant about whose status there is no clear evidence was personally free. *CRR* iv. 234 (Sussex 1206) is a doubtful example; *SS* lvi. 228 (Lincoln eyre 1219) a better one.

free status, as the later connotations of 'freeholder' indicate. The sensitive author of the *De legibus* therefore tried to safeguard lords' rights over their villeins by a fresh distinction. Villeins enfeoffed with free tenements did not thereby become free,[113] he said, for they did not hold freely, just for free service.[114] Consequently, if ejected, they could not recover by assize since they had no seisin as of free tenement. The case cited in support of this distinction was a mort d'ancestor in which the jurors reported that the plaintiff's father 'held the aforesaid land by free service, but he was a villein by birth and held other land in villeinage from the abbot of Coggeshall as the abbot's villein'. Not surprisingly they were unsure whether the plaintiff could be his heir and the assize was deemed to fail.[115] The decision may, even at this date, be due to the influence of the *De legibus* or its author.[116] The facts of the case strongly resemble those in others where the decision went the other way. If there were special circumstances in this one, no trace remains on the rolls. There are cases which show villeins holding free land, apparently licitly, but tenure was in practice usually so short-lived that the lawyers' analyses hardly mattered. A Lincolnshire villein called Reyngod, for example, married Emma a rich freewomen, and bought a free holding with her money, which the couple held until ejected by Reyngod's lord.[117] The other plea-roll references to villein tenure of free land are all from eastern England,[118] an area over-represented in early thirteenth-century plea rolls and marked by a precocious peasant land market. Eastern peculiarities may have had an exaggerated impact on the *De legibus*.[119] Cases from

---

[113] Unless the enfeoffment was made by the villein's lord and mentioned his heirs; if so a manumission was implied, above, Chap. 5.

[114] *Br.*, ff. 24b, 199, and *addicio* (a rubric not discussed by Woodbine, i. 397; see iii. 106n.). Revisers may have been at work in these passages, though clear indications are lacking.

[115] JI 1/229, m. 3d (Essex eyre 1227), cited *Br.*, f. 199.

[116] See above, n. 62, for the suggestion that this case was interpolated by Professor Thorne's first reviser.

[117] JI 1/482, m. 8d (Lincoln eyre 1245).

[118] *BNB* 1833, 1837 (Norfolk eyre 1227), *CRR* xiv. 336 (Norfolk 1230), *BNB* 1256 (Norfolk 1238–9), JI 1/482, m. 43d (Lincoln eyre 1245).

[119] See my 'The Origins of a Peasant Land Market', *Ec. H.R.*, 2nd s. xviii (1970), 24 ff. The justices were not always confident of their answers. When a lord challenged his free tenant's enfeoffment of someone else's villein whom he ejected, no judgement was ever enrolled for the ensuing assize of novel disseisin, although damages were assessed, JI 1/560, m. 26d = 561, m. 29d (Norfolk eyre 1250).

other parts of the country were generally decided against the villeins. This is what one would expect, since the royal courts did not on the whole accept the Bractonian view that exceptions of villein status were only valid when made by the villein plaintiff's own lord. A good example is the story of a royal villein called William, who left his native village, Barton Stacy in Hampshire, and crossed the Channel to the Abbey of St. Victor which held a manor in the village. The canons granted him a free holding back home for his service, but he never obtained manumission from the king. Consequently, when his son Geoffrey was disseised of pasture rights pertaining to the holding and sought to recover them by assize, he failed.[120] A very large number of cases testify to the rule that a villein could not be seised of a free tenement; in the 1240s, the number of such cases rises noticeably.[121]

The legal position remained unclear. Laymen were uncertain whether villeins could not sometimes hold free tenements legitimately, and lawyers would always argue the point for a client. These uncertainties can occasionally be seen on the plea rolls. The novel disseisin between William Herward and Peter de la Derme, for instance,[122] is an illustration. The jury found that William held freely but was a villein, 'but they do not know whether he can have a free tenement or not'. Only after some hesitation did the court deem the assize to have failed on the grounds of William's status.

The Bractonian distinction that might have guided the courts seems, like the *exceptio spoliationis,* never to have become unchallenged law within the period surveyed. Bestenover's Case was apparently the key event in its genesis. The author of the *De legibus* may have been moved by the decision in that case to work up his distinction. Or just possibly he was among those to develop it for the purposes of this awkward case.[123] Either

---

[120] JI 1/775, m. 8d (Hants eyre 1235–6). Cf. *V.C.H. Hants,* i. 452, 498, for Barton Stacy.

[121] Early examples are *LRS* xxii. 54, 155 (Lincoln eyre 1202), *CRR* xiii. 851 (Cambs. 1228), JI 1/863, ms. 2, 3 (Surrey eyre 1225), *BNB* 1902 (Suffolk eyre 1228). I have noted the rule in cases from the eyre rolls of Beds. (1247), Berks. (1244–5), Bucks. (1241), Devon (1243–4, 1248–9), Lincs. (1245), Norfolk (1250), Oxon. (1241), Surrey (1248).

[122] JI 1/536, m. 2. (Middlesex eyre 1234–5), for which see above n. 71. The Norfolk case noted on p. 100f. is another example.

[123] The germ of this idea could derive from Anger son of Hugh's Case, *SS* liii. 176 (Lincoln eyre 1218), discussed above.

way, the learned innovation was most useful apropos of peasant
tenures complex enough to raise questions about the effect of
status on tenure, or vice versa. That this was more common in
eastern England than elsewhere may explain why cases from
that part of the country stand out among the sparse authority
for the Bractonian distinction. The jurors who reported the
tenurial facts in court undoubtedly had their own views about
the location of justice, affected by local conditions and custom.
Perhaps, then, the distinction between tenure and status owes
something to pressure from below, the encouragement of East
Anglian jurors.[124] To administer it, the courts had to determine
whether villein services were owed 'ratione tenementi' or because of unfree status. This heavy burden of local detail was a
practical defect that would have slowed down the courts; possibly, this told against acceptance.[125] Around 1200, neither
villagers nor their lords knew on what legal basis services were
performed. Courts had to waste time on humble peasants and
puny parcels of land. Jury verdicts were unsatisfactory for the
lawyers' hopes of decisions based on repeatable principles. The
distinction between tenure and status was one plausible
attempt at a simplification. An equally defensible alternative
probably emerged from other confrontations between justices
and jurors. The presumption that families could become villein
by virtue of dwelling on villeinage land for a given length of time
might have been incorporated into the Bractonian theory of
villeinage.

The decision not to accept this prescription against free blood
in the *De legibus* must therefore have been made consciously and
under the influence of Civilian learning.[126] Later in the century,
many lawyers were prepared to allege villein status from the
fact of tenure in villeinage. Thus for many free peasant families,
the acquisition of customary holdings was a stage in their loss of
freedom. John le Coke, a smallholder who once held half an acre
and a rod of land freely, is one example. He took up a virgate of

[124] The plea rolls are no help here. The judicial habit of questioning jurors before
proceeding to judgement, noted elsewhere in this book as fairly common at this time,
gave local views on right and wrong an airing in court. The point may be of much wider
validity.
[125] All the same, the courts did have to accept the need for greater precision over
services in deciding tenurial questions, below Chap. 11.
[126] His own line on the status of the children of mixed marriages boils down to the
view that the child takes the status of the land on which he was born, below Chap. 10.

villeinage land in the same village 'ad firmam . . . per servilem condicionem', and later 'necessitate compulsus' sold his free holding by charter to another freeman.[127] John's status was undoubtedly in danger by this stage. Fear of a similar descent into villeinage may be the reason why Roger Aselak was unwilling to do the servile customs due from his villein holding and was therefore ejected by his lord.[128] Strong forces were at work. Just as land hunger impelled free men to marry villein 'heiresses' for their inheritances, lords too, with their own economic problems, were tempted to try and convert their free tenants into villeins in the hope of increasing their revenues.[129] A Lincolnshire *monstravit* illustrates this.[130] Walter Gamel, claimed as a villein, tried to defend himself by telling the court how his grandfather had taken over a villein holding some time earlier, and after this his father, Simon, and his uncles had all been forced to marry villein girls and to perform villein services, as villeins, on account of the fear in which they held their lord, Thomas of Moulton, and quite simply in order to retain their lands. Walter's story was probably true, for he came into court at the hearing when a jury was to have given its verdict and put himself on Thomas's mercy. Thomas then quitclaimed him of all naifty and paid him five marks 'pro donacione', and the court even remitted to him the mark which he had proffered to obtain a favourable jury.[131] The problem for Walter and those like him was to retain the right to leave the villeinage and its restrictions when they wished.[132] Marriage to a villein girl lost them this right for the duration of the marriage, and probably made their children unfree for good.[133]

Not surprisingly therefore, the freeman holding in villeinage never acquired his own label,[134] and the courts did not always exclude pleadings about tenure in cases about status, or vice

---

[127] KB 26/200B, m. 10 (*coram rege* 1270).

[128] JI 1/560, m. 20d = 561, m. 25 (Norfolk eyre 1250), discussed above, Chap. 6.

[129] E. King, *Peterborough Abbey, 1086–1310*, Chap. 6, documents some of these possibilities in some detail.

[130] JI 1/482, m. 33 (Lincoln eyre 1244–5), discussed further in Chap. 10, 000 below.

[131] JI 1/62, m. 16d (Bucks. eyre 1232), JI 1/176, m. 1d (Devon eyre 1248–9), and perhaps JI 1/870, m. 4d (Surrey eyre ?1248), referred to above, are cases which may reflect similar situations.

[132] Above, Chap. 4.

[133] *Glanvill*, v. 6; 'Glanvill revised', p. 75; *Br.*, ff. 26, 194.

[134] Vinogradoff, *Villainage*, pp. 143–4, comments on this.

versa. Thus, for example, a lord might prove that his tenant was his villein during an action begun by writ of customs and services alleging that the holding was in villeinage. The *De legibus* sanctions this procedure, and a case where the Abbot of Battle established his claim to a villein in this way is copied into the *NoteBook*.[135] Another such case was an appeal of robbery and imprisonment against Thomas de Lascelles brought by Nicholas son of Bernolf. The burden of Thomas's defence was that Nicholas was his villein, and that the cause of the trouble was the arrears owed from Nicholas's term as his reeve. He thought it worthwhile to add that Nicholas had recently failed to recover from him by assize of novel disseisin the holding where the violence occurred, because the jury had found that it was not a free tenement.[136]

Such were some of the limitations to the Bractonian view. It seems, however, that not until quite late in the century did courts seriously consider the alternative view, that long residence on villeinage made a man legally unfree. Prescription of this kind may have been a matter of course until the *De legibus* made the subject controversial, but according to cases available in print, it was under Edward I that legal controversy arose about the possibility of prescription against free blood and the length of the required presciption period. Possibly because of the *De legibus,* as Maitland suggested, the better opinion appears to be against the possibility of prescription. Britton, for example, argued along Bractonian lines to deny that a freeman holding by villein services could ever be reclaimed by writ of naifty. Right, he averred, would not allow that long seisin of villeinage could enserf a freeman any more than long seisin of a free tenement could change a villein's condition to free. Elsewhere he cited an imaginary case in which the alleged villein traced his lineage back to the sixth generation in order to prove his freedom.[137] Others, however, disagreed and differed only as to whether four or five generations on villeinage land were necessary to change a tenant's status.[138]

The available cases fail to make the legal position clear,

---

[135] *Br.*, f. 192; *CRR* xi. 1600 = *BNB* 1005 (Oxon. 1224), of which *CRR* xi. 850, 865, are earlier stages.
[136] *SS* lvi. 1024 (York eyre 1218–19).
[137] *Britton*, I. xxxii. 3, 19 (i. 196, 206).
[138] Vinogradoff, *Villainage*, p. 63; *P&M*, i. 425, 427.

although the most decisive of them is authority for the Brac-tonian view. This was a *ne vexes*[139] which, as the justices pointed out, might have remained confined to tenure had the plaintiff so wished. The defendant claimed that the plaintiff's family had been his family's villeins since time immemorial.[140] Both justices present observed that seisin may be wrongful and sug-gested that a litigant in an action pleaded in the right, as this was, ought not to be allowed to take advantage of seisin that might have originated wrongfully and been extended to the present time by illegal distresses.[141] Hengham, J., finally pro-nounced that 'prescription of time did not reduce free blood into servitude, because it was impossible for a freeman to have servile offspring'.

The only contemporary judgement known which went the other way was made by auditors of complaints, who reversed as false an earlier decision by assize justices in the country. This judgement was itself called into question. The King's Bench considered the case afresh at the time of the great Edwardian judicial scandals, without, so far as is known, coming to any decision. The case is obviously unsafe as authority but the facts are of interest.[142] The assize plaintiff, Martin son of Osbert le Provost, came from the fifth generation of his family to live on villeinage land at West Somerton, Norfolk, and had married there. The Prior of Butley excepted against his assize that Martin was his villein. The first set of justices had rejected the exception for reasons similar to Hengham's in the later case, but the auditors listed this argument among the three errors for which they reversed the result of the case; the view that pre-scription did not run against free blood was quite false, they said. Naturally, the prior shared their opinion, as he told the justices, whose reaction is, alas, unknown.

These cases about prescription against free blood reveal no thirteenth-century law on the subject that can be expressed in a simple formula. There was a certain pressure towards the doctrine as a simplifying alternative to the Bractonian theory,

---

[139] *YB 33 and 35 Edward I* (R.S.), pp. 10–15 (1305).
[140] See Sayles, *Select Cases in K.B.* iii (*SS* lviii), no. 61 (Yorks. 1301), for a similar plea.
[141] There are further remarks about wrongful seisin in *YB 32 and 33 Edward I* (R.S.), pp. 514–5 (1304).
[142] Sayles, *Select Cases in K.B.* ii (*SS* lvii), no. 41 (Norfolk 1292); the pleas in favour of prescription are on pp. 94, 96.

and it long remained an argument which a claimant lord might try on the courts with some hope of success.[143] But these very seignorial hopes perhaps provoked a countervailing backlash. No man could view with complete equanimity the possibility that freemen might sink unjustly into servitude, an important point which calls for further examination in a later chapter.[144]

Certainly prescription against free blood would have facilitated seignorial control of a dependent peasantry, but so too would court acceptance of the distinction between tenure and status. The procedure by which they had to attempt proof of villein status was archaic and full of legal pitfalls. In any event many actions of naifty arose from tenurial disputes,[145] for all the most valuble rights of lords over their villeins could be put into tenurial terms. Thus lords simply preferred to litigate (or act so as to invite their villeins to litigate) on tenure and the customs and services due from villeinage holdings. Once lords had established their right to these, the common law would give them all the assistance they could desire towards their implementation. Hence the exclusion of status, and proof by suit of kin, from their pleas was much in their interests. The author of the *De legibus* may have understood this and been more influenced than has been realized. His complex rules about the status of children of mixed marriages, when properly understood, are open to a similar interpretation.[146] Of course, tenants too could bring pleas about their customs and services, by acquiring writs of *ne vexes* for example, and this will have been especially valuable after the early thirteenth century when they were no longer able to initiate actions of naifty to prove their liberty.[147] But the lord must usually have had the whip hand. If all else failed, his greater financial resources permitted him to sue later in the right, and no lawyer ever seems to have sug-

---

[143] See also *YB 30 and 31 Edward I* (R.S.), pp. 136–9 (Cornwall eyre 1302), where Hengham's view prevailed, and Sayles, *Select Cases in K.B.* iii (*SS* lviii), no. 61 (Yorks. 1301), and Fitzherbert, *Villenage* 24 (1376), which tend in the other direction. During the fourteenth century, proof that an ancestor had arrived in the village as a stranger (*adventcius*) was held to create a counter-presumption that the family was free however they held their land, below Chap. 12, pp. 209 ff.

[144] Chap. 12.

[145] Below Chap. 10, pp. 163, 165; cf. my 'The Action of Naifty', *LQC* xc (1974), 340.

[146] Below Chap. 10.

[147] See below Chap. 10, pp. 165 f.

gested that a villein (*stabuliber* though he might be) could succeed against his lord in the right. The distinction between
tenure and status clearly was very handy for lords.

The point just made about the significance of *ius* is important
outside the distinction between tenure and status. Bracton's
whole system of villeinage law may have been more favourable
to seignorial power than appears at first glance. While it is true
that the relativity of villeinage would have permitted men to sue
at common law for seisin of land without putting their pretensions to free status at risk, *ius* and the all-important right to
villein customs and services, untrammelled by common-law
supervision, was clearly quite a different matter. The *De legibus*
nowhere extends the relativity of villeinage to actions of
right.[148] The author explicitly states that a lord could prove his
tenant unfree by birth in an action of customs and services,
whose issue was supposed to hang on the question of tenure. He
stops short at the point where pursuit of legal logic would have
upset seriously the existing order. On balance, then, lords faced
by any 'manorial crisis' in the thirteenth century would have
gained appreciably from the Bractonian system.

One further general point may be made about the *De legibus*
and its treatment of villeinage before we attempt to draw together some conclusions. Now that Professor Thorne has clarified the processes by which the treatise was written and published, it is no surprise that the Bractonian theory of villeinage
proves highly specific to one period of the early 1220s. We have
seen how rarely cases from later in Henry III's reign follow the
Bractonian line. It is equally true that the system would have
been inconceivable at an earlier date. If, for example, Glanvill
had taken it into his head to attempt something similar, the
result would have been very different. Glanvill had no conception of freedom and servitude as things which could be owned,
and this was essential to the relativity view. For Glanvill, villeinage was rather a public condition from which the villein can
never fully escape. These differences of outlook between the two
writers can be conveniently illustrated by a brief comparison of
their treatments of manumission.[149] The Bractonian position

---

[148] It might be argued that the *exceptio spoliationis* was the relativity of villeinage
applied to claims of right, but only about status not land.
[149] See on this Vinogradoff, *Villainage*, pp. 86–8; *P&M*, i. 427–9.

was entailed by his system. It accepted the implications of the commonplace opinions that all men were naturally free and servitude but a relationship between lord and villein. Thus manumission by the lord merely removed the last check on the freedom of one who had previously been free against everyone in the world but his lord. The former villein became free for all purposes, for all time and against the whole world;[150] the manumission was the final *datio libertatis*.[151] Glanvill could never have used a similar phrase. For him, villeinage was permanent; the villein can never escape his birth. The most he can hope is that a 'lord, wishing him to achieve freedom from the villeinage by which he (the villein) is subject to him (the lord), may quitclaim him for himself and his heirs; or he may give or sell him to another with intent to free him'. The effect of the lord's act is only to 'make his villein free against himself and his heirs, but not as against others'. A villein thus enfranchised could still be successfully challenged later if he were produced in court as suit, even though he might have been knighted in the interval.[152] Nor did Glanvill's view disappear as swiftly as one might imagine; it was still pleaded in court in two cases of 1226,[153] and a lawyer of the 1250s could still include among his 'Casus et judicia' a quite independent expression of the same view.[154]

Glanvill is very unlikely, then, to have toed the *De legibus'* line about exceptions of villein status to assizes. He seems to have felt that anyone tainted with servility had no right to be heard in the royal court 'si nativitas sua et uillenagium in curia obiecta fuerint et probata'.[155] He gives no hint that it might matter whose villein the excluded litigant was. Villein condition meant

---

[150] As a matter of fact this was never completely true, for few freedmen escaped all obligation connected with their former servile status.

[151] *Br.*, f. 4, following Azo. An early fourteenth-century gloss (Cambridge Univ. Library, MS Dd vii 6, Woodbine's CA) terms it *detectio libertatis*, *Bracton and Azo*, p. 123, which is perhaps a more exact formulation.

[152] *Glanvill*, v. 5 (ed. Hall, pp. 57–8).

[153] The first in *CRR* xii. 2529 = *BNB* 1749 (Wilts. 1226); earlier stages *CRR* xii. 945, 1465, 2140, 2149. The marginal annotation strongly disapproves of the judgement (though the court included Martin of Pateshull himself; cf. *CRR* xii, p. xiv), for good Bractonian reasons. The second in JI 1/1172, m. 4d = Vinogradoff, *Villainage*, pp. 421–2 = *Ab. Plac.*, p. 104 (Assize at Shrewsbury 1225–6); here the plea was unsuccessful.

[154] *Cas. Plac.*, p. lxxxiv/83 (*c.* 1252/6). Cf. the editor's comments ibid., pp. xxvi ff., and G. D. G. Hall, *Selden Registers*, pp. lxii–lxiii.

[155] *Glanvill*, v. 5.

that one could not possess the legal rights of a freeman, the *lex terre*.[156]

A generation later, such views looked rather crude to the author of the *De legibus* on his more advanced educational plane, though he willingly used Glanvill as a source to be rewritten in modern terms. His Bractonian theory of villeinage must now be summarized, its influence assessed, and its place in the history of common-law villeinage defined. The first requirement is to draw together the evidence for the date it was thought out. However long the individual parts took to emerge, the whole must have coalesced at one moment of time,[157] which can roughly be ascertained from the cases examined in this chapter. The theory crystallized some time before 1224 but no earlier than 1218, [158] although seeds may have been sown by the loose drafting of Magna Carta, c. 39, in 1215.[159] The process could only be dated more precisely if it were possible to be sure who the author was and how far the ideas were his own. Although this knowledge may never be available, we do know enough to envisage a judicial establishment used to differences of opinion on doctrine. The great name of the period was undoubtedly that of Martin de Pateshull, chief justice of the Bench. How far he approved of the *De legibus'* line on villeinage remains unclear. His last eyres saw a number of clear Bractonian decisions, some of which seem to have been incorporated into the treatise as revisions.[160] On the other hand, courts under his presidency also decided cases along lines that contradict the *De legibus*.[161] Similarly, a number of Bractonian decisions on villeinage pleas made under the aegis of William de Raleigh a few years later confirm Professor Thorne's suggestion

---

[156] Ibid., v. 5, 6. This phrase, which sometimes meant merely the right to make proof, is discussed below, Chap. 9.

[157] Above p. 98. The coexistence of conflicting views within the judicial establishment ensures that the pattern cannot be simple, and our evidence is of course deficient.

[158] The theory can hardly have preceded Bestenover's Case (pp. 56 ff., 110) by much. It seems to have been complete by the time of Pateshull's last eyres, 1226–8, and the last exception of villeinage to specify that the plaintiff was *his* villein dates from 1224, above n. 76.

[159] Above Chap. 6.

[160] Cf. above nn. 65–6, 115–6, and below pp. 148 ff.

[161] e.g. *BNB* 1030 (1224), above pp. 60 f., JI 1/863, m. 2 (1225), above n. 70, *BNB* 1749 (1226), on facing page.

that the treatise was known and used by his circle,[162] yet
Raleigh too did not invariably toe the Bractonian line. One
topic like villeinage is no sound basis for generalizations, at least
until much more is known about interactions between senior
and junior judges.[163] Nevertheless, the return of 'Bractonian'
ideas on villeinage in the late 1240s at the same time as the
judicial career of Henry de Bracton flowered is hardly likely to
be due to chance alone,[164] especially since the treatise was not
published for another ten years or so. Further research on a
wider range of doctrine will no doubt clarify Henry de
Bracton's personal role and reveal how lasting and complete
the De legibus' impact was to be.[165]

So far there are no good hints about the identity of the
original author. Certainly this study in no way contradicts
Professor Thorne's choice of Raleigh's circle as the most likely
place of origin.[166] Indeed it strengthens Thorne's case by
furnishing substantial, new internal evidence of the author's
methods and aims. At first sight, the theory of villeinage
appears an English solution to a set of English problems. Behind it lurked undeniably hard cases to puzzle justices and
stimulate the jurist's mind.[167] Bestenover's Case, for example,
is an obvious crux. And it certainly seems that the anomaly of a
freeman holding in villeinage encouraged the suggestive
Bractonian analogy with the Ancient Demesne's villein sokeman.[168] We have seen that even the attempt to retrace the
logical steps of the theory's formation suggests familiar concepts
of English land law.[169]

Yet the scent of the two laws is more pervasive still. The
author's learned legal education must surely be the source of
the systematizing urge itself. He had to render respectable
English common law in general, in something of the same way
(though more sophisticated now) that Glanvill's prologue once

---

[162] Above pp. 105 f., and Thorne, Br., iii, xxx etc.
[163] Cf. above pp. 85 f.
[164] Examples above nn. 77, 94, 110–11, and below pp. 179–80.
[165] See above pp. 32 n. 40, 35, 75 and below pp. 137–8, 179–80, 211, for Bractonian
rulings followed in Edward I's reign.
[166] Thorne, Br., iii. xxx–xxxiii.
[167] Above, pp. 100, 112.
[168] Above, pp. 56 ff.
[169] Above, pp. 90–3.

essayed to equate unwritten custom with Rome's *ius scriptum*.[170]
This is shown, for example, by his care to find English parallels
for all of Azo's prescriptions.[171] Roman-law influence alone can
explain such choices as the invention of the *exceptio spoliationis*
from such sparse English material, and the preference for the
distinction between tenure and status over the alternative prescription against free blood.[172] All in all, the *De legibus* strives
more for internal consistency than to refute alternative arguments.[173] The author guages his learned reordering finely, to
streamline doctrine without disturbing the *status quo* to an
unacceptable degree.[174]

The *De legibus* is certainly not the product of the social
theorist I once thought I saw behind it. This comes out most
clearly in the absence of seignorial apologetics. Though the
Bractonian theory of villeinage clearly has something to offer
serf-owning lords,[175] its social viewpoint is essentially conventional. It saw nothing morally wrong with servitude,[176] and no
reason therefore to seek release from their burdens for the
enserfed. A more real danger was the wrongful enserfment of
the rightly free.[177] A royalist lawyer[178] writing a general treatise
De legibus et Consuetudinibus Angliae is unlikely to include a social
tract on villeinage. The author's hopes for his own advance-
ment tempered his tendencies to extremes of moral fervour.
Even if he was in orders (like Raleigh and Henry de Bracton, for
instance), he had still to ensure his own income.[179] Future
research will no doubt extend Professor Thorne's insights to
teach us a great deal more about the predilections that shaped
the *De legibus*. In the meantime, the main impression left with
the student of villeinage law is of a learned legal education and a
technical task. A Romanizing spirit conceived of the theory of

---

[171] Above pp. 93 f., cf. below p. 176.
[172] Above pp. 102 ff., 114 ff.
[173] Above pp. 94, 99, 110.
[174] Above pp. 96, 118, and cf. above p. 85.
[175] e.g. above p. 119.
[176] The definition of servitude in *Br.*, f. 4b, is of course taken from Azo, *Bracton and Azo*, pp. 45–6, 51.
[177] Below Chap. 12.
[178] Cf. below pp. 126 f., 260 ff.
[179] For William of York see R. E. Latham and E. K. Timings (recte C. A. F. Meekings), 'Six Letters concerning the Eyres of 1226–8', *EHR* lxv (1950), 492–504.

villeinage to rationalize the existing law into a more defensible system the courts could administer with confidence.

9

THE VILLEIN AS LITIGANT AND SUBJECT

The relativity of villeinage now stands revealed as a rather special theory of villeinage law, a personal creation specific to Henry III's minority. Historians cannot rely on it as a guide to court practice outside a narrow period. However, one lesson at least is clear: the common law had no intention of attributing to lords absolute power over their villeins' lives. Chattels they might be to the lord; they were also human beings, whose survival concerned both church and king. This chapter examines the result of these different influences on the villein's legal rights, if any. It falls into two separate parts. The first, about the villein's rights against his lord and other individuals, is fairly straightforward. The other, on the villein's rights and duties *vis-à-vis* the whole community, the State if you like, is rather more complex. Contemporary decisions on relevant matters tended to be *ad hoc* and badly recorded, if at all. Moreover, all talk of the villein and the State begs the question of the origins of common-law villeinage which is reserved for Chapter 13. Thus the brief discussion here will merely survey some selected topics which illustrate the villein's position as a lowly subject of the king, whose public duties are rather more prominent than his rights.

First of all, an objection must be noted. Some would wish to deny to the unfree villein any legal rights. Is he not rightless almost by definition? Maitland, indeed, said of the villein: 'In relation to his lord, the general rule makes him rightless [while] criminal law . . . protects him in life and limb.'[1] Legal scholars have often disputed whether slaves or serfs within particular legal systems were rightless or not. Maitland would call a slave 'rightless' even when his life was legally protected against his master's violence. After all, modern English law protects domestic animals against maltreatment without giving them any legal right of redress against their masters. This view,

---

[1] *P&M*, i. 415.

though not beyond argument, seems sensible enough.[2] Clearly an object, dog or villein, may be protected by the law without having the ability to initiate itself legal proceedings to enforce that protection.[3]

Thus the fact that a slave, as chattel, has no rights against his master does not necessarily mean that the master can do anything he wishes. The limits will be determined by the attitude of the particular legal system towards private property in general and the ownership of slaves in particular. Developed legal systems seldom allow slave-owners absolute rights of property over their human chattels. One possibility is for the master to have absolute property rights over his slave as regards other individuals, but to be prevented by the State from treating him in too arbitary a fashion or with such violence as would injure him beyond recall. This, more or less the position of a dog-owner today, is obviously an extremely harsh rule for the ownership of men. In a society like medieval England where peasant serfs were far from being chattel slaves, it could never have been maintained in practice. Nevertheless, the *De legibus* proffered a view of the legal relationship between lord and villein, an extension of his Roman-law influenced theory of villeinage law analysed in the last chapter, not very different.

(I) VILLEIN RIGHTS AGAINST THE LORD AND OTHERS

The author of the *De legibus* considered the lord's rights over his villein absolute against all other individuals but, where necessary, subordinated by law to the public interest. The heavy Roman-law influence behind his statements may conveniently be approached by the consideration of a casual reference outside any systematic discussion of villeinage. He described the legal position of the monk as analogous to the villein's, a kind of civil death.[4] He tells his readers that masters had once had powers of life and death over their *servi* but that, as a result of their harshness, the king had assumed their mantle in this respect. Even so, *servi* who escape their masters' *potestas* 'breathe somewhat as if resuscitated to life'. The main point was that monks and villeins—like the dead—possessed no property

---

[2] D. B. Davis, *The Problem of Slavery in Western Cutlure*, p. 104, adopts it.
[3] The author of the *De legibus* may have thought in terms of an analogy between villeins and domestic animals, see *Br.*, f. 6b, and above Chap. 4.
[4] *Br.*, f. 421b.

rights.[5] This monk–*servus* comparison was almost a common-place among Roman and Canon lawyers,[6] among whom the idea clearly originated. The view of servitude as a kind of civil death, on which the comparison rested, appeared right at the beginning of the treatise.[7] *Servi* were set under their lords' power by the *ius gentium*. This power, once extended to life and death, was now limited by the *ius civile* under which the life and members of the *servus* were brought under royal control.

All this, including the 'recent' history, comes from Roman-law discussions about the nature of slavery and the relationship of *ius naturale* with *ius civile* and *ius gentium* which were already old in Justinian's day.[8] The idea of a time in the past when a master could kill his slave with impunity was part of the lawyer's justification of the institution of slavery in the face of the objection that all men were free by *ius naturale*.[9] Medieval Civilians reworked the story and concluded that masters were permitted reasonable correction of their *servi* but were to be punished if they killed them.[10] Even in twelfth-century England, according to the author of the *Leges Henrici Primi*, a lord who killed his *servus* was responsible for both his sin and the legal offence.[11] The *De legibus* combined the Civilian texts with the idea of civil death already current in English law.[12] Its author, a royal servant, may not have been unhappy to give the king an implied right to intervene when lords bore down too heavily on their villeins. Britton, whose abbreviation of the *De legibus* retains a personal flavour, certainly understood the implications for seigorial power.[13] When prisoners taken at war were conserved, the

[5] *P&M*, i. 433–4.
[6] P. M. Blecker, 'The Civil Rights of the Monk in Roman and Canon Law: the Monk as *Servus*', *American Benedictine Review* xvii. 2 (1966), 185–98. Cf. *Proverbia Sententiaeque Latinitatis Medii Aevi*, ed. H. Walther, iv, no. 28176a; 'servitutem mortalitati fere comparamus'.
[7] *Br.*, f. 6; cf. *Fleta* i. 5(2) and below for *Britton*.
[8] *Inst.*, i. 8; Buckland, *Slavery*, p. 4.
[9] *Br.*, f. 4b: 'servitus . . . dicitur a servando . . . Antiquitus enim solent principes captivos vendere, et ideo eos servare et non occidere'. This is from Azo, *Summa Institutionum*, cited *Bracton and Azo*, pp. 66–7.
[10] See R. W. and A. J. Carlyle, *A History of Medieval Political Theory in the West*, ii. 34–40. Azo (in his *Summa Codicis*, not used in the *De legibus*) and Placentinus took a stronger line against homicide by a master than the older view.
[11] *LHP*, 75.4. The source is Mosaic law (Exod. 21:20) through Alfred's code.
[12] *P&M*, i. 434–5
[13] *Britton*, I. xxxii. 1 (i. 195). Cf. especially *Br.*, f. 5, and *Bracton and Azo*, pp. 45–7, 51.

death sentence was only postponed and could be re-imposed at the master's will. Thus the slave was perpetually at his master's mercy. Then, Britton's version runs, because some treated their slaves with great cruelty, the masters should no longer be allowed to kill them; thenceforth the serfs' life and members were to be in the hands of kings and princes like those of freemen. In the illuminating words of the early fourteenth-century Longueville gloss,[14] the king now had a kind of 'fee sutyl en noun de seigneurie' in each man, so that the lord became a sort of mesne between the king and the serf whom he ought to treat 'pur lui enprower e ne nie dampner'. Possibly this would have seemed too much for the author of Bracton, in whose time royal contacts with villeins were still developing. But the *De legibus* certainly valued the public interest highly, and like Azo justified royal protection of the *servus* with the maxim that 'expedit . . . rei publicae ne quis re sua male utatur'.[15] This argument could be applied to almost any state interference in individuals' rights. The author would probably have been pleased to provide the king with an entrée into the internal functioning of lordships.

There is, of course, a most unpromisingly Romanesque flavour to all these discussions. Yet the Bractonian learning generally corresponds to the contemporary legal position. A lord might apply reasonable correction to his villein, up to a point roughly defined by custom. Villeins were not, however, to be maimed or killed and could themselves institute successful proceedings against their lords for excessively violent treatment. Indeed, the villein's rights against his lord, although limited, were little worse than his chances of redress against strangers who harmed him, a state of affairs which the *De legibus* tried to amend. The common law's limitations on seignorial treatment of villeins and such rights of action as were permitted them must now be examined in greater detail.

Glanvill never clearly states his views about villein rights; they must be inferred from one casual statement. A freeman who marries a villein woman and goes to live on the villeinage,

---

[14] Printed in a footnote, *Britton*, i. 195.
[15] *Br.*, f. 6; cf. *Bracton and Azo,* pp. 66–7 and n. 3. The near contemporary Simon of Hinton quoted the same maxim to very similar effect (lords can tallage their villeins at will but are subject to criminal law), Bodleian Library, MS Laud. Misc. 2, f. 86v; cf. below, Chap. 11, p. 192.

he said, 'legem terre tanquam nativus amittit' for as long as he remains bound to the villeinage land.[16] Since the freeman becomes a villein to all intents for the duration of his marriage, the implied principle is that villeins lack the *lex terre*. What does this mean? Close examination of other occasions when Glanvill used the phrase suggests that the connotations it held for him are inadequately summarized by a simple translation as 'legal rights'[17] or the like. The phrase *lex terre*[18] is susceptible of two rather different interpretations: in the wider sense which most scholars attribute to its appearance in Magna Carta,[19] or in a more narrowly legal sense connected with 'Lex' meaning proof by wager of law, the making of a solemn oath. The distance between the two is not as far as first impressions suggest. If the second sense is broadened a little to include methods of proof in general, deprivation of *lex terre* entails the loss of legal and civil rights.

Probably Glanvill intended this meaning on most occasions when he used the phrase.[20] Only once, when stating what happens when a champion is proved to have offered his services for reward, does he describe the consequences of losing *lex terre*.[21] One might deduce from this Glanvill's view of the villein's rights. Probably villeins could not appear in court as witnesses or jurors or to make proof for other men or themselves. They might however defend themselves against appeal, or even perhaps appeal others for any *atrox iniuria* committed against them in breach of the king's peace.[22] This tentative suggestion is at least compatible with another of Glanvill's remarks about villeinage. Because in his view manumission by

---

[16] *Glanvill*, v. 6.
[17] As offered by Hall, op. cit., p. 58.
[18] *Status integritas* is also used, *Glanvill*, ii. 7, v. 6.
[19] F. M. Powicke, 'Per Judicium Parium vel per Legem Terre', *Magna Carta Commemoration Essays*, ed. H. E. Malden (London, 1917); J. C. Holt, *Magna Carta*, p. 227. The special interest of the phrase at this period is that it marks the transformation of a system including personal laws into a territorial common law; cf. E. M. Meijers, *Études de droit international privé* (Paris, 1967), pp. 64 ff.
[20] *Glanvill*, ii. 3, 19; v. 5; xiv. 2. The exception is vii. 17 where it means 'due process of law' or something similar; cf. *BNB* 1203.
[21] *Glanvill*, ii. 3 (ed. Hall, p. 25). The ex-champion will never again be admitted to make proof in court for anyone else. He may only fight to defend himself (against appeal), to prosecute 'an *atrox iniuria* to his own body amounting to a breach of the lord King's peace', or to defend his right to his fee and inheritance.
[22] For *atrox iniuria*, see below.

the lord does not constitute complete enfranchisement, Glanvill notes that a villein freed in this way, if 'produced in court to make proof as a champion against a stranger *vel ad aliquam legem terre faciendam*, he can lawfully be excluded if his villein status is raised as an objection and proved'.[23] Clearly, Glanvill has the making of proof in mind here. One other reference also under-lines the importance of the *lex terre*. Perjurous knights of the grand assize were severely punished. In addition to loss of goods and a year's imprisonment, by the loss of their *lex terre* 'they rightly incur the lasting mark of infamy', Glanvill asserted.[24]

Glanvill's undoubted influence on the treatment of villein rights in the *De legibus* is disguised by the later writer's learned language.[25] The author talks not of *lex terre* but whether villeins have 'personam standi in judicio', standing in court.[26] 'Villeins', indeed 'have a right of action (*legem*) against their lords; they may proceed against them in court in matters where the punishment is that of life and members, because of their lords' violence, or because the wrong is an insufferable one, as where the lords so strip them that their wainage cannot be saved them.'[27] Thus, in his view, villeins sometimes had stand-ing in court, and could also sue strangers for the seisin of land they held freely.[28] Certainly, villeins are to be found on the plea rolls in the thirteenth century. If they had never pleaded in the royal courts, this book could not have been written. Few, however, succeeded in gaining much by their appearance there.

First of all, how frequently did villeins defend themselves against the actions of others? Britton at the end of the century said that villeins were always answerable as defendants.[29] But

---

[23] *Glanvill*, v. 5 (ed. Hall, p. 58); v. 6 implies the same for the child of a villein mother and free father.

[24] *Glanvill*, ii. 19. *Infamia* may bear a technical Roman-law sense here (cf. Hall, p. xxxvi) but the word is common in early medieval texts generally; cf. J. Goebel, *Felony and Misdemeanour* i (New York, 1937), pp. 61–81, 250–1, 255–76.

[25] *Br.*, f. 185, is a good illustration. Glanvill's dictum on perjury just mentioned is restated in more modern terms which, unexpectedly, make clear that Glanvill was relying on a tradition that went back to the Old English state and its concept of the 'law-worthy man'.

[26] *Br.*, f. 24b (ed. Thorne, ii. 85). The phrase is very close to II *Cnut* 37: 'ne stande his gewitnes sythan for aht'; closer than to its extant Latin translations, on which see Downer, *LHP*, pp. 321–2.

[27] *Br.*, f. 6 (trans. Thorne, ii. 34).

[28] Above, Chap. 8.

[29] *Britton*, I. xxxii. 7 (i. 199).

this statement is quite inadequate as a description of the early thirteenth-century situation. Any villein defendant in a royal court put his—that is, his lord's—chattels at risk. Lords expected to 'justice' their villeins in their own courts. To retain this power, they might be prepared to stand responsible in the royal court for acts of their villeins which caused loss to others. The only obvious exception to this theory was that the king had the right (or duty) to repress and punish breaches of his peace and other pleas of the crown irrespective of the offender's status. Thus villeins were probably subject to the criminal law like anyone else, but individual's claims would normally be barred by the defendant's admission that he was of villein status. Confirmation of this theory is difficult. The plea rolls alone rarely reveal whether a defending party was a villein. Even when they do, the cases are seldom clear authorities.

The villein's criminal liability, however, is pretty clear. In the early twelfth century, the *Leges Henrici Primi* had stated its opinion that *servi* guilty of homicide and other capital crimes died for them just like freer offenders.[30] This must have remained true. The writers of most later law books simply omit mention of status from their accounts of crime or the pleas of the crown. The exception is the *Dialogue of the Exchequer*, an early witness (*c*.1179) whose main interests are not legal. Its author, Richard FitzNeal, assumed that men of any condition were criminally liable and thus their chattels were forfeit to the king on conviction or flight. But both his Master and Pupil express the view that this rule was unfair on the lord of an *ascripticius* who would thus lose some of his own goods without being himself at fault. The Master explained that royal peacekeeping policy, as embodied above all in the Assizes of Clarendon and Northampton, demanded this. There was also another reason. Without the rule, lords might wrongly engineer their villeins' conviction in order to get hold of their goods, a possibility which the king's 'generalis . . . cura subditorum' moved him to prevent.[31] The Pupil raises no queries about the main point, whether royal jurisdiction covered villein pleas of the crown; it

---

[30] *LHP*, 59.23–5a, 68.11, 70.2, 85.4, 4a; the offender's status had certain effects on procedure.
[31] *Dialogus*, II. x (97, 101–2).

was beyond question.[32] The few plea-roll entries relevant are
sufficient to confirm that this remained so in the thirteenth
century. To defeat a claim of borough privilege in an 1198
appeal, the appellant Hubert of Anesty was quite happy to
allege in court that Roger son of Mabel had been a villein at the
time he committed the theft.[33] In 1210, Simon de Lindon
impleaded Maud of Biham (whom he had recently been claiming as his villein by writ of naifty) and an accomplice of making
a false appeal of homicide against him.[34] Neither Hubert nor
Simon felt that villeins could not be appealed. Occasionally,
too, juries of presentment revealed that some fugitive was a
villein,[35] an in 1227 when a convicted villein homicide was
hanged, the only difference his status made was that the king
received the offender's chattels without the usual year's tenure
of his land.[36] The evidence, though scanty,[37] bears out Vinogradoff's conclusion that 'in the criminal law of the feudal
epoch there is hardly any distinction between free men and
villeins'.[38]

The same was not true of civil law. Civil suits against villeins
in the royal courts normally failed. The general rule was that a
defendant's admission of villein status barred the action.[39]
Redress for wrongs committed by a villein had to be sought
from his lord. The evidence for this is not wholly clear. There
are some anomalous cases, and no doubt more defendants were
unfree than admitted their status in court.[40] Villein trespasses

[32] Ibid. II. xiii (107), mentions villein debts to the king 'pro excessu', which probably
means for an offence. *P. Roll 21 Henry II*, p. 198 (1174–5), is a probable example
concerning an unsuccessful appeal aginst two *rustici* for arson.
[33] *CRR* vii. 343, 344 (Yorks. 1198).
[34] *CRR* vi. 52, 105, 106, 107 (Lincs. 1210). See also below.
[35] *SRS* xi. 131 (Somerset eyre 1225) is an example. An unusual case about a villein
fugitive or homicide is revealed by *Cal. Pat. R., 1266–1272*, p. 658 (1272). A Cumberland
villein had crossed the border claiming to be on the run and had thus gained the King of
Scots' protection. His lord obtained a pardon for the villein and hoped no doubt that
the protection would now be removed.
[36] *SS* lix. 728 (Coventry eyre 1221); cf. ibid. 416.
[37] See also *PRS* xiv. 84 (Wilts. eyre 1195), *LRS* xxii. 631, ibid. 1016 (Lincoln eyre
1202), *NRS* v. 686 (Northampton eyre 1203), *SS* lix. 1340 (Shrewsbury eyre 1221).
[38] Vinogradoff, *Villainage*, p. 64.
[39] Examples of land actions where this happened: *CRR* i. 145, 194 (Middlesex 1200),
JI 1/731, m. 5 (Salop eyre 1203), *CRR* vii. 228 (Norfolk 1214), *SS* liii. 237 (Lincoln eyre
1219), JI 1/1172, m. 4d (Salop eyre 1226), JI 1/775, m. 11d (Hants eyre 1235–6).
Assizes are discussed below.
[40] A confession of villein status, once made, bound the villein for good; below, pp.
148 ff.

may have been actionable. The feeling was perhaps that a lord ought not to be held responsible for the quasi-criminal offences of his villein tenants whose lives he did not constantly supervise. One illustrative case is known from a casual reference to its progress in 1295,[41] but there is very little evidence of other actions which villeins may have used too.[42] It is impossible to prove the point for personal actions against villeins; as with crime, too much is taken for granted in the rolls. Assizes ought to be relatively clear. They centred on free tenements which a villein could hold (if at all) exceptionally and for a very short period. The usual pattern was that lords speedily took over their villeins' acquisitions, and assizes against the villeins were then barred by pleas of villeinage tenure. Clearly, villeins could not be permitted to lose their lords' property. But in fact a few assizes did succeed against villeins. In 1203, ten plaintiffs, eight of whom were unfree, sued nine villeins in novel disseisin. The unfree plaintiffs were excluded but the assize proceeded 'per licensiam' (possibly because the land was Ancient Demesne) for the one surviving free plaintiff and he recovered seisin.[43] In 1227 another novel disseisin went ahead in spite of the defendant's admission that he was villein to a third party. Not only did he lose his seisin to the plaintiff, but he was also amerced and assessed for five-shillings damages.[44] Three other similar cases are known from this circuit,[45] but these cases are quite exceptional.[46] Assizes barred by a confession of villein status

[41] *Rot. Parl.*, i. 134b.

[42] In *CRR* xii. 2353 (Essex 1226) some villeins were attached for rasing the Abbot of Waltham's forest dyke, but this was a special action based on breach of recent royal commands (and not the assize of nuisance as one would expect); cf. *Cal. Pat. R. 1225–1232*, pp. 2, 69–70; *Cal. Charter Rolls (Henry III, AD 1226–57)*, (London, 1903), i. 28–9, 100. It is also possible that actions to enforce suit of mill against villeins were occasionally permitted in the early thirteenth century, but this action came to be formulated against the villeins' lord. Cf. *Novae Narrationes*, pp. cxff. The defendants in KB 26/124, m. 1d (Leics. 1242), had been villeins until freed by their lord soon after he sold the mill off; cf. also *BNB* 161. After the first decade of the thirteenth century nuisances of this kind were often heard in the county court (Sutherland, *The Assize of Novel Disseisin*, pp. 63, 216–17) where it may have been possible to sue villeins.

[43] *WSS* iii. 110 (Lichfield eyre 1203). The village of Sutton may be included in Mere which was *terra regis* in 1086, *DB* f. 246a.

[44] JI 1/819, m. 28d (Suffolk eyre 1227). The defendant's admission was not framed as an exception to the assize.

[45] Cf. below p. 149.

[46] *SS* lxviii. 144, 145, 432 (Cornwall eyre 1201), can be subsumed to the normal rule if the defendant against whom the assize proceeded was lord of one of the villeins. The plaintiff of JI 1/818, m. 32d (Suffolk eyre 1240), must have received bad advice.

alone are not plentiful,[47] but no one seems to have argued successfully that they were insufficient to bar the assize, the one eyre visitation of 1227 apart.

Thus villeins were rarely forced to answer suits in the royal courts. Naturally in these circumstances, admitted villeins seldom initiated pleas there. Certainly they could not hope to recover property against their lords for the familiar reasons, but what of the lord's common-law duty not to kill or maim his villein? Surely the villein could enforce this through the courts. In theory he probably could, but the early thirteenth century was a time when private appeals before royal justices (where, alone, historians can study them) were ceasing to be an effective remedy for maltreatment in the face of judicial disapproval and strict constructionism.[48] Some form of public prosecution was preferred, and an appellee against whom the appeal had been held null would often find his alleged breach of the peace put to an inquisition all the same. Even this might be dropped if the appellants withdrew or failed to return to court, and villeins were very vulnerable to a repeat dose of the treatment which had induced them to come before the justices in the first place. The alternative, a suit in trespass, had its own problems. Lord–villein disputes almost always involved property rights which were of course not actionable. Great care was needed in making accurate pleas and rehearsing the facts in the best order. Although this affected the defending lords too, the parties' positions were not equal. Most justices held conservative views about society. Lack of sympathy from the bench can occasionally be detected. And for villeins, the failure to obtain a judgement meant complete defeat.

Yet, despite all these obstacles some villeins did achieve at least some kind of satisfaction against their lords. Villeins may have fared better against strangers, but the evidence is scarce because villeinage was seldom raised as an exception. A villein's formal legal rights were hardly greater against strangers than against their lords. An exception of villein status defeated property claims, no matter who the defendant was. Thus, although

---

[47] *RCR* i. 376 (Berks. 1199), *SS* lxviii. 847, 860 (Suffolk 1202), *WSS* iii. 114 (Lichfield eyre 1203), *CRR* iv. 276 (Essex 1206), *CRR* iv. 169 (Middlesex 1206), *SS* liii. 257 (Lincoln eyre 1219), all mort d'ancestors, and an unspecified assize *SS* lxviii. 797 (Essex 1202). The absence of novel disseisin is noteworthy.

[48] C. A. F. Meekings, *Crown Pleas of the Wilts. Eyre of 1249* (*WRS* xvi 1961), pp. 64 ff.

the law forbade criminal acts against villeins, it afforded them few legal opportunities of redress, and remote chances of success if they tried.

According to the books, the villein could appeal his lord in two types of case.[49] In the first place anyone can bring an appeal of sedition, providing he is not himself an obvious traitor. This is for straightforward reasons of royal interest. There is no reason to doubt that this facility was open to villeins although no actual case is known.[50] The villein could also appeal his lord of death or serious physical injury.[51] Bracton concedes that the villein has standing against his lord for matters which are 'contra personam eius', since everyone may appeal 'de atroci iniuria' where the action concerns their life and members or robbery. The phrase *atrox iniuria* denoted in Roman law an *iniuria* of an especially serious kind; its victim was afforded additional remedies at law. Harm done to a *servus* was actionable at Roman law only if the praetor decided that it amounted to an *atrox iniuria* (or if the master too had suffered the *iniuria*); the law provided no redress for a simple *iniuria*.[52] Glanvill may not have comprehended this technical meaning,[53] but the author of Bracton, more thoroughly versed in the learned laws, certainly did. His account of the topic follows the *Institutes* closely.[54] In Roman law, an offence might qualify as an *atrox iniuria* because of the place where it was committed, the importance of the victim, or the parts of his body assaulted. The *De legibus*, when speaking generally of the occasion when an action might be had for wrongs done to a *servus*, had merely said that the *servus* himself had standing against anyone 'de iniuriis sibi factis contra pacem domini regis'. Its author probably saw the

---

[49] *Cas. Plac.*, p. lxxix/38 (Casus et judicia), does not indicate a third type; those who had received manumission charters were no longer villeins.

[50] *Glanvill*, xiv. 1, *Br.*, ff. 118b, 141, 155b. Cf. Richardson, *Bracton*, pp. 124–5, for the Civilian source behind f. 118b, and *CRR* xii. 1055 (Northants 1225) a case correctly cited on f. 141.

[51] *Pace P&M*, i. 415 n. 3.

[52] W. W. Buckland, *A Manual of Roman Private Law* (2nd ed., Cambridge, 1957), p. 328; cf. Buckland, *Slavery*, pp. 79–82.

[53] *Glanvill*, ii. 3 (for which see above p. 129), ix. 1 (on which cf. Hall, *Glanvill*, p. 105), neither of which passages refers to villeins.

[54] *Glanvill*, xiv. 1, *Br.*, ff. 118b, 141, 155b. Cf. Richardson, *Bracton*, pp. 124–5, for the *Letters, Henry III* ii (ed. W. W. Shirley, R.S. 1886), p. 649, mentions an incident described as an *atrox iniuria*: rebels besieged in Kenilworth in 1266 cut off the hand of a royal messenger as a gesture of defiance.

villein's right to sue his lord as similar but less extensive, in that it was limited to cases of serious personal injury. The villein cannot bring against his lord an appeal of robbery or any action alleging the wrongful taking of goods. The lord is not liable for taking his own goods, nor can a villein institute proceedings against a stranger for taking goods which do not belong to him. Villeins thus came amongst those not entitled to appeal for larceny or robbery since the goods taken belonged to someone else.[55] In the Bractonian view, then, with the sole exception of allegations of sedition or the like, the villein's rights of action in the royal courts are limited to cases where he has suffered personal injury in circumstances against the king's peace.

Homicide is relatively simple. Three cases are known where men were impleaded for causing the death of their own villeins. In 1210, Simon de Lindon alleged that Maud of Biham and her accomplice Roger de Eston had impleaded him of the death of her son, falsely too since the boy was still alive. Simon knew well that Maud had been struggling to establish her freedom for a dozen years and had once acknowledged villeinage in court. He had himself claimed her by writ of naifty a few years earlier. Yet neither party saw fit to mention this at the hearings of the appeal.[56] At the same session, Thomas son of William appealed Andrew of Horbling of causing the death of William his father by maltreating him in prison.[57] This is exactly the kind of case Bracton had in mind. Andrew argued that the dead man and his son were his villeins, and declared that William had died 'de propria morte', not as a result of his imprisonment. He then offered two marks for a jury on this; the case was adjourned, and no more is known. Proof of the deceased's villein status was a good defence for the imprisonment only; it probably would not have defended him on the homicide. In the third appeal,[58]

---

[55] Br., f. 146; for the case cited there see below pp. 139 f. The author might have sought to justify an appeal of robbery by a villein, had he so wished, on the grounds that the breach of the peace was of the essence and the villein did have some interest in the goods taken even if he did not own them. He never took this step; cf. Br., ff. 103b, 141b.

[56] CRR vi. 52, 105, 106, 107 (Lincs. 1210). Cf. CRR i. 22; v. 49, 77 (before 1196, 1207), for the two actions of naifty against Maud. H. Cam discusses the cases in 'Thirteenth Century Peasant Pedigrees', Liberties and Communities in Medieval England (Cambridge, 1944), Chap. VIII, pp. 124–35, with some inaccuracies. For Simon de Lindon see Early Yorks. Charters, iii. 181.

[57] CRR vi. 106 (Lincs. 1210).

[58] SS lvi. 1024 (York eyre 1218–19).

Nicholas son of Bernolf alleged that Thomas de Lascelles and his servants arrested him when he was on his way to replevy some distrained animals and put him in prison. While he was there they killed his son and committed other violent acts. Thomas's defence was simply that Nicholas was his villein and reeve, and this was confirmed by the jurors. But the jury verdict first covered the child's death and stated that Thomas was not guilty of this. The court's view seems to be that a lord had to answer his villein about homicide but was immune to some at least of the lesser accusations. If a lord could not plead his victim's villein status as a defence to homicide accusations, strangers obviously could not either. No actual cases have been identified from the rolls but a chronicle account of an appeal at a York eyre conveys the right flavour. A villein servant of Sir Saer of Sutton, a neighbour of Meaux Abbey, was killed by the House's men in the course of a skirmish over land which the men claimed to have been given. Sir Saer proceeded to lay a most serious plaint before the royal justices, and the dead man's widow and brother brought an appeal. Neither came to trial, however, for the monks did a deal with Sir Saer and he prevailed upon the family to drop its suit.[59] Such cases left no trace on the plea rolls.

Villeins were affected by the endemic violence of their world in other ways too. If they defied their lords and tried to run away from the fee, alienate or otherwise reduce their holdings' value, or refuse services, lords frequently reacted with violent attacks on their homes and persons; arrest and imprisonment might follow.[60] Out of such contretemps emerged various kinds of appeal and trespass suit for false imprisonment.[61] The *De legibus*[62] would have us believe that lords could only imprison villeins of whom they had been in actual recent seisin. In this view, a lord had to claim his runaway within a year before he gained seisin of liberty as a *statuliber* who could bring a plaint of

[59] *Chron. Monasterii de Melsa* ii, ed. E. A. Bond (R.S. 1867), pp. 6–8, cited by N. M. Hurnard, *The King's Pardon for Homicide before A.D. 1307* (London, 1968), p. 199. The date is 1235/49.

[60] See generally R. B. Pugh, *Imprisonment in Medieval England* (Cambridge, 1968), pp. 52–5, 88, 250.

[61] S. F. C. Milsom briefly discusses the trespassory action in 'Trespass from Henry III to Edward III', *LQR* lxxiv (1958), 209–10.

[62] *Br.*, f. 7 and *addicio*. Cf. also *Fleta* i. 42 (60).

imprisonment if he were arrested. This probably became law late in the thirteenth century, perhaps as a result of the *De legibus'* publication.[63] Cases from the early part of the century never turn on seisin; rather, they illuminate the rule of thumb by which the courts decided whether violence on a villein was legitimate. At that date the lord's right to imprison his villein was limited only by his ability to prove his title to him in court.[64] Many appeals[65] and other pleas of imprisonment[66] thus failed when those who brought them were shown to be villeins.

So the lord can imprison his villein, but how much force can he use to get him there or keep him inside? Local practice often supplied the answer,[67] but there was also a more general *consuetudo* on the subject by which the lord could put his villein in stocks but not apply more severe discipline. The earliest mention of this custom was in an appeal of robbery and imprisonment which came before the justices in 1212.[68] Ivo de Bamburch alleged that Henry son of Walter had first robbed him, then taken him 'et infermavit firgis proprii equi sui' and kept him in prison until released by the sheriff. Ivo may have anticipated Henry's reply, that Ivo was his villein who had been arrested quite legitimately for refusing to find sureties and that 'eum posuit in ceppo et non in firgis, sicut consuetudo fuit ponere villanum'. Although the result is unknown, the case establishes the existence of a customary distinction between the use of stocks and irons. From the middle of Henry III's reign at the latest, the custom can be traced through the various intercon-

---

[63] *YB 21 and 22 Edward I* (R.S.), pp.446–9 (Middlesex eyre 1294), *YB 32 and 33 Edward I* (R.S.), pp. 54–7 (1304). By this time it was customary to plead seisin in any villeinage allegation by a claimant lord.

[64] As early as 1174–5, a Warwickshire lord was amerced the large sum of 15 marks 'quia incarceravit hominem quem voluit probare rusticum et non potuit', *P. Roll 21 Henry II*, p. 178.

[65] e.g. *CRR* iii. 324; iv. 37 (Essex 1205), *CRR* vi. 349 (Lincs. 1212), *BRB* vi. 444, 658 (Buckingham eyre 1227).

[66] *CRR* i. 22 (Lincs. before 1196), *SS* lxxxiii, 972 (York county court 1203, Assize at Bridgenorth 1204), *CRR* iv. 148, 305 (Cambs. 1206), *CRR* xii. 75 = *BNB* 1041 (Norfolk 1225), KB 26/126, m. 9 (Staffs. 1243).

[67] In *CRR* xi. 2141 (Bucks. 1225) the arrest of a villein for being in arrears on his service was said to have been made according to the custom of the manor.

[68] *CRR* vi. 349 (Lincs. 1212).

nected practitioners' aids like *Casus Placitorum*[69] and remained standard doctrine at the end of the century.[70]

Was a lord permitted to whip or beat or assault his villein?[71] Probably not, but few relevant cases can be identified. The interconnected issues of violence and property rights are not easily disentangled by either contemporaries or historians. The plea rolls convey the uncertainties that faced villein litigants. One such case is an arson appeal of 1220, to which the *De legibus* rightly directed readers in search of material about villein robbery appeals.[72] Roger de Kirkele was a prosperous tenant of a Suffolk manor which enjoyed the relaxed customs of the Ancient Demesne.[73] He ignored seignorial disapproval of his daughter's choice of husband, Thomas de Bradley, and celebrated the marriage of the couple. Consequently, one night early in Lent 1220, Roger's lord, Henry de Vere, came himself to the house looking for the daughter. He broke down the door and searched all over the chamber for her. She was not to be found, for her mother had helped her to escape through the window. Still in hot pursuit, Henry now broke into the locked grange where the family stored its barley, which then caught fire from his lighted torch and burnt down the whole house. Roger with his son-in-law's assistance appealed Henry of arson and breach of the king's peace in the county court, and their suit reached the Bench. Henry began his defence by making a

[69] The earliest known statement of the custom is *The London Eyre of 1244*, ed. H. M. Chew and M. Weinbaum (London rec. soc., 1970), no. 346, written 1246 or soon after. Also *Cas. Plac.*, p. 4/16, of which MS T is said to contain the pre-Edwardian tradition (*Cas. Plac.*, p. xiii) and which attributes it to an opinion of Simon of Walton, J. (fl. 1251/7); and *Brev. Plac.*, p. 124/23, of which MS E is said to contain a revision of *c.* 1270/5 (*Brev. Plac.*, pp. xxi ff.). All versions agree that stocks are permissible but opinions differ on whether it is irons and fetters or prison altogether that must be avoided. The London eyre roll and the Royal MS of *Brevia Placitata* explain the distinction in terms of the royal interest in the villein's life and members, which was discussed at the beginning of this chapter.

[70] *WSS* vi. 1.193 (Staffs. 1290), *Sel. Bills in Eyre AD 1292–1333*, ed. W. O. Bolland (*SS* xxx 1914), no. 40 (Salop eyre 1292). Cf. *Fleta*, i. 42 (60).

[71] As early as Henry I's reign a man was amerced 'pro rustico verberato', *P. Roll 31 Henry I*, p. 55 (Essex). Nothing is known of the relationship between the two men.

[72] *CRR* ix. 336, (cited *Br.*, f. 146); x. 150 (Suffolk 1220). Cf. Hilton, *Past and Present* xxxi (1965), pp. 16–17, for a slightly different account, and Thorne, *Br.*, ii. 413 n. 5.

[73] For Mutford, see *DB* ii, f. 283, *Book of Fees*, i. 135–6, 392, 403, and A. Suckling, *The History and Antiquities of the County of Suffolk* (London, 1846), i. 269 ff., where an inquest on lord's rights and tenants' customs, temp. Edward I, is printed. Henry de Vere was lord of a moiety only.

general denial of any breach of the peace or felony as well as the arson charge. The house caught fire by accident, he explained, but Roger was his villein and had brought the appeal maliciously and out of spite ('per odium et atiam') because his daughter's marriage plans had failed to receive assent. He then objected formally to the appeal on the grounds that it was 'de combustione alterius domus quam sue' and because Roger was his villein. The justices were not at once convinced and questioned both parties, apparently to see if they might evade a decision on the legal point by holding the appeal null for some technical defect. When this proved out of the question, they ruled that because Thomas had appealed 'de combustione alterius domus quam sue' and Roger had acknowledged that he held from Henry when the house was destroyed, no appeal lay—a rather unsatisfactory judgement. An enquiry into the alleged breach of the peace, however, was then ordered. But it never occurred because in the next term, Roger and Thomas came into court, withdrew from their appeal (again!), and were gaoled. The oddities of the plea-roll record of the case are quite illuminating indications about the justices' attitudes.

As the *De legibus* rightly indicated, Roger's failure does suggest why villeins could not succeed in robbery appeals, but is also a reminder that the appellee is on trial for his threats or violence too. Other similar appeals reinforce the lesson that this was the wrong kind of action for a villein to bring.[74] Roger's case suggests that robbery appeals brought by villeins could always be defeated by those appealed. A requirement that appeals of this kind were valid only if brought for the taking of the appellant's own property was not removed when the appellant was some stranger. Although none of the extant cases explicitly proves this to have been the law, strangers sometimes took advantage of the villein's lack of property rights to defeat appeals of robbery. Adam son of Henry's defence to an appeal by Nicholas Selage was that Nicholas was a villein of the Abbot of Bury who, when he heard that Nicholas was planning to leave the fee, had taken his land into hand and demised it to Adam. The abbey servant who had carried out the transfer was present in court and corroborated Adam's story. Nicholas's

---

[74] *CRR* i. 126 (Surrey 1200); *CRR* xii. 1579, 1639 (Bucks. 1225). In neither case were the judges forced to make a decision.

appeal failed for technical reasons, but in any event Adam's plea was probably adequate as far as the robbery charge was concerned. He was not of course covered for violence and was amerced on a jury verdict that he had smashed Nicholas's teeth, though Nicholas himself did not benefit from this.[75]

All these cases were appeals. A villein did not improve his chances of success by bringing his grievances before the justices by some other means. A lord whose house-breaking had been presented to eyre justices was pardoned his amercement when they learnt that the house belonged to a villein.[76] The rules seem to have been no different in cases of trespass or those heard under special judicial commissions. One group of cases for which a royal commission of oyer and terminer was acquired is worth extended treatment. At the end of the thirteenth century, tenants of the Abbot of Bec's manor of Weedon in Northamptonshire rebelled against their situation and claimed free status. Their presumption was savagely repressed, but a group of them persisted to get royal writs for oyer and terminer and also to secure interim peace. One was John de Brockhall, a member of a prosperous family whose engrossment of land in the village continued steadily throughout the century before the Black Death. He had tried to leave the fee with his goods, but was caught and manhandled by William de Grafton, the abbot's seneschal, and two of the bailiffs. More tenacious than some of the others, he pursued his complaints as far away as the King's Bench and set his damages at a notional £40. He received a carefully drafted answer:

And the aforesaid William and the others come and defend force and injury etc. And as far as the beating is concerned, they say that they are in no way guilty. And as far as the imprisonment is concerned, they say that the aforesaid John is a villein of the abbot of Bec Herlouin, tallageable high and low at his will. And they say that . . . because the aforesaid John of Brockhall was rebellious against his lord and denying the services which he ought to do to the aforesaid abbot his lord . . . [they] put that John de Brockhall in to stocks on a dung hill, as the abbot's villein, until he was willing to be justiced at the abbot's will, without having done any wrong ('transgressionem') to the same John.

The careful plea paid off for the abbot. John put in his claim to free status, but the jury predictably found him to be the abbot's

[75] JI 1/818, m. 42d (Suffolk eyre 1240).
[76] Richardson and Sayles, *Procedure without Writ*, no. 120 (Cambs. 1261).

villein. Then, questioned further by the justices, the jury declared that William de Grafton alone was guilty of beating John wrongfully and assessed his damages at forty shillings. Because the beating had been in breach of the king's peace, the court held that John should receive his damages and William had to find twenty shillings more for his amercement.[77]

This decision shows that something not unlike the Bractonian rule could be followed around 1300. But was this always so? The circumstances surrounding such cases did not favour the emergence of clear doctrine to be followed consistently. The justices aimed above all to punish offenders against the peace to secure royal interests. But by this time enough property was involved in many villeinage disputes to justify the employment of expensive lawyers with a nose for legal and procedural novelties that produced some unexpected decisions. A trespass case of 1306 based on the familiar kind of violent treatment of a villein was reported in a Yearbook under the Latin heading 'How a lord should defend against a nief'. Its argument illuminates the lord's pleading difficulties in a way plea-roll entries virtually never can. Bereford J.'s magisterial directions for the best plea against several allegations, only some of which can be met by a villeinage defence, give his not un-Bractonian view of the law. He thinks that proof of an exception of villeinage defeats allegations of taking chattels or wrongful imprisonment but not accusations of assault etc. The counsel in the case mistakenly pleaded a general denial of all accusations before making the exception of villeinage.[78] But the pleader ought to clarify the allegations to which he addressed his exception of villeinage. Failure to observe the correct precautions with precision might leave a lord forced to take his stand on the untenable general denial of allegations, with the probable consequence that he enfranchised the plaintiff, his former villein.

---

[77] Cal. Pat. R., 1292–1301, pp. 462–4, 466 (1299), KB 27/169, m. 13d (Northants, coram rege 1302), cited by M. Morgan, The English Lands of the Abbey of Bec (Oxford, 1946), pp. 109–12. One may doubt whether John received his money.

[78] YB 33 and 35 Edward I (R.S.), pp. 296–9 (1306). Bereford J.'s model plea was as follows: 'Neither as to the carrying off of the chattels nor as to what he says about imprisonment does the plantiff have to be answered, for he is our villein and we are seised of him etc., and [what happened was that] because he wanted to flee from us (or did something else against our will), we put him in stocks (ceps) and took his chattels as we [were entitled to do] etc., and as to the beating and wounding, we did not do it and are ready [to prove this] etc.'

Few villeins managed to bring their complaints of seignorial maltreatment before royal justices. Even more rare was the villein litigant who could afford good legal advice. But on the infrequent occasions when well-advised villeins did reach court, they could pose problems of an extremely complex kind to lords who had thought they were acting well within their legal rights in seeking to justice their villeins.

This survey of legal remedies available to villeins demonstrates that even their few legal rights exceeded any real chance of success. Two suggestions of the *De legibus*, which if justified, would have given further legal rights to villeins, must be examined to conclude this section of the chapter. The famous aside about the villein's wainage will first be considered, and then the remarks on contractual rights which he thought villeins could sometimes enforce even against their lords. These add little to villeins' rights as set out already, but do reveal something more about the author of the *De legibus*.

At the end of the summary description of villein rights quoted above, the *De legibus* had said that villeins had an action against their lords 'because the wrong is an insufferable one, as where their lords so strip them that their wainage cannot be saved them'.[79] No action to enforce this right of wainage is known, and historians have tended to dismiss the remark, probably rightly, as irrelevant to court practice.[80] Yet here the author departs from Azo, his guide through most of the Roman law in the early part of the treatise.[81] This was probably deliberate. What might he have had in mind?

The answer is clearly to be sought in Magna Carta, c. 20, which limited the amount of judicial amercement according to the seriousness of the offence and the extent of the offender's resources, and helped to formalize the assessment procedure. The villein and his wainage were included within the scope of this provision not to give the villein any new rights against his lord, but to safeguard the lord against loss due to excessive mulcting of his villeins, for in origin it covered amercement in

---

[79] *Br.*, f. 6, quoted above, p. 130.
[80] Vinogradoff, *Villainage*, pp. 74–6; *P&M*, i. 416; Novae Narrationes, p. cci.
[81] Cf. *Bracton and Azo*, p. 71.

royal courts only.[82] Quite soon, however, it applied in seignorial courts too, and eventually came to be identified with all
courts not of record,[83] which may have encouraged a feeling
that Magna Carta had intended to grant tenants, including
villeins, some protection against seignorial excess. In addition,
the common-law remedy for contravention of the provision, the
writ *de moderata misericordia*,[84] recited the protection of villein
wainage even when, as normally, it was brought by one of the
other protected groups,[85] and similar ideas seem to have been
canvassed in actions of waste at about this time.[86] Bracton's
dictum perhaps reflects these abstract ideas, but apparently not
practice: no cases brought by villeins with the writ *de moderata
misericordia* are known, partly because the writ was not invented
before the last years of Henry III's reign.[87] At least one early
reader of Bracton's treatise felt unable to accept that the remark
about wainage was true of all villeins. An *addicio* no later than
the early fourteenth century averred that the statement held
only for *servi* of the Ancient Demesne; as for other villeins

[82] This is established by a comparison of Magna Carta 1215, c. 20, with the 1217
reissue, c. 16 (= 1225, c. 14); royal villeins were excluded because the king like other
lords was not to be limited in what he could take from his villeins. See also above Chap.
3 and cf. Stat. Westminster I (1275), c. 6.

[83] *Novae Narrationes*, p. cci. Cf. *Feodarium Prioratus Dunelmensis* (Surtees soc., 1872),
p. 215, from 1229, cited A. L. Poole, *Domesday Book to Magna Carta* (2nd ed., Oxford,
1955), p. 476 n. 2.

[84] On which cf. Milsom, loc. cit., but the procedure is more complicated than he
realized. The first of the two writs is addressed to the lord or his bailiff and is a
prohibition; cf. *Selden Registers*, CC 99a, *Fleta*, ii. 66 (147–8), *Reg. Omn. Brev.*, f. 86v. The
second was to the sheriff and seems to have changed its form at the end of the thirteenth
century. The earlier form recites the prohibition and amercement; *Selden Registers*, CC
99a, *Fleta*, ii. 66. The later form is a writ of summons (not attachment), calling the lord
or bailiffs before the Bench; *Selden Registers*, R 243, *Reg. Omn. Brev.*, f. 87r.

[85] Most writs say 'salvo contenemento suo et villanus salvo waynagio suo' but the
form in the Berne MS (*c*.1272) is 'salvo contenemento suo et villanis villenagio suo'.
This suggests that the much controverted 'wainage' was sometimes understood as
denoting the villein holdings at this period (cf. *Mirror of Justices*, pp. 79–80), though, as
Dr Ian Kershaw reminded me, the connotation in manorial accounts is more often
what the holdings produced, i.e. crops and arable output.

[86] Cf. Vinogradoff, *Villainage*, p. 75. Dr Paul Brand brought another example to my
attention, KB 26/164, m. 12d (Norfolk 1260), where reference was made to an agreement by which a tenant in dower bound herself not to amerce the tenants except by
judgement of their neighbours and according to Magna Carta principles.

[87] The earliest example comes from the Luffield Register whose material dates
mostly from the 1260s. *Selden Registers*, pp. xliv ff., CC 99, 99a. Dr John Maddicott has
pointed out to me that *Cl. R. 1251–2*, p. 491, and *1253–4*, p. 139, probably mark the
origin of the writ.

'whenever the lord pleases, he can take away from his villein his wainage and all his goods'.[88]

So much, then, for the villein's wainage, which does not modify the previous verdict that villeins had remarkably few rights of action at common law. It is likely, therefore, that they could make valid—that is, legally enforceable—agreements with anybody? Bracton was inclined to think they could—even with their own lords.[89] The plea rolls lend little enough support to this view, but one must be clear what they can prove. Agreements were far more rarely framed with the courts' enforcement and interpretation in mind during the Middle Ages than now. Moreover, the common law was prepared to deal with a minority of *convenciones* only. Most agreements were made and adjudicated elsewhere,[90] and villeins probably made all kinds of agreement outside the royal courts more or less like others of their class. Examples abound in archives and cartularies,[91] including a number between villeins and their lords.

Royal justices were certainly aware of this. Some of the final concords by which naifty cases were ended resembled continuing agreements of this kind.[92] An assize utrum between Master John de Reigate and Geoffrey de Rishenden went even further. It emerged from the jurors' verdict that Geoffrey held of the fee of Master John's church, but was a villein of Earl William de Warenne's and held from him in villeinage. After Geoffrey admitted this, the parties concorded on terms by which Geoffrey paid two marks to hold the land for life for the same rent as before but recognized it as the church's frankalmoign. Earl William was, however, to be consulted before the concord was

---

[88] *Br.*, f. 6 (Vulgate ed. only). Cf. *Bracton and Azo*, p. 67, Woodbine, *Br.*, i. 372, and Vinogradoff, 'The Text of Bracton', *LQR* i (1885), 197–9 = *Collected Papers*, ed. H. A. L. Fisher, i. 87–9.

[89] *P&M*, i. 418–19; Vinogradoff, *Villainage*, pp. 70–4, is more positive.

[90] Cf. Milsom, *Historical Foundations of the Common Law*, pp. 211–15; A. W. B. Simpson, *A History of the Common Law of Contract* (Oxford, 1975), Part I.

[91] *P&M*, i. 418 and n. 6, gives some references. Cf. *The Hylle Cartulary*, ed. R. W. Dunning (SRS lxviii 1968), no. 60 (1402): 'And although R. W. is a *nativus* this agreement lacks nothing but is good.'

[92] Many such concords, of course, merely recorded the victory of one of the parties over the other, but in JI 1/909, m. 10 (Sussex eyre 1248), Gilbert de Cumpton recognized that he was a villein 'ita tamen quod libere possit ire et redire, et sibi perquirere ubicunque voluerit dum tamen reddeat eidem T. [domino] tota vita sua vi d. per annum'.

finalized.[93] He is unlikely to have been pleased. Wise lords tried to prevent their villeins' participation in final concords before royal justices, since this solemn act—even more than to receive a hearing in their own cause—might be construed as proof of their freedom. Thus, when Richard son of Godfrey sued Hervey de Cruce, William de Colville's seneschal intervened before the suit could be compromised to claim Godfrey as his master's villein who 'non potest cirographum facere in curia domini regis', and apparently began naifty proceedings against both men.[94]

That the royal courts would enforce a villein's agreement was thus rather a remote possibility, but the argument of the *De legibus* is characteristically ingenious. The author seems to have hoped to incorporate into the common law something of the villein's capacity in the outside world to make valid agreements. If a lord can manumit his villein for all purposes, he declared, then he can also manumit him for a single specific purpose. He probably had in mind agreements about land (especially leases), despite his knowledge that the common law was prepared to exercise very limited jurisdiction over such matters. If a lord broke an agreement of this kind, his villein could sue in covenant, according to the *De legibus*,[95] and answer an exception of villein status by pointing to the deed, when the lord's *ius* in the land will not avail him since 'volenti non fit iniuria'. The lord, by making the *convencio*, tacitly renounced his right to use the exception of villeinage in actions concerning it. He cannot even plead his ignorance of the villein's status at the time when the agreement was made, for one ought to know the status of one's covenantee.[96] The argument's premise is that tenants by *convencio* owe certain, that is fixed, services, and therefore approximate to

---

[93] *CRR* xi. 1775, 2889 (Essex 1224).

[94] *CRR* ii. 238; cf. *CRR* ii. 133, 139, 142; iii. 32, 39 (Cambs. 1202–3). William later recognised in open court that both men were free. He must have had good warning of their intentions since the suit seems to have been initiated by writ of right. Both M. M. Postan, *Carte Nativorum*, p. xlii n. 4, and Richardson and Sayles, *Law and Leg.*, p. 141 n. 1, cite this case and also *CRR* iii. 29, 260—but fail to point out that the court's uncertainty about status refers not to the fine's principals but to tenants who would have to acknowledge their services on the day. On this see above Chap. 2.

[95] Neither a villein (above) nor a lessee (Sutherland, *Assize of Novel Disseisin*, pp. 13, 32–3, 135) could recover his holding with an assize, though the *De legibus* did of course allow the assize to a *statuliber*, above Chap. 8 (ii).

[96] *Br.*, ff. 24b, 208; cf. f. 194b.

the privileged villeins of the Ancient Demesne.[97] Cases already discussed confirm that the author probably saw himself as extending rules already in use of the Ancient Demesne.[98]

Most of the evidence tells against adoption of this Bractonian line as doctrine during the period surveyed. Villeins could, however, probably make perfectly valid agreements with strangers, but neither party had any legal protection against the villein's lord. Thus one plea-roll entry records that fifteen men of John de Bovill held a certain meadow in common, as had their predecessors, for a rent agreed with the owner, William de Avranches. The enrollment recorded that thirteen of the men were John's villeins in order to protect his rights.[99] Two covenant actions confirm the impression of ultimate control remaining with the villeins' lord. The earlier was concorded on terms by which the plaintiff confessed to being a villein and his lord then renounced the disputed land to the defendant.[100] In the other, the plaintiffs alleged that they had been ejected from land held on a lease. The defendant acknowledged the covenant but denied ejecting the plaintiffs whom she declared to be villeins ousted by someone else for whom she could not answer.[101] Very probably, both of these cases arose from similar situations where villeins who had leased land from strangers were ejected by their own lords come to take the property in hand. They had, of course, no legal remedy.

Villein agreements with strangers were, then, liable to be disturbed by the intervention of the villein's lord. Clearly, to enter into agreements with villeins was unsafe in practice. What possible legal rights could their parties enjoy? But royal justices did exceptionally enforce agreements of this kind. Consider first the position of the free partner. Britton had stressed that valid obligations required a unity of will and consent, and denied that a villein partner could supply his share. Thus, in his opinion, if sued in debt, the villein defendant could plead that the deed ought not to harm him: he was a villein when he made it, so

[97] Cf. *P&M*, i. 405, for the 'conventioners' of the Ancient Demesne and below, Chap. 11, for the use of the uncertainty criterion in assessing sets of services.

[98] Above Chap. 6.

[99] *CRR* viii. 8 (no county given 1219).

[100] JI 1/775, m. 8d (Hants eyre 1235–6). The plaintiff's lord appears to have stood surety for the defendant's concord payment.

[101] JI 1/696, m. 22 (Oxford eyre 1241).

whatever he had belonged to his lord. The plaintiff had to refute these facts or fail.[102] The principle behind Britton's view,[103] that a free partner's action can be barred by the villein's confession of his status, holds for most land cases.

To bar the suit, villein defendants often pleaded both villein status and villeinage tenure of the land sought. The plaintiff took nothing and was amerced, but might go on to sue the villein's lord by another writ.[104] The plea of status alone in bar was naturally much rarer. Properly advised litigants preferred, if they could, to admit villeinage tenure alone, for confessions of villein status made in the king's courts could never afterwards be denied there.[105] Nevertheless, pleas in bar of villeinage tenure and status together are common and a few litigants simply confessed their villein status.[106] Most of these were genuine villeins, who made their acknowledgements under pressure from their lords, but a fraudulent confession of villeinage could be a useful device to defeat legitimate claims. Anyone who knew what he was doing would not voluntarily foreclose his chance of future liberty except for a very good price. Better to fight the case, for success was always possible and might later be pleaded as persuasive evidence of freedom, even if the court had never directly considered the question of status. Nevertheless, tenants sometimes did shelter behind their lords in this way.[107] Cases from Martin of Pateshull's eyres show the danger of the device which did not always succeed. At the very end of the century the jurors of Wakefield manor court told of a case in which a litigant at one of Martin of Pateshull's York eyres had conspired with his lord, Earl William de Warenne, to defeat the claim of the rightful heir to a

---

[102] *Britton*, I. xxix. 6, 25 (i. 158–9, 168–9).

[103] No such debt cases, however, have been found on the plea rolls.

[104] The plea-roll entry often reminded the defeated plaintiff of his rights, e.g. JI 1/229, m. 12 (Essex eyre 1227).

[105] *Br.*, ff. 277b, 421, citing *CRR* viii. 92 (= *BNB* 1411), 98, 265, 361 (Dorset 1220). Cf. also *RCR* i. 153 (Hertford eyre 1199), *CRR* viii. 321 (Bucks. 1221). For discussion see Chap. 10.

[106] e.g. *CRR* i. 145, 194 (Middlesex 1200), JI 1/732, m. 5 (Salop eyre 1203), JI 1/1172, m. 4d (Salop eyre 1226), *SS* liii. 257 (Lincoln eyre 1219), JI 1/775, m. 11d. (Hants eyre 1235–6).

[107] Cf. Vinogradoff, *Villainage*, pp. 68–9, *P&M*, i. 420–1.

holding by a false confession that he was the earl's villein.[108]
Did this happen often? The question is unanswerable from the
plea rolls, and other evidence is hard to find. That great judge
Martin of Pateshull may have felt that it happened a little too
often. Four cases from his last eyre circuit to East Anglia show
that the strategem did not always work. These are especially
interesting because they display judicial reasoning very similar
to the views expressed in the treatise *De legibus*. In two Suffolk
novel disseisins, the defendants asserted that they were villeins
of St. Edmund's Abbey; yet the actions were allowed to continue until juries had confirmed the story.[109] Not surprisingly,
the other case was copied into *Bracton's NoteBook* for its clear and
inescapable message. John del Frid brought an assize mort
d'ancestor for his father's old holding against Richer Brunger
who confessed in court that he was Roger of St. Denis' villein.
John answered that this ought not to harm him since, whatever
Richer now said, he had enfeoffed John's father with the land in
question 'as a free man and without any protest from his lord'.
Not until the death of John's father had Richer taken the land
into his hand—as lord of the fee. The court forced Richer to
answer 'de facto suo' and the jury rejected both his new defence
and his attempt to claim villein status.[110] One can only hope
that Roger did not take advantage of Richer's failure to claim
him as his villein!

Thus generally strangers seem unable to enforce their agreements against villeins, perhaps, as Britton suggested, because
no agreement with a villein was valid at common law. If so, the
corollary, that villeins could not enforce agreements, ought to
be equally true. This is borne out by the cases—with one
exception. Apart from the two cases mentioned above,[111] no
examples of identifiable villeins suing in covenant are known.
Thus, how the justices would have treated an exception of
villeinage is uncertain. Nor is there any evidence of the use of

---

[108] *Court Rolls of the Manor of Wakefield*, ed. W. P. Baildon and J. Lister ii (*YAS* xxix),
p. 78 (1297). The case, which must have been at the 1218/19 or 1226 eyres, shows the
danger of the trick: the family then drifted into real villeinage.

[109] JI 1/819, ms. 17d, 28 (Suffolk eyre 1227). The roll specified that the second case,
at least, was decided by a *jurata*. All four villein plaintiffs were pardoned their amercements for poverty. Another assize on m. 28d was similar; above p. 133.

[110] *BNB* 1833 (Norfolk eyre 1227).

[111] JI 1/775, m. 8d (Hants eyre 1235–6), JI 1/698, m. 22 (Oxford eyre 1241).

other personal actions (such as debt or *ejectio firme*) which could have been tried by a frustrated villein. As for land actions, their vulnerability to exceptions of villeinage had already been fully demonstrated.[112] Yet one exceptional case does exist, again from Martin of Pateshull's East Anglian circuit, the one direct authority for the Bractonian position. This was an assize of novel disseisin which arose out of the grant by a Norfolk lord, Roger de Suffordia, of a messuage and two small parcels of land to William Scissor, the son of one of his villein tenants who had recently died. William Scissor had paid a mark for the grant by which he was to hold freely in return for 8*d.* rent a year and forinsec service. After Roger's death, William went to his widow and son and paid them five shillings to continue the arrangement, and, when Roger's son ejected him a little while later, successfully recovered the holding by assize. How could a villein's son who does not seem to have been made free succeed by assize against his lord? The annotator in *Bracton's NoteBook* explained that 'the villein's son recovers . . . land which his father held in villeinage, because the lord gave it to the villein's son by his charter even without manumission'.[113]

That all the Bractonian decisions come from Pateshull's last eyre is a fact of some significance to students of the *De legibus*. But whether the influence travelled from the author and his book, as seems more likely, or in the other direction, matters little here. There was no lasting effect on the main stream of English law. Though their status cannot have prevented villeins from dealing with their neighbours on the same everyday basis as everyone else, after Pateshull's death the common law never again felt the need to recognize or rule on the resulting agreements. Villeins did not participate in the *lex terre*. They were for most purposes outside the common law, not worthy of their law as an earlier age would have said. Nevertheless, they were entitled by legal theory to institute proceedings in royal courts for certain kinds of civil and criminal wrong. They had in the thirteenth century the legal capacity to sue even their own lords for sedition, homicide, and really serious physical maltreatment. Against strangers their rights of action may have

[112] Above Chap. 8(ii).
[113] *BNB* 1814 (Norfolk eyre 1227).

been slightly more extensive; at any rate the strangers had to establish their status to the court's satisfaction, a task which cannot always have been easy without the lord's co-operation. In land actions, on the other hand, villein status was virtually always an insuperable barrier to success, though again strangers cannot have found it easy to establish their opponent's unfreedom to the courts' satisfaction unless they could secure the lord's co-operation. Even where villeins were permitted to bring actions, they needed exceptional luck and perseverance to succeed in practice. On the other hand, villeins were only answerable in the royal courts for criminal offences, pleas of the crown. Of course, this in no way hampered lords who could justice their villeins as they wished, untrammelled by most of the requirements of the common law. And the almost total lack of legal capacity may have humiliated the aspiring few. But some may have welcomed on occasion the immunity their status gave them in the royal courts. In sum, rightlessness at common law was a condition with great drawbacks for the few prosperous peasant families who had a chance to rise in the world, and occasional advantages too. Only as regards the villein's lord was he rightless in any complete sense, and this was true of the common law only. Its full significance can be assessed only in the context of all possible methods of securing rights and property, in other court-rooms and in the world of family and social relations, of horse-dealing and violence.

(II) THE VILLEIN AS SUBJECT

Excluded from the common law, the villein had to rely mainly on public power to enforce any rights he might claim and to protect him against seignorial excess or strangers' violence. The interest of the State (to hazard an anachronism) was omnipresent but never strong. In the face of theories of chattel ownership, it insisted that the villein too was a royal subject. The thirteenth-century villein could not shelter behind his lord from royal obligations such as peacekeeping, taxation, and (up to a point) military service. The monarchy now reached directly to him in these important respects. Angevin governmental expedients had forced their inventors to conscript the contributions of social classes previously untouched except through the mediation of their lords.[114] Hence, the later twelfth century saw an ideological transition away from an early medieval conception of unfreedom as an overriding submission to lordly control that excluded the unfree from participation in public life.[115] The Angevins were confident that their *generalis cura subditorum*[116] extended over all classes, free or not; all inhabitants of their lands owed them fealty and its associated duties.[117] The present chapter, then, argues that the villein as subject was created out of the needs of Angevin government.

Royal taxation of villeins is first seen among the arrangements for the carucage of 1198. Normally before the 1160s, the resources of the unfree were not tapped directly. All earlier royal aids and gelds were taken from the free, who no doubt took compensatory aids or tallages of their own from dependent cultivators. Thirteenth-century levies on movable goods were, in contrast, applied to all who possessed the taxable minimum of wealth, whatever their legal status.[118] This may have been intended even earlier than 1198.[119] Villeins, whose payments were perhaps not greater than before, were now more directly exposed to extortion from their neighbours or the new royal officials.[120] But the distinctions of status did not entirely disappear. The penalty for concealment of taxable goods, for

---

[114] This phenomenon is familiar at a higher social level. See, for example, A. B. White, *Self Government by the King's Command*, (Minneapolis, 1933) and N. Denholm-Young, 'Feudal Society in the Thirteenth Century: the Knights', *History* n.s. xxix (1944), 107–19, reprinted in *Collected Papers of N. Denholm-Young* (Cardiff, 1969), pp. 83–94.

[115] Below, Chap. 13, for full discussion of this point.

[116] The phrase is from *Dialogus*, II. x (101). Royal control over the villein's life and members is very much to the point, see above.

[117] The Assize of Northampton 1176, c. 6, called for fealty from all 'etiam rusticis' (Stubbs, *Charters*, p. 80). See also Howden, *Gesta Henrici Secundi*, ed. W. Stubbs (R.S. 1867), ii. 4 (1170). The exaction of general oaths was of course very ancient (cf. J. Campbell, 'Observations on English Government from the Tenth to the Twelfth Century', *TRHS* 5th s. xxv (1975), 46–7, but had been restricted to freemen. See below for the connection with defence.

[118] J. Willard, *Parliamentary Taxation on Personal Property 1290 to 1334* (Cambridge, Mass., 1934), pp. 164–7. See also J. R. Maddicott, *The English Peasantry and the Demands of the Crown, 1294–1341* (Past and Present Supplement, i 1975), an excellent pioneering study; pp. 6–15 deal with taxes on movables. Also Stubbs, *Charters*, pp. 351–3, 356, 358, and *Cl. R., 1231–4*, pp. 155–6; *1234–7*, pp. 543–5, for the royal writs etc.

[119] Cf. Stubbs, *Charters*, pp. 189, 249, and below pp. 157 ff. for the Assize of Arms.

[120] Maddicott, *The English Peasantry and the Demands of the Crown*, but note that he implies that the peasants' burden was comparatively light before the war pressures of the 1290s.

example, accepted the lord's claim to at least a share of his villein's substance.[121] But if the villein as subject looks to modern eyes incompatible with the villein as chattel, contemporaries remained unruffled. Royal advisers did not even bother to give the same justifications for successive levies. Thus *villani* number among those said to have 'granted' the fortieth of 1232, but the 1237 thirtieth was conferred by the various free classes 'pro se et villanis suis'.[122] Sometimes a lord petitioned against what he considered to be double taxation[123] or for the right to supervise the assessment and collection over his own villeins. Occasionally, then, 'an older idea of responsibility was followed'.[124] These exceptions show only that money, not theory, was the crux. Villeins paid at least their share, and had to take their turn as sub-taxors etc. too.[125]

The barriers broke down more quickly in taxation than elsewhere. Villeins, sworn to carry out taxation duties on one occasion, at another found themselves excluded from other comparable public tasks. Jury service is of particular interest, and quite well documented. The basic rule is clear and stable: villeins were ineligible to serve as jurors in royal courts.[126] Some of the very earliest cases saw the dismissal of jurors found to be unfree and the amercement of those responsible for empanelling them.[127] Villeins were officially 'useless' as jurors.[128]

---

[121] Stubbs, *Charters*, p. 250.

[122] Ibid. 356, 358. The writ for the 1235 scutage did not mention villeins at all, ibid. 357.

[123] e.g. *Chertsey Abbey Charters*, II. 1 (Sussex rec. soc. xii 1958), no. 1244 (17 Edward I).

[124] Willard, loc. cit.

[125] Stubbs, *Charters*, p. 250. *A Lincolnshire Assize Roll for 1298*, ed. W. S. Thomson (*LRS* xxxvi 1944), pp. xlvi, 163, 250, furnishes one certain example of a villein sub-taxor; the editor estimated that poor freemen were more common in the area than villeins, pp. cii–ciii, cix–cx.

[126] In France the serfs' incapacity was not confined to royal courts. P. Petot, 'Serfs d'eglise habilités á témoigner en justice', *Cahiers de civilisation mediévale* iii (1960), 191–4, attributes their exclusion to ancient perceptions of their moral inferiority and suggests that by the thirteenth century this was being rationalized in terms of the serfs' lack of independence. Only royal serfs were exempt from the ban, but the Capetians would occasionally grant out a similar privilege in an exercise of prerogative for the benefit of some church.

[127] *RCR* i. 306, 312 (Kent 1199), *RCR* i. 35 (Northants 1194), *PRS* xiv. 38 (Beds. 1194), *LRS* xxii. 166 (Lincoln eyre 1202), *CRR* iii. 276 (Rutland eyre 1205), *CRR* vii. 26 (Devon 1213), ibid. 288 (Norfolk 1214). Cf. also *P. Roll 31 Henry II*, pp. 161, 221 (Devon, Middlesex 1184–5), and *A Lincs. Assize Roll for 1298*, p. 74, no. 323, for a villein who had to bribe his hundred bailiff 'ut non poneretur in assisis nec iuratis'.

[128] *CRR* xii. 1465 (Norfolk 1225), xiv. 2349 = *BNB* 883 (Norfolk 1232).

Therefore, a plea of having served as a juror might be expected to have been a common answer to villeinage accusations. In fact, only one clear example has been noticed. Bela, a widow, was seeking her dower by her former husband Simon son of Achard. The tenant answered that Simon had been a villein and had held the land in question in villeinage. He had been free, Bela replied, and had held freely 'et ut liber homo fuit in recognicionibus et assisis coram justiciariis'. Once, indeed, he had been convicted of making a false oath and had to redeem himself. Her opponents compromised the action, although Simon's name does not appear among the jurors on extant records.[129] To Bela, service in the royal courts implied freedom. A dissenting Berkshire juror only a few years later took a similar view. Ten of his fellows accepted the legitimacy of the array of villein services the Abbot of Abingdon claimed from his men of Winkfield. He demurred, saying that he had never seen such customs done, but had seen Winkfield men swearing on assizes before the justices and therefore considered them free.[130] Villeins were not the only people useless for jury service; poverty was equally a bar.[131] Villeins and the very poor might be easily corruptible. William clerk, for instance, who sought special legal protection as a villein sokeman, naturally objected against those of his jurors who were what he claimed not to be, customary tenants at the will of his adversaries and lords, the monks of Fontrevault.[132] In a later case, a hundred sergeant related to one of the parties had empanelled ten useless villeins on the jury, presumably to help his kinsmen.[133] Susceptibility to influence was then the layman's explanation. The lawyers, prompted by the *ordines judiciarii*, eschewed such rationalization. Legal status debarred the unfree from testifying. Glanvill explicitly adopted the canonical rules for the admission of *testes* and applied them to juries. For him servile status was one disability out of a mixed bag that included age, sex, enmity, and

---

[129] *SS* liii. 802 (Lincoln eyre 1219). Bela may have confused royal and other juries, perhaps on purpose.
[130] *CRR* xii. 1031 (Berks. 1225); cf. JI 1/36, m. 3, for earlier stages at the eyre.
[131] *P&M*, i. 621 n. 5; cf. W. A. Morris, *The Early English County Court* (Berkeley, Calif., 1926), p. 108.
[132] *PRS* xiv. 38 (Beds. 1194).
[133] *CRR* xii. 1456 (Norfolk 1225).

infamia.[134] The *De legibus* characteristically followed its own system to distinguish the *statuservus*, removable on the simple word of an objector, from the *statuliber* whose removal required the oaths of free and lawful men.[135] The simpler procedure was probably the more normal[136] but voucher of lawful men as allowed in one early case.[137]

Nevertheless, villeins frequently served on juries outside the common-law courts. They regularly participated on manorial court juries in cases that did not involve influential freemen. Nor was their exclusion from royal juries total. They may have served in the county court[138] and probably in juries of presentment before eyre justices.[139] According to Fleta, they also served on coroners' juries, on the assizes of bread, ale, weights and measures, etc., and, provided they possessed seals,[140] on the special juries into coroners' own misdeeds.[141] Indeed, many of these juries could not have performed their functions without villein assistance.

Mere mistrust does not explain the ban on villein jury service in royal courts. The villein's status excluded him from sitting on civil juries just as it denied him the standing of a civil litigant. Exclusion from juries was part and parcel of the general denial

---

[134] *Glanvill*, ii. 12. He did not bother to list the canonical rules. His readers would have had to turn to such works as Peter of Blois, *Speculum Iuris Canonici* [Chartres, 1180], xxxiv (ed. Reimar, p. 65), or Ricardus Anglicus, *Ordo Judiciarius* [probably by Richard de Morins, later prior of Dunstable, but written at Bologna, *c*. 1196], ed. C. Witte (Halle 1853), pp. 25–9); *Dictionnaire de droit canonique*, vii. 1174. In the next century, Hostiensis, *Summa Aurea* II, tit. de testibus, no. 2 (ed. Venice 1574), explains the exclusion of *servi* as due to their frequent suppression of the truth for fear of their lords.

[135] *Br.*, ff. 185, 190b, 197.

[136] Cf. Sutherland, *The Assize of Novel Disseisin*, p. 70 n. 1. In *RCR* i. 35 (1194) the unrefuted confession of one juror was enough to adjourn the assize. Ricardus Anglicus, loc. cit., held that testimony from one alleged to be servile but who claimed to be free was acceptable pending further argument later.

[137] *PRS* xiv. 38. *RCR* i. 306, 312 (1199), may be another example.

[138] Dr Paul Brand suggests, mainly from thirteenth-century evidence, that the right to put freemen to their oath as jurors was a royal monopoly in the twelfth century; cf. *Glanvill* xii. 25. The rule would be akin to that by which no freeman had to answer for his free tenement without a writ. If so, juries in the county court would be rare; cf. L. E. M. Walker, 'Some Aspects of Local Jurisdiction in the Twelfth and Thirteenth Centuries . . .' (unpublished London Univ. MA thesis, 1957), pp. 255–64.

[139] *P&M* i. 421; Morris, *Early English County Court*, pp. 100–1. Certainty about jurors' status is unattainable. Morris used a rule of thumb that equated the poor with the unfree, which itself suggests that status was not so important.

[140] See the end of Chap. 5 above.

[141] *Fleta*, i. 18(20), ii. 12(74); cf. *Statutes of the Realm*, i. 21.

of the villein's right to sue and make proof at common law, to participate in the *lex terre*.[142] The assertion of the *De legibus*, that the lord's production of his villein in court as a villein 'ad disrationationem vel legem aliquam faciendam vel purgationem' enfranchised him, summarized the author's opinion of the law. The villein was incapable of making any kind of proof as 'a free man',[143] which is how witnesses produced in royal courts were customarily described. They were sometimes challenged as villeins, in much the same manner as jurors. In one disseisin plaint, the alleged unfree condition of suit was put to an inquest.[144] The only case noted in which a villein was refused permission to wage his law explicitly because of his status was a plea of debt in the anomalous county court of Chester.[145] Of the other forms of proof, the only one to require separate treatment is the ordeal, retained by the common law until 1219 for determination of criminal indictments. Villeins continued to face it at least as frequently as freemen. Glanvill declared that the form of the ordeal ought to depend on the accused's status: water for villeins, the hot iron for freemen. Of course, his formula, suspiciously neat, cannot be verified from the available evidence,[146] because the ordeal, rejected by almost all respectable thinkers, was declining. At the turn of the twelfth and thirteenth centuries, there were, however, still many in government and law schools prepared to retain its vulgar proof for use *ad terrorem* on the poor and unfree.[147] Distinctions between

---

[142] This accords with Petot's view on parallel developments in France. The influence of the learned laws no doubt played a part on both sides of the Channel.

[143] *Br.*, f. 194, following *Glanvill* v. 5; some Bracton MSS have the variant reading 'disrationandum'. Cf. also *Br.*, f. 156.

[144] *PRS* xiv. 48 (Essex 1194); cf. also ibid. 40 (Beds. 1194).

[145] *Cal. of County Court, City Court and Eyre Rolls of Chester, 1259–97*, ed. R. Stewart-Brown (Chetham soc., 1926), p. 18, no. 119 (1260).

[146] *Glanvill*, xiv. 1, purports to treat treason procedure but is generally accepted as authority for presentments under the Assize of Clarendon too. Uncertainty surrounds the details of criminal procedure during this period. Cf. *Dialogus*, II. vii (87); the editors of the 1902 edition, p. 217, disagree with J. B. Thayer, *A Preliminary Treatise on Evidence* (London, 1898), pp. 36 ff., even on the relative frequency of the two forms of ordeal, though the 1166 assize had specified the cold water.

[147] See J. Gaudemet, 'Les Ordalies au moyen âge; doctrine, legislation et pratique canoniques', *Recueils soc. Jean Bodin* xvii (1965), 126, and R. C. Van Caenegem. 'La Preuve au moyen âge: rapport de synthèse' ibid. 740–1, for references, and now my own paper in *On the Laws and Customs of England: Essays in Honor of Samuel E. Thorne*, ed. T. A. Green *et al.* (Univ. of North Carolina Press, 1980).

forms of proof on the grounds of status were therefore common and shifting.

In taxation and the making of legal proof, then, equality with freemen was confined, incomplete, and seemingly advantageous to anyone but the villein himself. Similarly, the achievement of some kind of parity with freemen in the bearing of arms exposed villeins to burdens. Earlier attitudes towards the arming of the unfree, which amounted to a kind of disability, were now abandoned. The grant of symbolic arms may have been a familiar part of manumission ritual,[148] for the old ideas of freedom in its fullest sense viewed the freemen as fyrd-worthy and obliged to defend the realm.[149] As knightly prestige increased, to dub men of servile background became more unthinkable, but twelfth-century practice was not clear-cut.[150] In Glanvill's view, the dubbing of a villein made him a knight alright, with a substantially higher status, but did not entitle him to make proof in a royal court as a freeman.[151] Good enough to fight and die for king and country, he was not yet good enough to swear for them.

Meanwhile in 1181, Henry II had associated the two tasks of defence and oath-swearing in his Assize of Arms, by which all freemen were to be sworn to arms.[152] The unfree were specifically excluded,[153] and in 1198 the claim to have been sworn to arms was raised by an alleged villein in defence to an action

---

[148] A. L. Poole, *Obligations of Society in the XII and XIII Centuries*, p. 33, and Richardson and Sayles, *Law and Leg.*, p. 138. The existence of prosaically worded charters does not preclude the use of ceremonial as well.

[149] See the material cited by Richardson and Sayles, *Law and Leg.*, pp. 100–1, 138, 148 n. 5, which seems to contradict their refusal to accept the existence of such an obligation before 1176 (or 1181); and cf. J. Scammell, 'Freedom and Marriage in Medieval England', *Ec. H. R.*, 2nd s. xxvii (1974), 527–8.

[150] *Red Book of the Exchequer* ii, ed. H. Hall (R.S. 1869), p. cclxxix, is not to the point, despite the mistranslation in *English Historical Documents*, ii. 447; I am grateful to Mr J. O. Prestwich who saved me from error here.

[151] *Glanvill*, v. 5.

[152] The traditional date is convincingly defended by J. C. Holt, 'The Assizes of Henry II: the Texts', in *The Study of Medieval Records*, ed. D. A. Bullough and R. L. Storey (Oxford, 1971), pp. 90–1.

[153] Stubbs, *Charters*, pp. 183–4. It is not quite impossible that the provisions were intended to apply to *all* with more than 10 marks p.a.; cf. c. 11, and the fictional air of the final oath which is severable from the rest of the document. The whole emphasis is on money, not status. But cc. 2–3 are telling evidence the other way, and the closely related *Leges Edwardi Confessoris*, c. 32A.9 et seq. (*Gesetze*, i. 656), of the early thirteenth century begins 'debent autem' universi liberi homines totius regni'.

of naifty.[154] Yet in 1225 the royal writ for the collection of a tax on movables envisaged the possibility that some villeins were sworn to arms,[155] and reissues of the Assize from 1230 onwards administered it on freemen and villeins alike in terms of wealth alone.[156] If any single express decision brought the villein into the assize, it was made in 1205 when fear of invasion led John to link military obligations directly with the taking of a general oath of fealty.[157] Since no text of that year's assize has survived, the possibility of a more gradual development should not be excluded. Sheriffs under pressure from the government or mindful of their own profit perhaps infiltrated villeins into the assize, gradually and at first illegally. The king's men then turned the innovation to their master's profit. Something like this probably happened in the earldom of Chester at least,[158] and if the process was more or less general the continued uncertainty into the 1220s would be comprehensible.

Returning from the siege of Bedford in 1224, one Adam le Kenteis was captured by his lord, Walter of Woughton, with whom he had been conducting a prolonged dispute over his villeinage. Adam's efforts to free himself produced an action at Westminster in the Michaelmas term of that year, when the local sheriff had to clear himself of Walter's allegation that he had wrongfully freed the allegedly villein Adam from prison.[159] Three years later at the eyre, Adam brought an appeal against Walter on the ground, among others, that he had robbed him of a lance and helmet to which he had been sworn under the assize of arms.[160] Walter's initial exception, that Adam was his villein, was ultimately abandoned, whether for legal or factual defects the plea-roll entry does not explain. On the other hand, Adam never tried the obvious argument that he must be free since he

---

[154] *CRR* i. 45, 67 (Northants 1198).

[155] Stubbs, *Charters*, p. 352.

[156] *Cl. R. 1227–1231*, pp. 395 ff., 398; Statute of Winchester 1285, c. 6=Stubbs, *Charters*, p. 466: 'chescun home'. Cf. *Fleta*, i. 24 (36).

[157] This is the argument of Richardson and Sayles, *Law and Leg.*, pp. 136–8, who consider the 1230 assize a mere 'reissue' of the lost document of 1205. See also M. R. Powicke, *Military Obligation in Medieval England* (Oxford, 1962), pp. 58–60, and note that 1205 is the first occasion since Domesday Book when penalties for default of military obligation are known to have been taken, an index of the goverment's fears.

[158] 'Magna Carta of Cheshire' (1215/16), c. 4, ed. J. Tait, *Cartulary of Chester Abbey* (Chetham soc. lxxix 1920), pp. 101 ff.

[159] *CRR* xi. 2141 (Bucks. 1224).

[160] JI 1/54, ms. 12, 18 = *BRB* vi. 444, 658 (Buckingham eyre 1227).

was sworn to arms as a freeman. Both parties lied during the trial,[161] but Adam may well have been both a villein and sworn to arms in 1224.

That there were villeins at the seige of Bedford is likely enough. In order to defeat Faulkes de Breauté the bishops had made a special grant of men, money, and siege machines. Those sent from episcopal demesnes to pull the machines, at least, will have included villeins among their number.[162] Service with armies was very much wider in scope than would appear from the assize of arms or speculation about knighthood. Peasants— villeins included—participated in military affairs throughout the twelfth and thirteenth centuries, but in dishonourable and exposed positions.[163] Ultimately, peasants bore most of the burdens of state anyway, whatever the theory. Faced by emergencies, kings lost interest in legal niceties. In 1213, for instance, John summoned to his aid as wide a selection of men as possible. Two chroniclers thought that there were villeins among those who responded.[164]

There is good reason, therefore, not to exaggerate the importance of the early thirteenth-century changes in military recruitment. Even in 1181, the whole weight was on financial resources, and a century later many villeins must still have been too poor to come within its scope.[165] Throughout the period under consideration here, the villeins' military role was dishonourable and subordinate, and the legal writers maintained the incompatibility of villeinage and knighthood right to the end.[166]

---

[161] The jurors found no robbery, as alleged by Adam. Walter's account of the happenings before the Bench in 1224 was probably false, for he later renounced it.

[162] *Pat. Rolls, 1216–1225*, pp. 464–5 = *Registrum Antiquissimum* i (*LRS* xxvii 1931), no. 222.

[163] See for an earlier period, E. John, *Orbis Brittanniæ* (Leicester, 1966), pp. 136–9. The ninth-century Carolingian enactments about military service, from which the Angevin assize of arms is in a general way descended, sometimes reached beyond freemen to demand assistance from the unfree.

[164] Matthew Paris, *Chronica Majora*, ed. H. R. Luard (R.S. 1872–4), ii. 538–9, calls them 'homines diversae conditionis' but William of Newburgh's continuator said that some were *rustici*, *Chronicles of Stephen, Henry II and Richard I*, ed. R. Howlett (R.S. 1885–90), ii. 514. Villeins may also have been called up in the crisis of 1169, Powicke, *Military Obligation*, p. 50.

[165] This is the impression given by *Fleta*, i. 24 (36).

[166] *Fleta*, ii. 51 (111), *Britton*, I. xxxii. 8, 22 (i. 200, 208); cf. *Br.*, ff. 190b, 198b, and *P&M*, i. 429. England boasted no *ministeriales* (serf-knights?) in the period and English historians have never felt inclined to analyse sergeanty in such terms; but cf. Scammell, *Ec. H. R.* 2nd s, xxvii (1974), 528.

In 1300, then, if the villein could not hope for the unrealistic splendour of knighthood, he did have a public role that had been denied to the slave of the early Middle Ages. Even if his oath was still not as weighty as his betters', the king would willingly accept his money and his blood. The villein as subject had significantly higher pretensions than his predecessor of two centuries before had been permitted to have. Thirteenth-century government distributed its burdens on a means test and left legal unfreedom on the whole to the lords. How far such changes penetrated village life is not the question here. The more weighty fact is that the shift which occurred in the fifty years centering on 1200 was an absolute prerequisite for any theory, like Bracton's, which sought to make the villein free and equal in public but an unfree serf to his lord.

PART III

VILLEINAGE AND THE COMMON LAW

Part II has examined the villein's status and legal rights, both through the idiosyncratic eyes of the treatise *De legibus* and from the records of actual cases. Even at common law, the villein was not quite without rights. In his more usual village environment, he might indeed be relatively well protected from everyday oppression; but once common-law standards were invoked, the legal disablities of villeinage significantly affected his life. The manorial lord had to take an interest in the common-law standing of his peasant tenants. Proof of their servility sometimes had a direct money value for him. Little bothered by the lawyer's distinctions between tenure and status, practical men sought the most effective method of securing services due or demanded. Chapter 10 will demonstrate how the archaic action of naifty (the basic procedure for the determination of common-law status) diverted litigation from status into tenure which was, no doubt, the parties' main concern anyway. Chapter 11 briefly surveys the common-law doctrines of villeinage tenure. This broad theme of seignorial freedom to manœuvre implies another: the efforts of peasant groups to seek free status, or (more simply) emancipation from their more onerous obligations on their own initiative. Chapter 12 examines the fairness and preconceptions of the common-law system, when it treated questions of villeinage, and assesses the effect on peasant initiatives of the supposed bias towards liberty.

10

THE ACTION OF NAIFTY AND PROOF OF VILLEIN STATUS

Villeinage status frequently arose as an interlocutory issue in actions about property rights or other matters. A special procedure, the action of naifty, existed to determine disputes over common-law freedom. This action, endowed by its origins with certain slightly unusual characteristics, had important consequences on villeinage law.

Three writs were used.[1] The claimant lord normally began proceedings by acquiring a writ *de nativo habendo* (writ of naifty) which ordered the sheriff to deliver up to him someone whom he alleged to be his villein. The sheriff did not execute this command without a judicial hearing in the county court, during which a rival lord might put in a claim to the fugitive. If at any time during the hearing, or trial of title, however, the alleged villein claimed to be free, proceedings had at once to be ended. They could be restarted only by transfer to a royal court, effected by the acquisition of one of two other writs. The claimant might obtain a *pone de nativis*, a variant of the writ *pone*, the standard means of transferring cases to royal courts. Or the alleged villein himself could seek a writ *de libertate probanda*, which in the thirteenth century and afterwards was generally termed a *monstravit*, from its initial word.[2] The issue of status could then be tried and determined by the royal justices. Cases that proceeded all the way from purchase of the writ of naifty to final judgement were, however, a minority. To understand why, the writs themselves must be analysed.

The common-law writ of naifty resembles in form those writs

---

[1] If one excludes the Ancient Demesne, questions about villein status appear to have been raised by plaint seldom if at all. A. Harding, 'Plaints and Bills in the History of English Law, mainly in the period 1250–1330', in *Legal History Studies 1972*, ed. D. Jenkins (Aberystwyth, 1975), pp. 65–86, might have led one to expect otherwise.

[2] Which it shared with certain other writs. See my article on 'The Action of Naifty in the Early Common Law', *LQR* xc (1974), 327, 331. What follows is summarized in the main from this article, where full references can be found.

issued by twelfth-century kings to assist favoured beneficiaries in the recovery of fugitives asserted to have wrongly left the lordships. Executive and abrupt in tone, the twelfth-century writs often sought the runaways' physical return in the confident expectation that no court proceedings were required; the issue in resulting lawsuits was never status, but title to the fugitives, disputed perhaps by some rival lord who also desired to profit from their surplus product in the form of rents and services.[3] Such cases, treated by Glanvill, appear briefly on the early plea rolls but soon disappear in the thirteenth century. The writ brought the disputed villeins into court, where they might all too easily raise a claim to liberty, which, however absurd, had considerable nuisance value. Wiser lords now preferred to sue in trespass or, most often, by real actions for the land itself.[4] By the first decade of the thirteenth century, the writ of naifty was already used almost exclusively to initiate trials of status.[5] During the reign of Henry II, drafting changes transformed the writ. By the end of the twelfth century, its continued superficial resemblance to the older executive orders belied the fact that the writ *de nativo habendo* was now a common-law originating writ to initiate status suits in the royal courts.[6]

Contemporaries hardly noticed the change. Royal justices faced with villeinage decisions relied on their own social in-

[3] *Early Yorks. Charters*, vii. 171 (*c.* 1175/95), concords one such case 'de hominibus'. Similar French disputes over men remained a matter for private settlement well into the thirteenth century. G. Langmuir, ' "Judei nostri" and the beginning of Capetian Legislation', *Traditio* xvi (1960), 203–39, and especially in an unpublished paper, ' "Tamquam servi": the Change in Jewish Status in French Law about 1200', demonstrates clearly that non-retention agreements and competition for manpower extended far beyond those of definitely servile condition. Also *Beaumanoir* paras. 472 et seq.

[4] *LQR* xc, pp. 342–3. *SS* lxviii. 1187 (Shrewsbury eyre 1221) is a trespass plea for unjust detention of *homines*. There is no way to tell which land actions masked disputes about the ownership of villeins. Nor does it matter much. Land litigation was normally about the right to receive rents and services, not to cultivate the land personally. Title to villeins could still sometimes be the real issue in naifty actions; cf. JI 1/1046, ms. 25, 66d (York eyre 1251).

[5] For a sheriff to take literally the writ's command and hand over the fugitive without prior court proceedings, would now be an obvious abuse of power. In the 1270s, the sheriff of Oxfordshire took a writ of naifty 'sine cognicione alicuius placiti nativitatis' to Woodstock and persuaded the bailiff of the liberty to hand over to a claimant a man dwelling in North Leigh 'pretextu cuius mandati'. In KB 27/45, m. 7 (1279), the King's Bench condemned his act and awarded the man damages for trespass, in spite of an exception of villeinage from the claimant; see further below, p. 211.

[6] These changes are treated below, Chap. 13.

stincts and local custom. Men treated as unfree in their home villages and lordships were left to the justice of their lords, subject to minimal supervision. Yet these judgements of the royal courts in effect created new definitions of legal freedom, equated with the right to remedies under the nascent common law, that is entitlement to royal jurisdiction and protection.[7] The extent of the king's jurisdiction was his business or his justices'. It was far too important to be left to the sheriff and the county court. This fact, and not the rationalizing guesses of thirteenth-century writers,[8] explains why actions of naifty had to leave the county court, once liberty was claimed, and move to a royal court.[9] The choice of the writ of transfer now needed (the claimant's *pone de nativis* or the alleged villein's *monstravit*) was crucial and sometimes turned into a race. A note in some thirteenth-century registers of writs advised that priority (apparently a matter of prior delivery to the sheriff) was *perutile* to the successful party. The choice of venue and chances of a swift outcome were thereby determined. As soon as the sheriff received a writ of *monstravit* he had to grant royal peace and protection pending trial to the alleged villein. No longer could the claimant lord seize his tenant's person with impunity, or attempt to exact the customs and services at issue. Breach of royal protection was an offence, and he had to await trial, generally at the next eyre, perhaps several years off. A *monstravit* could indeed take the case to Westminster, or even in theory *coram rege* (though a proffer might be required), but most alleged villeins welcomed the respite behind a royal guarantee of peace, before submitting even a strong case to the uncertainties of the courts. The weaker the case, the stronger the premium on delay. Even when the evil day at last came, villeins knew they might yet default and postpone matters further, or perhaps take advantage of some technical defect to defeat the claimant's action.[10] To exclude all this expense and loss, the claimant had

[7] Below, Chap. 13.

[8] For which see *LQR* xc, 388–9 (add *Glanvill*, i. 3–4, to the references there cited), and below Chap. 12.

[9] The trial could be *coram rege*, before the Bench at Westminster, or locally before the eyre justices. Some writ forms etc. envisage other itinerant justices, commissioned to hear assizes etc., but I know of no case examples.

[10] JI 1/954, m. 6 (Warwick eyre 1263) is a good example. The alleged villein admitted under questioning that he had no proof of liberty but escaped without day when he pointed out that the writ of naifty did not mention the claimant's wife, through whom he derived his claims.

to purchase and deliver his *pone de nativis* first. Then the trial would be at his convenience; he could select its date.[11] Many villeinage disputes were effectively decided once the sheriff had taken delivery of a *pone* or *monstravit*.[12]

The claimant's difficulties are emphasized here, because naifty actions were generally begun on his initiative. Rightly or wrongly, he probably envisaged himself as acting in defence of ancestral rights against peasant reluctance to fulfil their liabilities. Sometimes this was fair enough; naifty disputes were not always between powerful lord and defenceless peasant. But many claimants had the advantage long before the case came to trial. Their greater power and influence permitted the speedier purchase of their writ and hampered opponents' countermeasures. In the early thirteenth century, a vigorous lord had a good chance of successfully raising his rent demands without any challenge in the royal courts. In response, independently minded peasants had to seek freedom or practical relief by departure to a freer holding, rent strike,[13] or—if they had the means—the purchase of a writ such as *ne vexes*.[14] The end result might be a declaration of legal freedom, for example, if the lord was stirred into an unsuccessful action of naifty, but this time the advantages of delay were with the lord.

Could a peasant tenant ever begin a naifty suit on his own initiative against his claimant lord? Professor van Caenegem has suggested that Glanvill at one point envisages an alleged villein's licit acquisition of a writ *de libertate probanda* without the prior existence of a writ of naifty.[15] Glanvill's words are obscure, and the few relevant cases hardly constitute the flood one might expect if the procedure had been available to alleged villeins around 1200. Nevertheless, lords probably did, in the late twelfth and early thirteenth centuries, have to face some naifty suits which they had not started. The alleged villein's writ given by Glanvill, which differs from the *monstravit* of all extant registers of writs, may be the missing link.[16] Glanvill's writ lacks the *monstravit's* explicit references to a naifty plea in progress at the shire court, but rather treats the alleged villein

[11] *LQR* xc, 336–8, 342–3.
[12] There were procedural advantages for the trial too; see Chap. 12.
[13] *LQR* xc, 340 n. 83, gives some examples.
[14] Below, Chap. 11.
[15] *Van Caenegem*, pp. 343–4, on *Glanvill*, v. 4 (ed. Hall, p. 56).
[16] Compare *Glanvill*, v. 2, with *Selden Registers*, Hib. 31, CA 18, CC 103–4.

as plaintiff, with the claimant a defendant to be summoned before the justices.[17] This writ, available perhaps into the second quarter of the thirteenth century, probably enabled naifty suits to be commenced against claimant lords. On the other hand, the *monstravit* (which may have existed in Glanvill's day too despite the author's silence) was always interlocutory, and after about 1230 was the only writ the alleged villein could get.[18] Thenceforth naifty actions could begin only when a claimant obtained a writ of naifty.[19]

So in the developed action of the thirteenth century, the claimant was likely to be the party who wished to hasten matters along. He next had to secure his opponent's body in court for trial and judgement. All medieval litigation offered almost endless opportunities for delay; yet the common law never willingly resorted to default judgements. The law tried to encourage or compel litigants to appear in court. The parties had to give security of some sort for their appearance on the day of the hearing: the plaintiff promised to pursue his claim, the defendant that he would make his answer in court. If the defendant defaulted, the plaintiff's only hope was that the sheriff could coerce him to come by mesne process.[20] A naifty claimant had to give two sureties when he purchased his writ of naifty and renew the security on adding a *pone*.[21] Similarly, an alleged villein gave sureties if he acquired a *monstravit*.[22] On default both the principal and his sureties were in mercy. The claimant's default ended the present suit, though he might hope to restart it with a new writ at a later date.[23] Default by the alleged villein, however, not only permanently foreclosed his right to offer proof of liberty, but also allowed the claimant to

[17] *LQR* xc, 327 n. 9, 328–30, 346, but note also the consequences of the alleged villein's default at the eyre, ibid. 345.
[18] The best course of action if you were wrongly treated as a villein was to sue by assize and await the lord's exception of villeinage, which he would have to prove. See *SS* liii. 1057 (Worcester eyre 1221) and the editor's comments.
[19] *LQR* xc, 334 n. 50, 336; just possibly a *monstravit* was interlocutory in some action other than naifty, such as trespass.
[20] D. W. Sutherland, 'Mesne Process in the Early Common Law', *LQR* lxxxii (1966), 482–96, is a recent survey.
[21] *LQR* xc, 340–1, 343.
[22] Ibid. 329, 345.
[23] Ibid. 346–7. This is the position from Glanvill's day into the thirteenth century. Britton perhaps thought that the alleged villein was enfranchised and this view was still being canvassed in the early fourteenth century.

offer his proof of title later at the county court, if necessary, and the sheriff would assist him to secure the villein's presence.[24] This mesne process, probably no more effective in naifty actions than in others, encouraged rather than satisfied seignorial hopes, thereby occasionally inciting recourse to violent self-help.[25]

Rather infrequently, the two parties to a naifty suit arrived together in court to argue their respective cases and make their proof. Fresh difficulties met them there. 'If the working of the action has puzzles for us,' a modern commentator has observed, 'its nature perplexed contemporaries.'[26] Was it real or personal? Should the claimant count in the right or in seisin? The conflicting views were still debated in Edward I's reign.[27] Earlier in the century, few cases were pleaded exclusively in either right or seisin. Before the 1240s at the earliest, the rules were less insistent. The action was probably felt to lie in the right. The *De legibus* and its followers, in their discussion of the permanence of status decisions, categorized naifty cases in the right,[28] and some cases support this view.[29]

In addition, various exceptions could be raised against villeinage claims. Two based on the wording of the writ of naifty are especially interesting. The first is a plea of residence on royal demesne or in a borough, borough privilege. A case from 1231 will serve as illustration. Robert Grub declared that he was a king's burgess in Grimsby, that he had lived there for twenty years without any claim by his opponent in the suit, the Abbot of Selby, and that he had there land, a house, and a wife. His

---

[24] Ibid. 345, 347–8.

[25] *Britton*, I. xxxii. 10 (i. 201–2) seems too favourable to the claimant and cannot be verified from cases; cf. *LQR* xc, 341.

[26] Milsom, *Novae Narrationes*, p. cxlvii.

[27] *Cas. Plac.*, pp. lxxxvii/36, 79/20; *YB 32 and 33 Edward I* (R.S.), pp. 430–5, 512–14 (1305, 1304). Cf. *YB 30 and 31 Edward I*, pp. 164–9 (Cornwall eyre 1302), *YB 32 and 33 Edward I*, pp. 202–5 (1306), which bear on the question of counts in seisin. *Britton*, I. xxxii. 15 (i. 204–5), says that the writ was about possession of chattels. This is doubtful; the context is his idiosyncratic view about the villein as 'purely' his lord's chattel, above, Chap. 1. On his own telling, claimants did count in the right. He warns that they may end up with the great inconvenience of battle or the grand assize, neither of which are known to have been used in naifty cases of this time.

[28] *Br.*, ff. 190b, 192–3, 197b–8, 199–201b, 289b–90; *Fleta*, iv. 11 (236–9), v. 22 (336–7); *Britton*, II. xviii. 2, 6–8 (i. 322–3), IV. x. 2–3, 5–6 (ii. 278, 280–2).

[29] *BNB* 1828 (Norfolk eyre 1227): claimant as a minor could not decide questions touching ownership of right; *NAS*, p. 159 (Northumberland eyre 1269): count seisin 'ut de feudo et iure'; JI 1/483, m. 57d (Lincoln eyre 1271–2): a complete (?) count on seisin of self and father 'ut de feudo et iure'.

monstravit succeeded and he went free, because the abbot failed to produce any kin against him and also because he lived in a royal borough.[30]

Since before Glanvill's day, the writ of naifty had contained a clause which restricted the sheriff's duty to hand over the fugitive to his claimant; he was to do so 'nisi sit in dominico nostro'.[31] This clause enabled the fugitive to except in the county court that his claimant ought not to have him since he had reached the royal demesne.[32] The sheriff probably then had to stay the plea.[33] The idea was not to assist runaways, but to reserve the king's right to profit from them if he could. But in 1238 a new line was adopted with the invention of a new writ, which ordered the sheriff to stay the plea in the county only if the alleged villein had been on the royal demesne for a year and a day, unchallenged by the lord.[34] No doubt the facts were ascertained from a jury of neighbours.[35]

From the beginning, the defence of residence on privileged soil was pleaded in a way that went beyond the strict wording of the writ formula. Boroughs were included,[36] despite the recent

---

[30] JI 1/1043, m. 22d (York eyre 1231); cf. M. Beresford and H. P. R. Finberg, *English Medieval Boroughs: a Handlist* (Newton Abbot, 1973), p. 137.

[31] *Van Caenegem*, no. 122 (1175/80), has 'in dominico meo'; *Glanvill*, xii. 11, and all later forms are as in the text.

[32] Assize of Clarendon, c. 10, suggests that the town was already a likely alternative to a mere change of lords.

[33] The working and effect of the defence at this time remains entirely obscure.

[34] The writ first appears on the Close Roll under the date 22 September 1238, *Cl. R.*, *1237–42*, p. 104, under the rubric 'De loquela nativi non remanenda'. This probably marks its introduction but Corpus Christi College, Cambridge MS 297, f. 90v, col. 1 (a register of writs from the Channel Islands written in 1300 but containing material from the 1230s), has what may be an earlier example. See *Selden Registers*, p. ci. There are no earlier references to the plea on the rolls; one would expect few, since cases would not normally reach the royal courts; cf. *BNB* 1228 (Hants, *coram rege* 1237–8) for one case. Later writs found in *Selden Registers*, CC 101, *Fleta*, ii. 51 (111), *Reg. Omn. Brev.*, f. 87, are identical with the 1238 exemplar but for the omission of one 'et'.

[35] This was probably not normally available in the county at this time; see above, Chap. 9 (ii), p. 155.

[36] *Glanvill*, v. 5, on which cf. J. Tait, *The Medieval English Borough* (Manchester, 1936), pp. 220, 225, and Hoyt, *Royal Demesne*, p. 187; 'Willelmi articuli Londoniis retracti', c. 16 (*Gesetze*, i. 491) of *c.* 1210 (but cf. Richardson and Sayles, *Law and Leg.*, pp. 120–1); 'Glanvill Revised', MS cit., p. 75.

definition of the royal demesne,[37] but royal boroughs only;[38] unchartered Wycombe conferred no protection.[39] The stay on the privileged land had to constitute residence for at least a year and a day,[40] openly (that is, without challenge by the lord) and in a manner acceptable to the burgesses.[41] The exact requirements are hard to define. Some years in Bedford, with land, house, and wife were enough for one escapee.[42] Another successfully pleaded Salisbury custom that a year and a day in the city 'without any challenge, and in the merchant gild as a burgess' freed him for ever.[43] This variation in the customary requirements necessitated local confirmation of the rule, as here. Landlords had every reason to move carefully; their negligence could permanently foreclose their rights, though not apparently convey full freedom to the former villein.[44]

Interestingly, the clause 'nisi sit in dominico nostro' was never redrafted to comprehend the range of pleas the courts

[37] See on this Hoyt, *Royal Demesne*, pp. 144–6, B. P. Wolffe, *The Royal Demesne in English History* (London, 1971), pp. 17–24, 30–2, and P. D. A. Harvey, 'The English Inflation of 1180–1220', *Past and Present* lxi (1973), 9–13.

[38] See the pleas about Bedford and Grimsby in *BHRS* iii. 54, 336 (Bedford eyre 1227), and JI 1/1043, m. 22d, respectively.

[39] Compare JI 1/62, m. 24d (Buckingham eyre 1232), and *BNB* 1167 (Bucks., *coram rege* 1235–6), whose later stages were *CRR* xv. 1344, 1434. Wycombe's charter dates only from 1558, though a fine of 1226, confirmed by Henry III in 1239, was thereafter treated as one, Beresford and Finberg, *English Medieval Boroughs*, p. 72.

[40] For this rule familiar all over Europe, see *Glanvill*, 'Glanvill Revised', loc. cit.; *Br.*, ff. 190b, 198b; *Fleta*, ii. 51, iv. 11 (111, 235); *Britton*, I. xxxii. 8, 24 (i. 200, 209). Express references became rarer, Ballard and Tait, *British Borough Charters, 1216–1307* (Cambridge, 1923), pp. 136–7; M. Weinbaum, *British Borough Charters 1307–1660* (Cambridge, 1943), pp. xxxi–lv. Hoyt, *Royal Demesne*, pp. 187–8, explains this as due to generalization of the rule between 1210 and 1238. Cf. also A. H. Thomas, *Calendar of Plea and Memoranda Rolls of the City of London, A.D. 1364–81* (Cambridge, 1929), pp. xxiv–xxvi, and 'Magna Carta of Cheshire', (1215/16), c. 13, ed. Tait, *Chetham soc.*, lxxix, 101–9.

[41] *Glanvill*, v. 5: 'quiete . . . ita quod in eorum communam scilicet gildam tanquam civis receptus fuerit', on which see Tait, *Medieval English Borough*, pp. 222–4. 'Glanvill Revised', loc. cit., adds 'sine aliqua rec' domino suo'.

[42] *BHRS* iii. 54, 336 (Bedford eyre 1227); cf. *CRR* xii. 513 (1226) for the burgesses' claims.

[43] *WRS* xxvi. 467 = JI 1/996, m. 20 (Wilts. eyre 1249).

[44] Though *Glanvill*, v. 5, talks of freeing him from villeinage, the freedom was only valid against the lord and his heirs. *Br.*, ff. 190b, 198b, 200b–201 (and cf. ff. 6b–7), describes the effect of the defence as creating life protection for the villein who, however, remains as a *statuliber* technically unfree. The two different views (on which see *P&M*, i. 427–9, and Vinogradoff, *Villainage*, pp. 86–8) come to the same thing here in practice. See also *Fleta*, ii. 51 (111), iv. 11 (235), and the complex *Britton*, I. xxxii. 8, 24 (i. 200, 209).

allowed to be based on it. Another clause also offered something to a good pleader. Writs of naifty always stipulated that the alleged flight had taken place since some recent event, such as Henry II's first coronation.[45] Two defences were thus made possible: that the alleged fugitive had never left the land at all, and that his flight had taken place earlier than the limitation period. Surprisingly, both pleas are rare, though many writs of naifty must have been served on men still occupying their customary holding.[46] At the 1257 Suffolk eyre, for example, William Cheling' answered William de Cyressy's writ of naifty with the confession that he was his villein but 'he had never fled from the land of William his lord'. William de Cyressy, who was experiencing difficulties with several tenants at the time,[47] had to concede this and was amerced for a false claim, but was awarded his villein with chattels and *sequela* all the same.[48] A few years before in 1238, Joan de Brai had been claimed as a villein by Richard son of John, who produced suit of her kin. She had once been a villein, she admitted, but had married a freeman forty years before and lived with him as the wife of a freeman, and was therefore freed herself;[49] 'nor did she ever flee from his land, either before the term or after'. Richard answered that she had married within the term[50] and offered a mark for a jury on the point. Unfortunately the verdict is unknown.

Apart from these specialized exceptions, most argument in the royal courts revolved around the substantial question of the alleged villein's status. The most important method of trial

---

[45] The example given is from *Glanvill*, xii. 11. The limitation periods were changed from time to time, *Selden Registers*, pp. xxxv–xxxvii.

[46] It is the genuine flight which is hard to demonstrate; cf. *LQR* xc, 340 n. 81. *Britton*, I. xxxii. 16 (i. 205), advised that suit of kin might be questioned whether the alleged villein had ever been on the claimant's land and within his seisin.

[47] JI 1/820, m. 15 (Suffolk eyre 1257), contains a naifty action against an alleged villein who did not appear and had to be attached, as well as this case.

[48] JI 1/175, m. 29d (Devon eyre 1243–4), is a case where the alleged villeins excepted against the writ on the ground that they had never been 'manentes' on the claimant's land. They succeeded on other grounds, as also happened on the occasion recalled in *Cas. Plac.*, p. 28/79 (Temp. Edward I).

[49] JI 1/174, m. 24 (Devon eyre 1238). Richard apparently challenged this view and the court, unsure of the rule, hesitated; the roll had 'ad judicium' at this point.

[50] He alleged that the marriage took place four years after Richard I's first coronation, which, according to Hall, *Selden Registers*, p. xxxvii, was the material date for writs issued between 1229 and 1237.

called for the production in court of the alleged villein's relatives
to acknowledge their status and, by inference, establish his.
This 'suit of kin' was considered the correct method for proof of
status. A Yearbook note from the first years of Edward I suggests
that a claimant who could count his own seisin need not
produce kin, but even this concession was denied a claimant in
1304.[51] In practice, the only real alternative was to render proof
superfluous by pleading either a previous confession of villeinage status or proof in an earlier trial by royal justices.[52] A
brief account of these possibilities is required before suit of kin
is examined.

The treatise *De legibus* said that confession of unfree status in
the royal court or any court of record sufficed to prove exceptions of villeinage for good.[53] The author cited a case between
Hugh de Gundeville and Hamelin son of Ralph. Hamelin had
once confessed his villein status before eyre justices in John's
reign, to bar an assize of mort d'ancestor. Yet, a few years later
he brought an assize of novel disseisin against Hugh, his lord, at
another eyre and was allowed to succeed. Hugh had Hamelin
summoned before the Bench to explain why he, a confessed
villein, should now claim the rights of a freeman. Hamelin tried
to argue that he had merely acknowledged holding in villeinage,
but the rolls confirmed that he had fully confessed villein status.
The novel disseisin verdict was therefore overturned and the
sheriff ordered to hand Hamelin, when he was found, over to
Hugh.[54] Acknowledgements of villeinage in the county court
similarly bound those who made them,[55] and clearly, fines in
royal courts were at least excellent evidence of villein status.[56]
Occasionally notes of such acknowledgements were enrolled for

[51] *Cas. Plac.*, p. 101 (*c.* 1273/8); *YB 32 and 33 Edward I*, pp. 512–14 (1304). Cf. *NAS*
p. 159 (Northumberland eyre 1269) where the claimant counted his seisin 'ut de feudo
et iure' but could not prove it.

[52] *Novae Narrationes*, p. cxlv. An *addicio* to *Br.*, f. 210 (ed. Woodbine, i. 397), points out
that to bring suit a second time would be superfluous.

[53] *Br.*, ff. 200b, 277b *addicio*, 421.

[54] *CRR* viii. 98, 361; ix. 92 (= *BNB* 1411), 265 (Dorset 1220).

[55] *CRR* xi. 965, 2486; xii. 1413, 1859 (Oxon. 1226). See S. E. Thorne, 'Notes on
Courts of Record in England', *West Virginia Law Quarterly* xl (1934), 347–59, and
'Courts of Record and Sir Edward Coke', *Univ. of Toronto Law Journal* ii (1937), 24–35.

[56] *CRR* xii. 1579, 1639 (Bucks. 1225), refers to *Bucks. Arch. Soc.*, iv. 28, the fine of 1205
which concorded *CRR* i. 95; iii. 119, 123, 129, 150.

future reference.[57] An acknowledgement would probably bind the villein's son and grandson as well as himself.[58]

The plea that the alleged villein had previously been proved unfree was very similar. The claimant might vouch the county court to establish his plea that a confession had been made there, as Jordan de Wik' once did in an exception against a *monstravit*. Hugh son of Herbert answered that he had brought the *monstravit* in response to Jordan's suit against him in the county court which he in his turn vouched. The knights of the shire reported that the case before them had concerned three carucates of land, 'but Hugh always made himself out to be free'. Jordan was amerced for a false plea and the hearing moved on to other issues.[59] In the very early period, until about 1200, royal justices could be vouched to confirm proofs made at the eyre too,[60] but before long reference to the rolls themselves became the standard procedure.[61] The claim to have made proof could also be put to a jury.[62] Some kind of confirmation was essential. An assize exception failed because the defendant neither said where and when he had made his proof nor vouched the justices.[63] In his turn, an alleged villein might plead that the claimant had previously tried to prove him unfree and had failed. One assize of mort d'ancestor succeeded when the jurors declared that the defendant had impleaded the deceased 'de servitute' but could never convict him so that he died free.[64] Some alleged villeins tried the less powerful plea that they had

[57]   e.g. *CRR* x. 68 (Notts. 1221).

[58]   As the cases cited above suggest. Milsom, *Novae Narrationes*, p. cxliv, had some doubts, which receive some support from *BRB* vi. 378 (Bucks. eyre 1227), an exceptional case (cf. above, p. 61 n. 4) where a father's acknowledgement did not prevent his daughter recovering his holding by assize of mort d'ancestor. In *BNB* 1139 (Bucks. 1235–6) a husband's confession of villeinage, allegedly made under duress, defeated his widow's assize of novel disseisin, because the disseisin took place while he (and therefore she as his wife) was unfree. She recovered the next year by action of right, *BNB* 1185. Cf. Thorne, *Br.*, iii. xvii.

[59]   JI 1/300A, m. 3d (Hertford eyre 1221). Also *RCR* i. 153 (Herts. 1199), *CRR* viii. 271, 321 (Bucks. 1221).

[60]   *RCR* i. 366 (Norfolk 1198).

[61]   JI 1/560, ms. 12, 53d (Norfolk eyre 1250). JI 1/909, m. 13d (Sussex eyre 1248), was concorded (*Sussex rec. soc.*, ii 1903, no. 493) before the record had been checked. In *RCR* i. 92 (Hants 1194) 2 marks were offered to have the rolls.

[62]   *CRR* vi. 168 (Beds. 1211), *SS* lix. 156 (Gloucester eyre 1221).

[63]   *RCR* i. 84 (Lincs. 1194).

[64]   *SS* liii. 137 (Lincoln eyre 1218), with 'Bractonian' sidelining.

succeeded against the claimant by assize, without specifying the grounds of their success.[65]

Such pleas were never frequent. Suit of kin was the primary method of status proof and the central episode of most naifty cases that came to trial.[66] The procedure was a very ancient one that can be traced back to Carolingian Francia[67] and most probably entered the common law from local courts.[68] In its simplest form, doubts about a man's status were resolved by bringing into court as many as possible of his relatives. On their testimony as to his (and their) status, the court made its judgement. Continental evidence for the actual workings of the procedure is too slight for any full understanding.[69] The English material, though describing its common-law dotage only, tells rather more.

The relatives were treated at common law as a special kind of *testis*, summoned to attest almost exclusively to their own status and relationship to the alleged villein. Each party might proffer such a suit, and whichever was deemed to be 'sufficient'[70] won the case. The production of suit of kin actually constituted proof in such cases—an unusual use of suit, for the received view insists on a distinction between complaint-witnesses (suit) produced to establish that there was a case to answer, and proof-

---

[65] JI 1/62, m. 15 (Bucks. eyre 1232). JI 1/231, m. 19d (Essex eyre 1248), was a mort d'ancestor brought by an elder brother after his younger brother had tried and failed because of his villein status; he too failed.

[66] What follows is based on my paper, 'The Proof of Villein Status in the Common Law', *EHR* lxxxix (1974), 721–49, where full argument and references will be found.

[67] *EHR* lxxxix, 722–3, and especially *LHP*, 89 (ed. Downer, pp. 276–7) taken from a capitulary of 803.

[68] *Glanvill*, ii, 6, recommends its use to determine right to land in cases where the tenant could not have the grand assize because the parties were of common stock. No doubt this had been the procedure locally too.

[69] See N. Brussel, *Nouvel examen de l'usage général des fiefs en France* (Paris, 1727), ii. 1003–7; P. Petot, 'La Preuve de servage au Champagne', *RHDFE* 4e s. xiii (1934), 464–98; L. Verriest, 'Le Servage dans le comté de Hainaut', *Acad. royale de belgique, classe des lettres*, 2e s. vi. 3 (1910), 101–5; F. L. Ganshof, 'La Preuve dans le droit Franc', *Recueils soc. Jean Bodin* xvii (1965), 72–3, and also J. F. Niermeyer, *Mediae Latinitatis Lexicon Minus*, s.v. 'procinctum'.

[70] *EHR* lxxxix, 727–8. The term 'sufficient' derived, like much else in the rules, from Romano-Canonist procedure. *Decretum*, C. 35, q. 6, cc. 1–3, suggests that Canonists found the procedure acceptable as a means of establishing kinship for other purposes. There was however a doubt about the admissibility of *servi*, C. 35, q.6, c. 3 gl. *bonae famae*.

witnesses.[71] Suit of kin was exceptional in other ways too. Only kinsmen might be produced, and they remained open to examination as long as the procedure survived. Both of these points impeded the making of proof. People without a blood relationship to the alleged villein were inadmissible as suit. Thomas de Santon objected to two of the suit whom Adam de Aywood proffered in support of his *monstravit* that they were 'not of his kin' and offered half a mark for an inquisition. Since the two in question were Devonshire born, the case had to be adjourned there for a jury of locals. Only when this had confirmed Thomas's plea could the court find for him.[72] 'Examination' of suit involved questioning them to compare their stories and qualifications. This procedure fell into desuetude in most common-law actions after the early thirteenth century,[73] though it continued in the Courts Christian. In actions of naifty, suit of kin apparently continued to be treated seriously even into the fourteenth century. As late as 1326, two men produced by a claimant as cousins of the alleged villein were examined in court. They were asked if they were the claimant's villeins and then *seperatim* how each was related to the alleged villein. The report notes that their answers accorded with the claimant's count, and the court then went on to consider other arguments.[74] In the thirteenth century, though the plea rolls seldom record the fact, justices habitually questioned the suit produced by the parties, who frequently challenged each other's suit. The alleged villein might declare, for example, that his kinsmen's confession of villeinage was their own choice and ought not to harm him, or the claimant might deny that his opponent's suit were entitled to the liberty they claimed.[75] The court could not avoid interrogation of suit if it were to be able to pronounce upon the sufficiency of each side's case. When the challenges were done, suit had to contain at least two *testes* of the right kind, that is male (for a male alleged villein) and of the status alleged

---

[71] J. B. Thayer, *A Preliminary Treatise on Evidence at Common Law*, pp. 10–12; *P&M*, ii. 606–7. And see further below.
[72] JI 1/756, m. 12 (= *SRS* xi. 729), JI 1/175, m. 32 (Somerset and Devon eyres 1243). Cf. *EHR* lxxxix, 726.
[73] *P&M*, ii. 609–10.
[74] *YB 19 Edward II*, ff. 651 ff. = Fitzherbert, *Villenage* 32 (1326).
[75] *EHR* lxxxix, 726–7.

by its proponent, or it failed automatically.[76] Where both suits were prima facie sufficient the choice between them was left to a jury.[77]

Even around 1300, the cases were still hard fought. The practical difficulties for the claimant were quite daunting. Transport of the alleged villein's relatives before the justices, for example, perhaps at Westminster, was awkward to arrange and involved the loss of their labour for several days at least. *En route* they might choose to follow their kinsman into flight. Once in court, they might change their minds and claim to be free, in the hope that their kinsman's success would gain liberty for the whole family, for the claimant lord would have no suit left to produce![78] Undoubtedly, a lord would be well advised to sue in tenure if he could.

The whole procedure of suit of kin assumed a far stabler rural community than existed in most regions of thirteenth-century England. Hereditary in theory, legal status could be, and was, changed in men's lifetimes. Lords freed their villeins. Freemen sometimes became villeins by their own acts, for gain, or even out of malice.[79] Involuntary enserfment as a penalty was still possible.[80] Villagers who served as suit or on juries were confused by all these shiftings, and perhaps too by the comparatively recent and unfamiliar categories of common-law villeinage.[81] Some even found in court—to their astonishment—that they now differed in status from families with whom they habitually intermarried in the past. Certainly many families whose affairs the royal courts scrutinized brought with them pedigrees studded with 'mixed marriages' between partners of different common-law status. No doubt the plea rolls exaggerate the

---

[76] Ibid. 727–9. Female suit may have been admissible to prove a woman's status, but no cases are known, just as women rarely appear as *testes*. Women were occasionally produced as suit anyway.

[77] Cf. *Decretum*, C. 35, q. 6, c. 2.

[78] This possibility was raised in argument in *YB 32 and 33 Edward I*, pp. 512–14 (1304). JI 1/180, m. 6 (Devon eyre 1238), contains a case where the claimant, Alicia de Valletorta, experienced difficulty in finding suit against a father and his two sons who produced twelve relatives in all. She first tried to rely on the testimony of the knights of the county but eventually secured an adjournment to the next visitation so she could produce a third son. I am unclear why there is not more evidence of such happenings.

[79] *EHR* lxxxix, 725–6, gives some cases where this was alleged to have occurred.

[80] See above p. 36 for John's threat of 1205 and end of this chapter for an early thirteenth-century penal agreement. Cf. also *LHP*, 78.2.

[81] If the view propounded in Chap. 13 is correct.

frequency of such complexities in the villages—single-status families seldom required actions of naifty—but sorting out the hard cases was the courts' job. Suit of kin demanded a simpler model of lordship than was usual in the thirteenth century. Rules were therefore needed to ascertain the appropriate status of an alleged villein from one of these mixed families. The jurists naturally turned for help to the obvious sources: the learned laws, which had long since framed sophisticated answers to similar problems. Glanvill adopted the vulgar Roman-law rule of *status deterioris*, by which the worse blood prevailed. Thus for him, all children of mixed marriages were unfree, a simple rule of rough justice his compressed style has concealed from most modern readers.[82] The more sophisticated approach of the treatise *De legibus* demonstrably owed much to the learned laws. Though Glanvill was by his side while he wrote, the author was equally influenced by the *Summa Institutionum* of Azo of Bologna (ob. 1220). The crucial passage on f. 5 purports to follow and reconcile the two sources, an important point not previously appreciated. The author deals with each of Glanvill's points in the same order and under a very similar rubric ('Qualiter nascunt servi et qualiter fiunt'). But at the same time, he considered each of Azo's comments on the relevant title of the *Institutes* (I.4).[83]

A unique combination of doctrine resulted. Those born 'extra matrimonium' took their mother's status. The child of an unfree mother and a free father 'ex matrimonio' was, however, free as long as he had been born outside villeinage in a free bed, and legitimate children generally followed their father.[84] In practice a different rule held. Status depended on the land where the child was born, more properly on whether he was within a lord's *potestas* at birth. In the Bractonian view, seisin of status, rather than rightful status, mattered. The alleged villein's seisin of

---

[82] *Glanvill*, v. 6, expounded in *EHR* lxxxix, 732–3. His source remains a problem. Canon law is a possibility, e.g. Ivo of Chartres or Gratian, but an unlikely one. Vernacular law is more likely, though not perhaps the *Leges Henrici Primi* (discussed *EHR* lxxxix, 731), whose compiler certainly knew the vulgar rule, because Glanvill does not seem to have consulted twelfth-century English legal writings; see *Glanvill*, pp. xxiv–xxviii, Richardson and Sayles, *Law and Leg.*, pp. 80–2.

[83] Maitland, *Bracton and Azo*, p. 55, missed this.

[84] *Br.*, f. 5; *EHR* lxxxix, 735. 'Glanvill Revised' (*c.* 1229?) seems already to have held the same view, loc. cit.

liberty or his lord's seisin of him as a villein made him either a *statuliber* or a *statuservus*.[85] A child was unfree therefore if born within the lord's power, on the villeinage where he was seised of at least one parent as his villein and where both resided. Birth on a free holding outside the lord's power left the child free. This solution, though apparently original to the *De legibus*,[86] owed much to the two laws. Canonists in particular had for some time expressed concern in their writings about the dangers seignorial control over serfs' family life posed for the souls of both parties.[87] Their discussions prompted the *De legibus* to argue that the married couple ought to share the same legal status for the duration of their marriage. If they resided on the husband's holding, the wife took seisin of his status, and the child did so too. When the matrimonial residence was on the wife's land, a different argument applied. Despite the fact that 'Homme puet franchir femme mes pas femme homme',[88] the husband's genuine status was 'obscured' for the duration of the marriage; it followed that the child took the status of his mother and her holding.[89] Different arguments, but the same conclusion. The *De legibus* required this special pleading to reconcile Glanvill with Azo. Glanvill's dictum, that a freeman living on villeinage and married to a villein wife became 'tanquam nativus', was his guide and native authority,[90] but the idea came from Azo whose discussion of *fideicommissaria libertas* reveals an apparent exception to the general rule that a child's status at Roman law followed his mother's. *Fideicommissa* (an institution with no obvious English parallel) was a direction in a will or codicil that some slave should be freed, for example by the *heres*. Until it was executed, he or she remained unfree. Yet a child born of a woman in this situation was held to be free.

---

[85] See above, Chap. 8 for this; the equation of *potestas* with seisin is noted above, p. 96.

[86] In the present state of knowledge, with so few works of the learned laws in print, the possibility of a direct source cannot be excluded.

[87] P. Landau, 'Hadrians IV Dekretale "Dignum est" (X, 4.9.1)', *Collectanea S. Kuttner* ii = *Studia Gratiana* xii (1967), 512–53, cites a number of pertinent texts on the marriage of *servi* and compares the views of contemporary theologians.

[88] *Brev. Plac.*, p. 117.

[89] *EHR* lxxxix, 736–8.

[90] Compare *Glanvill*, v. 6, with *Br.*, ff. 26, 194, which says that a freeman living on villeinage retained his personal freedom and right to leave at will unless 'obumbrabatur' by marriage to a villein wife. Also *EHR* lxxxix, 733 n. 2.

The law interpreted the mother's claim to be given liberty in the future as already fulfilled, for the purpose of deciding her off-spring's status.[91] Azo drew attention to this exception to the general rule of Roman law and reminded his audience that *consuetudo* could even make the child of a free mother and a *servus* father a *servus* himself.[92] This is the origin of the Bractonian rule, that the child of a 'mixed marriage' took his father's status, which was also acceptable to the English courts of his day.[93] Azo cautiously refused to attempt an explanation; he would not ask whether the *ancilla*'s child was free 'ex persona matris' or 'ex voluntate hominis'. This reluctance provided the *De legibus'* author with the cue for his often misunderstood theory of 'tenemental influence'.[94] His fusion of Azo and Glanvill into a blend utilizable by the English courts is as remarkable for close adherence to the sources as for ingenuity. Alas, his successors never comprehended this part of his system, and no reformulation of common-law doctrine in the light of the concepts of the two laws ever materialized. Britton and Fleta abbreviated the argument and omitted its whole rationale with all talk of tenemental influence. For them, the child of a mixed marriage simply took his father's status: the *De legibus* minus Romanesque frills.[95]

Set into the context of decisions in actual cases, the achievement of the Bractonian scheme perhaps shrinks a little. The alleged 'tenemental influence' is a case in point. Behind this argument clearly lies the kind of presumption, occasionally countenanced by the courts, by which birth in a certain area was held to imply a certain status. Birth in Kent, for example,

---

[91] Buckland, *Slavery*, pp. 513 ff., 617–18, 620. The concession resembles that by which the child of a mother who had been free at any time between his conception and birth as held to be free.

[92] *Bracton and Azo*, pp. 52, 54. Azo's words are 'ex generali tamen consuetudine regni'. The reference is obscure; it certainly does not refer to England, but perhaps to Norman Sicily.

[93] See below. He may also have consulted the *Leges Henrici Primi* (for which see *EHR* lxxxix, 731) which could have led him in the same direction.

[94] In *EHR* lxxxix, 733–9, I argued that Bracton (or a source) had amended the Roman rule of mother-right to father-right, to take note of the fact that *servi* of his day contracted lawful marriages so that their offspring were no longer 'quasi vulgo concepti' and could therefore follow the status of their fathers. I had not then noticed the relevance of Azo on *Inst.*, I.4. The simpler argument in the text is much the more compelling.

[95] *Britton*, I. xxxii. 4, 9 (i. 197, 200); *Fleta*, i. 3.

carried the presumption of freedom.[96] The disputes that occurred in two neighbouring Lincolnshire villages in 1271 may
display this kind of presumption in the act of birth. Jurors in one
case declared that 'in the village of Bilsby there are two fees . . .
and all those born in the Falconer fee are free, but all those born
in the Peverel fee are villeins'. The action of naifty then failed
because the two brothers whose status was in question came
from the Falconer fee.[97] The proceedings in the second dispute
were more complex, involving four separate actions against
Herbert Pecche, lord of Coleby, who excepted against each of
them on the ground of villeinage. He alleged that an inquisition
held some years earlier before the court *coram rege* had found the
whole village outside the Falconer fee to be in villeinage. Despite
his offer to put this plea to proof from the appropriate rolls, the
eyre justices took no heed and found against him, with damages, in one novel disseisin. While the other actions were still
pending, he appealed to the king and procured a writ which
censured the justices and ordered the records of all four actions
with their parties to be sent *coram rege* in Hilary term 1272. At
the resulting hearing, the tenants denied that they had ever put
their lands or status on any inquisition. Their view was that any
previous jury verdict bound only the parties to the case and was
incapable of establishing a 'Bractonian' presumption. No judgement in the case has been found, perhaps because Herbert
Pecche died a few months later.[98] Even so, the incomplete
report suggests a pattern by which a presumption of status like
that in Kent could evolve, in a court system that badly needed
workable rules of thumb. The essence was to remove the need
for fresh juries by reference to a past verdict between other
litigants. Significantly, the only three relevant cases noted from
an earlier date all come from the only eyre visitation (that of
1246–8) in which Henry de Bracton is known to have partici-

---

[96] *EHR* lxxxix, 736.

[97] JI 1/483, m. 3 (Lincoln eyre 1271). The royal falconer, Walter de Bavent, held
half the vill in serjeanty 1212, *Book of Fees*, i. 161, 168.

[98] JI 1/483, m. 5 (Lincoln eyre 1271), KB 26/205, ms. 13, 13d (*coram rege* 1272). This
account supersedes that in *EHR* lxxxix, 741. Herbert's 'appeal' writ was dated 8
November 1271 and he died before 7 September 1272, *Cal. of Inquisitions Post Mortem . . .
(Henry III)* i, (London, HMSO, 1904), p. 285. The inquisition on which Herbert relied
was held 'tempore G. de Haxton G. de Segrave et H. de Batonia', which sets the likely
date as 1241/54, probably 1249–51 or 1253–4 when Henry of Bath was chief justice of
King's Bench.

pated as a royal justice.[99] Their Bractonian arguments indicate
his familiarity with the *De legibus*. The action of naifty in which
Thomas de Moulton claimed Walter Gamel as his villein at
Lincoln, before a panel of eyre justices which included Bracton
himself, can be our example.[100] Walter's grandfather, of the
same name, had apparently been free but had married his four
sons off to villein women on the Moulton fee. The young men
then performed villein services for their wives' holdings 'and for
fear of losing the lands which they held of Thomas, they dared
not say that they were free'. Consequently, Walter Gamel junior
was in great danger of a judgement that he was unfree. After
considerable argument, Thomas was persuaded to accept the
family's liberty. What the court would have decided had the
case been fought to a finish is hard to know, but the grandsons
of the freeman Walter Gamel senior, the offspring of villein
women born on villein holdings, might well have been adjudged
villeins.[101]

Plea rolls of the earlier thirteenth century rarely contain
sufficient detail to test the Bractonian assertions, perhaps
because the justices were not at first interested in the questions
they raised. This seems to have been true also of decisions about
suit of kin, whose primary emphasis was on male suit of the
paternal blood. Females produced as suit, and suit *ex parte matris*
generally, were sometimes expressly rejected in pleading.[102]
Yet father-right never developed into a strict rule of agnatic
descent. Maternal kin were produced when available, without
any obvious concern for logical consistency. Litigants tried to
bring into court as many *testes* as they could, to establish in a
general way their case.[103] Too often, the justices' problem was
the plethora of information before them. Not infrequently, each
party produced suit of several relatives and after the determination of all exceptions, each suit still looked 'sufficient'. The
court had to reach a decision on the basis of rules too simple to

[99] They are discussed in *EHR* lxxxix, 739–41.

[100] JI 1/482, m. 33 (Lincoln eyre 1245).

[101] Not necessarily. See above p. 115, for another discussion of the same cases in
terms of the distinction between tenure and status, by which Walter Gamel was free
after all. The case would have turned on the justices' manipulation of the concept of
seisin. Perhaps that is why it was concorded.

[102] *EHR* lxxxix, 742–3.

[103] This approaches Thayer's view, above n. 71.

cover these complex family relationships. Ideally the justices would deduce the status of the alleged villein's parents from that of the various suit produced. The alleged villein's status then followed logically. But on what basis to make the initial selection? Around 1200, the primary criterion was probably proximity to the alleged villein, on the analogy perhaps of the selection of a 'nearest' heir for the assize mort d'ancestor. Glanvill advised that the question be put to a jury of neighbours. In two cases litigants pleaded that their suit was related to the alleged villein in a particular degree (*gradus*), possibly a reference to the Romano-Canonist affinity rules known in England, but not apparently applied to the descent of property.[104] From the 1240s, however, if not earlier, the courts were borrowing from the parentelic system which did govern the descent of property. The plea would often state that the alleged villein and those produced in suit shared a common male ancestor, who was named and whose descent group (*parentela*) was then outlined.[105] The court established the status of this agnatic ancestor from that of his descendants; both males and females were admissible in evidence. The alleged villein took his status by strict father-right. Cases of the 1240s warrant Bracton's deductions from his Civilian guide, and were no doubt the ultimate reason for his choice. How far earlier cases support this position is another matter.[106] Legitimate children did therefore take their father's status.

The evidence that illegitimate children followed their mother's conditions, as the Civilians and the *De legibus* held they should, is also quite strong. The relevant cases more or less follow this rule,[107] and are supported by an early fourteenth-century text of *Brevia Placitata*.[108] Not until the second quarter of the fourteenth century did the courts adopt the 'absurd, if humane conclusion' that all bastards ought to be free. An illegitimate child could not inherit his father's villein status.[109]

---

[104] *EHR* lxxxix, 744; cf. esp. *Glanvill*, v. 4, and also ii. 6.

[105] Plucknett, *Concise Hist.*, pp. 714–17, sketches the parentelic system.

[106] *EHR* lxxxix, 744–5.

[107] See ibid. 745–6 for cases of the 1240s. *YB 5 Edward II*, pp. 121–3 (Yorks. late Edward I), shows that the Bractonian views were now well known: the alleged villein objected to three brothers produced against him as villeins that they were born of a free father and 'in legitimo toro, et ea racione debent sequi patrem et non matrem'.

[108] *Brev. Plac.*, p. 214.

[109] *EHR* lxxxix, 746.

The early common law again remains obscure. From the 1240s the courts followed rules about bastards and mixed marriage in general, that quite closely resembled those of the *De legibus,* a further indication that the treatise had an influence before its publication.[110]

From this study of the action of naifty and its procedures, significant conclusions emerge. The numerous procedural subtleties and opportunities for delay were all part of the way the competitive game of litigation was played. A shrewd lord might well decide to leave the courts alone, and rely instead on self-help and force. Perhaps the action of naifty's defects were obvious particularly early because of the anachronistic proof by suit of kin, a device inherited from quite a different world. The courts recognized its imperfections, but mostly toyed with petty improvements. The treatise *De legibus* essayed a more fundamental reordering early in Henry III's reign, apparently without lasting success. Then about the middle of the century, the *De legibus'* system began again to find favour in the courts, almost certainly through the advocacy of Henry de Bracton. Royal justices were prepared to recognize presumptions that the inhabitants of certain areas were free unless proved otherwise. Many welcomed this development, for the action of naifty's snags were becoming glaringly obvious. If continued, it would have simplified decisions and fewer alleged villeins would have escaped servitude. But even in the mid-century years some of Henry de Bracton's colleagues preferred to apply descent rules borrowed from land law. The *De legibus* had perhaps clothed its clever solution in a learning too opaque for later scholars. Its abbreviators at the end of the century grossly simplified the now misunderstood system. But this came too late to save the action of naifty. Seignorial litigants had long voted with their feet to desert status litigation altogether and sue in tenure. It is time to follow their lead.

---

[110] It is noteworthy that the *De legibus* and the courts coincide only from the 1240s, which is about right for Henry de Bracton's own judicial career.

AN EARLY THIRTEENTH-CENTURY AGREEMENT PROVIDING FOR PENAL
ENSERFMENT[111]

Sciant presentes et futuri quod talis est convencio inter Nicholaum de Sefeld
[Sheffield-in-Burghfield, Berks.] et dominum suum Alanum de Englefeld
[Englefield, Berks.] videlicet quod si[112] ita contigerit quod ipse Nicholaus
terram suam quam tenet de predicto Alano relinquerit vel alio modo remiserit
vel redditum suum plenarie annuatim non reddiderit scilicet viginti solidos.
Ego Nicholaus et totus exitus meus nosmet ipsos obligamus servos et nativos
ipsius Alani et tota terra predicta revertet predicto Alano vel heredibus suis
libera et soluta de dicto Nicholao et de heredibus. Ita quod ipse Nicholaus vel
heredes eius nunquam possint clamorem vel calumpniam in terra predicta
habere vel ius aliquod in predicta terra postulare. Et ut hoc mea presens carta
quam feci predicto Alano rata et stabilis permaneat sigilli mei apposicione
eam corroboravi. Hiis testibus. Domino Ricardo capellano de la vele. Jordano
de Bideford. Roberto de Wiston'. Ylgaro de Englef'. Hugone amis. Petrus [sic]
de Englef'. Willelmo Bernard. Stephano Bernard. Alano clerico. Et multis
aliis. (P.R.O., E210/3348. Seal tag through two slits.)

Alan succeeded to the manor of Englefield before 1219 and died soon after
1226.[113] He owned the mill of neighbouring Sheffield and its villein millers, by
grant of 1197 to his predecessor William of Englefield.[114] Nicholas may be the
Nicholas f. Sexi, granted a little later to William of Englefield[115] and whose
son was William the miller of Burghfield. The seventh and eighth witnesses
may be two of the three sons of Bernard the miller of Sheffield sold to William
of Englefield in 1197.[116] This agreement might thus date c. 1215/25 and
concern an enfranchised but dissatisfied miller.[117]

---

[111] See p. 175.
[112] MS: om.
[113] See *V.C.H. Berks.*, iii. 402–6. *Rot. Lit. Claus.*, ii. 47, is a commission as justice.
[114] *PRS* n.s. xxxi. 108–9.
[115] PRO, E326/12169.
[116] BL, Add. Charter 20592.
[117] Drs Barbara Dodwell and Brian Kemp were kind enough to help with local
information. The document itself I owe to the characteristic kindness of the late
C. A. F. Meekings.

11

THE LAW AND VILLEINAGE TENURE

'La question de status . . . apparaît comme une excroissance sur la question essentielle de tenure.'[1] Professor Jouon des Longrais's reaction against the attempt of the *De legibus* to distinguish between tenure and status, though somewhat exaggerated, displays good common sense. The author of the treatise tried to separate villeinage tenure to facilitate the assimilation of English law to a Roman system oriented more towards status. He understood and approved of the centrality of tenure in men's minds. His proposed solution to the problem of mixed marriages in effect introduced a test based on the tenure of the child's birthplace. Tenure was always a central factor in villeinage cases. More often than not, even villagers summoned before the justices to act as suit of kin, in status actions, must have based their testimony on their knowledge of the alleged villein's family holding and its obligations. And the justices themselves frequently proceeded by a rule of thumb that compared alleged villeins with their neighbours: they would find him free if he were less burdened than the villeinage tenants around him.[2]

The common-law rules about villeinage tenure are thus germane to a book about status, but since tenure has generally been better covered by past scholars, the discussion here will be selective. The efforts of the courts to evolve effective tests of villeinage tenure are specially interesting for the way they were affected by popular ideas about servility in general and by the social changes of the time. Serfdom and villeinage were characterized in men's minds above all by their arbitrary nature, the uncertainty of their dependance. 'N'être pas libre c'était, avant tout, obéir à la volonté sans freins d'un autre homme.'[3] To hold

[1] F. Jouon des Longrais, 'La Vilainage anglaise . . .', 217.
[2] Examples are discussed below. Also *BNB* 1828 (Norfolk 1227), 1210 (Lincs., *coram rege* 1236–7).
[3] Bloch, *Mélanges,* i. 304; cf. R. W. Southern, *The Making of the Middle Ages,* pp. 103–4, and more generally pp. 103–10.

unfreely was to hold at the lord's will.[4] Interpreted at its sharp-est, this meant that a lord could make his villein tenants labour for him in whatever manner he preferred, literally at his will. In practice, of course, this now never happened. The volume of labour services actually exacted from peasants decreased dur-ing the twelfth century. Perhaps the pendulum was swinging back again towards the exploitation of labour services in the late twelfth century,[5] a time of increasing legalism, definition of obligations, and written record. But in the early thirteenth century week-work, the heaviest form of labour service, was rarer among the peasants of certain areas than the payment of money rents. In consequence, lords who wished to reverse past commutation of labour obligations or to impose work from scratch faced a dilemma if their actions were disputed. The best method of proving their ancient rights was to plead previous seisin of works. But long lapse of time and the absence of written record made this task hard or impossible.[6] In their difficulty, lords turned to certain supposedly servile customs that con-tinued to govern peasant families, irrespective of the form in which lords received their rent; they hoped that these would establish that their peasants held in customary and servile tenure. Even for those whose ancestors really had received labour services in the past, proof of servile tenure in this way was not easy. Custom about seignorial consent to marriage or the lord's right to levy extraordinary contributions in his hour of need, was itself undergoing a transformation which liberated many tenants from seignorial control. While the trend was all towards greater freedom, in the early thirteenth century most groups of villagers found themselves at some ill-defined point on the road from extreme dependance on the lord's will to a relatively autonomous family life. The line between servile and free customs was hard to descry outside the theorist's brain. Courts that wished to draw a strict distinction between villein and free tenure on the basis of the tenant's obligations to his lord had to polarize specific customs, by force as it were, or ask more general kinds of questions.

[4] Above Chap. 6.
[5] P. D. A. Harvey, 'The Pipe Rolls and the Adoption of Demesne Farming in England', *Ec. H. R.* 2nd s. xxvii (1974), 345–59.
[6] Below p. 197.

Historians, agreed that the key to tenure was its terms, have discerned two possible approaches for the courts.[7] They could first ask whether any peasant customs were so characteristic of villein tenure as to be incompatible with freehold. Proof that these were owed would then stamp a holding as villeinage. Or, more broadly, they could ask *how* the tenure's liabilities were to be performed: were they owed and to be performed in a servile manner? Actual cases, however, demonstrate that these two types of question were only partially distinct in practice. In the early thirteenth century, the first approach did not work; no precise tests of villeinage tenure existed at the time. The recent artificial creation of Common Law[8] ensured that peasant customs did not obligingly divide into free and villein items. The situation where the degree of dependence on the lord shaded off almost imperceptibly from one group of tenants to another persisted into the thirteenth century. Not until such obligations as merchet and tallage became more carefully defined, later in the century, were straight tests feasible. In this process of definition, royal court decisions on the comparatively few tenurial disputes that reached them played a significant role; their judgements on the first kind of question were based on the second approach, more specifically on popular conceptions of the characteristic uncertainty of servile tenure. This fact helps to resolve the old controversy between Maitland and Vinogradoff about the courts' use of uncertainty as a criterion. Their central text, the *De legibus*, was engaged in its usual task of recording and explicating anomaly. Uncertainty was a convenient means to characterize the special position of the villein sokeman of the Ancient Demesne. Unfree yet protected, this tenure had to be distinguished from the pure villeinage elsewhere.

The establishment of certain customs as marks of villeinage would have greatly facilitated the courts' treatment of cases. French historians once thought that three customs so functioned to prove serfdom in thirteenth-century France, but have

---

[7] Vinogradoff, *Villainage*, pp. 81 ff. Cf. *P&M*, i. 362, 368–76. Arguments based on the definition of freehold are necessarily circular and unhelpful here. See *P&M*, i. 360; F. Jouon des Longrais, *La Conception anglaise de saisine* (Paris, 1924), pp. 141–8; Plucknett, *Concise Hist.*, pp. 571–2; A. W. B. Simpson, *Introduction to the History of Land Law* (Oxford, 1961), pp. 69–70.

[8] To be considered in Chapter 13.

now dropped the idea.[9] Likewise, no English custom (apart perhaps from merchet) was conclusive proof of villeinage before the end of the thirteenth century. Nor was there any prerequisite of freehold whose absence established villeinage. Litigants relied on a range of liabilities as more or less strong evidence of unfree tenure. A jury verdict that a tenant's ancestors 'could give and sell their land, both in marriage and in any other way, and sell their foal and ox, cut down their oak, marry their son and daughter without licence, and they do not have to give tallage'[10] described a free tenement. Of the other customs sometimes pleaded,[11] only the two most important, merchet and tallage, will be discussed here.

With the benefit of hindsight, the historian can define merchet quite simply. A tenant subject to merchet required the permission of his lord before he could marry off his daughter—or sometimes his sister. For this permission, the lord could demand whatever he desired, though not apparently in medieval England the *ius primae noctis*.[12] In practice, the lord usually accepted money, but the possibility that he might withold his consent remained. The humiliatingly servile nature of the custom is well illustrated by references to it as 'ransom of blood'. Had such clear-cut arrangements been common around the year 1200, the royal courts would have classified holdings subject to them as villein (individuals as villeins by status too, no doubt) with the warm assent of most contemporaries. But convenient clarity of definition was comparatively rare, and a recent study suggests a possible explanation. Jean Scammell traced the carefully defined merchet of the thirteenth century back into manorial arrangements of the twelfth and thirteenth centuries.[13] Before this transition period, she suggests lords had exercised substantial control over the family arrangements of dependants at all levels of society. The peasant's obligation to

---

[9] M. Bloch, 'Liberté et servitude, *Mélanges*, i. 290 ff., 316; L. Verriest, *Institutions médiévales* i (Mons, 1946), 201–19; Ch.-E. Perrin, 'Le Servage en France et en Allemagne', *Relazioni del x congresso internazionale di scienze storice* (Florence, 1955), iii. 216–9, 224; G. Fourquin, *Seigneurie et féodalité au moyen âge* (Paris, 1970), p. 38. Cf. also below p. 241.

[10] JI 1/870, m. 8 (Surrey assizes 1248).

[11] See *P&M*, i. 374.

[12] See however the rather weak argument of H. M. M'Kechnie, 'Ius Primae Noctis', *Juridical Review* xlii (1930), 303–11, that the right was exacted in Scotland.

[13] J. Scammell, 'Freedom and Marriage in Medieval England', *Ec. H. R.*, 2nd s. xxvii (1974), 523–37.

pay his lord a tax when he acquired a bride did not therefore particularly distinguish him from men of other social categories. Increasingly from the eleventh century onwards, however, favoured groups emancipated themselves from direct seignorial interference at such times. During the same period peasant families came under pressure from the church courts[14] to conform to a christian model of lawful married life.[15] Lords viewed the resulting fines as the loss of 'their' money and chattels,[16] so they gradually moved away from taxes on new husbands in favour of levies on fathers. Mrs Scammell interprets their intention as an attempt to stimulate the exercise of paternal authority to restrain the premarital activities of their daughters.

This interesting if rather fragile hypothesis rests rather unsteadily on the sparse and very difficult evidence for manorial arrangements before the late twelfth century.[17] It ought to be tested in further research,[18] but obviously the concentration on marriage as one of the crucial moments for peasant freedom

[14] J. Scammell, 'The Rural Chapter in England from the Eleventh to the Fourteenth Century', EHR lxxxvi (1971), 1–21, argues that the exercise of moral jurisdiction was restarted in lay courts.

[15] Servile peasant liaisons were not consistently recognized by the Church as lawful marriages before the Ius novum of the later twelfth century. P. Landau, 'Hadrians IV Dekretale "Dignum Est" (X, 4.9.1.)', 512–53. Thus peasant family arrangements were often unstable and transient.

[16] Above Chap. 3.

[17] Thus documentary backing is necessarily thin. Classical merchet may rise too soon to be explained as a reaction to the Gregorian expansion of moral jurisdiction, as Mrs Scammell appears to suggest. Moreover, there is something paradoxical about the idea that a husband of a supposedly unstable marriage was the person to stabilize the marriages of the next generation. Where would he find the required authority? Mrs Scammell's highly compressed formulation of her model requires the reader's close attention.

[18] Eleanor Searle, 'Freedom and Marriage in Medieval England: an Alternative Hypothesis', Ec. H. R. 2nd s. xxix (1976), 482–6, accepts Mrs Scammell's dating of merchet's introduction but questions her interpretation that this relieved the burden on the peasant, and indeed the whole connection with ecclesiastical marriage policy. She proposes that 'the function of merchet was to control land tenure and to tax the dowries of peasant girls'. Mrs Scammell's 'Wife-rents and Merchet', Ec. H. R. 2nd s. xxix (1976), 487–90, is an effective refutation of her much abbreviated argument. One point may be added. Dowries only took peasant property outside the lord's hands, when the girl married either a freeman or someone from another lordship (cf. French formariage). Professor Searle's hypothesis thus does not explain why ordinary intra-manorial marriages were subject to merchet. Perhaps at first they were not. The view in the text should now be compared with Professor Searle's full formulation 'Seignorial Control of Women's Marriage: the Antecedents and Function of Merchet in England', Past and Present lxxxii (1979), which appeared too late for consideration. Her interesting arguments certainly modify my opinions expressed above, but I hope to comment elsewhere.

is correct. Lord and tenant alike were alive to the opportunity presented for each to assert his view of their relationship. Only a tenant's death had a comparable ability to release normally concealed tensions and permit disputes or occasionally violent flare-ups. When, for example, Roger de Kirkele married off his daughter to Thomas de Bradley in the Suffolk village of Mutford, he knew that his lord, Henry de Vere, opposed the match. Nevertheless he proceeded, confident that, as a free socager not subject to merchet, he was free to act as he wished. Henry's response was to break into Roger's house at dead of night in a furious search for the girl that left a burnt-out ruin behind.[19]

Violent episodes forced merchet on men's attention. Lawyers were happy to advise their seignorial clients to plead merchet in court, when they could establish that someting like the model servile custom was due. The transition was, of course, far from complete in 1200. Thirteenth-century payments for marriage range from token registration payments to substantial sums for 'ransom of blood'.[20] Undoubted freemen from Northumbria and elsewhere owed merchet *ipso nomine*[21] while the courts had to accept that fixed marriage payments were quite compatible with free tenure.[22]

These were exceptional. Normally, popular opinion considered submission of a tenant's marriage arrangements to a lord's will as clearly servile. Although merchet could not, in theory, prove villein status (since it might be due 'ratione tenementi'),[23] its absence convinced eyre justices of a man's free status on one occasion.[24] On tenure, merchet was usually accepted as conclusive,[25] and the well-advised lord would allege that his adversary was a villein who held in villeinage and owed merchet.[26] Thus in a mort d'ancestor, the jurors found

---

[19] *CRR* ix. 336, x. 150 (Suffolk 1220), fully discussed above, p. 139f.

[20] W. O. Pike, *YB 15 Edward III* (R.S. 1891), pp. xv–xliii, and Scammell, 'Freedom and Marriage', 531–5, collect examples.

[21] *CRR* viii. 150 (Oxon. 1219) has free tenants liable to aid who cannot marry their daughters without the lord's consent.

[22] Examples are *CRR* v. 198 (Rutland 1208), JI 1/818, m. 33 (Suffolk eyre 1241), *BHRS* xxi. 250 = JI 1/4, m. 13d (Bedford eyre 1247); see also below, p. 196.

[23] *Br.*, ff. 26, 195, 208b; cf. *Fleta*, iv. 13 (193), *Britton*, I. xxxii. 3 (i. 196).

[24] JI 1/699, m. 9 (Oxford eyre 1247). According to the jurors, the plaintiff's deceased father had married off three daughters without the lord's licence or hindrance. There was some confusion with tenure.

[25] Vinogradoff, *Villainage*, pp. 82, 156; *P&M*, i. 372–3.

[26] *CRR* viii. 106 (Cambs. 1214).

that the deceased did not die seised as of fee etc. because he was the Abbot of Abingdon's villein 'so that he could not marry off his daughter without the abbot's licence and merchet at his will', and the assize of his two young unmarried sisters consequently failed.[27] A Norfolk trespass suit of the 1220s exemplifies in detail how valuable merchet could be to lords.[28] Peter de Nereford first distrained against, then arrested, his tenant Richard son of Thurkill for villein services due from his ten-acre holding in Panworth. In court, Richard put in his claim to be a freeman and the parties were assigned a day to bring their respective proofs of his status. At the same adjourned hearing, a recognition of the terms of Richard's tenure was to be made by a specially constituted jury of six villagers and six of his kinsmen, who were enjoined in particular to say whether Richard's sister Agnes had made fine with Peter's father for ten shillings when she married Geoffrey Baret. Peter's major interest was the disputed services. Proof of Richard's personal unfreedom would have been a convenient method of regaining them. Unfortunately for him, Thurkill, Richard's father, had been an outsider, not born in Panworth; Peter, therefore, had to argue that maternal suit sufficed as proof because Richard's holding had descended to him from Cristina his mother. But this ploy was unacceptable, and it fell to the jurors to break the impasse. They recorded that Richard and his fellow villagers (referred to as *villani*) owed light carrying and agricultural services without week-work. Tallage, however, was due on demand and Richard 'cannot marry off his daughter without his lord's licence', though the jurors did not know if Agnes had actually paid merchet. The justices seized on this. How did the jurors know that Richard owed merchet they asked? Had his ancestors ever given anything? The jurors answered yes: Cristina his mother had once given 18*d*. for a baby boy she had borne (as legerwite?) and two sisters had paid comparable sums to marry from the holding.[29] This apparently settled the matter. Richard appeared in court on a later day and admitted that he did owe the customs as

---

[27] JI 1/37, m. 20d (Berks. eyre 1241).
[28] *CRR* xii. 75 = *BNB* 1041 (Norfolk 1225).
[29] The roll says 'de eodem tenemento'. Probably Hugh clerk, the girls' father, had held a customary tenement like Richard's. The payment of merchet etc. by the women accords badly with Mrs Scammell's argument; Searle, art. cit., 484 n. 2, points out that payments were made for boys too sometimes.

recorded and was a villein. The court then handed him over to Peter as his villein.

Tallage never quite equalled the decisiveness of merchet. The wise litigant did not plead it on its own; he added merchet if possible.[30] Tallage was seldom more than good corroborative evidence,[31] and cases that turned on it alone are rare.[32] The lawyers' reaction to tallage's shortcomings as proof was to tighten up the manner in which it was pleaded. They advised pleaders to emphasize the tenant's submission to the lord's will, his uncertainty about the level and timing of seignorial demands. The well-presented count claimed that the lord had tallaged his tenants 'high and low' at his will.[33] Even so, the courts were not always convinced. When a jury of 1241, for example, returned that tenants owed no merchet and sold their animals at will, but gave tallage when the lord tallaged his villeins 'ad plus et ad minus pro voluntate sua', the court hesitated and the entry remains incomplete on both rolls.[34]

The explanation is similar to the one for merchet. Twelfth-century lords had seldom drawn a general distinction between their free and unfree dependants when making extraordinary levies. They took whatever custom and their own strength permitted. Limitation of this power to levy contributions at will began among the more noble dependants and gradually moved down society. At no specific moment was the line between servile tallage at will and free consensual aid precise enough to constitute a clear test for the courts. The terms 'tallage' and 'aid' each refer to the same 'fringe of vague obligations'[35] which every man owed his lord above and beyond his regular rent or

---

[30] e.g. JI 1/300A, m. 1 (Hereford eyre 1221), BNB 1225 (Salop, *coram rege* 1237–8).

[31] A typical reference is J. R. West, *St. Benet of Holme, 1020–1210* (Norfolk rec. soc. ii for 1931), no. 211, a memorandum that a tenant who already held free land by charter had been given (1175/1210) an additional 20 acres in villeinage 'without charter, for which however his heirs give no tallage'.

[32] JI 1/176, m. 1d (Devon eyre 1248–9) is one, though 'alia villana servicia' were also cited.

[33] *Brev. Plac.*, pp. 24, 70, 177, 215; *Cas. Plac.*, pp. 42/2, 79/20; *Novae Narrationes*, A 15–16, B 178, B 180, C 204. Among the earlier examples of stricter counts—the earliest date from the 1240s—are three from assizes pleaded before Henry de Bracton, JI 1/1178, ms. 18 (Devon 1250), 3d (Devon 1252), JI 1/1182, m. 10d (Devon 1254).

[34] JI 1/867, m. 11 = 868, m. 8d (Surrey eyre 1241). Cf. *CRR* xiii. 1024, *BRB* vi. 112 (Bucks. 1225), JI 1/818, m. 16d (Oxon. case from Suffolk eyre 1240).

[35] *P&M*, i. 349. See above p. 28 for a 1250 case about reasonable tallage taken annually.

service. This aid, sometimes sought in concrete as well as pecuniary form,[36] could be more or less honourable according to the custom of the lordship and what the lord felt he could exact. The style of the demand and even its name continued to matter. Royal writs dispatched to initiate the exploitation of vacant bishoprics for the crown began in the 1220s, for the first time, to distinguish between tallage of rustics and aid from knights and freeholders.[37] Royal writ draftsmen display an increasing sensitivity to the connotations of tallage from about this time.[38]

Some contemporary theologians too discuss what they call *tallia* in an indicative manner. Concern for the taxing lord's soul impels them to ask if he is guilty of robbery or must restore his gains as ill-gotten. The answer depends largely on the status of the payers. Several writers, Englishmen among them, specifically permit the tallaging of serfs at the lord's will, since they and their goods belonged to him anyway. A lord, who ought to obtain consent for exactions from his freemen to whom he had to expound his justification, had no such need with serfs. There were few limits on what he could take, even for moralists.[39] In the refined Aristotelian formulation of Richard de Mediavilla in the 1280s, the line to be drawn was between exactions from *servi*, at the lord's will and for his own use, and exactions from freemen which had to be for the 'common good'.[40]

Tallage presented the courts with an unresolvable circular argument. A decision whether a tenant was liable to tallage or to reasonable aid could be made easily only with prior knowledge whether or not his tenure was free. But this was too often

---

[36] e.g. *Early Yorks. Charters*, vi. 114 (1195/6).

[37] M. Howell, *Regalian Right in Medieval England* (Oxford, 1962), pp. 130–40.

[38] *Cl. R., 1227–31*, pp. 9, 574 (1227, 1231). Cf. *Cl. R., 1256–9*, p. 313, *Cal. Pat. R., 1247–1258*, pp. 560–1, for the reimposition of servile customs on an enfranchised tenant family under cover of a recent agreement with the king.

[39] J. W. Baldwin, *Masters, Princes and Merchants*, i. 235–8, ii. 172–4, esp. nn. 77, 79, 86, 90, for, among others, Robert de Courson and Robert of Flamborough, who both wrote *c.*1208/13, ibid. i. 19–25, 32–3. B. Smalley, 'The Quaestiones of Simon of Hinton', *Studies in Medieval History Presented to F. M. Powicke*, ed. R. W. Hunt, W. A. Pantin, and R. W. Southern (Oxford, 1948), pp. 210–11, for Simon who lectured at Oxford between 1250 and 1260. These writers all used *tallia* to cover both tallage/aid and royal taxation.

[40] Richard de Mediavilla, *Quolibeta*, III, q. 27 (edn. Brixen 1591, pp. 125–6). Richard produced these works in the course of Paris teaching, *c.* 1287; cf. P. Glorieux, *Répertoire des maîtres de Paris au xiiie siècle* (Paris, 1933), ii. 120–3, and above Chap. 7, p. 71 n. 25.

the question before the court. The parties frequently agreed that payments had been made in the past. All hopes for the future depended on their interpretation now. When they reached the courts, disputes followed a set pattern. The lord asserted that he had made his exactions arbitrarily as tallage, the tenants that they had given aid of their free will when the lord was in need. Pleadings made in the course of a long dispute about Fifhide-in-Leigh are a good illustration. The Prior of Merton claimed his customs and services from what he declared to be his villeinage. Among those specified with *auxilium* which he said ought to be paid when their fellows from Ewell (of which Fifhide was a member) paid theirs. The villagers answered with a claim to Ancient Demesne privilege, for Ewell had been royal demesne until Henry II had granted it to Merton. Each year they declared 'when the prior had need on account of his church's necessity, they aided him willingly and within reason, not because of villeinage but as of grace'. Although some of them were villeins, their common customs were not, in their view, villein. But the jurors thought otherwise. Their verdict on tallage as they called it (despite the parties' preference for *auxilium*), was that the villagers were rightly tallaged each year when men of Ewell were, 'not as of grace but by custom'.[41] The jury took into account the generally villein flavour of the other obligations, and thus both resolved interpretations for the future on that estate and, more generally, helped to spread the distinction between tallage and aid.

A substantial number of tenurial disputes were decided in the royal courts by the application of tests of this sort. Merchet, and to a lesser extent tallage, functioned quite effectively when the customs could be clearly established later in the century as ideas about common-law villeinage and servitude generally became more familiar. Custom gradually polarized into free or villein. The underlying equation of arbitrary treatment with servility lay deep in thirteenth-century consciousness. When in 1297 the Earl of Hereford declared at the Exchequer that 'nule chose ne met plu tot homme en servage qe rechat de saunc e

---

[41] *CRR* xi. 830, 1312 (= *BNB* 1661), 1496, 1829, 2893; xii. 699, 1378, 1635, 1811 (Surrey 1223–6). Merton Priory's troubles with Ewell and Fifhide went on over a long period. Other examples are *CRR* iv. 287, 297; v. 85 (Norfolk 1207), *CRR* vii. 104 (Northants 1214). The prior's writ was the unusual writ of customs and services in villeinage, for which see p. 264.

estre taille a volunte', his audience had no difficulty in seizing his meaning. This was not that Edward I had been exacting merchet and tallage from noblemen, but that the king's actions were too arbitrary. The earl chose his language to dramatize the revulsion felt at royal arbitrary prises and the like. Freemen were not to be treated in a manner fit only for serfs.[42]

These ideas could be applied to tenures which did not offer clear evidence of merchet or the like. The plea rolls do not reveal a large body of such cases, perhaps because the inclusion of judicial reasoning was so irregular. The *De legibus* appears at first to present uncertainty of tenure as the criterion of villeinage. 'A pure villeinage is one from which uncertain and indeterminate service is furnished,' he avers, 'where one cannot know in the evening the service to be rendered in the morning, that is, where one is bound to do whatever he is bid.'[43] As a factual description of the villein tenant's way of life this is of course nonsense. Most thirteenth-century peasants knew only too well, as the author was aware, their duties on the morrow and for that matter on most working days. Their working year was far more closely mapped out than that of most people today. Custom ruled in the countryside. The *De legibus'* dictum is explained by its context. The references to uncertainty all appear in passages concerned with the ancient demesne and its 'privileged' villeinage. This was an anomaly that required clarification. 'Pure' and 'privileged' villeinage—the Bractonian terms for standard villein tenure and the villein socage of royal demesne—could not be distinguished by the services they owed. Tenants performed the same servile works on each. The difference was that tenants of villein socage, some of whom ('conventioners') held by express agreement with their lords, were privileged by a form of legal protection against ejection and rent increases. Pure villeins lacked any comparable remedy. They were at their lord's will in the eyes of the common law, which therefore considered their tenure uncertain. The point now becomes clear. The author of the *De legibus* applied to

---

[42] J. G. Edwards, *EHR* lviii (1943), 155–6; H. Rothwell, *EHR* lx (1945), 34. Matthew Paris, *Chronica Majora* v, ed. H. R. Luard (R.S. 1880), p. 20, cited M. Clanchy, 'Did Henry III have a Policy?', *History* liii (1968), 207–8, puts similar imagery into Henry III's mouth.

[43] *Br.*, f. 26. Other relevant passages are at ff. 7, 168 *addicio* ('from Bracton', Woodbine, i. 392), 170, 200, 208b.

an awkward anomaly a guideline, new to the courts but derived from current popular theory and, perhaps, his reading in the two laws.[44] The certainty of a particular tenure indicated its relative freedom, without necessarily entailing that its tenants were legally free. The villein sokeman was a villein, on the wrong side of the line between *liber* and *servus* borrowed from Justinian, but yet possessed of special legal protection. The principle of uncertainty enabled the *De legibus* to recognize this and tackle other awkward cases. It was a guiding principle not a test of villeinage tenure in general.[45]

Maitland and Vinogradoff apparently did not notice the specific context of the uncertainty principle. Maitland, noting that free tenants owed labour too, thought the *De legibus* authority that 'any considerable uncertainty as to the amount or the kind of the agricultural services makes the tenure unfree'.[46] Vinogradoff demurred. He correctly observed that the cases did not turn on the lord's ability to allot tasks at his will. The courts must have administered a presumption, he suggested, that agricultural services were servile unless the tenant could show that he performed them 'in a certain and well defined manner, as if by convention'.[47] The scholarly disagreement was based on a shared error. The *De legibus* did not propose a new rule, like the merchet test. Uncertainty was simply a guiding principle for hard cases.

Royal justices used uncertainty as a tenurial criterion of this kind as early as 1228,[48] when the Bench at Westminster con-

---

[44] See the Appendix for examples of the kind of Canonist texts which may have encouraged him.

[45] There may have been a further point. It might be argued that by pleading his right to some customs etc., a lord renounced any other customs to which he laid no express claim. By the principle of uncertainty, Bracton could ensure that it sufficed to plead that a tenant held 'in villeinage', i.e. for uncertain, unlimited service, at the lord's will.

[46] *P&M*, i. 370–2. Maitland understood well of course the association between 'law and that general opinion of which law is the exponent'.

[47] Vinogradoff, 'Agricultural Services', reprinted from *Economic Journal* x (1900) in his *Collected Papers*, ed. H. A. L. Fisher (Oxford, 1928), i. 112–28. The merit of his contribution was to point out that uncertainty was not a convenient test and that labour, especially if of a demeaning nature, did indicate servility to contemporaries. At the end, though, he offers little different from Maitland.

[48] *CRR* xiii. 508 = *BNB* 281 (Warwicks. 1228), cited by *Br.*, f. 200. The problems of interpretation presented by the record are treated at the end of this chapter. Maitland had only cited it to illustrate the technicality of tenurial questions, *P&M*, i. 374 n. 2, but Vinogradoff discussed it in detail.

firmed an assize decision made by specially commissioned justices in Warwickshire. The Prior of Ruislip, who had excepted to the original assize that the plaintiff was a villein holding of him in villeinage, was in effect appealing against an unfavourable decision, that undoubtedly had been made (*inter alia*) on the criterion of how far the tenant's service to the prior was fixed and known in advance. Whatever the details of judicial reasoning, the plea-roll entry for the Bench hearing was good authority that one enfeoffed by certain and determined services could recover by assize if disseised. Yet both sets of justices were at least as interested in the marriage arrangements. Proof of a merchet liability would have rendered superfluous the more sophisticated arguments. The principle of uncertainty was second best. The rolls of the next dozen years contain no further examples,[49] but when cases do appear, they follow a similar pattern. The next one noted, from 1240, will suffice as illustration. William de Todenham had held two plots of land, one by a money rent, the other by fairly substantial labour services (mostly performed at the lord's expense) together with ten shillings for *convivia* and a fine for his daughter's marriage fixed by agreement at 12*d*. He recovered both plots by assize. The court found that he held the first 'per certum servicium denariorum' and the other 'per certas consuetudines ad cibum (domini)' without merchet.[50] Certainty was for the court, here and elsewhere,[51] a measure of the lord's ability to manipulate customary obligations at his convenience. To most minds the most certain service of all was an express money rent.[52] A jury finding that the lord 'never received any other service except only those four shillings' was enough for justices to declare one Suffolk

---

[49] *CRR* vi. 335 (Yorks. 1212) is an earlier example in which the absence of merchet was also as conclusive as the *servicium subscriptum*. Attaint of the jurors failed. Other early examples no doubt hide behind general verdicts.

[50] JI 1/818, m. 33 (Suffolk eyre 1240).

[51] Examples are JI 1/4, m. 13d = *BHRS* xxi. 250 (Bedford eyre 1247), JI 1/1253, ms. 2d, 5 (Surrey assize, *coram rege* 1281), and Sayles, *Select Cases in K.B.* iii (*SS* lviii), no. 26 (Norfolk 1296). *SS* lx. 74 (Surrey 1258) and Sayles, *Select Cases in K.B.* i (*SS* lv), pp. 14–15 (Bucks. 1275) both associated certainty of tenure with socage. The 'servicia nominata' of *BNB* 1210 (Lincs., *coram rege* 1236–7) were no doubt 'the services abovenamed' and cf. *RCR* ii. 25 (Oxon. 1199) for *certa servilia* claimed from a supposed free tenant.

[52] But cf. the argument on frankalmoign in Fitzherbert, *Counterple de vouch* 118 (1284–5).

holding free.[53] Money payments carried absolutely no connotation of servility. Labour always might do,[54] especially if it
involved dishonourable services such as the carrying of dung.[55]
The Church's rules of *opera servilia*, those activities forbidden to
christians on holy days,[56] illustrate ideas which they helped to
diffuse through society. In France, 'vilainage' was the characteristic term for land held by labour service.[57] Yet the English
royal courts could never simply adopt the popular notion as a
legal rule, for the presumption created by a money rent could
always be negatived by proof of previous commutation of (but
not enfranchisement from) villeinage customs.[58] This proof was
not always easy to achieve, for rents may have been paid for fifty
years or more.[59] The pleas must have stretched jurors' memories to breaking point and almost invited undue influence or
duress. No doubt there was much honest error too, for few in the
late twelfth century had the foresight to specify clearly whether
a relaxation of labour demands was to constitute an enfranchisement or not.[60] But generally, certainty, or at least the
degree of independence from seignorial interference in the performance of services, played a significant role in most villeinage
decisions.

This survey of the tenurial criteria administered in the royal
courts should not suggest that villein tenure was anywhere as
hard to establish as villein status. The doctrinal subtleties

[53] JI 1/818, m. 21d (Suffolk eyre 1240). Cf. also *SS* liii. 101 (Lincoln eyre 1218), JI
1/300A, m. 3 (Hertford eyre 1221), KB 26/123, m. 8 (Norfolk 1242).

[54] Cf. *The Chronicle of Jocelin de Brakelond*, ed. H. E. Butler (*NMT* 1949), pp. 28, 99,
and *SS* ii. 169 (Brightwaltham manorial court 1293).

[55] Vinogradoff, *Villainage*, pp. 170–1, *P&M* i. 370–2.

[56] *Dictionnaire de théologie catholique*, iv. 1311–22; Powicke and Cheney, *Councils*, ii. 2,
1020–1, 1063, 1096–7 (1287, 1291). Also M. D. Chenu, 'Arts "méchaniques" et œuvres
serviles', *Rev. des sciences philosophiques et théologiques* xxix (1940), 313–15, and P. Petot,
'L'Hommage servile', *RHDFE* 4ᵉ s. vi (1927), 102–3.

[57] Bloch, *Mélanges*, i. 321–2.

[58] e.g. JI 1/482, m. 12 (Lincoln eyre 1245).

[59] *CRR* vii. 60 (Northants 1214), *CRR* xii. 2275, xiii. 1024 (Bucks. 1228), JI 1/951A,
m. 14 (Warwick eyre 1232), KB 26/117B, m. 9 (Middlesex, *coram rege* 1237), JI 1/867,
m. 12d = 868, m. 10d (Surrey eyre 1241), JI 1/7, m. 8 (Bedford eyre 1276), etc.

[60] JI 1/7, m. 8 (Bedford eyre 1276), turned on the purchase of a villeinage by the
Prioress of Markyate. The sitting tenant, a freeman whose villein holding had been sold
by his lord over his head, came to an agreement with the purchaser, as his new lord. In
the court's judgement, this 'statum suum mutavit in annuum redditum denariorum
pro predictis servilibus serviciis solvendis', that is enfranchised the holding rather than
merely commuting the obligations 'in certam summam pecunie' as had been suggested.

discussed in this chapter can be traced only through the exceptional cases. The majority of disputes were probably decided by the courts on the more general bases of a rough test of services. The justices were satisfied if the customs exposed by jury verdicts looked right for villeinage, the sort of tenure in which royal justice did not bother to interfere. The plea rolls give bare details only. Easy cases produced simple, short plea entries. The legal interest of the relatively few hard cases lies above all in the way that perplexed royal justices reached out towards the ideas of ordinary men to find new doctrine outside the law. The historian must be careful not to confuse medieval popular conceptions of servility with the actual rules and principles that determined cases. Men imagined an ideal society in which villein tenants all held for indeterminate service. Theoretically, tenure 'in villeinage' allowed the lord whatever he chose to demand. In the thirteenth century, he would always take more than the money rent 'for all service' which was the mark of the free socager. This ideal model was obviously not suitable for wholesale adoption by the courts. The defect was not that the model was over-neat, but rather that the amount and kind of labour lords were to take from their tenants was precisely the point at issue in many disputes. Lords' demand for labour had shifted and increased on those estates which adopted direct exploitation of demesnes. Previous seisin of labour services, the obvious way to justify reimposition, was hard or impossible to plead. Where possible, the courts singled out servile customs as indicators of villeinage tenures. Merchet in particular was often decisive, where a clear liability to a servile form of marriage custom could be established—a requirement that was not easy to fulfil before the middle of the century. Around 1200 the vigorous process of customary definition and polarization was assisted by royal court decisions in villeinage cases.[61] Royal justices shared with lawmen the notion of uncertainty, by which lords were free to utilize their serfs as they preferred. The cases studied in this chapter thus both mark a movement of English rural custom in a direction convenient to lords and participate in the wider European movement towards greater legalism of which Magna Carta is the prime English symbol.

[61] Searle, *Ec. H. R.* 2nd s. xxix (1976), 474–5, appreciates this process well.

THE PRIOR OF RUISLIP'S CASE 1228[62]

Thomas son of Adam brought an assize of novel disseisin against the Prior of Ruislip and others who had, he complained, disseised him of his free tenement in Alderton, Warwickshire. The original trial was before three non-professional assize justices, not chosen from that core of full-time royal servants that staffed the central courts.[63] Their judgement in Thomas's favour displeased the prior, who had them summoned to bring their record to Westminster before the Bench for certification, a kind of appeal procedure. He then challenged their account of the first hearing on the ground that it omitted important details. The justices' version was as follows: the prior had objected to the assize because the holding was villeinage and Thomas his villein, who like his fellows owed villein services including merchet. Thomas had admitted owing some of the services alleged, but pleaded that they were performed at the lord's expense and that his other obligations were a money rent and a 'certum finem pro filia sua'. The jury on which he put himself found that he and his tenure were free. The prior agreed before the Bench that this had been their conclusion but not their whole verdict. The jurors had also said that Thomas had to give 12d. to marry off his daughter, and that he owed several other unspecified customs. They[64] then vainly sought from the justices an adjournment to have the assent of Lord Robert de Lexinton whether this was a free tenement 'ex quo scivit quid debuit facere vel non'.[65] The prior's plea failed. The Bench accepted the justices' denial of his story and upheld the original judgement.[66]

What was the point behind the prior's certification? According to the justices, the case turned on the issue of *how* the services were performed. The court held the tenure free because the jurors agreed with the plaintiff that, for example, he owed a fixed marriage fine and not merchet. Robert de Lexinton was an experienced royal justice, who had visited Warwickshire two years earlier on eyre, and might be expected to know the law better than part-time assize justices. The jurors (or the defendants) may have sought Robert's legal opinion whether the justices were right to decide the case on the principle of uncertainty, that the holding was free 'because [the tenant] knew what he ought to do'. If so, the Bench's confirmation of the verdict validates the uncertainty criterion for villein tenure as good law. But we cannot be sure that this was the point at issue.[67] Robert's opinion may have been desired simply because he was available and knowledgeable about local custom; if so, the case's authority is much weaker.

---

[62] See pp. 195f.

[63] They were not however without experience. *Cal. Pat. R. 1225–1232*, pp. 161, 165, 166, 167(bis), 206, 280, 281, record other commissions to them.

[64] The roll is ambiguous at this point. 'They' are probably the jurors but could be the prior and his fellow defendants.

[65] This is what the original roll says, but *BNB* has 'ex quo sciunt quid debuit facere et quid non', which significantly changes the sense.

[66] *CRR* xiii. 508 = *BNB* 281 (Warwicks. 1228).

[67] The version of the copy in *BNB* would stand this interpretation slightly more readily than that of the original roll.

One near-contemporary, the annotator of *Bracton's NoteBook*, thought the case turned on uncertainty. He viewed it in a very Bractonian way. He ignored the argument about merchet and thought (wrongly) that the exception had cited services as evidence of villein status; these were, he noted, 'certas, et bene scivit quid et quantum'. Thus the plaintiff was free as to his body despite the 'certain' villein services. And, he continued, a villein holding in villeinage cannot do (i.e., owe only) 'certain' services. His implication is that anyone who owed 'certain' services could not be a villein holding in villeinage. The connection with the treatment of the case in the treatise *De legibus* is close and obvious. The author[68] had been discussing his distinction between tenure and status and the question whether a freeman holding in villeinage could expect any common-law protection. A freeman who owes villein services, he says, may nevertheless have the assize if the services are certain, because this would show that the holding was free. Here as elsewhere,[69] he has the Ancient Demesne in mind and wishes to distinguish:

(1) free tenure, i.e. free socage, and
(2) villein socage on the Ancient Demesne, and
(3) villein tenure.

He shows first that villein socage (2) is similar to free tenure (1) in that both owe certain services, unlike pure villeinage (3). But neither tenants in pure (3) nor privileged (2) villeinage can benefit from the assize, because they hold *nomino alieno*. Here he cites our case. He thinks Thomas held by villein but certain services, after enfeoffment. The assize succeeded because the services were certain and therefore (implied) he held in his own name.[70] The reasoning behind the *De legibus'* conclusion, that 'if [the services] were uncertain, the tenement, whatever kind it was, will be villeinage', was not his clearest. Nevertheless, the author obviously considered the Prior of Ruislip's Case authority for the uncertainty principle.

---

[68] *Br.*, f. 200.
[69] Cf. Chap. 5.
[70] Bracton makes some assumptions about the facts behind the case which may not be justified. For instance, Alderton was not Ancient Demesne, *DB*, 239b.

12

'FAVOR LIBERTATIS': THE BIAS TO LIBERTY

Part II of this book, after expounding Bracton's theory of
villeinage, portrayed the villein's condition at common law,
with the compelling reality of villein disabilities, at least when
summoned before royal justice. Part III has surveyed the main
types of litigation by which villeinage disputes were brought
into royal courts, and thus modified our overall impression of
villeinage. A legal system that heeds precedent and rules of law
can always produce technical loopholes for the opportunist and
pitfalls for the unwary. The evolving common law did both, and
indeed moved in the direction of greater technicality during the
thirteenth century. The comparatively tight body of professional royal justices explained and justified their judgements
in terms of the law and its own logic. Quite often they reached
decisions by purely legal analysis and deduction. When difficult
points of law arose (or rather, were raised by litigants and their
advisers) in villeinage cases, the court's verdict was not always
predictable in advance. Lord and peasant alike at different
times found themselves denied enforcement of rights they had
been sure they possessed.

Viewed from this standpoint of villeinage suits, the nascent
common law somewhat resembles a fairly sophisticated fruit
machine, whose random factor is the unpredictability of legal
technicality. But gambling clubs can rig their machines. Was
the common law of villeinage rigged? The early common law
was far from impartial in any field. Its decisions in villeinage
matters were certainly not made at random. Although many
rules of villeinage became doctrine by chance inheritance from
the past—proof by suit of kin is one good example—the king
and his justices felt quite capable of making new law when
necessary.[1] Thus few historians have suggested that villeinage
law might have developed at random, or in a way calculated to
hold the balance between lord and tenant. Some social his-

---

[1] I refer to practice here, not to the theory behind, whatever that was.

torians, on the contrary, have dismissed royal law as irrelevant to the realities of life in the countryside. Village communities, in this view, on the whole regulated their own affairs, with little interference from royal government. Free and villein villagers lived alongside each other, intermarried, and earned their livelihoods in similar manners. What mattered was how much land and wealth each had, not what their common-law status was. Older proponents of such views tended to paint a rosy 'Merrie England' picture of village life.[2]

The legal material studied in this book heightens one's awareness of shadows in the picture: the closeness of violence and economic crisis to peasant life and so on. The very number of villeinage disputes that reached the king's courts demonstrates the seriousness of villeinage disabilities. The infrequency of royal court cases in a particular village does not prove that royal law lacked power and influence there. The occasional drama at Westminster could affect social relations between lord and peasant in the remotest hamlet of the realm.

Another approach to villeinage, associated with Marxist views, suggests that under the feudal regime of Angevin England the law functioned as an instrument of class repression and domination. Perhaps the ruling classes used the royal courts to coerce the labouring population to surrender unwillingly a higher share of their 'surplus'. Perhaps, too, the origins of villeinage itself lay in the resumption, from about 1180 onwards, of direct management of the great estates and their direct exploitation through compulsory labour services. The needs of the great landlords would have been well served by a royal law which offered the assistance of royal servants in the coercion of this peasant labour force. One obvious comment on this hypothesis leaps from the previous chapters. If villeinage was created to do this, the legislators had done a very bad job. The common law of the early thirteenth century did not function as an efficient instrument of compulsion. Other arguments on this view are best deferred until the next and final chapter, on the origins of villeinage.

No apology is offered for these twin caricatures of past approaches to the study of villeinage. A proper survey of the

---

[2] G. G. Coulton and H. S. Bennett were more careful to include villeinage and seignorial exploitation in their account of village life than some more recent writers.

past literature or a full assessment of the social changes of rural England in the twelfth century would each require a separate book. The present examination of the underlying assumptions behind common-law villeinage and its development commences with a critical assessment of the common law's self-image of its policy towards freedom and villeinage. Common-law judges of later times, looking backwards down their own history, believed that 'the procedure in trials touching the question of status was decidedly favourable to liberty'; the 'courts proclaimed their leaning "in favour of liberty" quite openly'.[3]

The perspective of the years misleads—at least so far as the thirteenth century was concerned.[4] To demonstrate this, we shall first examine the legend that the common law possessed an inherent bias toward liberty, perhaps borrowed from Roman law. We shall then consider the procedural details that supposedly attest to this bias to liberty, and finally, the possibility that the onus of proof in villeinage cases was habitually placed on the party who alleged villeinage.

The common law proudly boasted that the English courts had always had a leaning towards liberty—a good and humane quality. The *locus classicus* is Hargrave's learned and impressive speech in Somersett's Case, 1771.[5] He argued that the very extinction of villeinage resulted from 'the discouragement of it by the courts of justice. They always presumed in favour of liberty.' He further listed six 'instances of the extraordinary favour to liberty' of the common law, and this whole part of his argument was approved by the rest of the court, which proudly but wrongly believed that villeinage and the bias to liberty could be traced back to Anglo-Saxon England. They would have been chagrined to discover that their native principle had originated in Roman law. *Favor libertatis,* the general tendency to interpret rules and facts in favour of liberty, is associated with the wider principle of *benigniora praeferenda* (*Dig.*, 50.17.56), from which it was eventually said to have been derived. By its operation, the Law contrived both to favour freedom and to

---

[3] The words are from Vinogradoff, *Villainage*, pp. 83–5.
[4] Recent studies suggest also that the eighteenth-century courts were less favourable to liberty than they made out, but that is another story.
[5] Howell's *State Trials* xx at pp. 38–9.

protect the purity of *ingenuitas*.[6] The Roman rule that a child
was free if his mother had been free at any moment between his
conception and birth is a good example of its working.[7] The
principle was accepted by medieval glossators of both laws, who
turned to it when anomalies of slavery law required explanation.[8] The introduction of *favor libertatis* to English law in the
De legibus was effected with a similar object in mind, no doubt
because the author first encountered the idea during his study
of the learned laws.[9] The only explicit reference comes in a
passage where he is at a loss to explain why a writ of *monstravit*
could not be determined in the county court, although the writ
of naifty, to which it was *quasi incidens*, could. He did not know
why this should be 'nisi hoc sit propter favorem libertatis, que
est res inestimabilis, et que insipientibus et minus discretis
committi non debet'.[10] Later, in the section on assizes, he asked
what jurors should respond to an exception of villeinage, if the
plaintiff's status was in doubt, perhaps because he was personally unknown to them. 'In this doubt, judgement should be for
liberty, so that the interpretation falls *in benigniorem partem*, just
as it is presumed that every man is good until the contrary is
proved, and also because he who raises the exception about
villeinage does not prove it.' The final thought, which owes
nothing to *favor libertatis*, may have been the real clincher.[11]

The idea was entirely new to English law. Despite its respectable Romano-Canonist pedigree and its compatibility with
current theories, which explained servitude as a consequence of

---

[6] Buckland, *Slavery*, pp. 438–9; F. Schultz, *Principles of Classical Roman Law*, tr.
M. Wolff (Oxford, 1936), pp. 220–2; A. Berger, 'In dubiis benigniora (*Dig.*, 50.17.56)',
Seminar ix (1956), 36–49.

[7] Buckland, *Slavery*, p. 369, and cf. *Br.*, f. 5.

[8] e.g. *Decretum*, Dist. 54.19, gl. *officio*. Cf. *X*, 4.9.3, gl. *favore libertatis*, which asserts
that 'favore enim libertatis multa contra rigorem iuris statuta sunt', a borrowing from
Dig., 40.5.24.10; *Decretum*, C.12, q.2, c.68, is also cited. Cf. also *X*, 2.19.3, gl. *libertate*. The
Canonists consciously borrowed the idea from the Civilians; among the more promi-
nent citations were *Dig.*, 42.1.38, and 50.17.106, and *Cod.* 7.15.1 fin. And for *benignitas*,
cf. *X*, 5.41.2, *Sext*, 5.12.49.

[9] An educated man might pick up the odd reference elsewhere (e.g. John of
Salisbury, *Policraticus*, ed. C. C. J. Webb, Oxford, 1929, vii. 25), but Bracton's correct
usage seems another indication of his grounding in the learned laws.

[10] *Br.*, f. 105b, relied on the standard text *Dig.*, 50.17.106, as well as echoing his own
f. 1. Cf. *Fleta*, ii. 51 (111).

[11] *Br.*, f. 193, echoed by *Fleta*, iv. 11. Cf. *Br.*, ff. 200b, 239b: 'quotiens dubitatur an
quid sit, perinde est ac si non esset illud'. The *regulae* of *Sext*, 5.12.11, 65, support this
view of proof.

the Fall or of the *ius gentium*, no one had suggested previously that *favor libertatis* was law in England. Where the *De legibus* had been cautious in its introduction of the principle, subsequent usage progressively broadened it. Justices and legal writers employed it to justify a wide scattering of rulings otherwise hard to understand. Pleaders, short of strong arguments for their clients, cited *favor libertatis* to bolster their pleas. The note which appears in the Luffield register of writs is an early example from the 1260s. It stated that no more than two defendants might be named in a writ of naifty—'et hoc constitutum fuit primo in odium servitutis'—though a *monstravit* could name as many parties as the alleged villein wished—'et hoc in favorem libertatis'.[12] Apparently this statement records a minor innovation in mid-century, because early thirteenth-century writs of naifty quite frequently named more than two alleged villeins.[13] But in 1269 a claimant brought two separate writs against four alleged villeins.[14] The reference to *favor libertatis* perhaps reflects one man's reaction to a change that left some advantage with the alleged villein, whose writ remained unrestricted.[15]

An early fourteenth-century case illustrates well the way in which the principle of *favor libertatis* might lead in time to changes in the law. An action of naifty was brought into the Bench by *pone de nativis*, and the alleged villein was eventually constrained to appear in court by recourse to the grand distress. But when he finally appeared, the claimant himself defaulted. The court held that this default did not merely end the case: it enfranchised the alleged villein.[16] This judgement was quite exceptional, for the normal rule held that in these circumstances the alleged villein went without day (*sine die*) and retained the same status as before.[17] The reports reveal the

---

[12] *Selden Registers*, CC 100. Cf. *Brev. Plac.*, p. 214, of the early fourteenth century; it appears to be absent from a MS more or less contemporary with the register of writs, ibid. 91. Also *Fleta*, ii. 51 (110), *Reg. Omn. Brev.*, f. 87, 4th *regula*, *Vieux Natura Brevium*, 46, *FNB*, 78D.

[13] Close relatives in JI 1/558, ms. 11, 11d (Norfolk eyre 1208–9), JI 1/180, m. 6 (Devon eyre 1219), JI 1/174, m. 24 (Devon eyre 1238), but not in *SRS* xi. 515 (Somerset eyre 1243) or *WRS* xxvi. 162 (Wilts. eyre 1249).

[14] *NAS*, p. 156 (Northumberland eyre 1269), if I understand the entry correctly.

[15] e.g. *BNB* 1828 (Norfolk eyre 1227), JI 1/174, m. 21 (Devon eyre 1238), JI 1/614B, m. 7 (Northants eyre 1247).

[16] *YB Mich. 12 Edward II* (Selden YBB xxiii), pp. 90–2, (Warwicks. 1318).

[17] Above, Chap. 10, p. 166.

probable reason: the court had just given the claimant's attorney special leave to take his client's instructions when the alleged villein unexpectedly appeared in court. The holding of enfranchisement was no doubt given because a specially granted leave had been flouted, for the ordinary rule remained as before.[18] By Fitzherbert's day, however, the rule was that all such cases enfranchised the alleged villein, and he explained this as being 'en faveur de franchise'.[19] *Favor libertatis* had raised the exceptional to become the norm.

The pattern of development ought to be clear by now.[20] In 1347, an alleged villein was inspired to declare to parliament, in the course of a hard-fought suit with the Bishop of Ely, that 'the law rather favours the freedom of a man's body than to set him into servage'.[21] Although his principle was not followed on that occasion, the *favor libertatis* progressively established itself within the common law,[22] and was clearly the source of the later presumption or leaning towards liberty. *En route*, it contributed to the abolition of villeinage,[23] but the fact remains that the common law's bias to liberty, far from being a mark of its humanity, was really a measure of the harshness of the law of villeinage. The aim was to protect freemen against wrongful accusations of servility;[24] its backers were no doubt the same kind of people who were shocked when free women were disparaged, as they said, by marriage with unfree partners.[25] Set against this emotion was an opposite fear that villeins used legal trickery and procedural dodges to escape from their rightful

---

[18] Two of the MSS follow the case with one where the ordinary rule was administered, *YB Mich. 12 Edward II*, pp. 94–5 (Devon 1318).

[19] Fitzherbert, *Villenage* 28, to be compared with the more accurate citation in *FNB* 78F.

[20] Other illustrations are *Britton*, II. xviii. 6, developing *Br.*, f. 199, and *Mirror of Justices*, pp. 76, 79.

[21] *Rot. Parl.*, ii. 193a: 'si est la ley plus favourable a la fraunchise del corps d'ome que lui mettre en servage'.

[22] See *Vieux Natura Brevium*, 46v, Fortescue, *De Laudibus Legum Angliae*, ed. S. Chrimes (Cambridge, 1942), 42, p. 104, *Co. Litt.*, 139, and *FNB* 78D, 78G, for further material.

[23] See A. Savine, 'Bondmen under the Tudors', *TRHS* n.s. xvii (1903), 235–89. Cf. also W. W. Buckland and A. D. McNair, *Roman Law and Common Law* (2nd revd. ed., Cambridge, 1952), p. 30.

[24] As Savine concluded, art. cit., 256–60.

[25] See the references in *EHR* lxxxix, 730 n. 2.

lords and condition. These twin fears—of freemen wrongly enserfed and villeins wrongly enfranchised—long remained the common law's most prominent concerns in villeinage law. The total abolition of unfree status was not seriously proposed until 1381, when the lawyers, far from being in the vanguard of liberal change, were prime targets for rebel violence.[26] The fourteenth-century peasantry saw the courts as major props of the status quo. Paradoxically, one reason for the Law's reactionary stand was practitioners' pleas for alleged villein clients. By 1300, the professionals had arrived; their subtleties of pleading are well attested by the earliest Yearbooks. Rules designed to protect the free and virtuous appeared now to enable base villeins to deny their rightful status. So periodic attempts had to be made in parliament and elsewhere to block the loopholes in pleading practice. Lords complained about the procedural danger that a loose plea might be deemed to enfranchise their villein adversary. They sought that exceptions of villeinage should be tried where the jurors could be expected to know the circumstances of the alleged villein's birth, of which a newcomer's neighbours might be quite ignorant. The king's response did not always satisfy the complainants, but their gains, however small, were always more than the villeins'. Nobody has ever argued that parliament ever accepted *favor libertatis*.[27] The cases that fixed the common law's attitude to villeinage between the Black Death and 1381 were not always attempts by individual peasants or whole village communities to restrict their obligations, through claims of Ancient Demesne status and the like.[28] Significant though these were, *causes célèbres* involving

[26] On 1381 see R. H. Hilton, *Bond Men Made Free* (London, 1973), pp. 220 ff., with the documents translated by R. B. Dobson, *The Peasants' Revolt of 1381* (London, 1970) and my own comments in *EHR* lxxxv (1970), 609, and lxxxvii (1972), 611. On the legal evolution of villeinage tenure into copyhold, C. M. Gray, *Copyhold, Equity and the Common Law* (Cambridge, Mass., 1963), Chap. I, still seems to be a more acceptable account than the very uneven observations of E. Kerridge, *Agrarian Problems in the Sixteenth Century and After*, Chaps. 1–3.

[27] See *Rot. Parl.*, ii. 173b, 180a, 202b, 242a, 279b, 282b, 307b, 319b, etc., and Stats. 25 Edward III, c. 18, 1 Richard II, c. 6, and 9 Richard II, c. 2.

[28] R. H. Hilton, 'Peasant Movements before 1381', *Ec. H. R.* 2nd s. ii (1949) = *Essays in Economic History* ii, ed. E. M. Carus-Wilson (London, 1962), pp. 73–90.

substantial merchants and large sums of money caused even more stir.[29]

But this trend belongs to a later period. In the thirteenth century no one claimed *favor libertatis* as a specifically common-law principle. Most likely, men considered it a principle of *all* law, to ensure the protection of freedom. The slow popularization of the idea that followed its almost casual introduction reflects little credit on the common law for humanity and certainly establishes no leaning in favour of villeins.

Contemporary royal justices have left little direct information about their social prejudices. Study of their lives and careers will eventually clarify their links of employment and aspiration with the estate-owning classes; Henry de Bracton, who never served a great magnate as steward of his estates, was unusual.[30] Judicial sympathies presumably tended to favour the lords. Corruption too existed. Gifts and retainers to judges were common and must sometimes have influenced their conduct of cases.[31] But just how frequently 'coercion, bribery and the social sympathies of the courts helped the lords'[32] in the royal courts is another question. In default of good evidence, one can reasonably assume only that the supposed leaning of the common law towards liberty produced even less concrete benefits for alleged villeins than the most conservative estimate of the advantage to lords.

Vinogradoff, however, did not take this view. He believed that status procedure generally favoured the alleged villein, and

[29] *State Trials of the Reign of Edward the First, 1289–1293*, ed. T. F. Tout and H. Johnstone (Camden soc., 3rd s. ix 1906), pp. 90–1 (1287), a complaint against the infamous Adam of Stratton is a good early illustration. See also *YB 6 Edward II (SS* xvii 1902), pp. 11–13 (1308 case from Norfolk), *Rot. Parl.*, ii. 192a–3b (1347), and Dobson, *The Peasants' Revolt of 1381*, p. 126, for the incident which may have begun the troubles in Rochester.

[30] C. A. F. Meekings's many biographical studies of individual justices lie mostly alas unpublished; the tip of the iceberg only is revealed in such places as the introductions to *Crown Pleas of the Wilts. eyre, 1249 (WRS* xix 1960) and *CRR* xv. See the list of his writings in *Medieval Legal Records edited in memory of C. A. F. Meekings*, ed. R. F. Hunnisett and J. B. Post (London, 1978), p. 15. G. O. Sayles, *Select Cases in K.B.* i. (*SS* lv 1936), pp. xli ff., emphasizes the justices' extra-curricular roles as legal advisers on retainer. R. V. Turner promises a full study; see now his 'Clerical Judges in English Secular Courts', *Medievalia et Humanistica* iii (1972), 75–98.

[31] See *State Trials of the Reign of Edward I, 1289–1293, passim,* and F. J. Pegues, 'A Monastic Society at Law in the Kent eyre of 1313–1314', *EHR* lxxxvii (1972), 548–64.

[32] R. H. Hilton, 'Freedom and Villeinage in Medieval England', *Past and Present* xxxi (1965), 18. He produced no evidence.

proffered six illustrations.[33] First, one proof alone was accepted as conclusive, the production of 'suit of kin'. This is correct. But the retention of vigour by this form of suit, while others declined into mere formality, posed tricky problems for both parties in actions of naifty. The absence of any attempt to substitute a procedure less archaic and inappropriate was at most a recognition that claimants were turning to tenurial actions; more likely it was due to ordinary legislative inertia. Either way it owed nothing to any bias to liberty. Secondly, Vinogradoff noted the inadmissibility of women in suit of kin and the insufficiency of one man alone as proof. Both of these rules were, however, more ordinary than he realized.[34] Two more of Vinogradoff's points relate to the problem of the stranger. Proof of hereditary status was obviously much harder in the absence of a man's relatives. Vinogradoff declared the appropriate rule to be that an alleged villein was free if he could show that his father 'or any not too remote ancestor had settled on the lord's land as a stranger'. Moreover, the stranger was presumed free; uncertainty about his status was construed in favour of freedom.[35] Fourteenth-century courts were in fact prepared to presume the freedom of an *adventicius* in disputes over the status of a descendant, provided that the jurors were ignorant of his origins. A 1369 case, where it was argued on the alleged villein's behalf that 'il est greind reason en faveur de liberty', established the point.[36] To plead an *adventicius* ancestor was indeed not uncommon in the fourteenth century, though pleaders were generally careful to claim that the ancestor had been free as well as a newcomer to his village.[37] Many of these cases concern manors with Ancient Demesne connections[38] and pleas about

[33] Vinogradoff, *Villainage*, pp. 83–5. The main fault with Vinogradoff's argument was the lack of chronological precision; the criticisms that follow rule out the view for the thirteenth century, which is the central concern here, but do not necessarily refute his argument as of a later time.

[34] *EHR* lxxxix, 727–9, and above, Chap. 10.

[35] In a sense, it was up to the lord of his birthplace to keep him under surveillance, e.g. by taking chevage, above Chap. 4.

[36] *YB Hil. 43 Edward III*, f. 4, pl. 8 = Fitzherbert, *Villenage* 5, cited Vinogradoff, *Villainage*, p. 60.

[37] *Select Cases in K.B.* iii (*SS* lviii 1939). 61 (Yorks. 1301) is an example where the plea was successful. Note that the justices wanted details of the ancestor's arrival as a stranger, which the jurors were unable to furnish.

[38] As Milsom, *Novae Narrationes*, pp. liii–liv, pointed out. I see no evidence however that the defence originated on the Ancient Demesne, although this is the context of *Br.*, f. 26, the earliest reference to *adventicius* in this sense.

adventicii are rare before 1300.[39] But strikingly, the plea is absent from some apparently suitable mid-thirteenth-century cases. The courts would not yet presume that a stranger was free unless proved villein, or that proof of recent arrival protected a family from villein status.[40] That presumption's development can be explained without recourse to any theory about the law's leanings. Its roots are familiar rules of villeinage law. The practices of the claimant counting his ancestral seisin of the alleged villein's family,[41] and of argument about the alleged villein's *parentela* in clashes between rival suits of kin, forced several generations of the family on to the court's notice. New defences thus suggested themselves. One might argue, against the claimant's assertion of seisin of one's ancestors as villeins, that one of them, though free, had taken on a villein holding, perhaps by marriage to a villein 'heiress'. Or one might counter the claimant's suit of kin with the objection that a material ancestor had arrived in the village as a free newcomer.[42] Such a plea was peculiarly hard to check without evidence from the family place of origin.[43] At first the alleged villein had to meet counterpleas, such as the allegation that his family had sunk into villein status by prescription.[44] Gradually, however, the presumption that an *adventicius* was free when he arrived in the village came to be accepted by the courts, at about the same period and in rather the same way as the similar presumption that bastards were free.[45]

Vinogradoff's fourth point, also about newcomers to villages, was based on the *De legibus'* declaration that, where there was

[39] For *NAS*, p. 46 (Northumberland eyre 1256), the earliest I have noticed, see below n. 42. *NAS*, p. 159 (Northumberland eyre 1269), though the word *adventicius* does not appear in the entry, was similar. The pleas in both state quite explicitly that the ancestor was free. In KB 27/45, m. 7 (Oxon., *coram rege* 1279), justices opposed *adventicius* to villein in questioning jurors about an alleged villein's plea that he was free, but had resided for a period in the claimant's vill.

[40] See for example JI 1/482, m. 33 (Lincoln eyre 1245) and JI 1/56, ms. 14d, 19 (Buckingham eyre 1247), whose facts are retailed in *EHR* lxxxix, 740.

[41] This can be traced on the plea rolls from the 1240s, above Chap. 10, pp. 167, 181.

[42] This was the plea in *NAS*, p. 46 (Northumberland eyre 1256). The jury accepted the alleged villein's plea that his grandfather, the key link between him and the two villeins produced by the claimant, had come to the village of Mullsfen from Flanders as a 'liber homo et adventitius'. Mullsfen, held in chief as drengage, may have counted as Ancient Demesne, *Bk. of Fees*, i. 599.

[43] See below for later complaints about the difficulty.

[44] Above, p. 116 ff.

[45] For which see above, Chap. 10.

doubt, judgement was to be given for liberty.[46] After referring to *favor libertatis* (or more strictly the doctrine *benignitas*), Bracton had noted that doubt left the exception of villeinage unproved. The known cases of doubt[47] all tally with this down-to-earth interpretation. In a *monstravit* (possibly known to Bracton's author) brought by two brothers, Henry and Reginald, against the Abbot of Abingdon, both sides produced suit. The brothers denied that the abbot's suit were their kin, or even villeins at all; their own suit was free. The jury on which they put themselves did not quite agree. It found that the abbot's suit were villeins and related to the two brothers, but added that 'they do not know whether those kin whom Henry and Reginald produce to prove their liberty are freemen or villeins, but they do know that some of them are villeins . . . of others they know nothing'. Judgement was given for the abbot.[48] A rather later case has a pronounced Bractonian flavour. John de Laton' had persuaded the bailiff of Woodstock liberty to hand over to him Ralph Hereward as his villein. He achieved this with the aid of a slightly shady writ of naifty, acquired on the basis of Ralph's recent residence in John's vill of North Leigh. Ralph escaped and later sued John in trespass for imprisonment and loss of goods. John's defence, that Ralph was his villein, was put to a jury which confirmed Ralph's story in general but had to concede under questioning that 'penitus ignorant' whether Ralph had been John's villein and fugitive or 'in vilenagio tenens et adventitius'. Nevertheless the justices found for Ralph. John's admission that he was not in seisin of Ralph and the jury finding, that the arrest had been made outside the bounds of John's land, good conventional Bractonian points, sufficed to convince the justices, without any need to rely on *favor libertatis* or any similar principle.[49]

[46] *Br.*, f. 193.

[47] Few of the doubts raised found their way on to plea-roll entries. *CRR* ii. 122 (Surrey 1212) was a case of doubt about villeinage tenure (*pace* Poole, *Obligations of Society*, p. 18), in which the jurors assessed damages in anticipation of a judgement which may not have been reached. *PRS* xiv. 70 (Wilts. eyre 1194) is another case of tenurial doubt, where the plaintiff was authorized to have a new jury empanelled if he wished. Juries often declared the services and left the decision on villeinage to the court.

[48] *CRR* xv. 520 (Berks. 1233), sidelined like the case on the same membrane which became *BNB* 794. In *BHRS* xxi. 234 (Bedford eyre 1247), the doubt worked in favour of an assize plaintiff, when jurors were not quite sure that the deceased had been free.

[49] KB 27/45, m. 7 (Oxon., *coram rege* 1279).

Vinogradoff's fifth point suggested that few or no procedural restrictions hindered the alleged villein who sought to demonstrate his freedom. In particular, he might raise several different defences simultaneously, contrary to normal pleading rules. In fact, there is no good thirteenth-century evidence for Vinogradoff's view. In the fourteenth century, alleged villeins certainly claimed this right to make multiple pleas, and might support their argument with an appeal to *favor libertatis*, but the courts do not seem to have been swayed.[50]

Vinogradoff's sixth and final point was correct. Exceptions of villeinage were often tried by jurors from the alleged villein's residence, rather than men from his birthplace who were more likely to know about the family's status. This was so clearly to the alleged villein's advantage that lords strove in the fourteenth century to obtain a more favourable rule.[51] The point had arisen rarely in the previous century, no doubt because mobility was more restricted, though one case was adjourned into another county so that suit born there could be examined.[52]

Clearly Vinogradoff's conclusion that 'the procedure in trials touching the question of status was decidedly favourable to liberty' was mistaken, so far as the period before the end of the thirteenth century is concerned. The impossibility of deducing any clear trend in favour of alleged villeins, from the various points of procedure that do appear to favour one party or the other, is weighty evidence against any real external bias of the law. The system of rules in action was produced naturally by the operation of the standard rules of procedure, as modified by the efforts of imaginative pleaders to assist their clients. One further line of enquiry remains to test this 'technical' explanation of villeinage doctrine. Was there perhaps some general principle behind the common law of villeinage which laid the whole, or the heavier, burden of proof on the party that alleged villeinage? Although the answer is probably negative, the question illuminates the general direction in which pleaders influenced villeinage law.

---

[50] *YB Hil. 19 Edward II* = Fitzherbert, *Villenage* 32 (1326), cited by Vinogradoff, and *YB Hil. 43 Edward III* = *Villenage* 5 (1369) in which the alleged villein was particularly loath to concede the point.

[51] *Rot. parl.*, ii. 173b, 180a, 202b, 307b (1347–8, 1371).

[52] Above Chap. 10, p 174. The claimant was lucky that the circuit moved in the right direction!

Even today, the notion of a burden of proof causes difficulties.[53] In so far as the early common lawyers possessed the
idea at all, they had received it from the learned laws. The
Roman rule, taken over by the Canonists, held that the *onus
probationis* fell on the *actor* (plaintiff), but that, more generally, a
party who asserted a particular proposition or raised an objection had to establish it by positive proof or his adversary's
admission. As the maxim said, 'onus probandi incumbit ei qui
dicit'.[54] In practice, formulation of the dispute for litigation
could affect the burden's location. Where, for example, the
question of status arose through an exception from a *servus*
claiming to be free, the burden of proof became his.[55]

Common-law sources are not very explicit about the location
of the burden of proof. The defendant often had to choose
whether to plead a 'general denial' or to raise some kind of
exception. If he took the first, and no doubt primary course,[56]
the case turned on the plaintiff's offer of proof. If the second, he
had himself to offer proof, most normally by putting his case to a
jury.[57] But practice was seldom so neat, and the justices appear
to have exercised some discretion. Pleaders therefore ma-
nœuvred towards the award of an issue and proof favourable to
their client. In most actions, only one party made proof. Naifty
actions apparently differed. The claimant and alleged villein
could each offer and produce his proof, characteristically by suit
of kin.[58] If both proofs appeared 'sufficient', the decision
between them was put to a jury, in a way superficially resem-
bling modern court procedure. One might therefore expect twin
burdens of proof—on the claimant to prove his opponent villein
and on the alleged villein to prove his liberty. In practice, the
onus of proof in naifty actions lay primarily on the party whose
writ had effected the transfer into the royal court. Failure by

---

[53] Cf. J. B. Thayer, *A Preliminary Treatise on Evidence at Common Law*, pp. 353 ff., esp. p.
369.
[54] *Dig.*, 22.3.2. Cf. A. Berger, *Encyclopaedic Dictionary of Roman Law* (trans. American
phil. soc., Philadelphia, 1953), p. 652, s.v. *probatio*. The key texts for the reception by the
Canonists are *Decretum*, C.6, q.5, cc.1–2 and gl. *accusator*.
[55] *Decretum*, Dist. 54.10, gl. *diluere*, and Huguccio *ad idem* (MS Admont 7, fo. 78rb). C.
29, q.2, c.6 gl. *probare* finds this worrying, unless an alleged *servus* voluntarily undertook
proof of her liberty.
[56] *Novae Narrationes*, pp. xxxviii–xxxix.
[57] *P&M*, ii. 616, and generally 603–10.
[58] Above Chap. 10.

that party, the 'plaintiff' as it were, amounted to success for the other. And in assizes, ordinarily the party who raised an exception of villeinage had to prove it or lose his case. This succinct statement of the rules is the best demonstration possible that lord and villein were procedurally on a par in status cases. *Favor libertatis* played no observable role in the allotment of proof in the thirteenth century. These assertions must, of course, be confirmed from actual cases, first the naifty actions and then, with more difficulty, exceptions of villeinage in assizes. These two actions, the most important for status, suffice to establish the basic argument.

In simple naifty suits where the action reached the royal court as a result of the claimant's writs of naifty and *pone de nativis*, the onus of proof was his to discharge. When one early action failed, the court's reason for its holding did not mention that the alleged villein had produced suit. The entry stated simply that he could leave quit and free, because the claimant had produced no suit to convict him.[59] As Metingham, J., observed in 1294, there could be no higher answer to a writ of naifty than a flat denial.[60] One case even suggests that the claimant could not expect an answer at all unless he produced suit.[61] Yet by the late thirteenth century default by the claimant merely ended the present suit; it was not equated with a failure in proof and the claimant could sue again another day.[62]

When the alleged villein seized control of the suit by his writ of *monstravit*,[63] he probably also assumed the burden of proof. The assignation of the burden is less clear than in straight naifty cases, for there was some uncertainty which party was the 'plaintiff'. The alleged villein generally pleaded first, according to the plea rolls,[64] and had given security to prove his liberty when he acquired his writ.[65] He thus had the first opportunity

  [59] *CRR* iv. 60, 128 (Norfolk 1206).
  [60] *YB 20 and 21 Edward I*, pp. 446–9 (Middlesex eyre 1294); cf. *YB 32 and 33 Edward I*, pp. 512–14 (1304) and *Chetham soc.* lxxxiv, no. 81, p. 44 (Chester County court 1282).
  [61] *NAS*, pp. 274–5 = *Brev. Plac.*, pp. 215–16 (Northumberland eyre 1279): 'et quia predictus R. facit se responsabilem ad breve suum et narrationem [*et*] non producit sectam nisi . . ., consideratum est . . .' *P&M*, ii. 672, understands this differently; compare the French version.
  [62] Above, Chap. 10, pp. 165f.
  [63] I do not consider the 'Glanvill writ' (above, Chap. 10, p. 166) for lack of evidence.
  [64] *LQR* xc, 348–9.
  [65] Above Chap. 10.

(or duty) to prove his case.[66] A failure permanently ended his claim to freedom. But since this failure in proof was so close to proof of villeinage by the claimant, who may have produced his own suit of kin, talk of a single onus of proof is misleading. In practice, both parties did their best to make proof[67] and the alleged villein recovered his freedom when the claimant could not deny his suit.[68] Although the alleged villein's default or nonsuit curtailed his claim to liberty,[69] the claimant still needed to prove his title in the county. Similarly, in the thirteenth century, default or nonsuit by the claimant left the alleged villein's status as it had been prior to the case. He was not enfranchised for he had not yet made his proof of liberty, and the claimant might sue again later.[70]

If due allowance is made for the mixed character of *monstravit* hearings and the peculiarities of suit of kin, it is clear that naifty actions followed the standard rules about onus of proof. The assizes, furthermore, indicate that the same was true of procedure in other actions.[71] Assize plaintiffs' status commonly came under discussion in court, when an exception of villeinage was raised by the defendant, or the jurors 'discovered' villeinage in his family. Normally an exceptor had to offer proof of his exception (usually by a jury) and the plaintiff succeeded if the jurors found against his adversary. The Bractonian line on exceptions of villeinage was complicated by three factors. It aimed to protect genuine suits by freemen from difficulties due to frivolous villeinage exceptions. On the other hand, sometimes a villein was out to cause trouble; here the author would

[66] In JI 1/300A, m. 3d (Hereford eyre 1221), the alleged villein had a struggle to be allowed to fulfil the offer of proof in his count. His claimant alleged that he had proved him his villein in the county already, but the record of the county confirmed that the proceedings there had been the reason for the acquisition of the *monstravit*. Each party then produced his suit, before the alleged villein's freedom was acknowledged by concord.

[67] JI 1/273, m. 21 (Gloucester eyre 1248); 'Ideo consideratum est quod predicta Matilla in nullo probavit libertatem suam et quod predictus Petrus bene probavit ipsam esse villanam eius.'

[68] JI 1/454, m. 24 (Leicester eyre 1247): 'Et quia predictus Philippus nichil ostendit quod predictus Jordanus villanus sit nisi tantummodo simplex dictum suum et cognoscit quod parentes predicti Jordani, qui presentes sunt, sunt liberi homines, consideratum est . . .'

[69] *LQR* xc, 345.

[70] Ibid. 346–7; Chap. 10, p. 166.

[71] *Br.*, f. 192. There was of course an exceptional concern in the assizes to hasten proceedings; cf. Sutherland, *The Assize of Novel Disseisin*, pp. 18–20.

waive the usual rule and presume villeinage. Finally, he recognized the difficulty of proving someone else's villein unfree,
without the co-operation of the other lord, who had the kin
under his power.[72] For these reasons, he modified the normal
rule in accordance with his seisin-centred theory of villeinage.
The basic rule was to apply intact only to the *statuliber*, someone
in seisin of liberty before the challenge. The exceptor must offer
proof (by suit of kin or the assize) when he raised his exception
against him.[73] A *statuliber* was presumed free; the defendant had
to rebut the presumption by proof of his exception.[74] With the
statuservus, who had recently been in the defendant lord's power,
the presumption obviously worked in reverse. The exception
could best be confirmed by the assize.[75] The *De legibus'* conclusion that the onus of proof followed the plaintiff's presump-
tive status and seisin of liberty is not confirmed by the majority
of cases. Failure to produce some kind of proof certainly
invalidated some exceptions of villeinage,[76] including some
made by third parties intervening,[77] or by a plaintiff faced with
the defence that the land he sought was held not by the defendant but by his allegedly free sub-tenant.[78] But the rolls contain
no case where the onus of proof was on an assize plaintiff to
prove his freedom, because he was already within the defendant's power. Such cases can seldom have reached court. The
one example noted of the Bractonian plea, that the defendant
had held the plaintiff as his villein when he ejected him, was a
failure. The justices found for the plaintiff, when the defendant
admitted to them that the plaintiff had never acknowledged
being a villein.[79] The courts permitted no legal presumption of

[72] This is one reason why the *De legibus* denied the exception of villeinage to a
stranger; the villein was free against all but his lord. Above Chap. 8(ii).

[73] Since the assize procedure stressed speed, the rubric to f. 199 states that proof
must be *statim ad manum*, but the text left it to the justices' discretion.

[74] This accords closely with the supposed *exceptio spoliationis*, above Chap. 8(ii).

[75] This discussion is scattered over *Br.*, ff. 190b–201b, esp. ff. 191–192b. *Cod.* 4.19.15
and gl. *in possessione* suggests a Civilian parallel.

[76] *RCR* i. 84 (Lincs. 1194), *NRS* v. 663 (Northants eyre 1203), though the alleged
villein withdrew; *SS* liii. 137 and 176 (Lincoln eyre 1218), both entries with Bractonian
sidelining.

[77] *SS* lxxxiv. 4072, 4102 (Norwich 1209).

[78] *NRS* v. 769 (Northants eyre 1203), *SS* lix. 524 (Coventry eyre 1221). In both cases
the plaintiff was directed by the court to sue against the sub-tenant (from now on a
freeman), if he wished.

[79] *SS* liii. 1057 (Worcester eyre 1221), sidelined in 'Bractonian' style.

servility to defeat assizes; they may, however, have been more lenient about relatively thin evidence of villeinage brought to the attention of jurors by an influential defendant, wily enough to eschew a formal exception of villeinage.[80] This ploy of avoidance of formal exceptions may have gained popularity during the century.[81] Offers of suit of kin by excepting defendants certainly became rare,[82] in part because the procedure's defects were now widely recognized. Exceptions of villeinage tended to be put directly on to the assize,[83] as the *De legibus* had indeed allowed. All this time, pleading rules grew ever more restrictive and technical. Thus, a slight misformulation of an exception of villeinage often led to an unintended enfranchisement of the plaintiff.[84] Lords were well advised to forego the formal exception; better to raise villeinage and other possible defences informally, in or out of court, and hope the jurors took the hint.[85] Thus the accepted rules on the onus of proof, while retaining their legal validity, may have been evaded in practice, when tenants of doubtful status sued their lords.

This conclusion, if confirmed, clearly has an important bearing on the present enquiry into the common law's leanings in matters of status and of shifts in advantage. Seignorial pleading strategy itself perhaps evolved as a response to past assize defeats, when pleading errors enfranchised plaintiffs, who really ought to have been villeins. And the continuing struggle among pleaders to forward their client's interests may have

---

[80] The rolls never explain where the jury received their information. Assize failures because the plaintiff was a villein, where no exception had been made, are quite common. Others may hide behind a verdict of 'not disseised'.

[81] Sutherland, *Assize of Novel Disseisin*, pp. 19–20, 214, refers to exceptions of villeinage only in passing, which explains why his account does not do justice to the range of possibilities; but even so four of the villeinage cases he cites, p. 20 n. 1, do not seem to support him. My suggestions in the following lines are tentative, because I have sampled too few of the rolls from the later thirteenth century.

[82] JI 1/567, m. 2d (Norfolk eyre 1257) has a relatively late offer, not taken up by the plaintiff.

[83] As in ibid., ms. 7, 17d (Norfolk eyre 1257).

[84] e.g. *YB 30 and 31 Edward I*, pp. 136–9 (Cornwall eyre 1302). The reporter in *YB 21 and 22 Edward I*, pp. 166–7 (1293), proffers a *nota* to emphasize the care needed; a similar model plea for lords sued in trespass by their villeins was drafted at about the same time, above p. 142.

[85] *Select Cases in K.B.* iii (*SS* lviii 1939), 47–9 (Norfolk 1296). Informal statements of defence argument not amounting to an exception may appear on the rolls in words such as: '(the defendant) comes and says nothing why the assize should not be made, except that . . .' See Sutherland, *Assize of Novel Disseisin*, pp. 68–9.

produced, in the years around 1300, a small body of opinion prepared to argue for adjustment of the legal rules about onus of proof on the ground of *favor libertatis*. Previously the claimant's default on a *monstravit* left the alleged villein's status unchanged; at best he had seisin of liberty.[86] But Britton went beyond this. In his opinion, the alleged villein was enfranchised, because his *monstravit* was a 'bref de fraunchise'.[87] Although Britton's rule was eventually restricted to cases of departure in contempt of court, the fact that his view was canvassed in some early fourteenth-century cases[88] suggests that about this period *favor libertatis* was becoming a live force in the common law's treatment of villeinage, probably for the first time.[89]

The general conclusion of this chapter must be that, at least before the time of Britton, the common law exhibited no obvious bias or leaning towards liberty. The seductive Roman-law principle of *favor libertatis* was used only sparingly at first. In no way did it indicate a soft policy towards servility. Despite all talk of *benignitas*, the principle's Roman authors sought primarily to deter the wrongful enslavement of the free. This was equally the main attraction for English lawyers with anomalies to explain or weak cases to bolster. No doubt the high moral aura of *favor libertatis* carried an appeal to men educated in the tradition of a christian natural law. In the thirteenth century the argument was an oddity. During the century up to 1381, it influenced the battles of pleaders' skills that achieved minor modifications of villeinage law and elicited seignorial complaints in parliament and elsewhere. And ultimately it contributed to the eventual demise of villeinage.

Once the non-event of *favor libertatis* is removed from thirteenth-century villeinage law, what remains emerges as a formal structure of surprising impartiality. The rules about the onus of proof are the best illustration. If the common law ever felt tempted to bend its rules in favour of either lord or alleged villein, little was actually done. Of course, the legislators, lawyers, and justices involved, each with his mundane hopes

[86] Above, pp. 214f.

[87] *Britton*, I. xxxii. 12 (i. 202).

[88] *Novae Narrationes*, p. cxlvii.

[89] See also *Britton*, II. xviii. 6, where he develops a Bractonian point to declare 'en faveur de fraunchise' that no unwilling freeman could be compelled to put his status on the assize. Also ibid. IV. x. 5–6 (i. 280–2).

and ties, must have experienced temptation. Common-law 'impartiality' over villeinage possessed very considerable limitations. To say that the formal structure of doctrine was impartial tells little about the relative chances of one party or the other. The laconic and distorted nature of the legal materials (and the dispersed, uneven supplementary evidence available from outside the law) prohibits any attempt to make a scientific estimate of how much more likely the lord was to win than the alleged villein or vice versa. Clearly in practice extra-curial acts, power and influence in the county decided many villeinage disputes almost before they reached court. Flight to a secure new home beyond the lord's ken, for instance, could take the alleged villein beyond the range of a writ of naifty. But this must have been rare, for many reasons. In contrast, this book is replete with hints about lords taking the law into their own hands, justicing their peasants off their own bat, crushing without legal forms incipient aspirations to freedom. Where villeinage cases really were contested between a lord and a single peasant tenant, the advantage usually lay with the lord. In a legal study confined to the king's law, hints are the most that emerge.

PART IV

13
THE ORIGINS OF COMMON-LAW VILLEINAGE

The first three parts of this book have expounded the detailed legal evidence for the working of the law of villeinage within the thirteenth-century common law. This approach has constructed quite a minute picture of lawyers' attitudes towards the problems presented to the king by serfdom, through disorder, property disputes, and so on. The chapters also assessed as far as possible the significance of villeinage law to those most concerned by it, villagers classified as villeins (or in danger of such classification), their neighbours, and their lords. My early research, which had concentrated on understanding thirteenth-century villeinage as a legal system, minimized the problem of how that system came into being. To answer that question, the inquirer must reach back into quite a different world, adopt different approaches, and search very different sources. This enquiry can no longer be evaded. But, since the subject really calls for a book of its own, I offer here no more than a plausible hypothesis of the origins of villeinage, framed to fit the main lines of twelfth-century developments in government, law, and society as they appear to me.[1]

The comparatively 'hard' legal evidence about the action of naifty furnishes the starting point from which to introduce the hypothesis itself. I shall next establish the plausibility of my main assumptions (for they will remain assumptions) and try, within the limitations of the evidence, to date the stages by which common-law villeinage came into being. Finally, some

---

[1] R. H. Hilton, 'Freedom and Villeinage in England', *Past and Present* xxxi (1965), 1–19, first alerted me to the central importance of this topic, and I owe a good deal to Professor Hilton's stimulation, though I differ from him on many points. See also his *The Decline of Serfdom in Medieval England* (Studies in Econ. Hist., London, 1969), 9–17. Richardson and Sayles, *Law and Leg.*, pp. 138–48, present much relevant material, and E. Miller, 'La Société rurale en Angleterre (x^e–xiie siècles)', *Settimane di studio del centro di studi sull' alto medioevo* (Spoleto, 1966), 124–9, restates with some variations the traditional view.

possible explanations of the nature of the changes involved and
their effects on English society will be offered. The argument
will focus on the quarter of a century before and after 1200,
because the contention is that villeinage law was a by-product
of the emergence of the common law as a whole during those
years. Villeinage's origins have to be sought among the legal
traditions and political necessities of late twelfth-century
England, though the effects of the new doctrine were felt at all
levels of society and can only be understood in terms of the
patterns of social conflict and cohesion at the time.

Preliminaries over, let us begin the argument with the action
of naifty. Its working in the thirteenth century can easily be
expounded in terms of the conception of chattel ownership
considered in Part I. In effect, the law is ready to assist a lord, as
owner, to regain possession of his villein if he flees, or of his
service if he withdraws his obedience. The questions of title that
arose presented little serious difficulty to the courts. The only
snag in what would otherwise be an executive, almost administrative, matter[2] arose when the runaway claimed to be free
and thus beyond the lord's recall. The royal courts had procedures to deal with this, though they were archaic and none
too effective.[3]

The action of naifty almost seems designed for an England of
'classical manors' farmed for the benefit of their lord-owners by
the labour services of a predominantly servile peasantry; in
thirteenth-century sources, it appears virtually inseparable
from the chattel-ownership view of villeinage. But what of the
twelfth century? How long before 1200 can this action of naifty
be traced?

The question is hard to answer. Glanvill's treatise, completed
c.1187, is the first opportunity to see something like the whole
system of royal law, and most historians regard this as the first
view of a common law in existence. But two comments are in
order. First, the author was a very partial witness on the birth of
the common law. He wrote from within the circle of royal
advisers who had been reorganizing royal law, and he based his

[2] Cl. R., 1227–1231, p. 428, is an order for the return of a Gascon serf; Cal. Pat. R.,
1258–1266, p. 28 (and cf. Cl. R., 1256–59, p. 444), one for the return of a negro slave.
They show the direct way such matters might have been treated had not common-law
villeinage taken in at birth so much protective local custom.

[3] Above, Chap. 10.

account on those same royal writs through which the king offered justice to would-be litigants in *his* courts. Thus he certainly exaggerates the predominance of royal justice over other kinds in the country at this date. Secondly, any careful reader of Glanvill can discern that the customs and the court he describes are still in the process of rapid change.[4] Clearly, a writer from outside the royal camp would have seen the matter differently, and our author would have written a different account ten years earlier or later. Now Glanvill's Book V is dominated by the earliest and in many way the fullest account of the common-law action of naifty. In most respects this is the same action as that in the thirteenth-century plea rolls. No definite examples of naifty actions about status have been found before the date of Glanvill.[5] The action may have been very new indeed when Glanvill was writing, and perhaps only began in the 1180s. The common-law doctrine of villeinage itself can hardly be isolated earlier; in truth it emerged gradually from a series of changes which was not yet complete in 1187.

This crucial fact in the history of villeinage has been concealed from historians by the belief that the writ of naifty was of ancient origin, and had apparently changed little between the days of the Anglo-Norman kings and the thirteenth century.[6] Despite a close resemblance to Glanvill's writ, few if any of the earlier writs *de nativis* were intended primarily to introduce pleas about status,[7] nor were they directed solely at peasants. Glanvill's action of naifty was quite new, and study of earlier writs shows their progressive modification to make the emergence of the Glanvill action about status possible.

The purpose of the early precursors of Glanvill's writ of naifty becomes clear only when the wording of the writs is examined

[4] Book VII is an excellent illustration. Glanvill's account of inheritance, concentrated in this book, ranges from rules already virtually obsolete and moral sentiments about the way a father ought to treat his children, to other elements of the later common law of descent. His treatment of villeinage is open to similar comment, below p. 245.

[5] Pipe-roll entries may take the story back into the early 1170s; see below, nn. 37, 113.

[6] *Van Caenegem*, pp. 336–43, is a recent account with references to previous discussion; most of the twelfth-century writs considered below are cited from his edition. *Van Caenegem*, no. 124, is from *Glanvill*, xii. 11 (ed. Hall, pp. 141–2). *Novae Narrationes*, pp. clxii ff., is also valuable.

[7] Contrast the early rubric to *Glanvill*, Bk. V: 'placitum de questione status'.

on its own terms and within the context of the time. Preconceptions drawn from the later common-law action are misleading. On their own, the twelfth-century writs appear as grants of royal assistance, usually in general terms, to favoured beneficiaries who experienced difficulties with men from their lordships. In form they closely resemble the executive writs by which kings ordered the reseisin of land, also on behalf of privileged beneficiaries, often no doubt in return for some unmentioned *quid pro quo*. Writs about fugitives were often alternatives to writs for reseisin of land.[8] Behind them lay a world of fierce competition between lords, where power and position depended on the control of land and men. Land without men to work it was worth little, so the offer of holdings on attractive terms, to lure men from other lordships, was a common ploy in the early twelfth century.[9] When such strategems led to clashes, most lords relied first on their own resources. Under a king of limited power like Stephen, this was one cause of local private wars. In more controlled times, seignorial and local public courts heard consequential litigation over rights to men,[10] and there must have been local negotiations and agreements similar to those that occasionally dealt with land disputes.[11] But in twelfth-century England, the offer or threat of royal aid was always a useful ploy. These early writs about fugitives secured that advantage for one party.[12] Unfortunately, the precise situation which elicited a writ can rarely be discerned. The impetrant lord may have failed already to pre-

[8] A. Harding, 'The Medieval Brieves of Protection and the Development of the Common Law', *Juridical Review* (1966), 115–49, is an interesting if speculative attempt to argue that the origins of the action of right, trespass, etc. in Scotland lay in early royal writ-charters of protection—and ultimately in the king's peace. His ideas deserve a test against the English material. Cf. also J. S. Critchley, 'The Early History of the Judicial Writ of Protection', *Bull. Inst. Hist. Research* xlv (1972), 196–213, a more specialized study of a later period, and T. A. M. Bishop, *Scriptores Regis* (Oxford, 1961), p. 21.

[9] E. Searle, 'Hides, Virgates and Tenant Settlement at Battle Abbey', *Ec. H. R.* 2nd s. xvi (1964), 290–300, is one example; another may be the gradual increase in commutation to money rents on the Burton Abbey estates in the years after Domesday Book.

[10] See below, p. 239.

[11] N. M. Hurnard, 'Magna Carta, Clause 34', *Studies in Medieval History presented to F. M. Powicke*, pp. 157–63, surveys the evidence for land litigation in the twelfth century.

[12] Another method was for the man in possession to safeguard himself by a writ which forbade pleas against him. *Van Caenegem*, nos. 113, 161, are the only specific examples noted, but see also those writs cited ibid. 338, nn. 1–2.

vent tenants from leaving his lordship. Possibly he had watched impotently while a local rival lured men away from his lordship on to a neighbouring one, or more simply took over the land they cultivated. Or perhaps he just anticipated problems. In each eventuality, a royal writ could be thought worth the price.[13] Some of the earlier writs were worded to meet specific situations,[14] but most were phrased in general terms whose continuing value to the beneficiary explains their preservation in his archives. A newly elected prelate, whose consecration oath had bound him to recover any alienated possessions of his see, might, if shrewd, obtain from the king a privilege for the return of its fugitives when he also purchased a royal confirmation of all its property, or an equally general writ for the reseisin of allegedly alienated lands.[15]

Some unique documentation offered by the Bishopric of Durham, whose bishops were in the twelfth century building up what became one of the most independent of English liberties,[16] is invaluable here. The bishops' efforts to win or retain control over as many men as possible were exceptional only in the extra lawlessness of the border area. St. Cuthbert was certainly not averse to attracting men from other lordships. Reginald of Durham tells of a *pauper colonus* from Middleton-on-Tees who was heavily exploited by a greedy lord because he had retained the air of being well off. Eventually he could hardly continue to cultivate his land. Then St. Cuthbert, appearing to him in a vision, invited him to flee with all his possessions to Lindisfarne where he would enjoy the saint's peace and protection. Accordingly, he set off with his family and livestock in the depth of night. But the lord and his servants were not far behind, and had almost caught up with him by the time he arrived at the coast. Our fugitive now shrugged off a well-timed attempt by his wife and companions to persuade him to make for Lothian instead, and, preferring to trust in the saint 'potius . . . quam in

---

[13] Whatever that was; I know of no evidence.

[14] e.g. *Van Caenegem*, nos. 103, 110–11, where there had been genuine flights of which, significantly, the king's actions were at least a partial cause.

[15] *The Cartulary of Cirencester Abbey*, ed. C. D. Ross (London, 1964), i, no. 68, is a writ of naifty dated 1155/65, probably 1155, since no. 69 is a general confirmation of the abbey's lands dated by the editor 1155/8 and it resembles three writs of naifty from about 1155, *Van Caenegem*, nos. 114–16.

[16] Success, however, came slowly. See J. Scammell, 'The Origin and Limitations of the Liberty of Durham', *EHR* lxxxi (1966), 449–73.

terreno patrocinio', plunged on to the sands through the midst
of his enemies, whom the saint then rendered incapable of
either seeing or hearing the noisy procession. His successful
arrival on Lindisfarne brought him the raised status of a *civis*,
and in time his sons succeeded peacefully to the new holdings.[17]

This most illuminating anecdote highlights many of the key
factors behind twelfth-century writs of naifty. The ability to
leave an exploiting lord was a crucial escape route. The mere
knowledge that a man might move elsewhere, whether as of
right or because he could not be stopped, boosted a man's
power to bargain for a better tenurial deal. If one lord would not
let him prosper, there were, in an age when tenants were rarer
than land, others who would. Often the lord's answer, to chase
him and bring him back, sufficed, unless another lord was
involved. The foiled lord might then have sought outside help
from some more powerful ally, for example, or in the acquisition
of a writ of naifty granting the aid of royal ministers. That the
lord of Middleton did not do so is a reminder that royal assistance was for the influential few. The lord's right to retain
tenants against their will or retrieve them if they tried to leave,
though probably well accepted at the time, was normally his
own responsibility.

St. Cuthbert was, of course, often among these favoured few.
The wily and experienced Rannulf Flambard, bishop from 1099
to 1128, knew well how to play the game.[18] At different times he
received from Henry I three extant writs classed as writs of
naifty; much is known about the circumstances behind the issue
of each. One important point is immediately obvious: they all
concentrate on lands outside the bishop's liberty. The bishop
and his servants expected to handle troubles closer to home off
their own bat. The first writ dates from the beginning of the
reign. Henry had struck hard and quick at his dead brothers'
followers soon after his accession. Rannulf, more or less the
scapegoat for William Rufus's unpopular regime, was im-

---

[17] Reginald of Durham, *De Admirandis Beati Cuthberti Virtutibus* (Surtees soc. i. 1835),.
pp. 234–6.

[18] What follows is based on H. E. Craster, 'A Contemporary Record of the Pontificate
of Rannulf Flambard', *Archaeologia Aeliana*, 4th s. vii (1930), 33–56, with the comments
of R. W. Southern, *Medieval Humanism*, Chap. 10, pp. 197 ff., and H. S. Offler, *Rannulf
Flambard as Bishop of Durham (1099–1128)*, (Durham Cathedral lecture, 1971), esp.
pp. 4–7.

prisoned in the Tower, but escaped early in 1101 and supported Duke Robert so skilfully in Normandy as to win himself a place in Henry's amnesty later in the year. The first writ of naifty was then issued, in August, along with two others that restored the Durham lands to their state at the start of the reign.[19] With these writs Rannulf set out to recover the men and lands lost along with royal grace. But Henry and his brother were soon at each other's throats again, and Rannulf spent the next few years playing them off against each other from a Norman base. Thus the second writ dates from 1102 or 1103, when Archbishop Anselm absolved Rannulf and helped him to regain royal favour for a time. It ordered back all men who had left the diocese unjustifiably since the last bishop's death, men who had fled (as an accompanying writ said) 'on account of the money which the bishop gave me [the king]'.[20] After Henry's triumph at Tinchebrai in 1106, Rannulf, now firmly excluded from national politics, devoted himself perforce to the administration of his see. St. Cuthbert had still many losses to recover, so between 1114 and 1118 Rannulf procured a third writ to reclaim any other men who had fled with their goods 'on account of the money which I [the king] exacted from him'.[21] Clear evidence of Henry's approval was essential for Rannulf to remedy the situation. Tenants had been encouraged to flee elsewhere to better conditions, and rivals (like Nigel d'Aubigny) had sought pickings from episcopal lands. Though Rannulf's whole previous career led him to seek his primary remedy from Henry I, restitution was certainly not automatic. He may therefore also have acquired brieves of naifty from the king of Scots, who always wielded some power in the area.[22] Lords like the Bishop of Durham normally justiced their own men, but when necessary, used whatever outside help they could attract.

Of this recourse to outside help, the twelfth-century writs of naifty are our main evidence. The early 'writs of naifty' were merely a new kind of document conveying commands to enforce the long-established duty of one lord not to receive the man of

---

[19] Craster, nos. X–XII; *Van Caenegem*, no. 106.

[20] Craster, nos. XXIII–XXIV; *Van Caenegem*, no. 107.

[21] Craster, no. XXIX; *Van Caenegem*, no. 111.

[22] The cell at Coldingham did so before 1174, *The Acts of William I, King of Scots 1165–1214*, (*Regesta Regum Scottorum* ii, Edinburgh, 1971), nos. 44, 113 (before 1174).

another on to his lordship without the original lord's licence, for reasons above all of public order.[23] All extant writs about fugitives came from ecclesiastical archives.[24] Many were drafted by their ecclesiastical beneficiaries. What proportion of the whole they represent, or how typical they may be, is unknown. Nevertheless, already in the early twelfth century some genuine development can be traced, and during Henry II's reign the chancery stabilized writ formulas sufficiently to permit the expert to date writs within narrow limits by their diplomatic.[25] For much of the century, the writs' main concern is the restitution of men of their (allegedly) rightful lordship, thereby enforcing the claimant lord's title.[26] Any lawsuits over the execution of the writs were normally confined to the question of title, and were fought between great lordships. Status and the right to leave land were not a main concern of the writs, although the fugitives may exceptionally have tried to plead about these in some court.[27] Nor indeed were most writs acquired as a result of some trial of strength between a lord and an individual fugitive[28] or village. At this stage, lordship over men and over land were still much the same thing. Thus in the first years of Henry II's reign, when the king was issuing many land confirmations to remedy losses during the upheavals of the Anarchy, he also granted to several beneficiaries general privileges of naifty, to order the restoration of all their fugitives.

Quite soon, however, changes began to appear in the formulation of the writ. The first innovation can be detected as early as 1155.[29] Thenceforth, the writs describe the fugitives to be recovered as *nativi:* the claimant lord was to have restored to him 'omnes fugitivos et nativos'.[30] Although the significance of this change was perhaps not recognized immediately, the word

<hr>

[23] Below, pp. 235 f.

[24] *Van Caenegem*, no. 66/104 (1093/7), is a possible exception which all the same owes its survival to preservation among the archives of Colchester Abbey.

[25] Cf. Bishop, *Scriptores Regis*, pp. 20–2.

[26] Cf. M. Bloch, 'Liberté et servitude personnelles . . .', *Mélanges*, i. 353 n. 1, commenting on *Van Caenegem*, no. 114. Also above, p. 163 and n. 3.

[27] See below, pp. 236–9.

[28] *Van Caenegem*, nos. 109, 113, may be exceptions.

[29] The new regime may have introduced a number of these changes right from Henry's accession. For example, from 1155 grants in free alms were confirmed only if made *rationabiliter.*

[30] e.g. *Van Caenegem*, nos. 114 ff.

nativus carried the plain implication that the birth and hereditary condition of the fugitive mattered. The next small step was to conclude that fugitives ought to be returned to their lords, *only* if their birth precluded them from the right to leave freely, that is if they were hereditarily tied to the lordship. An intelligent lawyer or civil servant, who studied the writ carefully, might make the jump without difficulty. Other changes in wording are less precisely datable but may have been effective more swiftly. Their overall result is clear: they reduced the generality and scope of the favour to the beneficiary, the claimant lord. At first, writs could still be addressed to all sheriffs (not just to the sheriff of one county), but from the early 1160s the addressee was to obey the order for the fugitives' restitution only if they were found within his jurisdiction.[31] At about the same time the writs gained extra urgency by the addition of the phrase 'et sine dilacione',[32] and along with other 'judicial writs' of the common law, writs of naifty began to be sealed as letters close.[33] Probably, then, much of this work of amendment was implemented in the 1160s and 1170s. No writs are extant from the years immediately before Glanvill, to witness the final changes of the reign that produced Glanvill's own form.[34] This, unlike any known predecessors, ordered a single sheriff to surrender to a claimant lord one (or at the most two) fugitive *nativi*,[35] together with their chattels and *sequelae*, if found within his jurisdiction. This new formula is obviously connected with

[31] Ibid. 343.

[32] Ibid. 342. One earlier example is known, ibid., no. 108 (?1105). Cf. Bishop, *Scriptores Regis*, pp. 20–1, for the date of the change, which perhaps developed out of special proffers, as in *Dialogus*, II. xxiii. B (120).

[33] *Van Caenegem*, pp. 164–5; Bishop, op. cit., pp. 20–1; P. Chaplais, *English Royal Documents . . . 1199–1461*, (Oxford, 1971), pp. 6, 9, 11–12. This sealing change very probably coincided with the change of many writs (but not the writ of naifty) to a returnable form (on which see D. M. Stenton, *English Justice between the Norman Conquest and the Great Charter, 1066–1215*, Jayne Lectures for 1963, Philadelphia, 1964, pp. 32–3). This moment, about 1166, when for the first time judicial writs ceased as a group to be re-usable and had to be brought into court for use at the anticipated trial, is one candidate for nomination as the beginning of the common law; but see further below.

[34] One change of little significance here was the insertion of a warning to the sheriff not to touch the fugitives if they were on royal demesne. For its effect see above, Chap. 10, pp. 168 ff. *Van Caenegem*, no. 122 (1175/80), is the only example noted before Glanvill, although the appearance of similar formulas in Scottish brieves from 1164/75 (*Regesta Regum Scottorum* ii, nos. 44, 163, 387, 481) suggests that the refinement may have been earlier and associated with Henry's drive to consolidate royal-demesne rights.

[35] For the later common-law rule, see above, Chap. 12.

the rule in the assize of novel disseisin that a successful plaintiff recovered seisin not only of the tenement but also of its adjuncts, fruits, chattels, and so on.[36] Most important of all, perhaps, Glanvill is the first to reveal a settled procedure including a writ *De libertate probanda* by which the alleged fugitive could ensure that the case reached the king's court. This enabled the fugitive to plead in the course of proceedings commenced by writ of naifty that he was a free man, and thus not rightly returnable to the claimant lord against his will. Not until *c.*1187, therefore, could the writ of naifty definitely introduce into a royal court pleas of status.[37] Glanvill's pair of naifty writs and much of the procedure he presents in Book V seem very *au courant*.[38] Though naifty actions about the title to men continued in the royal courts for some considerable time,[39] the author of *Glanvill* probably wrote with recent memories of the royal prohibition of status pleas in the county court; certainly his reference is much more casual than the *De legibus'* later.[40]

Much of this account of the evolution of the writ *de nativis* and the court proceedings it could introduce must remain conjectural for lack of evidence. Comparison with the approach to the same problems in Scotland does, however, lend some support. At Henry II's accession, Scots royal law quite closely resembled English law, so that anyone familiar with twelfth-century England feels reasonably at home with contemporary Scottish legal documents. But Scotland never adopted the crucial developments that created the English common law over the next generation; its kings, less powerful than the Angevins, could not

---

[36] *Glanvill*, xii. 8–9.

[37] *P. Roll 21 Henry II*, p. 178 (1175), records that Osbert de Torp owed 15 marks (cf. *P. Roll 11 Henry II*, p. 49, for the same sum) for imprisoning a *homo* whom he wished to prove a *rusticus* but could not. This is the earliest likely reference to a naifty action on status in a king's court. For Osbert of Bustard-Thorpe see *Early Yorks. Charters*, i–iii, vi *passim*, and D. Greenway (ed.), *Charters of the Honour of Mowbray*, no. 379.

[38] The writs themselves are no help. Writs *de nativis* cease to be worth preserving once they become limited to one suit. No writs *de libertate probanda* have been found in seignorial archives.

[39] *LQR* xc (1974), 342–4; cf. *Glanvill*, i. 3–4, for the two types of action, called *questio status* and *placitum de nativis*.

[40] *Glanvill*, v. 1 (ed. Hall, p. 54), and above, Chap. 10. Glanvill can be very off-hand about recent innovations.

hope to centralize Scots law after the English model.[41] The brieves (writs) that have survived from the twelfth century include several about fugitives. They seem rather less standardized in form than their English counterparts (though the amount of standardization in England must not be exaggerated) and thus flexible enough to be tailored to the circumstances of a particular case.[42] The initial adaptations of English writs of naifty, up to the 1170s, were soon known and copied in Scotland.[43] Thus brieves using the word *nativus* are found from 1161–2,[44] and restitution 'absque dilatione' was ordered soon after the introduction of the equivalent English formula.[45] More significant are the changes which do not appear. Unlike the English writs, brieves of naifty continued for a long time to have multiple addressees,[46] amongst whom often stood *probi homines*,[47] as well as royal officials who could be told, for example, to act 'in cuiuscunque terra aut potestate' the fugitives were found.[48] Nor did the brieves gain the new formula about the fugitive's chattels and *sequela,* though some indeed continued to refer, in what was now an old-fashioned way by English standards, to the value of the fugitives' movable wealth, their *pecunia.*[49] Above all, the fugitive's own writ *de libertate probanda* never appears in Scotland; even in the fourteenth century when the lawbooks do describe status suits introduced by brieves of naifty, they mention no brieve for the fugitive himself.[50] The brieves retain a far more seignorial flavour than

---

[41] This has become something of a commonplace in discussions of medieval Scots law. That Scottish legal commentators continued to use Glanvill as their model into the fourteenth century is indicative. See A. A. M. Duncan, 'Regiam Majestatem: A Reconsideration', *Juridical Review* n.s. vi (1961), 199–217, and A. Harding, 'The Medieval Brieves of Protection and the Development of the Common Law', ibid. (1966), esp. 124, 127–9, 132 ff.; but note also G. W. S. Barrow, *The Kingdom of the Scots* London, 1973), Chap. 3, esp. pp. 85–94.

[42] e.g. *RRS* ii, no. 336, (1189/95).

[43] Cf. above n. 34.

[44] *RRS* i, no. 92: 'nativos homines terre sue aut fugitivos suos'. But cf. *RRS* ii, nos. 25, 248, 313, 326, 481.

[45] *RRS* ii, nos. 25 (1165/71), 248, but cf. ibid., nos. 44, 113.

[46] Even in the fourteenth century, those in *Register of Brieves,* ed. Lord Cooper (Stair soc., x 1946), pp. 38, 53, are to multiple addressees, though that in *Quoniam Attachiamenta* c. 56 (*Regiam Majestatem,* ed. Lord Cooper, Stair soc., xi 1947, p. 353) is to one only.

[47] e.g. *RRS* i, nos. 167, 188; ii, nos. 25, 337, etc.

[48] *RRS* i, no. 192 (1161–2); cf. *Van Caenegem,* no. 117.

[49] *RRS* ii, nos. 30, 248.

[50] *Register of Brieves,* pp. 36, 53; *Regiam Majestatem,* pp. 11–12, 353–5.

English writs. Essentially they remain royal confirmations of seignorial rights, warnings to rival lords; clauses ordering the return of fugitives were still inserted in general charters of confirmation and brieves of protection, long after such practices had ceased in England.[51] Some brieves show by their wording that the responsibility for finding the fugitive was the lord's and not the royal officials',[52] while others specify the lands to which the fugitives belonged.[53]

In sum, then, the Scots royal law about fugitives from lordships appears to have paralleled English developments until the mid-twelfth century. From about the middle of Henry II's reign, however, it diverged. Though an Anglocentric commentator might describe the Scots law as in suspended development for a while, the comparison highlights the significance of the changes that gave Glanvill's action of naifty to England. The task now is to assess the wider significance of the drafting amendments. Was the moment when the writ of naifty could for the first time introduce into the royal court suits about villein status also the birth-date of common-law villeinage? This idea, though attractive, is ultimately not quite convincing. Let us try to understand the implications of the question.

This book has sought to describe the common law's doctrine of villeinage. In it the terms 'villein' and 'villeinage' have been restricted as far as possible to those men and tenements considered by thirteenth-century lawyers to be unfree and therefore outside the common law, and to the group of common-law doctrines on the subject. A looser usage has, indeed, some contemporary warrant,[54] but the argument of this final chapter is primarily legal. The changes scrutinized here affected the way English society was viewed by lawyers, and ultimately worked to define the limits of legal jurisdiction etc. that the King was prepared to exercise. Of course the changes had significant social effects; indeed, this social context must not be

---

[51] Harding, 'The Medieval Brieves of Protection', 121, 124, 143; cf. *RRS* ii, nos. 30, 37, 248, 313, 481 (1208).

[52] *RRS* i, nos. 167, 188, 192; ii, nos. 25, 44, 113.

[53] e.g. *RRS* ii, no. 114 (1167/71); 'ad terram illam pertinentes'; also *RRS* i, no. 188; ii, nos. 44, 113, 163. Such formulas are already becoming rare in England under Henry I; compare *Van Caenegem*, nos. 109–10, with nos. 117, 119.

[54] There is some discussion of the meanings of *villanus, rusticus,* and *nativus* below, n. 113.

ignored. Yet the underlying social movements remain second-ary to the main purpose of this book. The suggested hypothesis is that 'villeinage', as a lawyer's body of doctrine for the people on the fringe of the common law or beyond it, originated in the late twelfth century. Any suggestion that English serfdom was only born at that late date is patently absurd, so I have strug-gled to confine my use of 'slavery', 'serfdom', and so on, to argument about social or economic context. They need not be defined closely, so long as one realizes that they were not legal categories.

Obviously the common law of villeinage was a kind of serf-dom law. But villeinage *ex hypothese* was quite new in 1200, while serfdom, as a social institution, had existed in England from time long out of mind. Most historians now agree that lordship and slavery each had roots deep into the Old English polity, and had perhaps featured in Anglo-Saxon society since the Invasions. So long as nobles possessed great landed estates, some inhabitants must have been too free to be properly re-garded as slaves, yet so dependant on their lords' will as to make no freemen. They may reasonably be termed 'serfs', unless their contemporary names are preferred.[55] The housing of a dom-estic chattel slave on a holding of his own off the manorial demesne, perhaps after his manumission, improved his con-dition and raised his status without removing all servility. Contemporary social nomenclature was not designed to make a modern sociological distinction between 'slave' and 'serf', and can mislead the incautious social historian. Hence, while west-ern Europe had clearly long moved away from the worst chattel slavery by the twelfth century, attempts to show how rapidly, or otherwise, slavery *disappeared* from England after the Norman

---

[55] See now H. P. R. Finberg, 'Anglo-Saxon England to 1042', esp. Chap. VII in *The Agrarian History of England and Wales*, I. ii, ed. Finberg (Cambridge, 1972). J. S. Scammell has promised a discussion of the 'twilight of subjection and personal limitation', in which she believes a majority of Old English society lived, *Ec. H. R.* 2nd s. xxix (1976), 487.

Conquest are beside the present point.[56] Historians can more usefully examine variations in the extent of lords' actual power over their men. Estate documents and the occasional literary reference[57] prove that many were still subject to a very complete control over the way they lived. Others were much freer, in one sense or other of the word,[58] though still submitted to seignorial restraints. In Carl Stephenson's words, 'all tenants who were not members of the feudal aristocracy were permanently subjected to manorial control, unless they could prove their title to an exceptional variety of freeholding'.[59] A good test of this assertion is the ability of lords to prevent their dependants from leaving their lordship. Indeed, the ultimate democratic right is to vote with one's feet.

The lord could threaten or actually exercise force. Presumably, this sufficed to cow many runaways and bring them back. Not all disputes ended so simply. How often could a lord and his court settle the matter satisfactorily, without the need for action outside the lordship such as negotiation with a neighbour, or an expedition against him, or an appeal for the king's aid? A lord's ability to justice his men without outside intervention depended on two factors: the amount of delegated (or usurped) royal

---

[56] Richardson and Sayles, *Law and Leg.*, pp. 142–3, argue that slavery survived well into the twelfth century in the west of England. Add to their references Gerald of Wales, *Expugnatio Hibernica*, I. xviii (*Opera* v, ed. J. F. Dymock, R. S. 1867, p. 258) on the Council of Armagh's pronouncement against the trade in English slaves to Ireland in 1170; *The Letters of John of Salisbury*, i, ed. W. J. Miller and H. E. Butler (*NMT* 1955), no. 87 (1148/61), and E. Bromberg, 'Wales and the Medieval Slave Trade', *Speculum* xvii (1942), 263–9. The arguments have always begun with the fall in numbers of Domesday *servi* between 1066 and 1086, but this may be an unreliable index of change, since the word *servus* penned by the same scribes at home across the Channel would be translated 'serf' by modern French historians! H. B. Clarke, 'Domesday Slavery (Reduced for Slaves)', *Midland History* i (1972), 37–46, on the other hand, rightly stresses the association of Domesday demesne ploughs and *servi*.

[57] e.g. Reginald of Durham, *De Admirandis B. Cuthberti Virtutibus*, p. 206, mentions William the miller of Thorpe a *homo dominio potestatis*, whose lord 'de ipso efficere libere potuit quicquid voluntarii animi motus de illo fieri vel praeordinare delegit'.

[58] G. R. Sitwell, 'The English Gentleman', *The Ancestor* i (1902), 91–7, remains valuable on the changing connotations of freedom. Hilton, 'Freedom and Villeinage', 4 etc., is a recent discussion. The use of *liber* to denote nobility appears rare in twelfth-century England; certainly in Magna Carta it bears the meaning of 'not villein' which was normal after the birth of the common law.

[59] This is the conclusion at the end of 'Commendation and Related Problems in Domesday Book', (1944), available as pp. 156–83 of his *Medieval Institutions* (Ithaca, N.Y, 1967). The denigration of Stephenson after his controversies with Maitland and Tait often missed the point of the questions he was posing.

power he could muster, and the territorial concentration of his lordship.[60] Judged by these two standards almost all English lordships fell far short of the contemporary French seigneurie. To approach their level of autonomy required time and exceptional opportunities. Thus, even at Durham far away on the Scots border, a string of able bishops, who understood how to exploit both St. Cuthbert's supernatural powers and the more mundane ones hired from the king, had to struggle for more than a century before palatinate status was achieved.[61] Lords who differed widely in the autonomy and physical resources at their disposal each struggled to avoid the loss of dependent tenants and their rents and incidents to others—or to gain more than they lost. The tenants were at the receiving end. The right to recede freely was therefore an important index of personal freedom. Lords could prevent the departure of most of their tenants in the twelfth century, so the right to leave was a valuable one. To determine who had that right, how and where it could be established, is a harder problem.

A long string of Old English laws deals with the man who leaves land without his lord's licence. Anyone who takes him in is liable to a heavy penalty. These laws were concerned with crime. They aimed to ensure that men were held to right by the lord they had been serving. All allegations had to be answered before a man was free to leave.[62] Presumably, though, the lord who could regulate by force the movements of all his men, on the king's behalf, could also do so when his own interests called for it. The laws most often used the word *mann* (Latin *homo*) which carried no taint of servility, though in a famous passage Wulfstan of York (or an early glossator) listed, among the evils

---

[60] J. H. Mundy, *Europe in the High Middle Ages 1150–1309*, (London, 1973), p. xiv and *passim*, makes some interesting comments on the usage of *potestas* and associated words to denote various kinds of authority derived from the decentralization of power abroad. Note particularly that *home de poosté* and its equivalents came to mean serf. And cf. above, pp. 35, 96, for the *De legibus*.

[61] H. Cam, 'The Evolution of the Medieval English Franchise', *Speculum* xxxii (1957), 427–42, and above, p. 000 ff.

[62] *Ine* 39, II *Edward* 7, II *Athelstan* 27, III *Athelstan* 4, IV *Athelstan* 4–5, V *Athelstan* 1.1, II *Cnut* 28, *Alfred and Guthrum* 4, 6 (*Gesetze*, i. 106–7, 144–5, 162–3, 166–7, 170, 330–1, 394). The texts are cited and commented upon by C. Stephenson, 'Feudalism and its Antecedents in England', (1943), *Medieval Institutions*, pp. 234–60. To other relevant material cited in my 'The Proof of Villein Status', *EHR* lxxxix (1974), 723 n. 8, add *Cartularium Saxonicum*, ed. W. de G. Birch (London, 1885–93), no. 559, and *Codex Diplomaticum Aevi Saxonici*, ed. J. M. Kemble (London, 1839–48), nos. 311, 1079.

caused by the Danes, the fact that 'free men are not permitted to have control of their selves, nor go where they wish, nor dispose of their own property as they desire'.[63] These laws were known in twelfth-century England[64] and can be seen, interpreted and elaborated, in the *Leges Henrici Primi*. Here matters are complicated by the existence of multiple lordship, itself an indication that the law was not solely concerned with impoverished peasants. In practice the real beneficiary was the liege lord on whose land the man was willy-nilly *residens*,[65] and who was ultimately responsible for holding him to right. The liege lord received the special penalty (*utleipa*) due from a man who left without licence.[66] He could dispossess a liege man who refused to be *ad rectum* or tried to take another protector against his will. However, if he did so, he might himself forfeit the liege *dominium* by taking back the land on which it was based.[67] The detailed treatment of these questions indicates that they were important as living law. That last point, on the essential endowment behind liege loyalty, could easily have been turned into a court exception against a writ of naifty, the fugitive pleading that he was entitled to leave since the lord had seized his fee.

But even in Henry II's reign a general right to leave at will was far from universal.[68] Who possessed this exceptional right, and how might it be claimed? At the highest levels of society, men who themselves owned manors or whole lordships had their affiliations changed by power politics, not law.[69] Quasi-legal argument about the rights and wrongs of departure or transfer from one lordship to another was more likely with lesser men. The customary rules, which once existed and were well

---

[63] *Sermo lupi ad anglos*, ed. D. Whitelock (3rd ed., London, 1963), p. 52 and note, translated in *English Historical Documents*, i. 856. The words quoted are an addition in MS C only, a mid-eleventh-century MS briefly described on p. 2 of the edition.

[64] e.g. *Leges Willelmi*, 48 echoes II *Cnut* 28.

[65] *LHP*, 55.1–3b; cf. ibid. 43.6–6a, 82.5, and p. 350 for the editor's speculations on the sense of *residens*.

[66] Ibid. 41.7–12, 85.

[67] Ibid. 43.2–4, 8.

[68] Assize of Clarendon, c. 10, warned town-dwellers not to receive any *homo* without manucaptors who was not in frankpledge. This clearly echoes the Old English laws already noticed.

[69] See p. 7 above for the case of the Count of Evreux early in the twelfth century. *Early Yorks. Charters*, ii. 114, illustrates the power a lord might exercise as late as the 1170s over men described only as *homines*, whose land grants he cheerfully approved on other occasions (e.g. ibid., no. 115).

known in the relevant locality, and now mostly lost beyond recall. Probably, like other status characteristics, the right to recede freely was associated with some social (and perhaps tenurial) groups but not others. Proof of membership in the group thus established the set of rights etc. to which one was entitled. Where this membership was inherited, a convenient method of proof in court was the *procincte*, by which the relatives of anyone whose status was in doubt were summoned to acknowledge their status (i.e. which group they belonged to) on oath. This procedure was certainly known in twelfth-century England.[70] There seems no reason why its use should have been restricted to cases of alleged servitude, for which alone it is documented. It seems equally appropriate in trials of the right to recede. Needless to say no actual cases have come to light. Among the scanty evidence for trials of status, *Domesday Book* is the most informative source.

King Williams's clerks and compilers strove hard to place in realistic categories the lowest classes, grouped as adjuncts to their manors, and had little difficulty with their accounts of the manors' French owners. Substantial numbers of independent freemen remained in the east and elsewhere, some with peasant tenants of their own, others attached to the manors of greater men. The test whether they could give, sell, or recede from their land without licence was the main division among these people, whatever name (freeman, sokeman, etc.) the clerks gave them. These three freedoms, of Old English origin and long known to mean the same however phrased, were vitally important in 1086. Land disputes, often reported under the head *Invasiones*, might turn upon the claim by one Norman lord that a particular English tenant had had the right to take his land where he wished, and had in fact put himself under new lordship. The court's finding was as important to the tenant as to his would-be lord, for the new lord's victory established his man in a status which enhanced his bargaining position, with the right (to be held in reserve) of moving on once more with his land. Determination of the issue between lords settled the tenant's status too. *Force majeure* was frequently the preferred method. An aggressor who already possessed soke of a coveted holding was in a good

---

[70] Above, Chap. 10.

position to cloak his usurpation with apparent legality by justi-
fying his action through his court.[71] During the Domesday
Inquest on the other hand, disputes were tried in court. In some
cases the king had previously (before or after 1066) ruled
already, ordering a tenant orally or by writ[72] to accept some
lord as his. Production of such a writ in court decided the case.
Where none was available, the court heard argument by the
parties supported by the testimony of suitors from the hundred
or shire courts and offers of proof by oath or ordeal.[73] The
Domesday Inquest was doubtless unique, but the suitors of
local courts who proffered their testimony before the com-
missioners will surely have participated in similar pleas at their
home courts during the next generation or so. The absence of
documentary record is easily explained. Reports of land cases
are few from this period. The great men or prelates for whom
these narratives or charters were composed wished to preserve
the details of their property in terms of the more permanent
bounds of land, not the ever-changing names of its tenants.
Thus some of our cases will be disguised as land pleas in the
records. In a certain proportion, one or both parties sought the
boost of royal writ, some of them writs of naifty. Even under
Henry I, writs of naifty may conceivably have introduced occasional pleas about fugitives to a court hearing, as they did
later in the century.[74] Already the executive order was qualified
with the adverb *juste*. Perhaps this word was intended merely to
warn the sheriff to be circumspect in his execution of the writ,
but recipients eventually understood it to mean that there could
be judicial inquiry into the question of whether the order was to
be carried out.[75] How soon this happened is disputed, and most

---

[71] Stephenson, 'Commendation', *Medieval Institutions*, pp. 157–9.

[72] Ibid. 165–6, 173–4. See also *DB*, ii. 187b, and F. E. Harmer, *Anglo-Saxon Writs*
(Manchester, 1952), pp. 149–50, for references to the career of Aelfric Modercope.

[73] The best known example is *DB*, i. 44b; also ii. 172–172b.

[74] *Glanvill*, xii. 9, included the writ of naifty among writs *de aliquo justiciando* which
initiated cases in the county court before the sheriff. G. D. G. Hall, *EHR* lxx (1961),
p. 319, and *Van Caenegem*, p. 206, see the significance of these writs in different ways.

[75] Milson, *Novae Narrationes*, p. cxliii, thought it just possible that *juste* alone sufficed
to introduce a case to court, but *Van Caenegem*, pp. 200, 274, 338, is very uncertain about
the word's effect. The argument in the text rests on general plausibility, especially with
the similar writs for land reseisin, and a very few cases (such as *Chron. Monasterii de
Abingdon*, ii, ed. W. H. Stevenson, R.S. 1858, p. 226, from 1166 and the Ramsey case
cited below, n. 78) that show discussion in court about the execution of writs in the form
of straight commands.

hearings due to writs of naifty would not be about the fugitive's status, as already explained.[76] Rannulf Flambard's second writ of naifty,[77] however, directed that he was to have back all men who had left in his time 'sine diracionacione et sine laga'. This wording surely implies the existence of men with the right to leave freely and the possibility of argument about who they were, culminating in a 'deraignment' in the bishop's court.[78] Given the evidence of Domesday Book and the twelfth-century laws, it is most unlikely that Durham tenants and Rannulf's writ were unique.

This examination of the twelfth-century writs of naifty in the light of other contemporary evidence about lordship has fruitfully established several points relevant to the origins of villeinage. Writs of naifty could initiate common-law actions about status in the thirteenth century only because of changes in their wording and function introduced by stages under Henry II. The writs had previously been exceptional royal favours granted to the few, to great lords who might benefit from royal assistance in the maintenance of control over their tenants against the occasional deliberate rivalry of neighbours. The fugitives claimed in the writs were by no means always peasants like the unfree villeins who figure in naifty actions later. Since lords expected to control (usually with their own resources) the movements of most of their tenants, including men up to the rank of quite important vassals, only men of some substance will have been able to register plausible claims to freedom of movement. The right to recede freely was at a premium in the highly competitive society of Anglo-Norman England. Disagreement about it led at times to violence, and occasionally to argument in court initiated by the royal dispatch of a writ of naifty.

Our next task is to demonstrate the deeper significance of the changes to the writs under Henry II. Once again, the legal evidence is first considered, before tackling the social context and attempting to assess the overall significance of common-

[76] *Van Caenegem*, no. 113 (1142/54), and perhaps no. 109 (?1106) are writs that envisage a trial of title. Nos. 104, 106, 110–11 are more clearly simple executive orders.
[77] Above, p. 227.
[78] *Van Caenegem*, no. 107. Cf. also no. 105 (1087/99) granted to Ramsey Abbey, whose abbot a little later tried in his court an issue raised by a resisin writ containing the word 'juste', *Cartularium Monasterii de Ramseia*, i. 138.

law villeinage. The proposed hypothesis interprets villeinage as an unintended by-product of the common law's birth during the period roughly from the 1160s to John's death. The legal reforms commenced under Henry II extended the range of remedy offered by the royal courts until their value was obvious to a far wider variety of subjects than ever before. For the first time large numbers of men who held no land directly of the king could think of the *Curia Regis* as their normal court for the redress of a growing (though never unlimited) list of possible grievances. This constituted a considerable extension of legal freedom. The number of litigants who sought the benefits of royal law cannot have been anticipated by the king's advisers and may have been unwelcome to many contemporaries.[79] Thus from an early stage in the common law's development, the king, his counsellors, and justices were faced with decisions about the topics the royal courts should treat and the types of complainant to whom they ought to promise a hearing. The unlimited extension of royal jurisdiction was never in question. No social revolution was envisaged. Yet the new policies of access to the courts raised echoes deep down in society. Quite humble men began to hope for redress of their grievances through royal justice. From time to time, peasant tenants who fancied themselves as free as their neighbours tried to sue their lords before royal justices who could not avoid deciding whether to offer remedies. The resulting decisions, to welcome some groups and refuse access to others, were often based on perfunctory reasoning, or derived from particular circumstances or personalities. Nevertheless, from the lost judgements of these early cases emerged the outlines of thirteenth-century villeinage law with its great circular arguments, of which perhaps the best example is the criterion of certainty as applied to the custom of merchet by the second half of the century.[80]

   The origins of English villeinage were just one part of a much wider European movement. During the twelfth century the 'rule of law' made great progress all over Europe, and custom was frequently delineated and reduced into writing. Many groups benefited by increased security against arbitrary treatment and more confidence in their rights and duties towards

----

[79] See the concluding section of this chapter.
[80] Above, Chap. 11.

their superiors and neighbours. The change is easily exaggerated; certain groups gained less or not at all, and, in effect, sank in their relative standing. The crucial need for ordinary non-noble landowners to achieve the right kind of classification in a centralized system like the common law is underlined by the substantial gains made by the successful. Magna Carta symbolizes this progress in England, with, for example, the redrafting of the famous c. 39 in 1217—to reiterate the exclusion from royal guarantees of security of villeins and the land they held[81]— as a further symbol of the truth that progress was uneven.

Leo Verriest's controversial studies of continental (mainly Flemish) society furnish a plausible pattern of change which ought to be tested against the very different kind of evidence from England.[82] The traditional French view had assumed that the three customs of *taille, mainmorte,* and *formariage* (corresponding to English tallage, and some forms of heriot and merchet) which were the marks of serfdom in late thirteenth-century France had been distinguishing characteristics of serfdom since time immemorial. The supporting evidence was scanty to say the least, and Verriest observed that most of the twelfth-century documents which referred to the three 'marks' of serfdom were seignorial grants to release various groups of dependents from the stricter control over vassals' property, succession, and marriage which lords previously had enjoyed. In the darker past, he inferred, with some exaggeration, seignorial control had been tighter over *all* dependants who were neither clerk, monk, or knight.[83] The evolution of the tests of villeinage tenure in thirteenth-century England is similar enough to merit a parallel explanation. The common law needed convincing tests badly. The delay before it adopted tallage 'high and low' and merchet surely occurred because men who were undoubtedly free at common law had only recently man-

---

[81] Magna Carta 1215, c. 39; 1217, c. 35. Cf. generally Holt, *Magna Carta*, pp. 19 ff., 63 ff.

[82] Verriest, *Institutions médiévales* t.1 (Mons, 1946), pp. 55–64, 201–19. Cf. Ch.-E. Perrin, 'Le Servage en France et en Allemagne', *Relazioni del x congresso internazionale di scienze storiche* (Florence, 1955), iii. 216–19, 224, which was one of the first studies to accept Verriest's view in essentials against that of Marc Bloch, 'Liberté et servitude personelles au moyen age . . .', *Mélanges*, i. 316 ff., and above p. 187, n.9.

[83] Cf. G. Duby, *The Early Growth of the European Economy*, tr. H. B. Clarke (London, 1974), pp. 172–3, 176.

aged to free themselves from seignorial control in such matters.[84]
And similarly, villeins felt their lack of common-law succession
rights the more keenly because their free neighbours could now
seek their inheritances in the royal courts even against their
own lords.[85] The spread of fixed, written custom and royal law
thus directly aided free dependents to escape seignorial restraints and generally improved their tenurial security and
condition.[86] Closer definition of the social groups involved is
difficult and not necessarily a desirable exercise, for contemporary social nomenclature certainly (very likely the membership
of the social groups themselves too) changed a good deal over
the twelfth century. The most sensible suggestion is a cautious
negative. One can fairly easily collect evidence of the rise and
fall of certain families or groups during these years—as in any
other period. Nevertheless, there is no prima-facie reason to
believe that a family, whose members were termed *villani* and
regarded as in some sense free (i.e. not *servi*) in 1100, would have
taken on an essentially changed condition by 1200, when a later
generation was once again called *villani* (or even *servi*) and
rejected by the common law as unfree.

This hypothesis about origins adequately explains the law of
villeinage of the more abundant thirteenth-century sources. It
is consistent with our knowledge of the early common law and
contemporary English society, but quite impossible to prove
conclusively. The best that can be offered is, first, a demonstration that important trends of the period can be understood
in the terms demanded by the argument and then a sketch of
patterns of change which may have followed.

A few unequivocal early cases would be the most effective
corroboration. A few years ago, Professor Hilton believed that
he could detect in plea-roll entries from the first decades of the
thirteenth century a 'feeling of immediate loss' which showed
how new and unexpected the common-law doctrine of villeinage

---

[84] Above, Chap. 11.
[85] Above, Chap. 7.
[86] Battle Abbey, perceiving this danger shortly after 1200, turned to forgery in an
attempt to maintain 'the old undifferentiated service tenures' and thereby stave off
common-law interference with its tenants, E. Searle, *Lordship and Community: Battle
Abbey and its Banlieu* (Toronto, 1974), pp. 102–5.

still was.[87] He may be right about the feelings, for plea-roll interpretation is a personal matter, but his argument cannot command acceptance for several reasons. No doubt emotions did run high in the courtrooms during the trial of villeinage issues, but the plea rolls reveal little about such happenings. Between the lines, one may read hints of violence outside courts or the special bitterness of defeated litigants. But this cannot be measured, or distinguished from much similar evidence on later, fuller rolls. As long as villein status continued to matter, villeinage disputes always generated heat. In any event, good evidence of a general depression of peasant condition at the end of the twelfth century has yet to be produced.[88] The argument of this chapter calls merely for a shift in the meaning of established terms which would be hard to spot, however luxuriant the documentation. The earliest plea rolls help the argument in two ways only. They confirm Glanvill's account of naifty by exposing the existence from the early and middle 1190s of naifty actions that turned on the determination of the alleged fugitive's status.[89] They also proffer a warning that ambiguities and uncertainties in villeinage doctrine, which would not have been tolerated later, remained common in the first decade of the thirteenth century.[90]

Clearly, cases from the crucial years before 1200 and the earliest common-law records will not impress the sceptic.[91]

---

[87] Hilton, 'Freedom and Villeinage', 14. Professor Hilton's treatment of these cases is sometimes open to question. See, for instance, his discussion (p. 16) of *CRR* xii. 1579 (Bucks. 1225) which does not make it clear that the villein later acknowledged his status and was amerced when he withdrew his complaint. That the villein's father had indeed admitted his unfreedom in court twenty years earlier, as Robert of Broughton said, is proved by the fine Robert produced, J. Hunter, *Fines*, i. 233 (= *BRB* iv, p. 28).

[88] The economic arguments are surveyed briefly below.

[89] *RCR* i. 84, 92, 153, 366 record cases from four different counties 1194–9 in which reference was made to previous proceedings in various courts. In *PRS* xiv. 73 (Wilts. eyre 1194) the question of whether a holding was *villenagium* or a free tenement was put to a jury. See also *CRR* i. 45, 67 (Northants 1198).

[90] *RCR* ii. 253, *CRR* ii. 25 (Norfolk 1200–1), and *SS* lxxxiii 905, 959 (York eyre 1204) are illustrations. Also J. R. West (ed.), *St. Benet of Holme, 1020–1210*, no. 211.

[91] S. F. C. Milsom, *The Legal Framework of English Feudalism* (Cambridge, 1976), appeared too late to be fully integrated into this book. Milsom's sensitive treatment of the early common-law materials—it amounts to a brilliant critique of the early plea-rolls as a source—is often very relevant to topics treated here. His argument often approaches that of this chapter very closely. He believes that many of the bare entries of land suits on the plea rolls conceal decisions about villeinage. See especially pp. 21–3, 83, 84 n. 2, 92 n. 4.

How might the changes have worked and why, for example, did they appear to proceed almost unnoticed by contemporary observers? Richard FitzNeal wrote his *Dialogue of the Exchequer* in about 1179, a few years before Glanvill—when royal justices and advisers must already have been at work sporadically on the creation of villeinage doctrine. The *Dialogue*'s scattered references to villeinage are all quite congruous with our view. Richard, who wrote to expound official Exchequer practice rather than to set out the law, had no special interest in villeins, or serfs, or hereditary rank as such. He was, however, concerned with the problems created for royal financial administration by seignorial property-rights over their dependants, social institutions which the royal administrators could not simply override. He is therefore an enlightening witness to social prejudice. For example, he favoured special strictness in the Exchequer's treatment of those engaged in trade, because they could so easily conceal their assets and thereby evade their obligations to the king.[92] Similarly, his references to serfs[93] are equally informative. An *ascripticius* was distinguished from other seignorial dependants by being 'de regni iure' more narrowly subject to his lord, who was 'lord of the man and the things'.[94] Nevertheless the king possessed an over-riding 'generalis . . . cura subditorum' even over serfs,[95] which entitled him, for instance, to have the goods of a royal debtor's *ascripticius* sold to meet his lord's obligation to the king, once the lord's own goods had been exhausted. This was unconnected with servility, for the king had similar rights over knights' property when collecting his scutage; formerly he had enjoyed even more extensive powers.[96] This same royal superiority also sanctioned the king's retention of the chattels (though not the land) of an *ascripticius* who had fled under suspicion of a crime punishable under the new procedures.[97]

---

[92] *Dialogus*, II. xiii (107–9).

[93] The term he generally used was *ascripticius*, for which see above, Chap. 4. The standard Exchequer term was *rusticus* (see below n. 113) but Richard preferred the more classical ring of *ascripticius* with its connotations of the bond to the soil. He also used *servus* once.

[94] *Dialogus*, I. xi; II. x (56, 97).

[95] *LHP*, 43.1, 1a, shows that this was no new idea.

[96] *Dialogus*, II. xiv (110–12); cf. above, Chap. 3.

[97] *Dialogus*, II. x (97).

To the pupil's objection that this rule contravened the lord's ownership of his serf's property, Richard answered that lords might otherwise engineer the death of their *ascripticii* in order to gain possession of their goods.[98] And finally, in another passage Richard casually emphasizes that part of the king's job was to protect men against their 'domestic enemies', the lords.[99]

Richard FitzNeal never betrays any awareness that he had been living through a great social upheaval among the peasantry or even that villeinage was a new legal doctrine. More surprisingly, even Glanvill a few years later did not conceive of villeinage as a new general doctrine either. Although his account treats the action of naifty for the first time as a means to determine legal status in court, he devotes almost equal attention to the older action about title to fugitives. Other details in the treatise strongly suggest that Glanvill too had yet to isolate villeinage as a separate entity. General ideas about villeinage could conveniently be expounded in a discussion of the exception of villeinage in civil actions like the assizes, as in the *De legibus* later. Various references *en passant* confirm that to Glanvill villeinage was a bar to suits in royal courts,[100] but assizes may not have been popular enough yet at the requisite level to merit extended discussion. At any rate, Glanvill never thought to set out the procedural details of exceptions on the grounds of status, still less to expound any general ideas about villeinage. Likewise, his treatment of the writ of customs and services looks vague. Later treatments and the writs themselves carefully specify whether the tenure is free or villein. Glanvill merely says that royal aid is available to any lord not powerful enough to justice his own tenants, and his sample writ leaves the kind of tenure unspecified.[101]

---

[98] This response illuminates, incidentally, seignorial influence on royal justice at the time. Cf. *Cal. Pat. R., 1272–1281*, p. 103 (1275), for a false accusation of theft from a villein made by the villein's lord, apparently in the expectation that he would secure the accused's land as an escheat.

[99] *Dialogus*, II. x (101–2). Cf. *Britton*, above Chap. 9(i), p. 128.

[100] Above, p. 120. Both the passages cited there are very short and allusive. *Glanvill*, xiv. 1, notes that a *rusticus* can bring an appeal, with the implication that other actions are prohibited.

[101] *Glanvill*, ix. 8–9; *Selden Registers*, Hib 36, CA 25, CC 149–149a. Cf. *P. Roll 18 Henry II*, p. 31 (1172); Roger de Verli owes 5 marks 'pro habendo servito de hominibus suis'; and see the end of this chapter.

These remarks of Richard FitzNeal and the author of Glanvill, two of the most intelligent and best informed men at Henry II's court, meaningfully corroborate the present hypothesis. The very gradual emergence of villeinage as a coherent doctrine prevented even the shrewdest observers from noticing it for a long time. What men did *not* see is, of course, impossible to document, but the case for a slow evolution can be strengthened by comparing the origins of villeinage with an associated change in royal administration (on which Richard FitzNeal is almost equally unhelpful). The Ancient Demesne of the later Middle Ages was formed from a late twelfth-century shift in attitudes towards the exploitation of royal lands. Since one consequence of the changes was the creation of a special kind of protected customary tenure, which the *De legibus* later termed 'privileged villeinage', the story has a double relevance to the origins of 'pure villeinage'.[102]

Royal estate management can often be compared usefully with that of other great lordships. All lords faced similar difficulties in dealings with their peasant tenants. The king wished to retain control over his customary tenants, whom he, like other lords, regarded as for the most part totally subject to his will. The great lords on the Council of the infant Henry III viewed the matter thus in 1217, when they promulgated the second reissue of Magna Carta, for one amendment to the provision restricting royal amercement of villeins added the words 'other than our own'.[103] The king, as manorial lord, had expected the same right to amerce his own villein at will as other lords had, for he shared the same theoretical view of lordship over human chattels: that he could dispossess them totally if he wished. On the other hand, ordinary lords had a certain interest too in preserving peasant prosperity on their lands, since they benefited from it through servile incidents. This particular argument was all the more attractive and cogent to the royal

---

[102] Hoyt, *Royal Demesne*, Chaps. 5–6, is the main source for the next paragraphs, but my own interpretation of the evidence has been deeply influenced by M. K. McIntosh, 'The Privileged Villeins of the English Ancient Demesne', *Viator* vii (1976), which I was able to study in an early draft. I am most grateful to Mrs McIntosh for her kind help.

[103] Magna Carta 1215, c. 20; 1217, c. 16. The same kind of concern for the king's own villeins was shown earlier by one of the amendments to the writ of naifty under Henry II, above, n. 34. See also SS lxviii. 393 (Cornwall eyre 1201) and *Fleta*, ii. 52 (113).

administration, because the Angevin kings never followed the lead of their more advanced subjects, who decided to manage their demesnes directly from the time of inflation in the 1180s and afterwards.[104] That labour services were in consequence less valuable to the king than to some other lords necessarily concentrated the attention of royal advisers on other potential revenues, and especially on tallage. No great acuity was required to notice that an age of rising prices reduced the real value of fixed money farms. Moreover, the right to this theoretically arbitrary tallage increased in value when lawyers extended it to alienated royal lands as well as current royal demesne. Royal self-interest thus urged the protection of tenants of former royal demesne too.[105]

The simplest way to effect this protection was perhaps to permit inhabitants of current royal demesne and 'ancient' demesne to utilize the common law. They were the king's tenants; why should they not sue in the king's courts? This probably happened for a while, until the growing sophistication of legal analysis around 1200 rendered such a confusion of jurisdiction unacceptable.[106] The common law had already rejected many customary tenants of other lords as villeins; clearly villeinage was also the natural classification for royal-demesne tenants of comparable condition. Actions they brought in the royal courts began to be opposed by exceptions of villeinage and, after occasional early hesitations, these were allowed by the justices.[107] The disappointed king's villeins were directed to submit their disputes for settlement 'according to the custom of the manor'. The subsequent hearing in the manorial court quite often satisfied affairs within the manor. Later

---

[104] P. D. A. Harvey, 'The English Inflation of 1180–1220', *Past and Present* lxi (1973), 9–14, discusses royal reactions to the problems posed by inflation.

[105] When and how this extension of royal rights was made is a question still to be answered. It is however outside the present purpose.

[106] B. Kemp, 'Exchequer and Bench in the Later Twelfth Century—Separate or Identical Tribunals?', *EHR* lxxxviii (1973), 559–73, marshalls evidence to argue that the division of royal jurisdiction into separate central courts took place in the later 1190s. But note that the boundaries were still far from clear in the next decades, R. V. Turner, *The King and his Courts . . . 1199–1240* (Ithaca, N.Y., 1968).

[107] See McIntosh, 'Privileged Villeins', Pt. III. Some exceptions were more specific to the Ancient Demesne and say something such as that 'the assize should not be made because that land is socage of the lord king's manor where no assize can be made'; see Hoyt, *Royal Demesne*, pp. 208–9.

in the thirteenth century, however, some great lords such as those of the abbeys of Bec and St. Albans became aware of the need for a central tribunal with power to oversee all the manorial administrations on their lands. But the king had no need to establish such a new tribunal. His justices had long inquired into the management of demesne manors during their eyre visitations,[108] and royal-demesne tenants usually managed to bring their complaints of maltreatment to the notice of one royal court or another. Consequently two new procedures enabled the common law to regulate the treatment of the king's villeins in his manorial courts without according them the protection reserved for freemen.[109] Customary tenants on both present and 'ancient' royal demesne, though disqualified by their villein status from the common law, enjoyed tenurial protection by the custom of the manor, supported by the little writ of right and the *monstraverunt* procedure.

Here are clear lessons for the origins of ordinary villeinage. The king's villeinage could not have been thought 'special' without the prior existence of 'pure' villeinage. The creation of privileged villeinage required more organized thought from royal advisers than did the birth of ordinary common-law villeinage. Its direct bearing on royal revenue expectations was important at a time when the administration of the royal demesne and royal finance generally were under close scrutiny. Even so, Ancient Demesne policy will have occupied little of the Council's debating time. Change resulted from a series of gentle drifts: access to the common law at first, then a gradual exclusion, and finally growth of the special procedures. The timing of each stage varied from one estate to another, both on royal demesne and on alienated lands, as individuals' complaints made decisions necessary.[110] In this process of chance

[108] Stubbs, *Charters,* pp. 176–7, 254–5, etc.

[109] See above p. 62 and no. 48 for the first appearance in 1224 of the little writ of right. The other special procedure, the *monstraverunt,* was less formal and slower to emerge. Its early history remains unstudied. Actions of customs and services in villeinage (see end of this chapter) and compromise agreements about ancient demesne land are not uncommon on the plea rolls of the early part of Henry III's reign. Each may have figured in *monstraverunt's* pre-history.

[110] Mrs McIntosh's study cited above concentrated on the royal manor of Havering, Essex, whose customary tenants sued at common law until 1212 at least, but gradually lost this right until the new procedures were first used there in 1234.

extension, the spread of demesne privilege must have resembled the earlier spread of villeinage classification itself.

The devices for the protection of peasants in whom the king had a direct financial interest resulted from a closely associated movement of legal and administrative innovation. Ways in which individual groups may have attained their status in the thirteenth century must now be expounded.

A large proportion of thirteenth-century villeins were from families who can never have hoped for freedom. Many customary tenants (certainly far more than can be explained as the descendants of Domesday *servi*) were so economically weak and subject to their lord's control that their classification as villeins involved merely a change of name, if that. Few possessed the resources to test the lord's right to that control in public courts; fewer still desired to risk the inevitable unpleasant repercussions. Individual challenges to their villein status were rare, except among the more prosperous who keenly felt the stigma and economic burden of unfreedom, and who led the village confrontations that were quite frequent later in the thirteenth century.[111] Smallholders and the landless rarely figure on the plea rolls; their status must normally have been clear. Angevin justices felt little need to search their hearts on the appearance of most other peasant litigants. Modern textbooks often fail to convey the medieval sensitivity to social distinctions; vast gulfs separated the different classes in the twelfth century.[112] Many peasants must have struck the jurors, let alone their social superiors, as laughably servile. Sometimes a lord's influence persuaded a royal court not even to bother going through the motions. For example, Bishop Gilbert Foliot received in the late 1160s a royal writ to begin a suit about half a virgate of land in his lordship, rent 12*d.* per annum. He returned it to his close acquaintance the chief justiciar, with a covering letter which explained that the matter was too trivial and the complainant

---

[111] That peasant resistance was an essential element of the seignorial regime is a major theme of Professor Hilton's book, *Bond Men Made Free* (London, 1973). I am in broad agreement with this view but note that much of the evidence for it shows negative reactions such as rent strikes and non-co-operation. Direct challenges to seignorial authority were rarer.

[112] My favorite illustrative text is the *De Arte Honeste Amandi* of Andreas Cappellanus, translated by J. J. Parry as *The Art of Courtly Love* (Columbia records of civilization, 1941).

fere rusticus; the command was surely not intended to be taken seriously.[113] Various signs convinced justices that litigants before them were too 'rustic' for their complaints to be entertained by the king's courts; heavy week-work,[114] for example, unpleasant or dishonourable services, the recent sale of a close relative, or the successful production of suit of kin. Cases that turned on such villeinage pleas can be glimpsed on the pipe rolls from 1170 onwards,[115] and may lie behind early plea-roll entries that record the failure of assizes, without proffering reasons.

Real rustics and yokels caused the courts few problems. Royal guarantees of their rights would have appeared patently absurd, but this was not true of all villagers. The crux for the law was around the borderline whose status might have gone either way. Their existence is directly implied by the mixed marriages of free and villein that so troubled the courts later.[116] Families who lived as neighbours and considered themselves equal enough to intermarry now found they were on different sides of a line of legal classification. Such arbitrary distinctions turned perhaps on some special or temporary circumstance, or even occasionally on a suit in a royal court where villeinage was not an issue and was never even mentioned. Success or failure in early civil actions at common law had consequences beyond the mere allotment of seisin in the disputed land.[117] Since royal justices did not record the reasons for their decisions, men soon forgot why Thomas had won or William lost. Only the fact of

---

[113] *The Letters and Charters of Gilbert Foliot* (Cambridge, 1967), no. 196 (1165 or 1166/8). *Rusticus* is frequently used on Exchequer documents from *P. Roll 31 Henry I*, p. 55 on, and certainly implied servility by the second half of Henry II's reign; it became the Exchequer equivalent of *nativus* in chancery documents and *villanus* on some early legal records. This must be the connotation here but see below, p. 252, for a less clear use, probably from the late 1150s. Other early official references to *rusticus* are c. 16 of Constitutions of Clarendon 1164 (Stubbs, *Charters*, p. 167) and c. 4 of the Crusading statutes 1188, Roger of Howden, *Gesta Henrici Secundi*, ii, ed. W. Stubbs (R.S. 1867), pp. 32–3; *Chronicon*, ii, ed. Stubbs (R.S. 1869), pp. 336–7. The original connotation must have been country-dweller, i.e. not in castle or town. See also now A. Murray, *Reason and Society in the Middle Ages* (Oxford, 1978), pp. 237 ff.

[114] This was unusual at the time; see most recently P. D. A. Harvey, 'The English Inflation of 1180–1220', 20–2.

[115] *P. Roll 16 Henry II*, pp. 149–50 (Lincs.), are the first certain references.

[116] Above, Chap. 10.

[117] The date from which civil litigation in royal courts was sufficiently common to have these consequences is still uncertain. Sutherland, *Assize of Novel Disseisin*, pp. 13–14, sees 'private prosecutions' from the late 1160s. I doubt whether they were frequent before the late 1170s, but once started they could have spread swiftly.

success or failure remained. So William's assize failure might suggest that his family had no right to bring assizes, or even perhaps to put their complaints before royal justice. When the assize was brought to contest the lord's control over his land and tenants, as was normal in the earliest period,[118] the suggestion of unfreedom was nearly irresistible. Inheritance claims were particularly significant. At a time when the king was setting the weight of his authority behind the principle of heritability,[119] failure to assert one's ancestors' rights in his court must have been responsible for the descent of many families. Or—to put it more accurately—at the moment of succession the issue of the existence of a right to inherit would often be the decisive battleground.[120]

Success in any of the early real actions might later persuade a royal court of one's free status.[121] Failure must have condemned some families to classification as villein, and perhaps social decline. This purely legal pattern of events was perhaps quite common, and could constitute an important determinant of eventual legal status, which was only remotely dependant on social mobility. One special case, that of the remnants of the former Anglo-Saxon aristocracy, supports this conjecture. Except for a few years under Henry I, Englishmen had suffered the discrimination to be expected by a conquered people ever since the arrival of the Normans. Memories of former glory did not die completely, however, and underwent some revival in the twelfth century.[122] On Stephen's death a number of English

[118] S. F. C. Milsom suggested this as the original function of the assize in his introduction to the reissue of *P&M* (Cambridge, 1968), pp. xxxvi–xliv; see now the doubts of Sutherland, pp. 30 ff., and the powerful restatement in Milsom, *Legal Framework of English Feudalism*.

[119] See Thorne, 'English Feudalism and Estates in Land', *Cambridge Law Journal* xvii (1959); Holt, 'Politics and Property in Early Medieval England', *Past and Present* lvii (1972), and now the important thesis of Milsom, *The Legal Framework of English Feudalism*.

[120] The family of William of Cirencester is an illustration, (see below), although the parties appear to have argued more openly about villeinage than in the kind of case posited here.

[121] See above, Chap. 10, p. 173, for naifty actions of 1232 and 1248 where this plea was raised.

[122] R. W. Southern, *Medieval Humanism*, Chap. 8, contains interesting comment on this. F. M. Stenton, 'English Families and the Norman Conquest', *TRHS* 4th s. xxvi (1944) is basic, and see also W. E. Wightman, *The Lacy Family in England and Normandy, 1066–1194* (Oxford, 1966), pp. 40 ff., and D. Greenway, *Charters of the Honour of Mowbray, 1107–1191* (London, 1972), nos. 392–5.

families joined the queue of hopeful litigants seeking justice from Henry II. In 1154, the disturbed tenurial situation left by the usurper Stephen and memories of the relative favour of the new king's grandfather, seemed to many English families to offer good grounds for optimism. Perhaps too many applied at once. At any rate, sometime before 1162 a *statutum* was apparently enacted to the effect that Englishmen could recover their lands only if they could establish that their ancestors had been seised on the day of Henry I's death in 1135.[123] An early writ of Stephen's to Burton Abbey provided a precedent. Intended to assist the beneficiaries by imposing unusually heavy burdens of proof on those who disputed their title to land, the Burton writ forbade *anglicani* to implead the abbot for any land he held at the date of its issue.[124] A somewhat similar writ of Henry II's prohibits the impleading of Colchester Abbey by a *rusticus* claimant of an inheritance.[125] Two others protect their beneficiaries against suits by *anglici* who could not plead seisin dating back to 1135, and one general confirmation writ contains a similar clause.[126] Only one of the writs actually mentions the *statutum*,[127] and there is only one reference to the rule later than 1170, a payment to get an issue under the rule put to a jury at the 1182 York eyre.[128] But if the rule was enforced during the intervening period, Englishmen will have been prevented from utilizing the new assize of novel disseisin[129] and could not have succeeded by action of right.[130]

---

[123] *Van Caenegem*, pp. 216–18; D. M. Stenton, *English Justice*, pp. 31–2. Southern, *Medieval Humanism*, p. 142, believed that Henry II's chancery removed the distinction between his French and English *fideles* in the address clause of his writs from 1155. This gesture would be relevant here, but later documents also address French and English.

[124] *Van Caenegem*, no. 165.

[125] *Van Caenegem*, no. 175. There is no certainty that this was issued first of Henry's writs under discussion, but the editor's date range of 1154/70 can be narrowed on the assumption that it was acquired at about the time the abbot obtained a writ of naifty (*Cartularium Monasterii S. Johannis Baptiste de Colecestrie*, ed. S. D. Moore, London, 1897, i. 40–1), identical in form to *Van Caenegem*, no. 116 (1158), except for its attestation by Becket as chancellor.

[126] *Van Caenegem*, nos. 169, 172, and p. 217 n. 2.

[127] Ibid., no. 169.

[128] *P. Rolls, 28 Henry II*, p. 45; *31 Henry II*, p. 66 (1182, 1185).

[129] An actionable disseisin had to have taken place recently; see Hall, *Glanvill*, p. 180, and Richardson and Sayles, *Law and Leg.*, p. 95 n. 2, for the limitation period.

[130] *Van Caenegem*, p. 218, thinks the *statutum* fell out of use; *British Borough Charters*, i. 73, cited in n. 3 does not seem relevant to me. Sutherland, *Assize of Novel Disseisin*, Chap. 1 does not consider the question. The well-known description of the effects of the Norman

The rule in this rather special case was especially dangerous, for English birth almost carried a presumption of servility. An Englishman skilled enough to be entrusted with the management of a Bury manor by Abbot Samson was nevertheless noted as 'glebe ascripto'.[131] In the next century one commentator equated villeinage with Englishry in the context of the *murdrum* fine,[132] while English customs which had once signified high birth before the Conquest now became characteristically peasant, if not tests of servility.[133] Clearly these Englishmen were a special case, but similar discriminatory rules may have eased the route of other groups towards villeinage.[134] Moreover, the Angevin government may have pursued similar policies against other substantial sections of the population. The possibility that, for example, they favoured repression of the peasantry in the interests of their lords, will be examined below.

In several different ways, then, a villein family in the thirteenth century might have attained its common-law status. The only reasonably well-documented family so far noticed fits none of the above patterns exactly.[135] During Henry I's reign a certain Hugh had held a tenement in Cirencester for the service of 20*s*.-a-year rent. He had probably been there when the king founded the abbey in 1133 and no doubt considered his tenure free; at any rate, his substantial holding was the only one of its kind in the vill. At Hugh's death his son William succeeded. Soon William encountered difficulties with the monks, who were unwilling to tolerate an anomalously free holding so close

Conquest in *Dialogus*, I. x (52–3), may allude to the rule: 'Communicato tandem super hiis consilio, decretum est ut quod a dominis suis, exigentibus meritis, interveniente pactione legittima, poterant optinere, illis inviolabili iure concederetur. Ceterum autem nomine successionis a temporibus subacte gentis nihil sibi vendicarant'.

[131] *Chronicle of Jocelin of Brakelond*, p. 33.

[132] Richardson and Sayles, *Procedure without Writ*, p. ccii: 'Anglecheria, ut dicunt quidam, proprie dicitur de vilano, murdrum de libero homine', briefly discussed by C. A. F. Meekings, *Crown Pleas of the Wilts Eyre 1249*, pp. 62–3.

[133] Heriot (above Chap. 7) is the most familiar example.

[134] *Van Caenegem*, nos. 159–78, on which see below n. 173, may contain hints about some of these other rules.

[135] The main sources are as follows: *The Cartulary of Cirencester Abbey*, i, nos. 36–40, and no. 67, a writ of *c*.1155 cited in two inquisitions of 1200/1 and 1202/3 held to see if the land in question ought to be a royal escheat. Royal interest in the case is no doubt connected with the vill's importance as a source of royal servants, and, more directly, the vacancy of 1186–7 when the House was in the king's hands. See also *Rot. de ob. et Fin.*, pp. 22, 221; *Rot. Chart.*, pp. 10, 132b.

to home. Soon after Henry II's accession, probably in 1155, the abbot secured a writ restoring to the House its land in the vill and singling out for mention ('nominatim') William's service and tenement. The abbey was to recover these lands 'sicut iuratum est per probos homines C.'. Though the terms of this verdict are lost, Williams's neighbours seem to have disappointed him.[136] The abbot pursued his advantage by twice compelling William to acknowledge before royal justices that he held in villeinage, once probably soon afterwards and again some time before 1177.[137] William then died, sometime before 1183,[138] and the abbey cellarer seized the land on the authority of Henry II's writ of c.1155. But shortly thereafter, William's brother Robert in his turn took the holding over 'sicut ille qui fecit se heredem'. No doubt he considered himself free enough to succeed to a tenement which had belonged to his family for over fifty years and had passed from father to son within living memory. But Robert's preference for self-help rather than the assize of mort d'ancestor suggests that he did not rate his chances before a royal justice highly, in view of his brother's recent confessions of villeinage tenure. His tenure was short, for the sheriff restored the abbey to seisin after the abbot had complained to the king. Possibly, Robert was then permitted to re-enter, on the abbey's terms, for the holding was still called William of Cirencester's early in the next century. The family, by then classed as villein, ironically may soon have begun to enjoy a protected tenure once more, since Cirencester was former royal demesne.[139]

---

[136] *Cartulary*, i, no. 20, is an extent from about this time which contains the note: 'Willelmus debet metere unam acram et fenagium.' If this refers to our man, it strengthens my inference that the jurors found for the abbey. There is reference to 'other customs' being owed for the holding in addition to the rent, which may mean merchet, tallage, and the like. For the customs of other men at Cirencester at this date see *CRR* xii. 896, 1477 (1225).

[137] The cartulary editor's dates are based on the known careers of the justices before whom the acknowledgements were made. D. M. Stenton, *Pleas before the King and his Justices* iii (*SS* lxxxiii 1966), pp. l–li, suggests that the first occasion may have been close to 1156, although four of those present appear to be identical with jurors of 1200/1.

[138] This must have been during the 1180s, at a time when the abbey may have experienced other tenurial disputes; cf. *Cartulary*, i, no. 73 (1172/89).

[139] In 1221 assize defendants claimed that their land was king's villeinage but the court accepted the abbot's plea that Cirencester was his borough, *SS* lix. 83. One of these defendants was Richard Noel, brother of the royal *serviens* to whom King John had committed the holding. Cf. *Cartulary*, i, nos. 37–8, 272–5.

So much for the role of the courts seen through the legal evidence. Our reasonably clear picture must now submit to brief examination from other standpoints. The comprehensive regional survey of peasant condition that would illuminate the local factors behind decisions which labelled different groups of tenants as free or villein, is clearly impracticable here.[140] Economic historians, however, have usually focused on broader questions such as the hypothesis of some kind of 'manorial crisis' in the early thirteenth century. Some scholars have suspected that seignorial financial difficulties led to the political repression of peasant labour in favour of the great estates. This chapter will conclude with some tentative suggestions on both topics, first on the impact of economic trends and then finally on the influence, if any, of conscious Angevin policy.

Current views of the economic trends around 1200 mostly begin from the arguments of Professor M. M. Postan. He emphasized the return from indirect to direct exploitation of demesne lands by great landlords whose sensitivity to economic fluctuations alerted them to their loss of profit under the old system.[141] Some recent commentators have doubted whether the necessary degree of economic wisdom and foresight existed at this date, but they do acknowledge the important change in land management methods.[142] The twelfth-century leasing of demesnes was probably an old established system, almost the only way to manage a great, widely scattered lordship in the absence of an educated administrative class. Many economic arrangements of the twelfth century, between lord and farmer[143] as much as between the demesne manager and the actual cultivators of the soil, were governed by slow-changing custom.

[140] R. H. Hilton, *The Decline of Serfdom in Medieval England* (London, 1969), pp. 17–24, is an acute preliminary sketch, but too little of the material has yet been studied from regional points of view. N. Stacy, 'The Estates of Glastonbury Abbey, *c*.1020–1200', (unpublished Oxford Univ. D. Phil. thesis, 1971), esp. pp. 201–16, is very helpful about one great lordship, in a study that calls for early publication.

[141] Professor Postan's views have undergone subtle reshaping over the years. See most recently his *The Medieval Economy: an Economic History of Britain 1100–1500* (London, 1972), Chap. 6, and the bibliography in *Ec. H. R.* 2nd s. xviii. 1 (1965).

[142] The following summary is based on E. Miller, 'England in the Twelfth and Thirteenth Centuries: an Economic Contrast?', *Ec. H. R.* 2nd s. xxiv (1971), 1–14, and 'Farming of Manors and Direct Management', ibid., 2nd s. xxvi (1973), 138–40, and P. D. A. Harvey, 'The English Inflation of 1180–1220', *Past and Present* lxi (1973), 3–30. N. Stacy, 'The Estates of Glastonbury Abbey', has also been of value.

[143] 'Farmer' refers here to those who farmed (i.e. leased) demesne land from a lord.

But this was not always so. The twelfth-century economy was far from stagnant. Great lordships opportunely shared in the expansion, by raising the rental due from their farmers;[144] otherwise, the chance to profit remained with the farmers who might themselves raise the level of feudal rent in cash or kind due from tenant cultivators. The existence of a 'real inflation of the currency' between 1180 and 1220, strongly argued recently, gave these questions a greater urgency for both lord and farmer. Importantly for our purposes, all estate managers began to recognize more clearly the increased potential of profits from lordship over men. A lord might react to pressure from an ever-rising expenditure, without changing to direct exploitation of his demesnes by, for example, withdrawing tenants' rents and incidents from the manorial farm.[145] Many large estates, however, did begin to change to direct exploitation. Their administrators certainly realized that inflation was reducing the buying power of their rentals, but equally they modified their approach to management problems as economic tightness forced them to become more business-like. Some of these methods which were transforming Angevin government could be applied to great lordships by men with experience of how they worked for the king.[146] 'Self-government at the king's command' was turned to good account, as enlightened self-interest nearer home. Historians have also stressed the associated change in the form by which feudal rent was taken. Some lords did exercise their option (as they saw it) to exact labour services from tenants accustomed to paying a money rent, which theoretically ought to have promoted the cheaper cultivation of demesnes once again under direct control. In actual fact, the evidence for this reversal of commutation is thinner than once thought, especially for eastern England. Reliance on heavy compulsory labour services to cultivate manorial demesnes cannot have been as widespread in early thirteenth-century England as theory might suggest. Lords perhaps recog-

[144] Miller, 'England in the Twelfth and Thirteenth Centuries', 8–10, and 'Farming of manors', 139, gives some examples. The royal demesne could provide others; cf. Hoyt, *Royal Demesne*, pp. 222–5, for Brampton, Hunts.

[145] Glastonbury Abbey did so; Stacy, pp. 100–2.

[146] Dr Henry Mayr-Harting has pointed out to me that to draw up records like the *Rotuli de dominabus*, ed. J. H. Round (*PRS* xxxv 1913) of 1186 implies quite an advanced interest in royal profit and loss, within a restricted part of the king's revenues.

nized the axiom that workers under duress seldom fulfil skilled tasks efficiently and used hired labour for the more straight-forward jobs.[147]

There are obvious implications for the origins of villeinage, but the relationship between the two sets of phenomena was never simple. Perhaps common-law villeinage originated in order to supply lords with the essential power and authority to coerce the compulsory labour force demanded by their new policy of direct exploitation of demesnes, especially if the four decades after 1180 saw an actual depression of peasant con-dition in the countryside. Proponents of this view disagree especially about whether lords ('the governing classes') acted to defend their diminishing real revenues or, more aggressively, to augment existing powers and revenues. The unacceptability of such a view, however, is clear. The twelfth-century reality was certainly less tidy, more complex. A comparison of estate sur-veys from different parts of the country between the eleventh and fourteenth centuries provides no obvious evidence for the material worsening of peasants' condition *vis-à-vis* their lords. That feudal rent did rise in real terms during the thirteenth century although a possibility, remains undemonstrated. Late twelfth- and thirteenth-century surveys detail obligations etc. much more carefully than their predecessors. More lords delib-erately distinguished carefully between the different categories of tenant on their lands, as they gradually realized how much they might lose by granting a charter to the wrong tenant or taking his homage. Common-law protection of 'free' tenants inhibited the seignorial freedom of action assumed until quite recently, and full records of existing custom were essential to avoid costly mistakes. Ironically, the peasants benefited too, since lords could less easily increase obligations defined by the villagers themselves under oath and perpetuated in writing.[148] Their continued submission to seignorial control even carried certain advantages, for villeinage tenants were fairly well pro-tected from extremes of social differentiation due to the land

---

[147] Harvey, 'The English Inflation', 21. Hilton, 'Peasant Movements before 1381', *Ec. H. R.* 2nd s. ii (1949) supports this point, by showing how disgruntled peasants could hamper demesne cultivation.

[148] A point spotted by Homans, *English Villagers of the Thirteenth Century*, pp. 270–2; and cf. Searle, *Lordship and Community*, pp. 102–5.

market. Where spare holdings were rare, the free tenant's easier engrossment of extra land may often have mattered less than his villein neighbour's customary security of tenure.[149] When lords began to appreciate the novelty of this doctrine of villeinage, the constant threat of supervision or hindrance from the royal courts must have struck them most forcibly. The new theory of their unlimited authority over their villeins added little to their real power. Occasional assistance from royal officials during village revolts, for example, was no doubt welcome,[150] but agricultural production geared to sale in the open market cannot be managed efficiently on the basis of regular recourse to coercion. Plantation slavery had no place in medieval England. Common-law villeinage merely retained for lords reduced powers over the tenants who did not escape as freemen. But even this diminished seignorial authority was valuable. The lord had an advantage in an emergency; he could assemble villagers swiftly to combat floods or fire on his property before permitting them to attend to their own. Long before the Statute of Labourers, the lord had an extra pull in competition for the hire of wage labour. And of course the royal justices' reiteration that villeins and all their possessions belonged to their lords enabled the lord, as far as the common law was concerned, to expropriate them with impunity. Lords reserved this power to pressurize peasant families at those most vulnerable moments —on the householder's death, for example, or when providing for the future disposal of the family holding, as at a daughter's betrothal. Manorial officials, vigilant for the fat windfalls that sometimes resulted, gathered a steady trickle of revenue in the manor courts. To maintain over customary tenants a degree of control now largely lost for the rest, these courts were the key institutions. The right to justice his own villeins was as valuable as any benefit of villeinage law; in practice it generally prevented damaging contact with other jurisdictions, not least the common law itself.

The uncertainties of nascent villeinage law afforded alert or unscrupulous litigants attractive opportunities to better them-

---

[149] Cf. E. A. Kosminsky, *Studies in the Agrarian History of England in the Thirteenth Century* (Oxford, 1956).
[150] The different kinds of royal assistance are listed at the end of the chapter.

selves at the expense of their tenants and local peasants.[151] In individual cases, bids for local power must have been crucial. For example, English manorial officials, like their continental counterparts,[152] sometimes usurped rights and dues from absentee owners to construct new lordships. The best illustration discovered, however, is on a slightly different pattern where the losers were the king and the royal foundation of Stoneleigh. Ketelburn was the richest of a group of Henry II's royal-demesne tenants at Canley in Warwickshire.[153] Each of them owed fixed money rents payable at Kenilworth Castle. Apparently at his neighbours' request (certainly with their assent), Ketelburn assumed the chore of carrying all the rents there when due. Meanwhile the king endowed all his demesne in the area, including the hamlet of Canley and its rents, on his religious house at Stoneleigh. Shortly after Henry's death, the crucial step in the creation of a new lordship occurred. In about 1190 Ketelburn married his son Peter to the daughter of Hugh Bardolf, constable of Kenilworth and sheriff of the county, and with Hugh's connivance began to divert the royal rents to his own use. The fact that castle treasury-receipts were outside Exchequer control certainly facilitated this alienation. At any rate, the new lordship was unchallenged until 1258, when Peter's son Robert brought actions of naifty against the current tenants to prove that they were his villeins. He failed, was amerced, and quitclaimed his alleged rights. Perhaps, simply unlucky, he failed on some technicality; the full story was not yet known. Stoneleigh Abbey had, however, been alerted, and in 1266 after the civil war purchased a special writ of *quo warranto*. No doubt the jurors were carefully primed and at the hearings, in Kenilworth and then Warwick, the above story was

---

[151] Tenants too might make things difficult for their lords. The awkward procedures of villeinage continued to embarrass lords, as already noted, above Chaps. 10 and 12. See *RCR* i. 224; ii. 44; Richardson and Sayles, *Law and Leg.*, pp. 140–1 (Gloucs, 1198–9), for Philip of Barrington, a villein miller of Llanthony Priory, who fined for permission to leave his job, together with his family and goods but failed to move out of his 5 acres 'service tenancy'. The prior had to use his influence with the justiciar, Hubert Walter, and commence proceedings in the Bench in order to get him out.

[152] Cf. M. Bloch, 'La Ministerialité en France et en Allemagne', *Mélanges*, i. 512 ff.; Mundy, *Europe in the High Middle Ages*, pp. 143–5.

[153] *The Stoneleigh Leger Book*, ed. R. H. Hilton (Dugdale soc., xxxiv 1960), pp. xxxiv–xxxv, 30–5, 197–8, discussed by Hilton, *A Medieval Society: The West Midlands at the End of the Thirteenth Century* (London, 1966), pp. 164–5.

told to refute Robert's claim to the lordship. The hamlet was taken into the king's hands and then returned to the abbey after a fortnight. Robert was compelled to renounce all his lands and claims, with the exception of a life tenure of his house only, in order to liquidate the £50 damages awarded against him. Significantly, he was not finished. He was rich enough to repurchase his property in a shady deal with the abbot, after friends had intervened. The family had profited so greatly during seventy years' usurpation of lordship that they were now secure against this small disaster. And interestingly, their wealth seems to have been derived not from the 30d. each tenant paid a year but from assarts, suit of court, and the incidents which they enjoyed as lords.

Peter of Canley's *coup*, although exceptional, cannot have been unique in view of the transformations of the legal system during the late twelfth century. Great lords recognized the dangers to their own power, and the continental evidence shows their concern to be well founded. There were, of course, two special factors about England: lords' interest in the management of their demesnes—which worked against usurpations—and the king's growing near-monopoly of *haute justice*. Having briefly considered seignorial concerns, we turn next to the influence of the Angevin kings and their advisers.

Was there an Angevin policy towards the peasantry? If so, was common-law villeinage the product of a conscious political decision to abandon some or all of the peasantrty to their lords? The answer to each question is 'Yes, but . . .' There was, of course, no Ministry for Peasant Affairs under the Angevin kings. The peasantry occupied little of the Council's time. Wider questions of lords and their men (landlord and tenant) did require a certain amount of attention, though much less than high politics, war, and diplomacy. The main context was Henry II's insistence on his right to realize as much of his country's resources as he could in emergencies.[154] Collectors of debts to the king sometimes had to make an administrative distinction between a debtor's different classes of tenant.[155] A similar need also arose in legal contexts. Lords in search of writs

---

[154] W. L. Warren, *Henry II* (London, 1973), Chap. 10.
[155] Above pp. 244 ff.

to help reclaim or justice their peasants expected their proffers and general standing in royal favour to persuade the king to enforce their views of their tenants' condition. Much more rarely, peasants too reached the royal presence to parade their grievances and plead an opposite case.[156] No plaints were rejected automatically. The king's coronation oath bound him to offer justice to all who sought it.[157] Moreover, voices that urged moderation or compassion for the poor were not uninfluential at court. When taxation was envisaged, royal interest could embrace peasant prosperity—especially if at the expense of others; concern for the poor and weak was indeed part of his royal role. His advisers included men familiar with the established ecclesiastical tradition that princes ought to support the *pauper* against the oppression of the of the *potentes*.[158] By *pauper*, the writers meant someone not necessarily destitute[159] or servile, but incapable of defending himself from knightly violence without assistance. In the tenth and eleventh centuries such ideas had contributed to the 'Peace' movement.[160] By the twelfth century the prince's duty to protect the poor under the Church's supervision had become a post-Gregorian commonplace.[161] Thus Richard FitzNeal apparently regarded lords, from an Exchequer standpoint, as the 'domestic enemies' of their tenants.[162] A little later Glanvill's prologue[163] included some conventional praise of the king who dispensed justice

[156] One such occasion was during the rebellion at Much Wenlock, Salop, in about 1163. The rebels secured some kind of royal writ and also sent representatives to the mother house in France. See *Cartulaire du prieuré de La Charité-sur-Loire*, ed. R. de Lespinasse (Nevers–Paris, 1887), no. 62, pp. 148–52, and the comments of R. Graham, 'The History of the Alien Priory of Wenlock', *Journal British Archaeol. Assoc.*, 3rd s. iv (1939), 124–5.

[157] P. E. Schramm, *A History of the English Coronation*, trans. L. G. Wickham Legg (Oxford, 1937), Chap. 7, remains the basic treatment.

[158] See K. Bösl, 'Potens und Pauper', in *Alteuropa und die Moderne Gesellschaft: Festschrift für O. Brunner*, ed. A. Bergengrauer and L. Deike (Göttingen, 1963), and R. Le J. Hennebique, '*Pauperes* et *paupertas* dans l'occident carolingienne aux ixe et xe siècles', *Revue du nord* 1 (1968), 169–87; J. C. Dufermont, 'Les Pauvres d'après les sources anglo-saxonnes du viie au xie siècles', ibid. 189–201, is disappointing.

[159] See above, p. 76.

[160] H. E. J. Cowdrey, 'The Peace and Truce of God in the Eleventh Century', *Past and Present* xlvi (1970), 42–67, notes that the movement made little headway in England.

[161] See above pp. 235 f. for Archbishop Wulfstan's thoughts about *earme men* and cf. *LHP*, 10.3.

[162] *Dialogus* II. x (101–2).

[163] *Glanvill*, p. 2.

without fear or favour and aided the poor against the rich and powerful. Henry II was, he thought, like that. John of Salisbury argued in his *Policraticus* (written before he entered government service for Henry) for a static, interdependent society, characterized by the organic metaphor of the body politic. This body's feet, those groups like the *agricolae* that discharged the humbler yet necessary offices, had to act within limits of public utility (i.e. the criminal law) and furnish *obsequium* to their superiors, who in turn owed them *necessarium subsidium*. The numerical size of these humbler classes made their protection important for the whole community, and government itself was instituted partly to ensure their preservation.[164] Henry must have been quite familiar with such well-meaning advice.[165]

Undeniably though, the main weight of selfish interest worked in the other direction, against special protection for the peasants. The king and his advisers all belonged to a nobility that assumed that peasants existed to work lands for their lord's benefit.[166] In this view peasant tenants were primarily their lords' concern; arbitrary treatment was restrained, if at all, only by the action of the criminal law. For much of Henry II's reign, these sentiments were certainly not focused into a policy. Questions of status or jurisdiction were considered as they arose, by the royal minister or justice on the spot. Only the rising bulk of civil suits brought by men who were not tenants-in-chief perhaps compelled the Council to think about royal jurisdiction.[167] Possibly this development, which still has to be dated, was associated with an anonymous legal writer's reiteration of Anglo-Saxon admonitions that plaints should not be brought to the king before the justice of the shire and county

---

[164] *Ioannis Saresburiensis Episcopi Carnotensis Policraticus*, ed. C. C. J. Webb (Oxford, 1909), ii. 58–9.

[165] J. W. Baldwin, *Masters, Princes and Merchants*, i. 236–7, and B. Tierney, *The Medieval Poor Law* (Berkeley and Los Angeles, 1959) give futher hints of contemporary ideas on poverty.

[166] J. Le Goff, 'Note sur la société tripartie ... du ixᵉ au xiiᵉ siècle', *L'Europe aux ixᵉ–xiᵉ siècles*, ed. A. Gieysztor and T. Manteuffel (Warsaw, 1968), pp. 63–71, argues for the narrowing down of the class of *laboratores* to mean a peasant élite which needed the new monarchies to keep the peace for it. G. Duby has recently posited a connection with Gregorian reform. Also M. David, 'Les Laboratores jusqu'au renouveau économique des xiᵉ–xiiᵉ siècles', *Études d'histoire de droit privé offertes à P. Petot* (Paris, 1959), pp. 107–19.

[167] *Glanvill*, x. 8, 18, is the most explicit case.

was first sampled.[168] Apart from maintenance of law and order, the king had little obvious interest in any massive extension of his jurisdiction. Furthermore, royal justices were disinclined to spend too long in exile on eyre;[169] their social prejudices and financial greed often resulted from actual or desired ownership of estates reliant upon peasant labour. All participated on occasion in the exploitation of estates on the royal demesne. Such men hardly bothered to justify the exclusion from their courts of peasants and others deemed unsuitable for access to the *beneficia* of royal justice. Lowly litigants simply lost their cases. [170] Yet, there was no wholesale exclusion of all under-tenants. It suited the royal book to offer protection against seignorial interference to an ever-increasing range of *pauperes'* holdings. This was indeed a major theme of Angevin legal reforms.[171] Henry and his sons lent a selective ear to the promptings of conscience.

The resulting rule-of-thumb distinctions, between peasants granted royal remedies and those who met with no response, is well illustrated by another section of the so-called 'Leges Willelmi' (cc. 29–32) which has been described as 'an independent statement of the law relating to villeinage' in Henry II's reign.[172] Chapters 30 and 31 envisage royal help in the justicing of *nativi* by their lords, but c. 29 adopts a different tone towards groups whose names have less servile connotations. *Coloni* and tillers of the soil are not to be harassed ('vexentur') beyond what they owe; so long as they perform services due, lords are not to eject them from their holdings. The term *colonus* (perhaps meaning sokeman or some fairly independent tenant here) is generally used in Roman law to emphasize that tenants were bound to the soil. Here, the opposite emphasis suggests that the anonymous author advocated royal protection against seignoral excess for those whose standing and tenure justified this. But routine royal assistance would be given to lords who needed to justice serfs. Around the time of Glanvill, writs for a tenant to seek a

---

[168] *Leges Willelmi*, 43; cf. II *Cnut* 17, 19, and its twelfth-century redactions. The dating of this text is very material to the chronology of the legal reforms.

[169] Cf. R. E. Latham and E. K. Timings (recte C. A. F. Meekings), 'Six Letters concerning the Eyres of 1226–8', *EHR* lxv (1950), 492–504.

[170] Above pp. 249 f. for one probable example.

[171] S. F. C. Milsom's argument to this effect, first presented in his introduction to the 1968 reissue of *P&M*, is deepened in *The Legal Framework of English Feudalism*. Sutherland, *The Assize of Novel Disseisin*, had expressed doubts.

[172] Richardson and Sayles, *Law and Leg.*, pp. 141–2, 171.

royal prohibition against his lord's undue harassment of his free tenement begin to appear.[173] This fact confirms one side of the anonymous jurist's statement. The other, that the king would assist in the justicing of serfs, demands a moment's examination.

The best proof that common-law villeinage was essentially a by-product rather than the result of a conscious policy of peasant repression, is the early common law's unhelpfulness to their lords. Apparently, once the line of exclusion was drawn, those excluded were simply abandoned to their lords. The common law did not mobilize royal power for the coercion of the peasantry on their lords' behalf. Thus royal writs of naifty did order sheriffs to restore fugitives, but by now the result was normally a suit about status which the lord might lose. When village discontent erupted into open violence, the sheriff no doubt helped in its repression, with or without express royal command, but he did not act to prevent revolts. In Glanvill's day, a lord incapable of justicing his own tenants might already seek the sheriff's help by acquiring a writ of customs and services. In the registers of the thirteenth century, such writs specified that the holding in question was free and often specified the disputed claim to services. One might expect a special writ for the lords to claim villein services, without the need to specify what was due. Writs of customs and services due from villeinage tenements were indeed issued in quite substantial numbers in the early thirteenth century, but never reached the respectability of known registers and were apparently restricted to the Ancient Demesne.[174] The writ *ubi non sufficit*, which ordered the sheriff to distrain villeins to do their services, was similarly available only to the privileged lords of Ancient Demesne manors.[175] Thus

---

[173] *Glanvill*, xii. 10. Milsom, *Novae Narrationes*, pp. xlvii ff. shows how the thirteenth-century *ne vexes* was the tenant's counterpart to the lord's writ of customs and services. Van Caenegem's description of his writs, nos. 159–78, as 'ne vexes' is misleading. Apart from no. 176 (1170/83), they notify royal officials of privileges granted to favoured lords which, unlike the common-law *ne vexes*, do not presuppose tenure between the parties. See now Milsom, *The Legal Framework of English Feudalism*, pp. 31–2.

[174] See above p. 193 for a good example. Other cases can generally be shown to concern land with claims to Ancient Demesne privilege. Cf. *Glanvill*, ix. 8–9.

[175] The earliest example noted is Cambridge Univ. Library, MS Kk v. 33, no. 78 (Maitland's CB); others are *Selden Registers*, CC 105, R 249; *Reg. Omn. Brev.* f. 87v, no. 5. That it was unavailable for pure villeinage lands is suggested by the writ's place on the registers (cf. Maitland, *Coll. Papers*. ii. 146, 157) as well as the lack of cases on the rolls. Less restricted issue may have been allowed at some later date.

private lords were expected to do their own dirty work. Since the action of naifty was unhelpful to claimant lords,[176] this royal unwillingness to aid lords probably encouraged resort to violence. At worst the lord's attempt to achieve his ends by force would lead to an amercement for freehold through a writ *ne vexes*. At best, he achieved a favourable judgement on tenure, which the sheriff was expected to enforce. That the Angevin kings never thought in terms of any fundamental reform of this situation, undesirable from several points of view, refutes once and for all simple theories of common-law villeinage as a means of class oppression.

[176] Above Chap. 10.

14

EPILOGUE

The common law of villeinage was the unnatural child of lawyers' ingenuity and of administrative convenience. Never consciously created, it was equally never abolished. After the period covered by this book, the rules changed little. Profound disturbances in society, not reform in English law, ushered in the one serious attempt to end villeinage and to transform serfdom during the Peasants' Revolt in 1381. Where that had failed, more than a century of decay by evasion and emancipation was to succeed.

The first century or so of villeinage's existence can be divided into four rough periods. The first, from the 1160s until Magna Carta, saw the gradual synthesis of a new system out of diverse materials of seignorial custom, royal convenience, and legal learning. The second, which witnessed a remarkable outpouring of legal creativity, ran through Henry III's minority and into his period of personal rule. The middle years of the century saw an equally remarkable intensification of pleading and conceptual analysis of the Law against a political background of disturbance and reform. Finally, towards the end of the century, the Yearbooks for the first time highlighted villeinage law through a haze of procedural tricks thrown up by gladiatorial pleaders, as a minor aspect of common law, far removed from the countryside but now including a great deal of Bractonian doctrine that had seemed aberrant in the 1240s.

The narrative of legal change during the century is still too little studied from actual cases in the plea rolls and Yearbooks. Only thus can one know which twists of legal doctrine demand elucidation in the wider context of more general historical trends. In the meantime, some preliminary questions suggest themselves for investigation. A legal hypothesis about the birth of common-law villeinage has to leave aside many sociological questions that are obviously important in the story. One wonders for example, how lords and their peasant tenants reacted in the early thirteenth century when they gradually became aware of the new common-law relationship in which they stood to each other? One does not naturally expect legal innovation to stimulate violent self-help. Yet lords, as I have suggested, once they recognized the strength of their new common-law position, must sometimes have been encouraged to meet their tenants' complaints with force. They knew that the odds were on their side in court, and that ultimately the sheriff would lend them his aid.

Similarly, we need to ask why the legal pace quickened in the 1220s and 1230s. John's too frequent personal involvement in the ordinary business of the courts may have hampered development before 1215. The baronial council of the Minority interfered less, and left the judicial establishment to go much its own way. The *De legibus* remains the best testimony to the resulting bustle of innovation and discussion, despite a waning of its authority in the 1230s. Until other Bractonian arguments have been followed through the plea rolls of the mid-century into the Edwardian Yearbooks, there is no way to know how typical was the evolution of villeinage law.[1] The increasing precision of pleading seen in villeinage cases of the 1230s and 1240s about kinship links, tallage, and merchet certainly looks normal enough. One might deduce that pleaders would find congenial the Bractonian direction that assize defendants specify their recent seisin as lord of their alleged villein plantiff, when excepting on the grounds of status. But the signs are that pleas of this kind were for long rare, which draws one back to extra-legal causes.[2]

The courts' ever-changing view of the shape of common-law villeinage will not easily find explanation in general terms. Political pressures cannot be excluded, for the crucial period covers both Henry III's personal rule and the revolutionary years after 1258. On the other hand, the development of villeinage doctrine may prove to have varied from the main line of

---

[1] Sutherland, *The Assize of Novel Disseisin,* Chaps. 1–3, and P. A. Brand, 'The Contribution of the Period of Baronial Reform (1258–67) to the Development of the Common Law in England', (unpublished Oxford Univ. D.Phil. thesis, 1974) will provide a good start, once the chronological patterns they uncover are amended to take account of Thorne's Bracton.

[2] Most of this is from Chap. 8 but see also the last part of Chap. 9(i) and pp. 167, 181, 191 above.

common-law development. One would then turn to village life
and seignorial customs and concerns for an explanation. Conceivably, even the intensification of precision in pleading could
reflect a heightening of tension on the manors, the frustrated
expectation of families left stranded by the tide of legal freedom.
The interrelation between legal and social change in mid-
thirteenth-century lordship and estate management remains a
rich and exciting field for research.

Less drama is to be expected from the end of the century.
Doctrine was more or less settled and accepted; no one anticipated significant change. But that did not prevent men from
struggling for advantage in the courts. Villeinage was not primarily a matter of classes. Indeed, viewed from the court,
thirteenth-century society was less a layer cake than a handicap
race. The stigma of villeinage rendered a family or the tenantry
of a particular village that much less capable of competing in
the struggle for subsistence. Villeinage cases in the courts were
contests in which individuals struggled to set or upset the odds.
Error, or an imaginative dodge dreamed up by a legal adviser,
determined how far an alleged villein was handicapped for the
future. The most obviously desirable research here is more
narrowly legal. One wants to know when, how fast, and how
completely the Bractonian theory of villeinage spread and became dominant in the courts, and to relate this to the Edwardian
judicature's increasingly formalistic and equity-less atmos-
phere. Thus this book ends as it began, facing the treatise *De
legibus et Consuetudinibus Angliae*, which will always be associated
with the name of Henry de Bracton. Its study remains central to
our hopes of understanding the ebb and flow of influence from
the common law to agrarian society, from King to Lords and
Peasants.

APPENDIX

THE 'ASCRIPTICIUS' IN THE TWO LAWS

The special status of the colonate of the Late Empire was created during the fourth century in order to retain essential cultivators on the great estates. Peasants, under various titles (of which *ascripticius* or *ad-scripticius* is one), had their freedom of movement etc. restricted in their landlords' interests, but remained legally free and distinguishable from *servi*.[1] Their condition, moreover, had its compensations: 'even if the *colonus* was tied to the land, he could not on his side be removed from it'.[2] Any conceptual clarity present at the colonate's origin had disappeared by Justinian's day, so that references to it in the *Corpus Iuris Civilis* presented medieval lawyers with some puzzles. The Civilians labelled the anomalous groups *servi glebae* and recongized, albeit dimly, a resemblance to the serfs of their own day. Marc Bloch showed long ago that French lawyers picked up the phrase *servus glebae* in the thirteenth century and used the ideas behind it to raationalize the terminology and institutions of the serfdom of their day.[3] The analogy, which answered their need to justify the 'attache au sol', had already been noticed by Canonists at least a century before. Lecturers sometimes explained to their students that the *ascripticii* and so forth of their texts resembled the *manants* of the vernacular ('manentes a manendo'), who were similarly not *servi* but unable to leave freely;[4] and one Englishman, the author of *Leges*

[1] Medieval commentators went to some pains to explain the difference between *coloni, originarii, inquilini, ascripticii*, and so on. H. Nehlsen, *Sklavenrecht zwischen Antike und Mittelalter*, Bd. I (Göttingen, 1972), pp. 129–31, cited by Pakter (below, n. 7), argues that their distinctions are artificial and unnecessary.

[2] A. H. M. Jones, 'The Roman Colonate', *Past and Present* xiii (1958), 1–13, and *The Later Roman Empire* (Oxford, 1964), ii. 795–803; R. Latouche, *The Birth of the Western Economy*, tr. E. Wilkinson (London, 1967 ed.), pp. 18–21.

[3] Block's two papers, 'Serf de la glèbe: histoire d'une expression toute faite' (1921) and 'Servus glebae' (1926), are reprinted in *Mélanges*, i. 356–78.

[4] Paucapalea, *Summa über das Decretum Gratiani*, ed. J. F. von Schulte (Giessen, 1890), p. 31, and Huguccio, MS Admont 7, fo. 78rb, both ad Dist. 54.11 gl. *originarios*. It is not improbable that Civilians made similar points.

Willelmi, used the term *colonus* in his contemporary account of English villeinage law.[5] By the early thirteenth century, glosses of the two laws contained a fairly wide range of comment on *ascripticii* etc., which must have been among Bracton's sources of inspiration for his theory of villeinage law.

Civilians and Canonists alike were forced to say something about the subject by occasional references in their set texts. For example, a lecturer faced with *Inst.* 1.3.1. that 'omnes homines aut liberi sunt aut servi' could feel impelled to ask in response 'quid de ascripticio?' Was he free or not? Similarly, the Canonists had to decide whether the prohibitions against the ordination of *servi* without the consent of their lords[6] and against Jewish ownership of Christian *servi*[7] applied to *ascripticii* too. Most Civilians agreed that the *ascripticius* was free. Among those who espoused this position were Azo, in his *Summa Institutionum* followed by the *De legibus*,[8] and Accursius in his authoritative Ordinary Gloss.[9]

A different school, however, stemming from Jacobus and comprising among others Vacarius, held that 'inter eos et servos nulla est differentia'.[10] Most Canonists considered the *ascripticius* free,[11] and Ricardus Anglicus, later Prior of Dunstaple, went so far as to declare that he could give testimony and

---

[5] Above Chap. 13, p. 263.

[6] *Decretum,* Dist. 54.7, 11, 20–1.

[7] W. J. Pakter, 'De His Qui Foris Sunt: the Teachings of Canon and Civil Lawyers concerning the Jews' (Johns Hopkins Univ., Maryland, Ph.D. thesis, 1974), pp. 109–10, 398–401, surveys the texts. The question of the Jewish ownership of agricultural serfs was not treated by decretists until Gregory the Great's 'Multorum ad nos' entered the set texts as *Comp. I,* 5.5.3. in *c.* 1190.

[8] *Bracton and Azo,* p. 44.

[9] See above p. 94 for his gloss on *Dig.,* 1.5.3., which probably inspired the theory of the relativity of villeinage. He rehearses the arguments ad *Inst.* 1.3.1. gl. *aut servi.* Cf. Carlyle, *Hist. of Medieval Political Theory,* ii. 39–49, for some other Civilians.

[10] E Seckel, 'Distinctiones Glossatorum', *Von Martitz Festschrift* (Berlin, 1911), pp. 352–3; *The Liber Pauperum of Vacarius,* ed. F. de Zulueta (*SS* xliv 1927), pp. 30–2. One Azo MS cites *Cod.,* 11.48.21, the text basic to this view, Carlyle, ii. 40 n. 1. See also E. Kantorowicz and W. W. Buckland, *Studies in the Glossators of Roman Law* (Cambridge, 1938), pp. 137, 279, for Rogerius, and R. W. Southern, 'Master Vacarius and the Beginning of an English Academic Tradition', *Medieval Learning and Literature: essays presented to R. W. Hunt,* ed. J. J. G. Alexander and M. T. Gibson (Oxford, 1976), pp. 257–85.

[11] The Ordinary Gloss of Johannes Teutonicus ad Dist. 54.21 gl. *originariis* followed Glossa Palatina (1210/15), MS Vat. Pal. Lat. 658, fo. 15va.

perform other *actus legitimi*.[12] The tenurial tie by which he was bound to the glebe naturally created some doubts about his freedom. A *servus glebae* was not however a *servus*, because his bond was to the land and not primarily personal;[13] his servitude was *ratione tenementi*, as the *De legibus* would say, not *ratione persone*. All the same, he could not recede freely from his land, where he had to perform agricultural service. The Church felt this to be incompatible with holy orders, which called for freedom from secular entanglements. A man unable to leave his holding, for secular purposes, could hardly leave the world and enter orders. Thus the Canonists would not permit the *ascripticius'* ordination, until freed by his lord, though the Civilians did.[14] All agreed on the *ascripticius'* bond to the soil, but the compensation of a kind of tenurial security was also recognized. The *ascripticius* was not to be sold, with or without his land,[15] and a lord who tried to shift him from his holding risked the loss of his own rights.[16] Some writers add that the *ascripticius'* obligations were fixed in advance, for he held *certa condicione*.[17] The links with the Bractonian treatment of *glebae ascripticii*, the villein sokemen on the Ancient Demesne, are quite clear.

The more general parallels with Bracton's system of villeinage law are equally obvious. They argue for his familiarity with this fairly recondite topic of the two laws. Probably the basic

[12] Pakter, p. 400. Ricardus wrote *c*.1196. Alanus Anglicus, another Englishman, expressed a similar view also at Bologna, *c*. 1203/6. Pakter, loc. cit. *Summa . . . Coloniensis*, ed. G. Fransen and S. Kuttner (Monumenta iuris canonici Ser. A.1 1969), i. 101 however, ranges *ascripticii* and *originarii* among the *servi persone*.

[13] Irnerius ad *Dig.*, 1.5.4; Carlyle, ii. 39. Cf. Kantorowicz and Buckland, pp. 137, 279, for Rogerius and the *Summa Vindoboniensis*.

[14] Gratian had included in the *Decretum*, as Dist. 54.20, Novel 123.26, which permitted the ordination of *inscripticios*, who retained the obligation to continue performing their agricultural services. *Summa Parisiensis*, ed. T. P. McLaughlin (Toronto, 1952), p. 50, accepts this. Other Canonists preferred to follow the authority of Dist. 54.21 which included *originarii* among those not to be ordained without consent; Ricardus Anglicus (above) is explicit in making the choice. Cf. below for other references.

[15] Dist. 54.12 gl. *originarios* again follows Glossa Palatina, MS cit., fo. 15rb.

[16] Apparatus 'Quia brevitas' ad *Comp. I*, 5.5.3. (Pakter, p. 398; 1198/1210) makes this point. Cf. the fourteenth-century epitome, E. Seckel, *Beiträge zur Geschichte Beides Rechte in Mittelalter* i (Tübingen, 1898), p. 415 n. 129: 'ascripticius glebe . . . nec invitus possit de iure compelli ut recedat'.

[17] Stephen of Tournai, *Die Summa über das Decretum Gratiani*, ed. J. F. von Schulte (Giessen, 1891), p. 81 ad Dist. 54.20 gl. *ascripticius; Summa Coloniensis*, i. 101; Rufinus, *Summa Decretorum*, ed. H. Singer (Paderborn, 1902), p. 144 ad idem, said that *censiti* were bound 'ad certum censum'.

analogy with the *acripticius* was obvious enough to the growing number of Englishmen with an education in learned law.[18] The prohibition of servile ordinations had been promulgated in English ecclesiastical councils,[19] some of whose canons specifically mention *ascripticii* as well as *servi*.[20] Here of course lies a further difficulty. The *De legibus* almost always refers to the villein as *servus*.[21] Its author cannot have regarded him as the equivalent of both Roman *servus* and *ascripticius* at the same time. The truth seems to be that wholesale transfer to the villein of the *ascripticius'* legal attributes was out of the question; the gap between their status was too great in spite of the general resemblance.[22] On the other hand, though Bracton 'used the worst word he had got, the word which, as he well knew, had described the Roman slave whom his owner might kill',[23] he was fully aware that the villein was no chattel slave. The comparison with the *ascripticius* furnished him with material to pare down the disabilities of the *servus* until he more or less resembled the villein of English law.

[18] In addition to S. Kuttner and E. Rathbone, 'Anglo-Norman Canonists in the Twelfth Century', *Traditio* vii (1949–51) and E. Rathbone, 'Roman Law in the Anglo-Norman Realm', *Studia Gratiana* ix = *Collectanea S. Kuttner* i (1967), 255–71, see now R. V. Turner, 'Roman Law in England before the time of Bracton', *Journal of British Studies* xv (1976), 1–25, and P. Stein, 'Vacarius and the Civil Law', *Church and Government in the Middle Ages: Essays . . . C. R. Cheney*, ed. C. Brooke, D. Luscombe, G. Martin, and D. Owen (Cambridge, 1976), pp. 119–38.

[19] e.g. Stubbs, *Charters*, p. 167 (Constitutions of Clarendon 1164, c. 16), Howden, *Chronicon* ii (ed. W. Stubbs, R.S. 1867), 74 (1175), and Powicke and Cheney, *Councils* II. 1.24–5, 60, 180, 186, 228 (1213/14, 1219/28, 1225/30, 1225/37).

[20] Powicke and Cheney, *Councils* II. 1.585, 681 (1258, 1261) on the enforcement of villein wills. W. Lyndwood, *Provinciale* (Oxford, 1679), III, tit. 13 De testamentis, cites Accursius' gloss, quoted above p. 94, in his commentary on the reissue of these canons by Archbishop Stratford.

[21] The direct references to *ascripticius* are on f. 4b (= freeman holding in villeinage; cf. *Bracton and Azo*, p. 49) and on f. 7b (= villein sokeman; cf. *P&M*, i. 389–91).

[22] Richard, Prior of Dunstable, would not have wished the villeins of his house to have the same condition, amounting almost to full *lex terre*, that he accorded to the *ascripticius*, see above.

[23] *P&M*, i. 412.

SELECT BIBLIOGRAPHY

I. PRIMARY SOURCES

A. MANUSCRIPT SOURCES

1. Plea rolls
All plea rolls extant in the Public Record Office from the period before 1250 were used, either in MS or in printed editions (below, B.2). Rolls from the second half of the century have been sampled.

Public Record Office
CP 40   Bench of Common Pleas (from 1272).
JI 1   Eyre and assize rolls, mainly from circuit.
KB 26   Plea rolls from the central courts.
KB 27   King's Bench (from 1272).

2. Charters
The main series searched for manumission and sale charters were British Library, Additional Charters and Harleian Charters.

3. Other legal material
Three manuscript registers of writs were consulted:
    Bodleian Library, Oxford, MS Douce 137;
    Cambridge Univ. Library, MS Kk v.33;
    H.M. Register House, Edinburgh, Berne MS on which see Lord Cooper, *Scot. Hist. Rev.* xxvii (1948);
(the last two from photographs).

'Glanvill Revised', Gonville and Caius College, MS 205/111, also Cambridge Univ. Library, MS Mm I 27. The date of the work and the relationship between the manuscripts are conveniently discussed in Hall's edition of *Glanvill*, pp. 195–8.

4. Miscellaneous (Consulted for individual items.)
Public Record Office
    CP 25(1)   Feet of fines.
    CP 52/1/1A   Original writs.
    E 210/3348   Charter.
    E 268/125   Memoranda roll 1250.

British Library
    Additional MS 46353   Cartulary.
    Arundel MS 221   Cartulary.
    Harleian MS 2110   Cartulary.

Leeds Central Library, 'Selby Abbey Cartulary'.
Bodleian Library, MS charters, Norfolk a. 6 (614). Will.

5. Canon Law MSS
Huguccio, *Summa*, MS Admont 7.
Glossa Palatina, MS Vat. Pat. Lat. 658, both from microfilm.

B. PRINTED SOURCES

(N.B. Where the year of publication and the year for which a volume was issued are not the same, the latter is preferred.)

1. Law books

BRACTON, HENRY DE, *De Legibus et Consuetudinibus Angliae.* The edition used is ed. G. E. Woodbine, 4 vols., New Haven, Conn., 1915–42, as reissued Cambridge, Mass., 1968–77, with translation by S. E. Thorne, whose editorial matter established that Henry de Bracton, J., was not the author, as had always been supposed. Citations are conventionally by the folios of the Vulgate edition, ed. H.N., London, 1569.

Brevia Placitata, ed. G. J. Turner and T. F. T. Plucknett, *SS*, lxvi, 1947.

Britton, ed. F. M. Nichols, Oxford, 1865.

Casus Placitorum, and Reports of Cases in the King's Courts (1272–8), ed. W. H. Dunham jr., *SS*, lxix, 1950.

COKE, SIR E., *The Second Part of the Institutes of the Lawes of England*, London, 1642.

Early Registers of Writs, ed E. de Haas, T. F. T. Plucknett, and G. D. G. Hall, *SS*, lxxxvii, 1970.

FITZHERBERT, SIR A., *The New Natura Brevium of . . . Mr. Anthony Fitzherbert.* Edition used, London, 1666, cited by folios of the early editions.

FITZNEAL, R., Bishop of Ely, *Dialogus de Scaccario,* ed. C. G. Crump, A. Hughes, and C. Johnson, Oxford, 1902. Cited by book and chapter, followed in parentheses by page number of the edition and translation by Johnson, *NMT*, 1950.

FLETA, *Commentarius Juris Anglicani*, ed. J. Selden, London, 1685. Vols. ii (Books 1–2) and iii (Books 3–4) of the edition by H. G. Richardson and G. O. Sayles, *SS*, lxxii, lxxxix for 1953 and 1972, have been used where possible. Citations by book and chapter, followed by page number of the 1685 edition in parentheses.

FORTESCUE, SIR J., *De Laudibus Legum Angliae,* ed. S. B. Chrimes, Cambridge, 1942.

Gesetze der Angelsächsen, ed. F. Liebermann, 3 vols., Halle, 1903–16.

GLANVILL, *Tractatus de Legibus et Consuetudinibus Regni Angliae Qui Glanvilla vocatur*, ed. G. D. G. Hall, *NMT*, 1965.

Leges Henrici Primi, ed. L. J. Dower, Oxford, 1972.

LYTTLETON, *Sir T. Lyttleton, his Treatise on Tenures*, ed. T. E. Tomlins, London, 1841.

The Mirror of Justices, ed. W. J. Whittaker with introduction by F. W. Maitland, *SS*, vii, 1893.

Natura Brevium in Frenche, ed. R. Tottel, London, 1557.

Novae Narrationes, ed. E. Shanks and S. F. C. Milsom, *SS*, lxxx, 1963.

Regesta Regum Scottorum=G. W. S. Barrow ed., *The Acts of Malcolm III, King of Scots, 1153–1165*, Edinburgh, 1960; *idem* and W. W. Scott, *The Acts of William I, King of Scots, 1165–1214*, Edinburgh, 1971.

Regiam Majestatem, ed. Lord Cooper, Stair soc., xi, 1947.

Register of Brieves, ed. Lord Cooper, Stair soc., x, 1946.

Registrum Omnium Brevium tam Originalium quam Judicialium, London, 1531.

Royal Writs in England from the Conquest to Glanvill, ed. R. C. Van Caenegem, *SS,* lxxvii, 1958–9.

2. Collections of case material

Bracton's NoteBook, ed. F. W. Maitland, 3 vols., London, 1887.

Calendar of the Roll of the Justices on Eyre [at Bedford] 1247, ed. G. H. Fowler, *BHRS,* xxi, 1939. English abstract.

Calendar of the Roll of the Justices on Eyre [Bucks] 1227, ed. J. G. Jenkins, *BRB* vi. 1942.

Civil Pleas of the Wiltshire Eyre 1249, ed. M. T. Clanchy, Wilts. rec. soc., xxvi, 1971.

A Complete Collection of State Trials . . . from the Reign of Richard II to the 16th year of the Reign of George III, 33 vols., London, 1809–28. Vol. xx, ed. T. B. and T. J. Howell.

Crown Pleas of the Wilts. Eyre of 1249, ed. C. A. F. Meekings, Wilts. rec. soc., xvi, 1961.

Curia Regis Rolls, 15 vols. to date, London, 1923–.

The Earliest Lincolnshire Assize Rolls, AD 1202–1209, ed. D. M. Stenton, *LRS,* xxii, 1926.

The Earliest Northamptonshire Assize Rolls, AD 1202 and 1203, ed. D. M. Stenton, *NRS,* v, 1930.

Evidences Relating to the Town Close Estate, Norwich (for Stanley and others v. Mayor and Corporation of Norwich), Norwich, 1887.

FITZHERBERT, SIR A., *La Graunde Abridgement,* Edition used London (?) 1516, cited by title and case number.

The London Eyre of 1244, ed. H. M. Chew and M. Weinbaum, London rec. soc., 1970.

The Memoranda Roll for the Tenth Year of . . . King John . . ., together with the Curia Regis Rolls of Hilary 7 Richard I (1196) and Easter 9 Richard I (1198) . . ., ed. R. A. Brown, *PRS,* n.s., xxxi, 1957.

Northumberland Pleas, from the Curia Regis and Assize Rolls, 1198–1272, ed. A. Hamilton Thompson, Newcastle-upon-Tyne rec. comm., Newcastle, 1922.

Placita Anglo-Normannica, ed. M. M. Bigelow, London, 1879.

Placitorum in Domo Capitulari Westmonasterii Asservatorum Abbreviatio, Temp. Regum Ric. I . . . Edw. II, Rec. Comm., 1811.

Plea Rolls, temp. Henry III. Suits affecting Staffordshire Tenants Taken from the Plea Rolls . . . and Abstracted into English, ed. G. Wrottesley, *WSS,* iv. 1883.

Pleas before the King and his Justices (1198–1212), ed. D. M. Stenton, 4 vols., *SS,* lxvii–viii, lxxxiii–iv, 1948 and 1966–7.

Roll of the Justices in Eyre at Bedford, 1202, ed. G. H. Fowler, *BHRS,* i, 1913.

Roll of the Justices in Eyre at Bedford, 1227, ed. G. H. Fowler, *BHRS,* iii, 1916. English translation.

Roll of the Justices in Eyre [Bedford], 1240, ed. G. H. Fowler, *BHRS,* ix, 1925.

Rolls of the Justices in Eyre for Gloucestershire, Warwickshire and Shropshire (1221–2), ed. D. M. Stenton, *SS,* lix, 1940.

Rolls of the Justices in Eyre for Lincolnshire and Worcestershire, ed. D. M. Stenton, *SS*, liii, 1934.
Rolls of the Justices in Eyre in Yorkshire, 1218–19, ed. D. M. Stenton, *SS*, lvi, 1937.
Rotuli Curiae Regis, ed. Sir F. Palgrave, 2 vols., Rec. Comm., 1835.
Selden Society, Yearbook series, 25 vols. to date.
Select Bills in Eyre, AD 1292–1333, ed. W. O. Bolland, *SS*, xxx, 1914.
Select Cases in the Court of King's Bench under Edward I, ed. G. O. Sayles, 3 vols., *SS*, lv, lvii–viii, 1936, 1938–9.
Select Cases of Procedure without Writ under Henry III, ed. H. G. Richardson and G. O. Sayles, *SS*, lx, 1941.
'*The Shropshire Eyre Roll of 1256*', ed. A. Harding, Oxford Univ. B.Litt. thesis, 1957.
Somerset Pleas . . . Close of the Twelfth Century—41 Henry III, ed. C. E. H. Chadwyck-Healey, *SRS*, xi, 1897.
Staffordshire Suits extracted from the Plea Rolls, temp. Richard I and King John, ed. G. Wrottesley, *WSS*. iii, 1882.
State Trials of the Reign of Edward I, 1289–1293, ed. T. F. Tout and H. Johnstone, Camden soc., 3rd s., ix, 1906.
Three Early Assize Rolls for the County of Northumberland, saec. xiii, ed. W. Page, Surtees soc., lxxxviii, 1890.
Three Rolls of the King's Court . . . AD 1194–1195, ed. F. W. Maitland, *PRS*, xiv, 1891.
Three Yorkshire Assize Rolls, for the Reigns of King John and King Henry III, ed. C. T. Clay, *YAS*, xliv, 1911.

3. Charters and non-royal legal material
Anglo-Saxon Writs, ed. F. E. Harmer, Manchester, 1952.
The Burton Chartulary, ed. G. Wrottesley, *WSS*, v. 1, 1884. Calendar in Latin and English.
Calendar of County Court, City Court, and Eyre Rolls of Chester, 1259–97, ed. C. Stewart-Brown, Chetham soc., n.s., lxxxiv, 1925.
Calendar of Plea and Memoranda Rolls . . . of the City of London, 1364–81, ed. A. H. Thomas, Cambridge, 1929.
Cartulaire du prieuré de La Charité-sur-Loire, ed. R. de Lespinasse, Nevers–Paris, 1887.
Cartularium Monasterii de Rameseia, ed. W. A. Hart and P. A. Lyons, 3 vols., R.S., 1884–94.
Cartularium Monasterii S. Johannis Baptiste de Colecestrie, ed. S. D. Moore, London, 1897.
Cartularium Saxonicum, ed. W. de G. Birch, London, 1885–93.
Cartulary of Chester Abbey, ed. J. Tait, Chetham soc., lxxix, 1920.
The Cartulary of Cirencester Abbey, Gloucestershire, ed. C. D. Ross, 2 vols., London, 1964.
The Cartulary of Missenden Abbey, ed. J. G. Jenkins, 2 vols., *BRB*, ii, x, 1938–55.
The Cartulary of Newnham Priory, ed. J. Godber, *BHRS*, xliii–xliv, 1963–4.
Charters of the Honour of Mowbray 1107–1191, ed. D. Greenway, Brit. Acad., London, 1973.
Chertsey Abbey Charters, ed. M. Guiseppi *et al.*, Surrey rec. soc., xii in 5 parts, 1915–63.

Codex Diplomaticum Aevi Saxonici, ed. J. M. Kemble, London, 1839–48.
The Coucher Book of Kirkstall Abbey, ed. W. T. Lancaster and W. P. Baildon, Thoresby soc., viii, 1904.
Court Roll of Chalgrave Manor, 1278–1313, ed. M. K. Dale, *BHRS*, xxvii, 1940.
Court Rolls of the Abbey of Ramsey, ed. W. O. Ault, New Haven, Conn., 1928.
Court Rolls of the Manor of Hales, ed. J. Amphlett, Worcs. hist. soc., 3 vols., 1910–33.
Court Rolls of the Manor of Wakefield, ed. W. P. Baildon, *YAS*, xxix, 1901.
Documents Illustrative of the Social and Economic History of the Danelaw, ed. Sir F. M. Stenton, British Academy Records of Social and Economic history, 1920.
Early Charters of St. Paul's, London, ed. M. Gibbs, Camden soc., 3rd s., lviii, 1939.
STENTON, F. M., *The Free Peasantry of the Northern Danelaw*, reprd. Oxford, 1969.
Historia et Cartularium Monasterii Sancti Petri Gloucestriae, ed. W. S. Hart, 3 vols., R.S., 1863–7.
The Hylle Cartulary, ed. R. W. Dunning, *SRS*, lxviii, 1968.
Leet Jurisdiction in Norwich, ed. W. Hudson, *SS*, v, 1891.
Luffield Priory Charters, ed. G. R. Elvey, *BRB* and *NRS*, 1968–.
Records of the Barony and honour of the Rape of Lewes, ed. A. J. Taylor, Sussex rec. soc., xliv, 1939.
Registrum Antiquissimum of the Cathedral Church of Lincoln, ed. C. F. Foster and K. Major, *LRS*, 11 vols., 1931–73.
St. Benet of Holme, 1020–1210, ed. J. R. West, Norfolk rec. soc., ii–iii, 1932.
Select pleas in Manorial Courts, ed. F. W. Maitland, *SS*, ii, 1888.
4. Fines
Devon Feet of Fines, vol. i, 1196–1272, ed. O. J. Reichel, Devon and Cornwall rec. soc., iii, 1912. English translation.
Feet of Fines for Essex, vol. i, AD 1182–AD 1272, ed. R. F. G. Kirk, Colchester, 1899–1910. English translation.
Feet of Fines for the County of Norfolk, . . . 1199–1202, ed. B. Dodwell, *PRS*, n.s., xxvii, 1952.
Final Concords of the County of Lancaster, Part I, AD 1196–AD 1307, ed. W. Farrer, Lancs. and Cheshire rec., soc., xxxix, 1899.
Fines, Sive Pedes Finium . . . A.D. 1195–1214, ed. J. Hunter, vol. i, Rec. Comm., 1835.
Pedes Finium . . . for the County of Somerset, 1196–1307, ed. E. Green, *SRS*, vi, 1892.
Pedes Finium . . . relating to the County of Surrey, ed. F. B. Lewis, Surrey arch. collns., extra vol. i, 1894.

5. Other public records
The Book of Fees, 2 vols. and index, London, 1920–31.
Calendar of Patent Rolls, London.
Close Rolls, Henry III, London.
Domesday Book, London, 1783, and Rec. Comm., 1816.
A Lincolnshire Assise Roll for 1298, ed. W. S. Thomson, *LRS*, xxxvi, 1944.
Pipe Roll Society publications. Pipe rolls cited from the Society's editions by King and regnal year, e.g. *P. Roll 31 Henry I*.
Red Book of the Exchequer, ed. H. Hall, 3 vols., R.S., 1896.
Rotuli de Oblatis et Finibus in Turri Londiniensi Asservati, Temp. Regis Johannis, ed.

C. Roberts, 2 vols., Rec. Comm., 1835.
Rotuli Litterarum Clausarum in Turri Londiniensi Asservati, ed. T. D. Hardy, 2 vols., Rec., Comm., 1833–4.
Rotuli Parliamentorum ut et Petitiones et Placita in Parliamento, ed. J. Strachey, 6 vols., London, 1767–77.
Royal Letters, Henry III, ed. W. W. Shirley, 2 vols., R.S., 1866.
Select Charters . . ., ed. W. Stubbs, 9th ed., revised by H. W. C. Davis, Oxford, 1913.
The Statutes of the Realm, 9 vols. and 2 index vols., 1810–28.

6. Roman and Canon law; theology
ANGLICUS, RICARDUS, *Ordo Judiciarius*, ed. C. Witte, Halle, 1853.
Azo, *Summa Institutionum*, Basle, 1563.
Corpus Iuris Canonici, ed. E. Freidburg, Leipzig, 1879–81.
Corpus Iuris Civilis. Various modern editions used. For the medieval gloss, the edition of Paris, 1517–18, 4 vols., was consulted.
Councils and Synods, with other Documents Relating to the English Church, vol. ii, ed. Sir F. M. Powicke and C. R. Cheney, Oxford, 1964.
Distinctiones Glossatorum, ed. E. Seckel, *Festschrift . . . Von Martitz*, Berlin, 1911.
HOSTIENSIS (Henry of Susa), *Summa Aurea*, ed. Venice, 1574.
The Liber Pauperum of Vacarius, Ed. F. de Zulueta, *SS*, xliv, 1927.
LYNDWOOD, WILLIAM, *Provinciale seu Constitutiones Angliae*, Oxford, 1679.
PAUCAPALEA, *Summa über das Decretum Gratiani*, ed. J. F. von Schulte, Giessen, 1890.
PETER OF BLOIS, *Speculum Iuris Canonici*, ed, T. A. Reimer, Berlin, 1837.
RICARDUS DE MEDIAVILLA, *Super Quatuor Libros Sententiarum Petri Lombardi quaestiones subtilissimae*, Brixen, 1591.
RUFINUS, *Summa Decretorum*, ed. H. Singer, Paderborn, 1902.
Selected Passages from the works of Bracton and Azo, ed. F. W. Maitland, *SS*, viii, 1894.
Summa . . . Coloniensis, ed. G. Fransen and S. Kuttner, Monumenta Iuris Canonici Ser. A.1, 1969.
Summa Parisiensis, ed. T. P. McLaughlin, O.S.B., Toronto, 1952.
THOMAS OF CHOBHAM, *Summa Confessorum*, ed. F. Broomfield, *Analecta Medievalia Namurcensis*, xxv, 1968.
TOURNAI, STEPHEN OF, *Die Summa über das Decretum Gratiani*, ed. J. F. von Schulte, Giessen, 1891.

7. Narrative sources
Annales de Dunstapalia, ed. H. R. Luard, R.S., 1866.
ADAM OF EYNSHAM, *Magna Vita S. Hugonis*, ed. D. L. Douie and H. Farmer, 2 vols., *NMT*, 1961.
Chronica Monasterii de Melsa, ed. E. A. Bond, R.S., 1866–8.
The Chronicle of Bury St. Edmunds, 1212–1301, tr. and ed. A. Gransden, *NMT*, 1964.
Chronicles of Stephen, Henry II and Richard I, ed. R. Howlett, R.S., 1885–9.
Chronicon Monasterii de Abingdon, ii, ed. W. H. Stevenson, R.S., 1858.
GIRALDUS CAMBRENSIS (Gerald of Wales), *Opera*, ed. J. S. Brewer *et al.*, 8 vols., R.S., 1861–91.

HOWDEN, ROGER OF (Roger of Hovenden = 'Benedict of Peterborough'). *Chronica*, ed. W. Stubbs, R.S., 4 vols., 1868–71.

HOWDEN, R. DE., *Gesta Regis Henrici Secundi*, ed. W. Stubbs, 2 vols., R.S., 1867.

JOCELIN OF BRAKELOND, *The Chronicle of Jocelin of Brakelond*, tr. and ed. H. E. Butler, *NMT*, 1949.

JOHN OF SALISBURY, *Ioannis Saresburiensis Episcopi Carnotensis Policraticus*, ed. C. C. J. Webb, Oxford, 1909.

—— *The Letters of John of Salisbury*, i, ed. W. J. Miller and H. E. Butler, *NMT*, 1955.

MATTHEW PARIS, *Chronica Majora*, ed. H. R. Luard, 7 vols., R.S., 1872–84.

ORDERIC VITALIS, *Historia Ecclesiastica*, ed. M. Chibnall, 6 vols., Oxford, 1968–, in progress.

REGINALD OF DURHAM, *De Admirandis Beati Cuthberti Virtutibus*, Surtees soc., i, 1835.

The Stoneleigh Leger Book, ed., R. H. Hilton, Dugdale soc., xxxiv, 1960.

WULFSTAN OF YORK, *Sermo Lupi*, ed. D. Whitelock, 3rd ed., London, 1963.

8. Dictionaries

BERGER, A., *Encyclopaedic Dictionary of Roman Law*, Trans. Amer. Phil. Soc., Philadelphia, 1953.

Dictionnaire de droit canonique, ed. R. Naz, 7 vols., Paris, 1935–65.

Dictionnaire de théologie catholique, ed. A. Vacant and E. Mangenot, 18 vols., Paris, 1899–1972.

EMDEN, A. B., *A Biographical Register of the University of Oxford to AD 1500*, Oxford, 1958.

Mediae Latinitatis Lexicon Minus, ed. J. F. Niermeyer, Leiden, 1976.

9. Miscellaneous

The Ancient Laws and Institutes of England, ed. B. Thorpe, Rec. Comm., 1840.

ANDREAS CAPELLANUS, *De Arte Honeste Amandi*, tr. J. J. Parry, *The Art of Courtly Love*, Columbia Records of Civilization, New York, 1941.

Capitularia Regum Francorum, ed. A. Borétius and V. Krause, M.G.H., LL., I, Hanover, 1883.

Documents of the Baronial Movement of Reform and Rebellion, 1258–67, ed. R. E. Treharne and I. J. Sanders, Oxford, 1973.

The Nibelungenlied, tr. A. Hatto, Harmondsworth, 1965.

Proverbia Sententiaeque Latinitatis Medii Aevi, ed. H. Walther, 6 vols., Göttingen, 1963–9.

Monasticon Anglicanum (Sir William Dugdale), ed. J. Caley, H. Ellis, and Revd. Bulkeley Bandinel, 6 vols. in eight, London, 1817; re-published Farnborough, 1970.

RÉMI, P. DE., Sire de Beaumanoir, *Les Coutumes de Beauvaisis*, ed. A. Salmon, 2 vols., Paris, 1899–1900, reissued 1970.

The Victoria History of the Counties of England, ed. H. A. Doubleday *et al.*, 1900– in progress.

II. SELECT SECONDARY AUTHORITIES

ADAMS, N., 'The Writ of Prohibition to the Court Christian', *Minnesota Law Review*, xx, 1936.

AULT, W. O., 'Village By-laws by Common Consent', *Speculum*, xxix, 1954.

BALDWIN, J. W., *Masters, Princes and Merchants*, 2 vols., Princeton, N.J., 1970.

BALLARD, A. and TAIT, J., *British Borough Charters, 1216–1307*, Cambridge, 1923.

BALON, J., 'Le Statut juridique des Colliberts du Val de Loire', *Revue bénédictine*, lxxvii, 1967.

BARTON, J. L., 'Bracton as a Civilian', *Tulane Law Review*, xlii, 1968.

BEAN, J. M. W., *The Decline of English Feudalism*, Manchester, 1968.

BERGER, A., 'In Dubiis Benigniora (*Dig.*, 50.17.56)', *Seminar*, ix, 1956.

BISHOP, T. A. M., *Scriptores Regis*, Oxford, 1961.

BLECKER, P. M., 'The Civil Rights of the Monk in Roman and Canon Law: the Monk as "Servus"', *American Benedictine Review*, xvii. 2, 1966.

BLOCH, M., *Mélanges historiques*, 2 vols., Paris, 1963.

BÖSL, K., 'Potens und Pauper', *Alteuropa und die moderne Gesellschaft: Festschrift für O. Brunner*, eds. A. Bergengrauer and L. Deike, Göttingen, 1963.

BRAND, P., 'The Contribution of the Period of Baronial Reform (1258–67) to the Development of the Common Law in England', unpublished Oxford Univ. D.Phil. thesis, 1974.

BRUSSEL, N., *Nouvel examen de l'usage général des fiefs en France*, 2 vols., Paris, 1727.

BUCKLAND, W. W., *A Manual of Roman Private Law*, 2nd ed., Cambridge, 1939.

—— *The Roman Law of Slavery*, Cambridge, 1908.

—— *A Textbook of Roman Law*, 2nd ed., Cambridge, 1932.

BUCKLAND, W. W. and McNAIR, A. D., *Roman Law and Common Law*, 2nd revised ed., Cambridge, 1952.

CAM, H., 'The Evolution of the Medieval English Franchise', *Speculum*, xxxii, 1957.

—— *Studies in the Hundred Rolls*, Oxford, 1921.

—— 'Thirteenth Century Peasant Pedigrees', in *Liberties and Communities in Medieval England*, Cambridge, 1944.

CAMPBELL, J., 'Observations on English Government from the Tenth to the Twelfth Century', *TRHS* 5th s., xxv, 1975.

CARLYLE, R. W. and A. J., *A History of Medieval Political Theory in the West*, 6 vols., Edinburgh and London, 1903–36.

CHAPLAIS, P., 'The Anglo-Saxon Chancery: from the Diploma to the Writ', *Journal Soc. Archivists*, iii. 1965–9.

—— *English Royal Documents . . . 1199–1461*, Oxford, 1971.

—— 'The Origin and Authenticity of the Royal Anglo-Saxon Diploma', *Journal Soc. Archivists*, iii, 1965.

CHENU, M. D., 'Arts "Méchaniques" et œuvres serviles', *Rev. des Sciences philosophiques et théologiques*, xxix, 1940.

CLANCHY, M., 'Did Henry III Have a Policy?', *History*, liii, 1968.

CLARKE, H. B., 'Domesday Slavery (Reduced for Slaves)', *Midland History*, i, 1972.

CORBETT, P. E., *The Roman Law of Marriage*, Oxford, 1930.

CRASTER, H. E., 'A Contemporary Record of the Pontificate of Rannulf Flambard', *Archaeologia Aeliana*, 4th s., vii, 1930.

CRITCHLEY, J. S., 'The Early History of the Judicial Writ of Protection', *Bull. Inst. Hist. Research*, xlv, 1972.

DAVID, M., 'Les Laboratores jusqu'au renouveau économique des xie–xiie siècles', *Études d'histoire de droit privé offertes à P. Petot*, Paris, 1959.

DAVIS, D. B., *The Problem of Slavery in Western Culture*, Ithaca, N.Y., 1966.

DOBSON, R. B., *The Peasants' Revolt of 1381*, London, 1970.

DODWELL, B., 'Holdings and Inheritance in Medieval East Anglia', *Ec. H. R.*, 2nd s., xx, 1967.

DOLLINGER, P., *L'évolution des classes rurales en Bavière depuis le fin de l'époque carolingienne jusqu'au milieu du xiiie siècle*, Paris, 1949.

DUBY, G., *La Société aux xie et xiie siècles dans la région maconnaise*, Paris, 1953.

DUNCAN, A. A. M., 'Regiam Majestatem: a Reconsideration', *Juridical Review*, n.s., vi, 1961.

FAITH, R. J., 'Peasant Families and Inheritance Customs in Medieval England', *Agric. Hist. Review*, xiv. 2, 1966.

FINBERG, H. P. R., 'Anglo-Saxon England to 1042', in Finberg ed., *The Agrarian History of England and Wales*, vol. i, Cambridge, 1972.

FLAHIFF, G. B., 'The Writ of Prohibition in the Thirteenth Century', *Medieval Studies*, vi, 1944; vii, 1945.

FOWLER, G. H. and HUGHES, M. W., 'Disseisins by Faulkes de Breaute at Luton', *BHRS*, ix, 1925.

GILCHRIST, J., 'The Medieval Canon Law on Unfree Persons: Gratian and the Decretist Doctrines, *c.*1141–1234', *Studia Gratiana*, xix, 1976.

GLORIEUX, P., *Répertoire des maîtres de Paris au xiiie siècle*, vol. ii, Paris, 1933.

GOEBEL, J., *Felony and Misdemeanor*, vol. i, New York, 1937.

GOFF, J. LE, 'Note sur la société tripartie . . . du ixe au xiie siècle', *L'Europe aux ixe–xie siècles*, ed. A. Gieysztor and T. Manteuffel, Warsaw, 1968.

GOURON, M. and A., 'Hommage et servage d'ourine: la cas des serfs d'Agde', *Mélanges P. Tisset*, Montpellier, 1970.

GRAHAM, R., 'The History of the Alien Priory of Wenlock', *Journal British Archaeol. Assoc.*, 3rd s., iv, 1939.

GRAY, C. M., *Copyhold, Equity and the Common Law*, Cambridge, Mass., 1963.

HALLAM, H. E., *Settlement and Society: a Study of the Early Agrarian History of South Lincolnshire*, Cambridge, 1965.

HARDING, A., 'The Medieval Brieves of Protection and the Devolopment of the Common Law', *Juridical Review*, 1966.

HARVEY, P. D. A., 'The English Inflation of 1180–1220', *Past and Present*, lxi, 1973.

—— 'The Pipe Rolls and the Adoption of Demesne Farming in England', *Ec. H. R.*, 2nd s., xxvii, 1974.

HEMMEON, M. DE W., *Burgage Tenure in Medieval England*, Cambridge, Mass., 1914.

HENNEBIQUE, R. LE J., *Pauperes et paupertas dans l'occident carolingienne aux ixe et xe siècles*', *Revue du nord*, 1, 1968.

HILTON, R. H., *Bond Men Made Free*, London, 1973.

—— *The Decline of Serfdom in Medieval England*, Studies in Econ. Hist.,

London, 1969.

—— —— 'Freedom and Villeinage in England', *Past and Present*, xxxi, 1965.

—— —— *A Medieval Society: the West Midlands at the End of the Thirteenth Century*, London, 1966.

—— —— 'Gloucester Abbey Leases of the late Thirteenth Century', *Univ. of Birmingham Hist. Journal*, iv, 1953–4, repr. in R. H. Hilton, *The English Peasantry in the Later Middle Ages*, Oxford, 1975.

—— —— 'Peasant Movements in England before 1381', *Ec. H. R.*, 2nd s., ii, 1949, repr. in E. Carus-Wilson, ed., *Essays in Econ. History*, ii, London, 1962.

HOLT, J. C., 'The Assizes of Henry II: the Texts', in *The Study of Medieval Records*, ed. D. A. Bullough and R. L. Storey, Oxford, 1971.

—— —— 'The Ballads of Robin Hood', *Past and Present*, xviii, 1960.

—— —— *Magna Carta*, Cambridge, 1965.

—— —— 'Magna Carta and the Origin of Statute Law', *Studia Gratiana*, xv, 1972.

—— —— *The Northerners*, Oxford, 1961.

—— —— 'Politics and Property in Early Medieval England', *Past and Present*, lvii, 1972.

HOMANS, G. C., *English Villagers of the Thirteenth Century*, Cambridge, Mass., 1942, repr. 1960.

HOYT, R. S., *The Royal Demesne in English Constitutional History, 1066–1272*, Ithaca, N.Y., 1950.

HURNARD, N. M., *The King's Pardon for Homicide before A.D. 1307*, London, 1968.

—— —— 'Magna Carta, Clause 34', in *Studies in Medieval History Presented to F. M. Powicke*, ed. R. W. Hunt, W. A. Pantin, and R. W. Southern, Oxford, 1948.

HYAMS, P. R., 'The Action of Naifty in the Early Common Law', *LQR*, xc, 1974.

—— —— 'The Origins of a Peasant Land Market in England', *Ec. H. R.*, 2nd s., xxiii, 1970.

—— —— 'The Proof of Villein Status in the Common Law', *EHR*, lxxxix, 1974.

JOLLIFFE, J. E. A., *Angevin Kingship*, London, 1955.

JONES, A. H. M., 'The Roman Colonate', *Past and Present*, xiii, 1958.

JOUON DES LONGRAIS, F., *La Conception Anglaise de saisine*, Paris, 1924.

—— —— 'La Portée politique des réformes d'Henri II', *RHDFE*, 4e série, v, 1936.

—— —— 'La Vilainage anglaise et le servage réel et personnel', *Recueils soc. Jean Bodin*, ii, Brussels, 1937.

KANTOROWICZ, H., and BUCKLAND, W. W., *Studies in the Glossators of Roman Law*, Cambridge, 1938.

KEMP, B., 'Exchequer and Bench in the Later Twelfth Century—Separate or Identical Tribunals?', *EHR*, lxxxviii, 1973.

KING, E., *Peterborough Abbey, 1086–1310*, Cambridge, 1973.

KOSMINSKY, E. A., *Studies in the Agrarian History of England in the Thirteenth Century*, Oxford, 1956.

KUTTNER, S. and RATHBONE, E., 'Anglo-Norman Canonists in the Twelfth Century', *Traditio*, vii, 1949–51.

LANDAU, P., 'Hadrians IV Dekretale "Dignum est" (*X*, 4.9.1)', *Studia Gratiana*, xii, 1967.

LANGMUIR, G., ' "Judei nostri" and the Beginning of Capetian Legislation,' *Traditio*, xvi, 1960.

LATHAM, R. E., 'Minor Enigmas from Medieval Records, 2nd Series', *EHR*. lxxvi, 1961.

LATHAM, R. E. and TIMINGS, E. K., (recte C. A. F. Meekings), 'Six Letters concerning the Eyres of 1226–8', *EHR*, lxv, 1950.

LENNARD, R. V., 'Agrarian History: some Vistas and Pitfalls', *Agric. Hist. Review*, xii, 1964.

MADDICOTT, J. R., *The English Peasantry and the Demands of the Crown, 1291–1341*, Past and Present Supplement, i, 1975.

MADOX, T., *Formulare Anglicanum . . .*, London, 1702.

—— *History . . . of the Exchequer*, London, 1711.

MAITLAND, F. W., *The Collected Papers of F. W. Maitland*, ed. H. A. L. Fisher, Cambridge, 1911.

—— and see POLLOCK, SIR F.

McINTOSH, M. K., 'The Privileged Villeins of the English Ancient Demesne', *Viator*, vii, 1976.

McKECHNIE, W. S., *Magna Carta. A Commentary on the Great Charter of King John, with an Historical Introduction*, 2nd ed., Glasgow, 1914.

MEEKINGS, C. A. F., see Latham, R. E. and Timings, E. K.

MEIJERS, E. M., *Études de droit international privé*, Paris, 1967.

MILLER, E., 'England in the Twelfth and Thirteenth Centuries: An Economic Contrast?', *Ec. H. R.*, 2nd s., xxiv, 1971.

—— 'The English Economy in the Thirteenth Century: Implications of Recent Research', *Past and Present*, xxviii, 1964.

—— 'Farming of Manors and Direct Management', *Ec. H. R.*, 2nd s., xxvi, 1973.

—— 'La Société rurale en Angleterre (xᵉ–xiiᵉ siècles)', *Settimane di studio del centro di studi sull' alto medioevo*, Spoleto, 1966.

—— 'The State and the Landed Interest in Thirteenth-century England and France', *TRHS*, 5th s., ii, 1952.

MILSOM, S. F. C., *Historical Foundations of the Common Law*, London, 1969.

—— *The Legal Framework of English Feudalism*, Cambridge, 1976.

—— 'Trespass from Henry III to Edward III', *LQR*, lxxiv, 1958.

MITCHELL, S. K., *Studies in Taxation under John and Henry III*, New Haven, Conn., 1914.

MORGAN, M., *The English Lands of the Abbey of Bec*, Oxford, 1946.

MORRIS, W. A., *The Early English County Court*, Berkeley, Cal., 1926.

NEILSON, N., 'Custom and the Common Law in Kent', *Harvard Law Review*, xxxviii, 1925.

—— *Customary Rents*, Oxford Studies in Social and Legal History, ii, Oxford, 1910.

OURLIAC, P., 'L'Hommage servile dans la région toulousaine', *Mélanges . . . L. Halphen*, Paris, 1951.

PAKTER, W. J., 'De His Qui Foris Sunt: the Teachings of Canon and Civil Lawyers Concerning the Jews', Johns Hopkins Univ., Maryland, Ph.D. thesis, 1974.

PEGUES, F. J., 'A Monastic Society at Law in the Kent Eyre of 1313–1314',

EHR, lxxxvii, 1972.

PERRIN, CH. E., 'La Servage en France et en Allemagne', *Relazioni del X congresso internazionale di scienze storiche*, iii, Florence, 1955.

PETOT, P., 'La Commendise personnelle', *Mélanges Paul Fournier*, Paris, 1929.

—— 'L'Hommage servile: essai sur la nature de l'hommage', *RHDFE*, 4e série, vi, 1927.

—— 'Licences de mariage et formariage des serfs dans les coutumes françaises au moyen âge', *Annales d'histoire de droit (Poznan)*, ii, 1949.

—— 'L'Origine de la mainmorte servile', *RHDFE*, 4e série, xix, 1941.

—— 'La Preuve de servage au Champagne', *RHDFE*, 4e série, xiii, 1934.

—— 'Serfs d'église habilités a témoigner en justice', *Cahiers de civilisation médiévale*, iii, 1960.

PIKE, L. O., *Year Books of the Reign of King Edward the Third, year XV*, R.S., London, 1891.

PLUCKNETT, T. F. T., *A Concise History of the Common Law*, 5th ed., London, 1956.

—— *Early English Legal Literature*, Cambridge, 1958.

—— *The Legislation of Edward I*, Oxford, 1949.

POLLOCK, SIR F. and MAITLAND, F. W., *The History of English Law before the Time of Edward I*, 2 vols., 2nd ed., 1898.

POOLE, A. L., *Obligations of Society in the XII and XIII Centuries*, Oxford, 1946.

POST, G., 'Bracton as Jurist and Theologian on Kingship', *Procs. 3rd International Congress of Medieval Canon Law, 1968*, Vatican, 1971.

POSTAN, M. M., 'The Charters of the Villeins', in *Carte Nativorum, a Peterborough Abbey Cartulary of the Fourteenth Century*, ed., C. N. L. Brooke and M. M. Postan, *NRS*, xx, 1960.

—— 'The Chronology of Labour Services', *TRHS*, 4th s., xx. 1937.

—— and TITOW, J. Z., 'Heriots and Prices on Winchester Manors', *Ec. H. R.*, 2nd s., xii, 1958.

POWICKE, SIR F. M., 'Per Iudicium Parium vel per Legem Terrae', *Magna Carta Commemoration Essays*, ed. H. E. Malden, London, 1917.

POWICKE, M. R., *Military Obligation in Medieval England*, Oxford, 1962.

La Preuve, Recueils de la Société Jean Bodin, xvii, 1965.

PUGH, R. B., *Imprisonment in Medieval England*, Cambridge, 1968.

RAFTIS, J. A., *Tenure and Mobility: Studies in the Social History of the English Village*, Toronto, 1964.

RATHBONE, E., 'Roman Law in the Anglo-Norman Realm', *Collectanea Stephan Kuttner i = Studia Gratiana*, xi, 1967.

RICHARDSON, H. G., *Bracton: the Problem of his Text*, SS supplementary vol. ii, 1964.

RICHARDSON, H. G. and SAYLES, G. O., 'The Early Statutes', *LQR*, 1, 1934.

—— *Law and Legislation from Athelbert to Magna Carta*, Edinburgh, 1966.

SAVINE, A., 'Bondmen under the Tudors', *TRHS*, n.s., xvii, 1903.

SCAMMELL, J., 'Freedom and Marriage in Medieval England', *Ec. H. R.*, 2nd s., xxvii, 1974.

—— 'The Origin and Limitations of the Liberty of Durham', *EHR*, lxxxi, 1966.

—— 'The Rural Chapter in England from the Eleventh to the Fourteenth Century', *EHR*, lxxxvi, 1971.

—— 'Wife Rents and Merchet', *Ec. H. R.*, 2nd s., xxix, 1976.

SEARLE, E., 'Freedom and Marriage in Medieval England: an Alternative Hypothesis', *Ec. H. R.*, 2nd s., xxix, 1976.

—— 'Hides, Virgates and Tenant Settlement at Battle Abbey', *Ec. H. R.*, 2nd s., xvi, 1964.

—— *Lordship and Community: Battle Abbey and its Banlieu*, Toronto, 1974.

SECKEL, E., *Beiträge zur Geschichte beider Rechte in Mittelalter*, vol. i, Tübingen, 1898.

SHEEHAN, M. M., *The Will in England from the Conversion of the Anglo-Saxons to the End of the Thirteenth Century*, Toronto, 1963.

SIMPSON, A. W. B., *A History of the Common Law of Contract*, Oxford, 1975.

—— *An Introduction to the History of the Land Law*, Oxford, 1961.

SITWELL, G. R., 'The English Gentleman', *The Ancestor*, i, 1902.

SMALLEY, B., 'The Quaestiones of Simon of Hinton', *Studies in Medieval History presented to F. M. Powicke*, eds. R. W. Hunt, W. A. Pantin, and R. W. Southern, Oxford, 1948.

SOUTHERN, R. W., *The Making of the Middle Ages*, London, 1953.

—— *Medieval Humanism and other Studies*, Oxford, 1970.

STACY, N., 'The Estates of Glastonbury Abbey, *c.*1020–1200', unpublished Oxford Univ. D.Phil. thesis, 1971.

STEIN, P., 'The Source of the Romano-Canonical Part of the Regiam Majestatem', *Scottish Hist. Review*, xlviii, 1969.

STENTON, D. M., *English Justice between the Norman Conquest and the Great Charter, 1066–1215*, Jayne Lectures for 1963, Philadelphia, 1964.

STENTON, SIR F. M. 'Early Manumissions at Staunton, Nottinghamshire', *EHR*, xxvi, 1911.

—— 'English Families and the Norman Conquest', *TRHS*, 4th s., xxvi, 1944.

—— *Transcripts of Charters Relating to . . . Gilbertine Houses*, *LRS*, xviii, 1922.

STEPHENSON, C., *Medieval Institutions*, Ithaca, N.Y., 1967.

SUCKLING, A., *The History and Antiquities of the County of Suffolk*, London, 1846.

SUTHERLAND, D. W., *The Assize of Novel Disseisin*, Oxford, 1973.

—— 'Mesne Process in the early Common Law', *LQR*, lxxxii, 1966.

SWINBURNE, H. A., *A Treatise of Testaments and Last Wills*, 5th ed., London, 1728.

TAIT, J., *The Medieval English Borough*, Manchester, 1936.

—— 'Waynagium et Contenementum', *EHR*, xxvii, 1912.

THAYER, J. B., *A Preliminary Treatise on Evidence at Common Law*, London, 1898.

THORNE, S. E., 'Courts of Record and Sir Edward Coke', *Univ. of Toronto Law Journal*, ii, 1, 1937.

—— 'English Feudalism and Estates in Land', *Cambridge Law Journal*, xvii, 1959.

—— *Henry de Bracton, 1268–1968*, Univ. of Exeter, 1970.

—— 'Livery of Seisin', *LQR*, lii, 1936.

—— 'Notes on Courts of Record in England', *West Virginia Law Quarterly*, xl, 1934.

TITOW, J. Z., *English Rural Society, 1200–1350*, London, 1969.

TURNER, R. V., 'Clerical Judges in English Secular Courts', *Medievalia et Humanistica*, iii, 1972.

—— *The King and His Courts . . . 1199–1240*, Ithaca, N.Y., 1968.

—— 'Roman Law in England before the Time of Bracton', *Journal of British Studies*, xv, 1976.

VERRIEST, L., *Institutions médiévales, introduction au corpus des records de coutumes et de lois de chef-lieux de l'ancien comté de Hainault*, t. i, Mons, 1946.

—— 'Le Servage dans le comté de Hainault, les sainteurs, le meilleur catel', *Académie royale de belgique, classe des lettres*, 2e série, t. vi, fasc. 3, 1910.

VINOGRADOFF, SIR P., *The Collected Papers of Paul Vinogradoff*, ed. H. A. L. Fisher, Oxford, 1928. Vol. i, historical.

—— *Villainage in England*, Oxford, 1892.

WALKER, L. E. M., 'Some Aspects of Local Jurisdiction in the Twelfth and Thirteenth Centuries . . .', unpublished London Univ. MA thesis, 1957.

WARREN, W. L., *Henry II*, London, 1973.

WEINBAUM, M., *British Borough Charters, 1307–1660*, Cambridge, 1943.

WOLFFE, B. P., *The Royal Demesne in English History*, London, 1971.

INDEX

Abingdon Abbey, 68, 154, 190, 211
accursius, 94, 270, 272n. *See also
corpus Iuris Civilis:* ordinary gloss
Achard, Simon f., Bela widow of, 154
actions, assize of mort d'ancestor, 18,
51n., 56, 62, 66, 67, 75–6, 111, 112,
134n., 149, 171, 172, 173n., 181,
189–90, 254; assize of novel disseisin, 11, 19, 38, 40, 41, 42–3, 44,
51–4, 60–1, 67, 68n., 95–103, 106,
110–11, 113, 116, 133, 171, 172n.,
230, 252; assize of nuisance, 133n.;
assizes, petty, 215–17, 245, 251;
assize *utrum*, 3, 145; covenant,
146–7, 149; customs and services,
119; debt, 147–8, 150; *de fine facto,*
14; *de homagio capiendo,* 14; dower,
76; *ejectio firme,* 150; entry *per villanum,* 41–3; entry *sur* disseisin, 43;
imprisonment, 30–1; intrusion,
18; mandrial suits in common-law
forms, 13, 49, 69; *monstraverunt,* 64,
65n., 248; naifty, xxi, 10–11, 29,
34, 56–7, 95, 96, 102–7, 115,
118, 132, 136, 146, 158, chap. 10
passim, 205, 209, 211, 213–15, 218,
222–32, 236, 238–9, 243, 259, 265,
defences to, 167–70, 210; *Quare deforciat,* 61; replevin, 20; right, 8,
146n., 172n., 224n., 252; trespass,
105–6, 132–3, 134, 137, 142, 163,
166n., 190, 211, 224n.; waste.
27–9, 144; *see also* appeals,
(criminal), writs
Adam, Thomas f., 199–200
adventicius, 34n., 118n., 209–10, 211
aid, 191–3
Alanus Anglicus, 271n.
Alderton (Warwicks.), 199
Alvergate (Norfork), 64
Alverstone, Alan of, 10
amercements, 29, 44, 52, 53n., 57, 76,
143–4, 246

Ancient Demesne, 26, 39n., 56, 62–5,
122, 133, 139, 147, 186, 193, 200,
207, 209, 210n., 246–8, 254,
264–5, 271
Anesty, Hubert of, 132
Angot, Richard, 3
appeals, (criminal), 8–9, 14–15, 41,
116, 132, 134–9, 158; *see also under
individual crimes*
Aquinas, St. Thomas, 93
arson, 132n., 139–40, 189
ascripticius, xx, 26–7, 37, 72, 88,
90, 94, 109–10, 131, 244–5, 253,
269–72, *see also colonus*
Aselak, Roger, 54, 115
assizes, petty, *see* actions
attornment of service, 5–10
atrox iniuria, 129, 135
Avaunt, Hugh f., 3
Avelina, Ralph f., 14
Avranches, William de, 147
Aynevill, Ralf de, 45n.
Aywood, Adam de, 174
Azo of Bologna, 85, 89–90, 93, 110,
123, 127n., 128, 143, 176–8, 270

Bacum, Walter, 76
Bagot, Simon, 8
Baicer, Nicholas f. Walter (Wim),
66, 76
Ball', John le, 75
Bamburch, Ivo de, 138
Bardolf, Hugh, daughter of, 259
Baret, Geoffrey, 190
Barrington (Gloucs.), Philip of,
259n.
Barrowden (Rutland), 62n.
Barton Stacy (Hants), 33, 113
Basset, Gilbert, 105
bastards, 181–2, 210
Bath, Henry of, c.j., 179n.
Battle Abbey, 116, 242n.
battle, trial by, *see* proof

Bavent, Walter de, 179n.
Bec, Abbey of, 141, 248
Becicet, Thomas, 252n.
Bedford, 158–9, 169
Beeton, Mrs., 102n.
Bereford, William, j., 142
Bernolf, Nicholas, f., 116, 137
Bestenover, Martin of, and his case, 27, 56–9, 110, 113, 121n., 122
Bigod, *see* Norfolk, Earl of
Biham (Lincs.), Maud of, 132, 136
Bilsby (Lincs.), 179
Bine, Richard, f., 9
Binham, Prior of, 43n.
Blithe, William and Agatha de, 52
Bloch, M., 26, 78n., 269
borough privilege, 132, 167–9
Bosevill, Simon de, 45n.
Bovill, John de, 147
Bracton's NoteBook, 58, 105n., 116, 149, 150
Bracton (Bratton), Henry de, j., xxn., 82–4, 101, 106n., 107n., 111, 122, 123, 179–80, 182, 191n., 208
Bracton, treatise attributed to, *see De legibus et Consuetudinibus Angliae*, treatise
Bradley, Thomas de, 139–40, 189
Brai, John de, 170
Bramley (Surrey), 39n.
Brampton (Hunts.), 256n.
Brancaster (Norfolk), 46
Brand, Dr Paul, 144n., 155
Breaute, Faulkes de, 63, 159
Bret, Simon le, 10
Brevia Placitata, 42, 139n., 181
Britton, 25, 36, 50, 87, 97, 116, 127–8, 130, 147–8, 149, 166n., 178, 218
Britton (treatise), 2
Brockhall (Northants.), John of, 141–2
Brok, David del, 105
Broughton, Robert of, 41, 243n.
Brunger, Richer, 149
Burton Abbey, 19, 224n., 252
Bury St. Edmunds (Suffolk), Abbey of, 31, 140, 149; Abbot Samson of, 253

Butley Priory, 117
Butterwick, Lincs., 8

Caen, Abbess of, 42n.
Canley (Warwicks.), 259–60
Canley (Warwicks.), Peter of, 76n.
Canley (Warwicks.), Robert of, 259–60; *see* Ketelburn
Canterbury, Archbishop of, 71, 227
Casus Placitorum, 12, 139
Chalfont (Bucks.), 11n.
Champion, Hugh, 11
charters, 12–13, 191n., 257; manumission, 31–2, 135n.; possession of, felt to imply freedom, 44–6; of sale of villeins, 3, 11, 45; to villeins, alleged villeins, 44–5, 66, 150; villeins not to use, 43
Cheling', William, 170
Chester, Earl of, 51–2, 158
chevage, 34–6, 209n.
Chiltun, Ralph de, 63
Chobham, Thomas of, 94
Cirencester (Gloucs.), William and Robert, f. Hugh of, 251n., 253–4
Cirencester Abbey, 253–4
Clanchy, M. T., 23n.
Clerk, Simon the, Christiana wife of, 111
Clerk, William, 154
Coggeshall, Abbot of, 99, 112
Coke, Sir Edward, c.j., 60n.
Coke, John le, 115
Colchester Abbey, 228n., 252
Coleby (Lincs.), 179
collibertus, 15n.
colonus, xx, 58n., 225, 263, 269–70; *see also ascripticius*
Colville, William de, 146
Compostella (Spain), St. James of, 33
Corpus Iuris Civilis, 85, 90, 269; *Institutes*, 135, 176, 270; ordinary gloss, *see* accursius
Council, King's, 105, 260, 263
Councils, English Church, legislation of, 71–2, 272
Courson, Robert de, 192n.

tenure, socage
Somerton, West (Norfolk), 117
statuliber, 57, 75, 97, 102–6, 119, 137, 146n., 155, 169n., 177, 216
statuservus, 97, 102, 106, 155, 177, 216
statute(s), *see* legislation
Staunton, William de, 32
Stephenson, C., 234
Steringe, Alexander de, 3, 30
Stoneleigh Abbey, 259–60
Stratton, Adam of, 208n.
Strete, Roger de la, 75
Struby, Nicholas de, 75
Suffordia, Roger de, 150
suit, witness, *see* proof
suit of kin, proof by, xxi, 171–6, 180–1, 190, 209, 211, 214, 216, 217, 237, 250
surety, *see* security
surrender and admittance, 39, 40, 43
Sutton (Staffs.), 133n
Sutton, Sir Saer of, 137

Tait, J., 234n.
tallage, 28, 57, 64, 186, 187, 190–4, 241, 247. 254n., 267
tallage, royal, 267
Taverham, Baudri de, 42n.
taxation, 19, 152–3, 261
templar, knights, 68
tenure: copyhold, 53, 60n., 207n.; dower, 28, 144n.; drengage, 210n.; frankalmoign, 23, 145, 196n., 228n.; freehold, 186n.; *per furcam et flagellum,* 46; sergeanty, 159n., 179n.; socage, free, 39n., 64, 71, 189, 196n., 198, 200; socage, villein, 26, 38, 56, 63, 65, 122, 154, 186, 194–5, 200, 271, 272n.; *see also* villeinage tenure
theft, 8–9, 116, 132, 136, 138, 139, 158
Thetford Priory, 68
Thorne, S. E., viii–ix, 82–6, 98, 99, 119, 121–3
Thorp, John of, 75
Thorpe (Durham), William the miller of, 234n.

Thorpe, Osbert of, 230n.
Thurkill, Richard f., 190
Thyning, John de, 45
Todenham, William de, 196
Tournai, Stephen of, viii
trades: carpenter, 33; merchant, *mercenarius,* 34n.
Travers, Hugh, 32
Turville, Richard de, 11

Udard, Richard f., 41

Vacarius, 58n., 270
Valletorta, Alicia de, 175n.
Vere, Henry de, 139–40, 189
Verli, Roger de, 245
Verriest, L., 78n., 241
villanus, 242, 250n.
villein(s): agreements with, 145–9; alienations of land, chap. 5 *passim,* 136; attached to lord's land, chap. 4 *passim;* cannot bring civil actions, 51, 132f.; can travel with lord's licence, 33–6; criminal law, subject to, 131; not devisable, 25; disputes over ownership of, 10, 224–30; family life, lord's control over, 10, 15–16, 177; flights, 29–31, 137, 140, 168, 170, 222, 225; heir, can neither be nor have, 66, 76–8; holding free land, 75, 101, 108n., 109, 112–13; holds at lord's will, chap. 6 *passim;* holds *nomine alieno,* 51, 200; itinerant, 33, *and see adventicius;* king's, 113, 144n., 246n., 254n.; *lex terre,* has no, 121, 128–30, 150, 156; no seisin of free tenement, 113; property rights, has no, 19, 126–7; prosperous, 77, 151; sale of, chap. 2 *passim;* subject of king, as, 151–60, 244, 261–5; taking of, appeal for, 14–15
villein status: by prescription, 115–18; suit of kin conclusive proof of, 209; tenemental influence on, 115–18, 178
villeinage: bars civil actions, 20, 132, 148; confessions of, in court, 47,

DATE DUE

FEB 1 1984			

DEMCO 38-297